Great Power Competition

The Changing Landscape of Global Geopolitics

Edited by
Mahir J. Ibrahimov

US Army Command and General Staff College Press
Fort Leavenworth, Kansas

An imprint of The Army University Press
Cover design by Dale E. Cordes, Army University Press.

Library of Congress Cataloging-in-Publication Data

Names: Ibrahimov, Mahir, 1956- editor. | U.S. Army Command and General   Staff College Press, issuing body.

Title: Great power competition : the changing landscape of global geopolitics / edited by Mahir J. Ibrahimov.

Other titles: Great power competition (U.S. Army Command and General Staff College Press) | Changing landscape of global geopolitics

Description: Fort Leavenworth, Kansas : US Army Command and General Staff College Press, 2020. | Includes bibliographical references.

Subjects: LCSH: Great powers. | Military policy. | Strategic rivalries (World politics) | International relations and culture. | United States--Foreign relations. | Russia (Federation)--Foreign relations.

November 2020

Editors
Diane R. Walker and Amanda M. Hemmingsen

Foreword

The world is changing at an ever-increasing pace. Modern communication with worldwide connectivity has brought together a global community. In this environment, we must be globally astute. We must understand the geopolitical and sociocultural aspects of regional affairs in any region in which we may be called upon to serve. Understanding the operating environment and associated regional cultures of our partners and competitors is essential to making military decisions that directly affect outcomes locally, regionally, and globally. Agile leaders must be able to recognize the cultural and geopolitical realities of operations and be prepared to adjust appropriately to achieve our nation's broader goals. The US Army's culture, regional expertise, and language programs provide a mechanism to prepare our troops to operate in and among a region's indigenous cultures.

This anthology, *Great Power Competition: The Changing Landscape of Global Geopolitics*, written under the auspices of the US Army Command and General Staff College's Cultural and Area Studies Office (CASO), expands on the previous volume, *Cultural Perspectives, Geopolitics, & Energy Security of Eurasia: Is the Next Global Conflict Imminent?* The first book gained significant positive traction among Army leaders as well as among scholars nationally and internationally. *Great Power Competition* expands the focus to include Latin America and Africa. Our authors provide insight and observations on the battle for influence in these important regions.

The articles that make up this work explore the cultural and regional implications of Chinese and Russian power projection in Eurasia, the Americas, and Africa; the rise of sub-state actors in their regions; and military applications of culture, area expertise, and foreign language proficiency in the operational environment.

As our Army refocuses to prepare for competition in complex future operating environments, the insights offered in this volume are important for all Army leaders. Future missions may vary, but all will include the need to understand the geopolitical and cultural foundations of regions in which we operate and the people we encounter around the globe.

All Army leaders should read this book.

Maj. Gen. Stephen J. Maranian
US Army War College Provost;
former Deputy Commanding
General for Education, US Army
Combined Arms Center, and
Army University Provost

Contents   *page*

Illustrations *page*

Introduction

Mahir J. Ibrahimov

Great Power Competition continues the discussion begun with the 2017 *Cultural Perspectives, Geopolitics, & Energy Security of Eurasia: Is the Next Global Conflict Imminent?*[1] This second volume undertakes a deep analysis beyond the obvious military strategic nexus to identify new spaces for planners and policymakers alike to consider. Similar to *Cultural Perspectives,* distinguished nationally and internationally known scholars in their respective areas discuss how emerging global and regional powers are trying to expand their influences in Eurasia, the Americas, and Africa, among other regions. The scholars, who bring a combination of academic and first-hand practical expertise, examine how the actions of adversaries such as Russia, China, and Iran in a greater Eurasia landscape and beyond have challenged the US National Security Strategy and National Defense Strategy. These actions include continuous efforts to challenge US interests in the Middle East, Southwest Asia, the Western Hemisphere and Africa, especially in the changing homeland security landscape in light of COVID-19 and recent societal unrest.

Like *Cultural Perspectives,* this book was written under the auspices of Cultural & Area Studies Office (CASO)—previously Culture, Regional Expertise, and Language Management Office—of the US Army Command and General Staff College (CGSC). *Cultural Perspectives* received significant attention from Army senior leaders as well as more broadly from scholars for its relevance to the rapidly changing operational environment and expertise of the contributors.

The concept of both volumes is that geopolitical affairs continue to develop at breakneck speed. Military leaders must come to grips with these affairs, especially social, economic, and cultural factors with which they are often unfamiliar and uncomfortable. As Maj. Gen. John S. Kem, former Army University provost, asserted in *Cultural Perspectives*: "Military decisions that directly affect strategic outcomes rely heavily on cohesively understanding the operating environment and associated regional cultures of our allies and our adversaries."[2] Kem and other senior military leaders understand that appreciation of a culture and regional expertise can directly affect the success of a mission. Through works like this volume and its predecessor, CASO helps fulfill its mission to prepare the Army to understand a region's indigenous cultures and achieve success wherever it operates:

> CASO serves the educational mission within the institution and across the Army and in conjunction with partner organizations, provides a mechanism to engage all CGSC constituencies concerning the importance of cultural, political, economic and social factors in shaping the operational environment. . . . CASO and its events create a sustainable advantage for Regionally Aligned Forces, Security Forces Assistance Brigades, Army schools, and Centers of Excellence by providing training and education tools that enhance Professional Military Education, Pre-Deployment, and Functional Training in support of the US National Security and National Defense Strategy objectives in a variety of regional contingencies across the spectrum of conflict including the possibility of Large-Scale Combat Operations. CASO's purpose is to assist in preparing globally responsive and regionally aligned forces that work with a variety of partners including host nation militaries and populations to execute the Army's Prevent, Shape, and Win strategic role.[3]

Source documents provide guidance for training in three broad areas.
1) **Core Cultural Competencies:** Core cultural competencies includes areas such as understanding culture, applying organization awareness, cultural perspective taking, and cultural adaptability.
2) **Regional/Technical Competencies:** Regional/technical competencies deal with applying regional information and operating in a regional environment.
3) **Leader/Influence Functions:** Leader/influence functions include strategic (cultural) agility, (cultural) systems thinking, cross-cultural influences, organizational cultural competence, and utilizing interpreters/advisors.
CJCSI 1800.01D (officer PME Policy) and CJCSI 1805.01A (Enlisted PME Policy).

Figure 0.1. CASO outreach extends across the Army, Department of Defense (DoD) and beyond through a variety of educational programs, including publishing, guest speakers, direct support to CGSC classes, live panels, video podcasts, international cooperation, and research. Created by Army University Press based on author information.

Great Power Competition continues the discussion and analysis of the Eurasia region, including Russia and other countries of the former Union of Soviet Socialist Republics (USSR). Several chapters provide detailed descriptions of regional and global realities, viewed through the prism of Russia's traditional military-strategic culture. As with all countries in the Eurasian region and elsewhere, Russia and its traditional strategic interests impact global and regional geopolitics and the socio-cultural situation.

Russia's intervention in Syria has changed the military and diplomatic dynamic in the regional crisis and forced the United States to search for a new approach. US influence in the region might be in jeopardy. Some traditional American allies are already talking with Moscow about how to resolve the crisis, which could potentially change the strategic landscape.

The insights offered in this volume will be important for Army professionals who lead soldiers in a variety of missions across the globe. *Great Power Competition* chapters address a wide range of regions such as Eurasia, the Western Hemisphere, Africa, and the Middle East. This broad approach reflects that regional and global geopolitics are interconnected socio-culturally, economically, and historically. Russia, with significantly fewer resources compared to the former USSR, is playing an increasingly active role in Eurasian and global geopolitics. One factor which influences current Russian foreign policy in Eurasia and beyond is Eurasianism.[4] While its significance has changed to a great extent, Eurasianism still suggests strategic rivalry and, most importantly, has historical and socio-cultural roots that have shaped Russian strategic and military thinking over the centuries. This book's editor traveled to Ukraine to participate in the US Army's recent Russian New Generation Warfare in Ukraine study as well as other Eurasia-related research. The research clearly identified significant gaps in achieving America's national security objectives in the region: shared historical, cultural, and language heritage between Russia, Ukraine, and other former Soviet satellites and some former Warsaw Pact countries that would be difficult to break.

At the same time, the United States lacks understanding of and appreciation for indigenous cultures, including those in the Eurasia region. The new generation of warfare is already ongoing in Ukraine and other regions. Operations are occurring within the "gray zone."[5]

Russians are effective in these areas because they have actively operated like this for centuries and have socio-cultural aptitude and common linguistic capabilities. Russians understand the value of culture and "soft power" from having experienced it during the Soviet period and before.

At a March 2019 conference on the future of Russian military strategy, General Valery V. Gerasimov, the Russian Army chief of the general staff, reiterated ideas that he initially laid out in a 2013 article in *Voyenno-Promyshlennyy Kurier* [The Military-Industrial Courier], a Russian army journal. He commented that "countries bring a blend of political, economic, and military power to bear against adversaries" and Russia's armed forces "must maintain both 'classical' and 'asymmetrical' potential (the mix of combat, intelligence and propaganda tools)," which the Kremlin deployed in conflicts such as Georgia, Syria and Ukraine.[6]

Gerasimov's views had never been made into doctrine. However, the consistency of his ideas over the past several years and their practical implications in different regions tell us that the Russian government is executing those concepts. Further, Gerasimov remains one of Russia's leading military intellectuals and is a close advisor to President Vladimir Putin.

China is another rising global power—rapidly expanding its influence mostly through trade, financial, and other soft power means of influence. At the same time, the increasingly expanding rapprochement of China, Russia, Iran, and Turkey—as well as some other mostly regional countries—is a profound threat to US National Security and National Defense Strategy objectives.

CASO and its partners would like to express special appreciation to Robert F. Baumann, former CGSC director of degree programs, for his useful advice and support. Also, sincere appreciation to Donald P. Wright, deputy director of Army University Press, and his team; Amanda S. Cherry, CGSC editor; Harry L. Sarles, Army University public affairs officer; the CASO team and its partners; Daniel O. Neal, Army University contractor; Casey L. Phillips, CGSC developer/system administrator; and the other faculty and staff who supported the project.

Special thanks to Maj. Gen. Stephen J. Maranian, former US Army Combined Arms Center for Education deputy commanding general and Army University provost; James B. Martin, CGSC dean of academics; and Jackie D. Kem, CGSC associate dean of academics, for their continuous support of CASO in general and this anthology in particular. CASO is also grateful to Thomas P. Wilhelm, director of the Foreign Military Studies Office (FMSO), US Army Training and Doctrine Command G-2, and his team, as well as Roderick M. Cox, president and chief executive officer of the CGSC Foundation, and his team for their continuous support.

Notes

1. Ibrahimov Mahir, Otto Gustav, and Gentile Lee, eds., *Cultural Perspectives, Geopolitics, and Energy Security of Eurasia: Is the Next Global Conflict Imminent?* (Fort Leavenworth, KS: Army University Press, 2017).

2. Maj. Gen. John S. Kem, Provost, foreword to *Cultural Perspectives*.

3. US Army Cultural and Area Studies Office (CASO), "Mission and Vision Statement," accessed 24 June 2019, http://usacac.army.mil/organizations/cace/lre.

4. Alexander Dugin, *The Fourth Political Theory* (London: Arktos Media, 2012). See also Alexander Dugin, *Eurasian Mission: An Introduction to Neo-Eurasianism* (London: Arktos Media, 2014).

5. Congressional Research Service, "Information Warfare: Issues for Congress," 5 March 2018, R45142, Version 5.

6. Tsenosti Nauki V Predvidenii, "Novie Vizovi Trebuyut Pereosmislit Formi I Sposobi Vedenia Boyevikh Deistviy [A Value of Science in Prediction: New Challenges Demand Rethinking the Forms and Methods of Carrying out Combat Operations]," *Voyenno-Promyshlennyy Kurier* [The Military-Industrial Courier] 8, no. 476, 27 February 2013, http://vpk-news.ru/articles/14632. See also Andrew E. Kramer, "Russian General Pitches 'Information' Operations as a Form of War," *The New York Times-Moscow*, 2 March 2019, https://www.nytimes.com/2019/03/02/world/europe/russia-hybrid-war-gerasimov.html; and William Darley, "Analyzing Toxic 'Fake News': Are Key Concepts Promulgated by Master Propagandists of the Past Still in Practice Today?," *Small Wars Journal*, accessed 13 Sep 2019, https://smallwarsjournal.com/jrnl/art/analyzing-toxic-fake-news-are-key-concepts-promulgated-master-propagandists-past-still.

Chapter 1
Russia's Soft Power Projection in the Middle East
Anna L. Borshchevskaya

Political scientist Joseph S. Nye Jr. defined soft power as "the ability to get what you want through attraction rather than coercion or payments. It arises from the attraction of the country's culture, political ideals, and policies. When our policies are seen as legitimate in the eyes of others, our soft power is enhanced."[1] For a state to be successful, according to Nye, hard power is necessary; but it is also important to shape long-term preferences of others and project values. Soft power projection helps attract partners and allies.[2]

Historically, the Kremlin always emphasized hard power. During the Soviet era, the following phrase encapsulated so many aspects of Soviet life it became a trope: "If you don't know, we will teach you; if you don't want to, we will force you."[3] In more recent history, Moscow has focused on hard power projection; the brutal suppression of Chechnya's struggle for independence, the 2008 war with Georgia, the 2014 annexation of Crimea from Ukraine, and the 2015 military intervention in Syria to save Syrian dictator Bashar al-Assad all highlight Moscow's preference for hard power. Indeed, in private conversations, Western policymakers often argue that Russia has no power to attract. The Kremlin has yet to treat its own citizens well—let alone those of other countries. An oft-cited example of Moscow's inability to attract is that generally people do not dream of immigrating to Russia; rather, they tend to dream of immigrating from Russia to developed democracies, contributing to Russia's brain drain.

In this context it may be tempting to conclude that Russia does not project soft power at all. Yet the reality is more nuanced. Moscow, while abusive to its own citizens, devotes a great deal to soft power projection—often more so than to hard power. However, it defines soft power on its own authoritarian terms. While much attention has been devoted to these activities in the West and the post-Soviet space, the Middle East provides fertile ground for Russian efforts, which have received far less attention. For nearly two decades under Vladimir Putin, Moscow consistently focused on soft power projection in the region and cultivated an image of a neutral powerbroker and peacemaker, as well as a business partner. In addition to diplomacy, trade and tourism, Moscow projects its influence through the Russian Orthodox Church, culture centers, major sports events, Chechnya's strongman Ramzan Kadyrov, and Kremlin-controlled propaganda outlets such as *RT* and *Sputnik*. Moscow cultivates attraction by projecting authoritarian values which resonate in a region with little history of democracy. Through this soft power projection, Moscow cements leverage to secure influence at the expense of the West.

Moscow's Authoritarian Interpretation of Soft Power

A major source of confusion about Russia and soft power is Moscow's interpretation of the term. According to Nye himself, the Kremlin is failing "miserably" because it is attempting to project soft power using the state, and with a zero-sum approach.[4] To succeed, Russia (and China) in his view, "will need to match words and deeds in their policies, be self-critical, and unleash the full talents of their civil societies. Unfortunately, this is not about to happen anytime soon."[5] Framed this way, it would seem the Kremlin and soft power just do not go together.

Yet Moscow has its own broad authoritarian interpretation of the term. It is ultimately pragmatic and aimed at building leverage. This includes projection of values—just not democratic ones. This is why it is zero-sum and government-led, and why this approach runs counter to Nye's definition. Indeed, both democracies and the Kremlin fund non-profit organizations—a soft power tool; but where democracies are open and transparent, those funded by the Kremlin are opaque and subversive. Russian pro-Kremlin academic Sergei Karaganov argues that the Kremlin definition of soft power is different from that of the West. "Russian political leaders have largely interpreted the soft power concept in a very instrumental and pragmatic way," he wrote; "many Chinese and Russian soft power initiatives often pursue overtly pragmatic, interest-based goals rather than aim to take into account international partners' interests."[6] Karaganov indicated that this broader interpretation of soft power "contradicts Nye's definition because [Nye] excludes coercion as well as economically driven influence ('payment' in his terminology) from soft power."[7] In the Russian interpretation, these are acceptable soft power instruments. Russian scholars note that the terms "soft power," along with "foreign policy image," have taken a prominent position in Russia's policy discourse; Russian analysts discussed over the years the need for Russia to better project soft power.[8]

Moscow always cared about its image—domestically, and internationally. Perception of legitimacy by others especially mattered to the Kremlin, though differently from how Western governments understand the idea and how to pursue it. In early years when the Bolsheviks consolidated power, they took small steps first then watched for outside re-actions; when there was little to none, they proceeded to larger domestic atrocities. Nye himself acknowledged that after World War II, the Soviet Union's communist ideology found an appeal in Europe and the Third World. The Soviet Union presented its ideology as a better and legitimate alternative to that of the West and pushed moral equivocation between the two. Leaders carefully cultivated select foreigners as "useful idiots" who would present the Soviet Union in a highly skewed if not entirely fictitious light. Among the most famous of these is perhaps Pulitzer prize-winning *New York Times* journalist and Stalin apologist Walter Duranty, whose re-porting helped Stalin hide from the world his 1932–33 crime of state-led famine in Ukraine. Furthermore, the Kremlin cultivated other sources of attraction. Russian analyst Innokenty Adyasov wrote, "Yury Gagarin was the best instrument of Soviet soft power: never, perhaps, in the post-war world was sympathy toward the USSR [Union of Soviet Socialist Repub-lics] so great . . . the personality of the earth's first cosmonaut had an impact."[9] The Soviet Union also used soft power tools like major sporting events as opportunities to improve its international image—and spared no expense, human or financial.

The Russian Diaspora as a Soft Power Tool

The Soviet Union fell but the Kremlin even under Boris Yeltsin had a policy toward Russia's diaspora, which it would soon instrumentalize as a soft power tool.[10] Israeli journalist and author Isabella Ginor recalled an interview she conducted with then-Russian foreign minister Andrei Kozyrev in 1995 in Jerusalem. It is illustrative of the difference between Western and Kremlin approaches to soft power regarding the country's "compatriots"—Russian speakers living abroad:

IG: You mentioned Russia's commitment to protect "Russian speak-ers" everywhere. I'm a Russian speaker. Does that include me?

AK: Of course.

IG: But I never requested Russia's protection.

AK: No one is asking you.[11]

The issue of Russians and Russian speakers is compounded by pro-found confusion about term definitions, which often gets lost in transla-tion. In English, "Russian" can mean either an ethnic Russian or a Russian citizen—there is no distinction. In Russian, "russkiy" means ethnic Rus-sian and "rossiyanin" is a Russian citizen. A Russian-speaking Ukrainian or Jew, for example, would be a "rossiyanin"—a Russian citizen—but not a "russkiy." Yet in official documents, people write "russkiy" rather than "rossiyanin" as a nationality.[12] Even in everyday speech, Russian speakers routinely use the two terms interchangeably. For the Kremlin, the Russian-speaking diaspora has been a soft power tool, yet as Mikhail Suslov writes, "The understanding of Russian 'compatriots' abroad' has never been the same."[13] When Putin presented his illegal Crimea annexation in March 2014 as a "rescue" of Russia's "compatriots" in Ukraine, he also played on and reinforced confusion over the definition of a Russian "compatriot;" he defined nationality in terms of language and ethnicity.[14]

Soft Power Emphasis under Vladimir Putin

Moscow turned to soft power early into Putin's first presidency, with a major focus on the immediate post-Soviet space. Fiona Hill, a prominent Russia scholar and former Russia advisor to President Donald Trump, wrote in August 2004 that Moscow's soft power projection efforts in the former Soviet Union produced clear results:

> There is more to Russia's attractiveness than oil riches. Consider the persistence of the Russian language as a regional lingua franca—the language of commerce, employment and education—for many of the states of the former Soviet Union. . . . Then there is a range of new Russian consumer products, a burgeoning popular culture spread through satellite TV, a growing film industry, rock music, Russian popular novels and the revival of the crowning achievements of the Russian artistic tradition. They have all made Russia a more attractive state for populations in the region than it was in the 1990s. . . . Instead of the Red Army, the penetrating forces of Russian power in Ukraine, the Caucasus, and Central Asia are now Russian natural gas and the giant gas monopoly, Gazprom, as well as Russian electricity and the huge energy company, UES—and Russian culture and consumer goods. In addition, private firms—such as Russia's Wimm-Bill-Dann Foods—have begun to dominate regional markets for dairy products and fruit juices.[15]

Indeed, the results of Moscow's soft power efforts were so significant in the early Putin years that, according to Hill, they outweighed Moscow's hard power projection. "Since 2000, Russia's greatest contribution to the security and stability of its vulnerable southern tier has not been through its military presence on bases, its troop deployments, or security pacts and arms sales," she wrote.[16] Thus Putin focused on image projection far more than observers may have realized; and in those years it appeared to pay off.

But these years also saw the rise of peaceful color revolutions in the post-Soviet space that the Kremlin perceived as orchestrated by the United States. They also touched the Middle East, with Lebanon's Cedar revolution. For the Kremlin, the most significant was Ukraine's Orange revolution of November 2004 to January 2005. In this context, Moscow increasingly worked in the former Soviet Union to consolidate power among Russia's "compatriots." For the Kremlin, "protection," or "rescue," of Russian compatriots from fictional enemies was the perfect pretext to justify aggression, and events to promote Russian language and culture served as a pretext for cementing leverage inside the target countries, positioning Moscow as a decision-maker. In this sense, compatriots were a soft power tool under the Kremlin's definition of the term; the Kremlin would protect them whether they asked to be protected or not.

The southern tier has been important both in terms of Russia's interest in what it called the "near abroad" and a "privileged sphere of influence," but also because it connected to the Middle East. Historically, the Kremlin considered itself vulnerable in this region. For this reason, both czarist Russia and the Soviet Union looked for ways to protect this "soft underbelly." For the Soviet Union and for Putin's Russia, this also meant undermining the North Atlantic Treaty Organization (NATO) southern flank.

As for Russian-speaking "compatriots," although the majority reside in post-Soviet space, the Kremlin talked about it in global terms. In the Middle East, immigrants from Russia and the former Soviet Union quickly added approximately one million to Israel's population; at the end of the Cold War, this total hovered just under five million.[17] In more recent years, Putin routinely emphasized that Russia and Israel had a "special relationship" primarily because of Israel's Russian-speaking immigrants.[18] Putin closely studied the fall of the Soviet Union, as did Yevgeny Primakov, former chief of Soviet security services and later Russia's prime minister in Boris Yeltsin's government. Both came to believe that from a purely strategic perspective, the Soviet Union made a mistake by antagonizing Jews, especially the Jewish population in the USSR.

The year 2004 saw not only Ukraine's Orange revolution but also Russia's return as an international donor; over the years, the country increasingly cultivated this role. These events had a profound effect on the Kremlin.

A reference to Russia in the West as a "re-emerging donor" became common.[19] In December 2005, Moscow also launched *Russia Today* ("Rossiya Segodnya" in Russian, eventually renamed *RT*) as its flagship propaganda outlet for projecting its narrative to overseas audiences and discrediting the West. "When we designed this [*RT*] project back in 2005," Vladimir Putin said in an interview years later, "we intended introducing another strong player on the world's scene . . . but also try, let me stress, I mean—try to break the Anglo-Saxon monopoly on the global information streams."[20] Thus, the Kremlin cast a wide net with its soft power projection.

Aggression Accompanied by Soft Power Projection

With time, Putin grew more ostensibly aggressive in his foreign policy—aggressiveness accompanied by efforts to improve Russia's image. Putin's February 2007 speech at the Munich Security Conference sent a clear signal of this more aggressive foreign policy posture.[21] Yet in June the same year, he approved the Concept on Russia's Participation in International Development Assistance, which presented "a strategic vision of the substance and priorities of Russia's policy concerning the provision of international financial, technical, humanitarian, and other aid to facilitate socioeconomic development of recipient countries, help resolve crisis situations caused by natural disasters and/or international conflicts, and strengthen Russia's international position and credibility."[22] The document listed regional priorities that went beyond the Commonwealth of Independent States (CIS) to include the Asia-Pacific, Middle East, Africa, and Latin America. With regard to the Middle East specifically, the document prioritized "strengthening of relations."

The following year, Russia's January 2008 Foreign Policy Concept focused not only on the Kremlin's traditional themes of a multipolar world, perceived American domination, and a stated goal for Russia to become "an influential center in the modern world;" it also emphasized soft power, in general, and its use to achieve these goals and strengthen Russia's international position:

> Together with the military power of States, economic, scientific and technological, environmental, demographic, and informational factors are coming to the fore as major factors of influence of a state on international affairs. . . . Economic interdependence of States is becoming one of key factors of international stability. . . . Strengthening of international position of Russia and solution of the tasks related to the establishment of equal mutually bene-

ficial partnerships with all countries, successful promotion of our foreign economic interests and provision of political, economic, information and cultural influence abroad require the use of all available financial and economic tools of the state and provision of adequate resources for the Russian Federation's foreign policy.[23]

Although the document addresses "mutually beneficial partnerships," it is important to remember to read between the lines. Moscow pays lip service to these ideas but, in reality, tends to see partners as subjects. Yet in this context it is clear that Moscow understood the importance of projecting soft power and was intent on using it to achieve its goals.

Following Moscow's aggression against Georgia in August 2008, the Kremlin launched a massive propaganda campaign to boost its international image, especially in the West. Russian officials discussed using soft power as a foreign policy driver that year and noted that Putin and Russian Foreign Minister Sergei Lavrov had done the same on multiple occasions.[24]

In September 2008, a month after Moscow's aggression that led to a war with Georgia, Putin issued a decree creating the Federal Agency on the Affairs of CIS Countries, Compatriots Living Abroad, and International Humanitarian Cooperation—Rossotrudnichestvo for short. By its own description, "the activities of Rossotrudnichestvo and its overseas agencies are aimed at implementing the state policy of international humanitarian cooperation, facilitating the spread abroad of an objective view of modern Russia."[25]

The next month, Lavrov gave an interview on the eve of a major international conference on Russian compatriots living abroad. He said that soft power is gaining greater importance, and highlighted that Moscow should be using it specifically in relation to its "compatriots." In the same interview, Lavrov described the victim as the criminal—he talked of Georgia's "aggression" against Southern Ossetia.[26] Rossotrudnichestvo's activities, for their part, raised concerns among law enforcement agencies in democratic countries about possible intelligence operations. Just as *RT* was a propaganda channel, Rossotrudnichestvo would be another instrument of the Russian state—anything but objective, contrary to its official pronouncements. Such methods stood in stark contrast to how democratic societies projected their values, yet they fit within the Kremlin interpretation of soft power.

The year 2012 marked several milestones in Russia—including with regard to the Kremlin's soft power projection. In late 2011 to early 2012, massive anti-Putin protests erupted throughout the country—the largest since the fall of the Soviet Union. In addition to famously blaming US Secretary of State Hillary Clinton for "giving the signal" for protestors to come out, Putin penned a series of articles in the mainstream Russian press. He outlined his vision for the country, including on economic and foreign policy fronts, and focused on Russia's problems, especially the Arab Spring. When discussing his foreign policy vision, Putin talked about improving Russia's image, including the need to promote a positive and "accurate" image of Russia abroad.[27] Soon after in July that year, he raised the importance of using soft power at a high-level meeting with Russian ambassadors and permanent representatives in international organizations:

> Let me remind you that "soft power" is all about promoting one's interests and policies through persuasion and creating a positive perception of one's country, based not just on its material achievements but also its spiritual and intellectual heritage. Russia's image abroad is formed not by us and, as a result, it is often distorted and does not reflect the real situation in our country or Russia's contribution to global civilization, science, and culture. Our country's policies often suffer from a one-sided portrayal these days. Those who fire guns and launch air strikes here or there are the good guys, while those who warn of the need for restraint and dialogue are for some reason at fault. But our fault lies in our failure to adequately explain our position. This is where we have gone wrong.[28]

Thus, in February 2013, Russia officially incorporated soft power into its foreign policy toolkit, while indirectly putting the blame on the United States for what it perceived as destabilizing soft power projection—a consistent Kremlin theme. This interpretation highlighted the Kremlin's own spin on the concept of soft power:

> Soft power, a comprehensive toolkit for achieving foreign policy objectives building on civil society potential, information, cultural, and other methods and technologies alternative to traditional diplomacy, is becoming an indispensable component of modern international relations. At the same time, increasing global competition and the growing crisis potential sometimes creates a risk of destructive and unlawful use of "soft power" and human rights concepts to exert political pressure on sovereign states, interfere in their internal affairs, destabilize their political situation, ma-

nipulate public opinion, including under the pretext of financing cultural and human rights projects abroad.[29]

Moscow's evolution in terms of soft power application coincided with a new stage of aggression in international affairs when it illegally annexed Crimea from Ukraine in March 2014 and began a covert war in Eastern Ukraine. Yet Moscow continued to care about its international image, orchestrating a referendum in Crimea under the barrel of a Russian gun to create a perception of legitimacy for its actions.

Moreover, *RT* channels began broadcasting in the United Kingdom, France, and Germany to continue promoting the Kremlin viewpoint in the West, which was rightfully outraged by Kremlin activities. Senior Russian officials such as Lavrov continued to talk about the importance of using soft power in the years after.[30]

Moscow's success (or lack thereof) in the post-Soviet space and the West warrants a separate discussion. As the Kremlin grew increasingly aggressive toward its neighbors over the years and employed a variety of tools to destabilize and divide Western democracies, Moscow's image became arguably mixed at best. Moscow succeeded in annexing Crimea and fighting a war in Eastern Ukraine, but it also brought Ukrainians closer together and consolidated their efforts to join the West. The overall feelings of Russian-speaking "compatriots" toward Russia itself tended to be mixed. That Russia remained under sanctions was also a testament to widespread negative Western views of Putin's Russia. The Kremlin continued to use its soft power tools through government-controlled organizations presented as non-governmental organizations (NGOs) or, more accurately, GONGOS (government-organized non-governmental organizations, a term that emerged in the post-Soviet space); culture centers; and information operations that continue to destabilize democracies and cement the Kremlin's influence in the post-Soviet space. This massive effort should be taken seriously. In this sense, the Kremlin's grip was growing. At the same time following Moscow's Crimea annexation, the G-8 kicked Russia out as a member; and at the time of this writing, an invitation for re-entry does not appear forthcoming. While US President Trump called for Russia's re-admittance, Germany and other European countries rejected such a move. That said, the situation may change as France and Germany continue to pursue a reset with Russia and if more voices in the United States and the West broadly call for a reset with Russia.[31] Regardless, the Middle East has been a different story.

Leveraging through Soft Power in the Middle East: Diplomacy, Tourism, and Trade

Once Putin succeeded Yeltsin, he worked steadily and consistently to return Russia to the Middle East, as envisioned some years earlier by Yevgeniy Primakov. A skilled Arabist who was Russia's prime minister in the late 1990s, Primakov held notions of a "multipolar" world also promoted by other Russian officials. In this view, Russia should not let the United States dominate any region, least of all the Middle East. Russia's June 2000 Foreign Policy Concept defined Moscow's Middle East priorities largely in terms of soft power—"to restore and strengthen positions, particularly economic ones"—and noted the importance of continuing to develop ties with Iran.[32] The January National Security Concept also highlighted "attempts to create an international relations structure based on domination by developed Western countries in the international community, under US leadership."[33] The November 2016 version highlighted the importance of the Middle East in Russian foreign policy and named "external interference" (a euphemism for the United States) as a major cause of regional instability.[34] These documents, together with those mentioned in previous sections, show both Moscow's intent to become a major player in the region from the very beginning, and its emphasis on soft power as a key instrument in achieving this aim.

Putin's approach to the region was pragmatic from the very beginning—not unlike his overall approach to soft power. He worked to build and maintain ties with virtually every major actor in the region and, by 2010, had built good relations with all regional governments and most key internal opposition movements.[35] Through Putin's efforts, Russia regained political, diplomatic, and economic influence in the region. Among his soft power instruments, he emphasized trade, especially arms and hydrocarbons but also goods such as foodstuffs, along with growing Russian tourism, diplomatic exchanges, and provision of high-technology goods such as nuclear reactors, and in some cases major loan forgiveness, such as $13.4 billion debt forgiveness to the Syrian regime. Over the coming years, Turkey, Egypt, and Israel emerged as top destinations for Russian tourists, which especially mattered to Turkey's and Egypt's economies. It was a tap Putin could turn on and off. When Russian tourists could not go to Turkey and Egypt, many went to Tunisia. Tunisian Tourism Minister Selma Elloumi Rekik said, "We also note that the growth of the Russian market is continuing; it was not a temporary phenomenon as some claimed but a real trend that we can capture and encourage."[36] Morocco aimed to attract as many as two million Russian tourists by 2020.[37] While initial numbers were in the tens of thousands, such stated aspirations matter.

Moscow also built leverage through construction of Turkey's and Egypt's nuclear power plants. Moscow's continued strategic search for port access also mattered in terms of Russia's strategic levers of influence. Moscow and Cairo signed an industrial free-trade zone; while the primary purpose was likely political, the economic dimension is also worth mentioning.

In the Persian Gulf area especially, Moscow's soft power projection focused on financial instruments, getting Gulf leaders more interested in Russian weaponry, encouraging sovereign wealth fund agreements, and organizing business councils and traveling exhibits that created forums for Russian-Arab commercial deals.[38]

Moscow paid pensions to former Soviet citizens living in Israel—even as it had no money to adjust Russian citizen pensions for inflation. This was another example of Moscow's pragmatic soft power projection that had little to do with genuine concern for people—compounded by the fact that the dollar value was largely symbolic, approximately $200 a month.[39] Moscow also recognized West Jerusalem as Israel's capital before Washington recognized Jerusalem in its entirety.[40]

Senior regional leaders routinely paid their respects to Putin in Moscow, and this trend increased over the years. Israeli Prime Minister Benjamin Netanyahu, for example, made more trips to Moscow than to Washington during the Obama and Trump presidencies. Israeli high-tech goods were an important component of Putin's relationship with the Jewish state.

In sum, Putin's pragmatic approach was more successful than that of the Soviet Union's ideological blinkering.[41] Unencumbered by ideology, Putin offered a clear and simple narrative as an alternative to the West—a narrative on an authoritarian, anti-Western great power that resonated with the region's leaders. Putin's September 2015 military intervention in Syria officially returned Russia as a key region player and positioned Putin as a regional powerbroker. Soft power alone could not do that. Yet without his previous years of investing in relationships and building influence as Putin had done, Putin would not have been able to take full advantage of the chance that Syria had presented him; he had invested in the groundwork that created receptivity to Moscow on a deeper level, and beyond Syria alone, and especially in the context of American retreat from the region that began under the Obama administration. Indeed, it is the broader overall emphasis on Putin as peacemaker, a regional powerbroker—in itself a projection of soft power, of Russia's image—that continued to play a key role in his success in the region beyond the use of his military. This earned him often-begrudging respect in the region for sticking to his guns—ironically, while simultaneously cultivating an image of a neutral broker—and also clearly picking a side in Syria and sticking by his promises. As *Jeune Afrique* noted, Moscow earned a reputation among the region's leaders for not intervening in domestic affairs and, most importantly, keeping its promises.[42]

Ironically, Moscow's success in the Middle East was an example of how soft and hard power reinforced each other—seemingly consistent with Nye's argument for soft power. Putin enabled and protected Syria's Assad, who was responsible for one of the worst humanitarian tragedies since World War II; and more broadly across the region, Moscow's influence perpetuated low-level instability and reinforced the region's anti-democratic proclivities, showing just how different Moscow's interpretation of soft power was from that of Western analysts like Nye. Ultimately, Moscow's soft power efforts were to build pragmatic, hardnosed leverage in the region. As prominent Lebanese journalist Hussam Ittani wrote:

> It was believed that Russia's intervention would completely wreck relations between it and Arab countries that support the Syrian opposition. Russian diplomacy, however, succeeded in shifting Arab attention towards issues that concern them both, such as energy. Russia has, throughout this period, maintained its policy on sensitive issues that concern Arabs, such as the Palestinian cause. Pragmatism, therefore, dominated Russian-Arab relations and both parties succeeded in averting a clash by adopting a list of priorities, although not ideal, that reflects the balance of power on the ground.[43]

Leveraging through Soft Power in the Middle East: the Orthodox Church and Cultural Outreach

Diplomacy and economic leverage are critical elements, but the Kremlin also resorted to other tools. The Russian Orthodox Church was a subtle and critically important soft power tool in the Middle East, in the backdrop of Putin's multipolar world vision for the Middle East—to counter perceived Western hegemony, imperialism, and moral degradation. The Kremlin aligned the Russian Orthodox Church with the state as both a domestic and foreign policy tool, and revived Russia's historical mission as the main protector of Eastern Orthodox Christianity in the Middle East. The idea was not entirely separate from "protection" of Russian "compatriots" abroad in a sense of presentation of both as under threat—a claim that could sound more credible in the Middle East than in the former Soviet Union.

Jerusalem always mattered to the Russian Orthodox Church, both to czarist and especially imperial nineteenth century Russia. At the time, the Church exercised influence over Greek, Armenian, and Arab Orthodox communities in the Ottoman Empire. It funded schools, churches, and hostels in Palestine and Syria.[44] Under Putin, the Russian Orthodox Church attempted to revive the idea, along with broader historic notions of Russia as the "Third Rome," with its own spin in terms of connections to state foreign policy of expansion into the Middle East. The church in this context presented itself as a unifying force for all Christians in the region and the main pillar of stability protecting Christian communities. This was among the many reasons why the church and the Kremlin cultivated ties with Israel.

In a 2015 presidential decree, Putin created the President Putin Palestinian Organization for Culture and Economy, a school in Bethlehem.[45] According to Israel Defense, approximately 500 Palestinian children attended in 2017. The school opened under the auspices of the Orthodox Imperial Society, originally founded by Czar Alexander III and restored in its official name in May 1992. Indeed, for Russian Patriarch Kirill, the reestablishment of the society was critically important; seven years earlier, the Israeli government returned to Russia a building associated with this society—a mark of Russia's prestige and influence in Israel.[46] In January 2019, Mahmoud Abbas, the president of the Palestinian National Authority, met with the head of the Orthodox Imperial Society of Palestine; according to Russian chief propaganda outlet *RT*, the society would work to bring more Russian pilgrims to Palestine.[47]

In Lebanon, Moscow courted the country's relatively large Christian community, mainly via the Orthodox Gathering (al-Liqaa al-Orthodoxi), founded in 2011. The most prominent member of this group, Elie Ferzli, was Lebanon's deputy parliament speaker and former information minister who was a long-time supporter of the Assad regime. In January 2014, a Russian parliamentary delegation—including Sergei Gavrilov, head of a Duma committee that focused on "defending Christian values," and Russian ambassador Alexander Zasypkin—stopped in Lebanon en route to Syria and met with members of the Orthodox Gathering and other figures. Gavrilov called on the stakeholders to form a joint council with the goal of "activating cooperation on all levels."[48] In October and November 2017, they held a spate of meetings that resulted in calls for closer cooperation with Orthodox entities in Lebanon, including the Orthodox Gathering.

According to Deutsche Welle, the Imperial Orthodox Palestine Society (IOPS)—a tsarist-era NGO that was revived after the fall of the Soviet Union—had become "the centerpiece of the Kremlin's activity" in Lebanon.[49]

The Church also played an important role in Russia's Syria campaign. Patriarch Kirill and other Russian priests praised Putin's efforts while some Russian priests blessed war planes that went to Syria and sprinkled holy water on missiles. They compared Russia's Syria campaign to "holy," or "sacred war"—characterizing the intervention as a fight against terrorism, a "holy" fight that should unite everyone.[50] Kirill also linked the fight against terrorism in the Middle East with the Soviet Union's fight against fascism during World War II—a critically important Kremlin theme to consolidate Russian society domestically; this also played a major role in its links with Israel. Kirill's May 2016 statement is illustrative:

> We know that the victory in the Great Patriotic War was a righteous victory. . . . This is why from the very beginning the Great Patriotic War was named as a sacred [or holy] war, that is the war for the truth. . . . God grant that this ideal of the Christ-loving army never leaves our people, our Armed forces. And today, when our warriors take part in hostilities in the Middle East, we know that this is not aggression . . . this is a fight against the terrible enemy in itself evil is not only for the Middle East, but for the whole human race. This evil we call terrorism today, . . . today the war on terror is a holy war.[51]

The church also continued to develop ties within Syria. In September 2018, for instance, Kirill met with the grand mufti of Syria.[52] In May that year, a group of children "of fallen Syrian soldiers" came to Moscow at the invitation of Combat Brotherhood, an all-Russian veterans organization. They met with Kirill at Moscow's Christ the Savior Cathedral and performed the famous Russian song from the World War II era, "Katyusha," in Arabic and Russian.[53]

In addition, the Russian Orthodox Church cultivated a perception of establishing "a stable relationship with all religious faiths in the region."[54] Thus, the church's efforts were not limited to the Christian world alone; it also cultivated ties with its Muslim counterpart in the region. For example, Kirill repeatedly described ISIS as an extremist organization that warped the true meaning of Islam and called for a broad alliance in the region to fight extremism—a call that was similar to Putin's calls for a broad multilateral coalition to fight terrorism.

Separately from religion, Moscow promoted Russian culture throughout the region, primarily through cultural centers run by Rossotrudnichestvo and the RusskiyMir Foundation. These agencies, however, may have had wider goals in mind pertaining to serving as intelligence fronts and tools for general subversion. Russian culture centers have become common throughout the region—for example, in Kuwait, Lebanon, and Tunisia—and their number is growing.[55] In Lebanon, for example, press reports indicated more would be forthcoming. Anecdotally, these centers often provide genuinely useful services, such as ballet classes. Several years ago, a Russian culture center in Kuwait hosted a Soviet movie night; to the surprise of many, the room was packed. As part of Moscow's growing relations with Morocco, the Russian departments of culture and foreign affairs planned a major festival of Russian artists in Agadir, while King Mohammed VI granted Moroccan nationality to a Chechen mixed martial arts (MMA) fighter, Mairbek Taisumov.[56]

Moscow's Syria intervention, not unlike interventions in the post-Soviet space, saw the rise of Kremlin attempts to improve its image with regard to its activities there. Thus, approximately a dozen Russian humanitarian organizations mushroomed in Assad-controlled areas of Syria, secular and religious, Christian and Muslim. The Russian Defense Ministry largely coordinated distribution of aid around Syria.[57] Moscow's main purpose for these organization was political, rather than humanitarian; while the miniscule aid distribution produced little substantive change, it generated positive news coverage for Moscow. These organizations did not go through the same level of scrutiny as Western organizations seeking permission to work in Assad-controlled areas. Indeed, this situation was reminiscent of Moscow's involvement in efforts to bring Syrian refugees home from Lebanon; the few who did return often faced brutal treatment from the Assad regime. The refugee situation remained unresolved—while Moscow positioned itself as indispensable and gained leverage over all parties.

Leveraging through Soft Power in the Middle East: Muslim Russia and Propaganda

Russia's very identity developed in close proximity to the Middle East and Islam. Moscow likes to present itself as a country that culturally understands the region better than the West, comes with no colonial baggage, and was an alternative to Iran. Moreover, as Russia's overall population declined, it's sizable Muslim majority of roughly twenty million has been growing, adding to the reasons why Moscow wanted to cultivate the Middle East. Moscow appealed to the self-interest of the region's leaders who felt comfortable dealing with Putin. Moreover, Middle East officials do not worry about the Russian equivalent of a Foreign Corrupt Practices Act when dealing with Moscow. Russia's ties to the Kurds went back approximately two hundred years and remained critically important.[58]

Chechen republic leader Ramzan Kadyrov has been another tool of Moscow's soft power projection. Putin installed Kadyrov in 2009; two years later, Kadyrov's horses began racing in the Dubai World Cup and he began to cultivate a positive image with Middle East leaders and make business connections.[59]

In May 2017, the United Arab Emirates-backed Sheikh Zayed Fund opened in Grozny and pledged $300 million to be spent over the next decade for small and medium business enterprises in Chechnya. The next year, a luxury hotel, The Local, opened in Chechnya. It was the first North Caucasus region hotel sponsored by a foreign funder, the Fabulous Abu Dhabi Hotel Management Company. Crown Prince Mohammed bin Zayed attended the opening ceremony. Egypt's national football team stayed in this hotel during the World Cup, which Russia hosted that summer. Kadyrov, just like the Orthodox Church and secular Moscow organizations, also funded humanitarian ventures in the Muslim world.

In 2020, the Muslim World League (MWL) for the first time launched an international conference on religious peace and coexistence in Moscow. The fifth session, held in Grozny, discussed the foundations of Russia's religious and ethnic relations and the country's relationship with the Islamic world.[60] The MWL chose Russia for the summit because, in its view, the country had been a model of religious and ethnic harmony in recent years. In April 2020, Moscow and Grozny hosted Islam: A Message of Mercy and Peace. Representatives of over forty three countries attended this conference on Islam and, according to Kremlin-run Regum, described Chechnya as one of the most "dynamically developing regions" and Russia as "the best friend of Islam and doesn't pursue a policy of double standards" (an indirect reference to the United States).[61] At the conference, Kadyrov received a number of awards and titles, such as "hero of Islam" and "star of Jerusalem."[62] It may be premature to talk about tangible achievements beyond lofty pronouncements, but Moscow's approach to working with the league contrasts with Europe's choice to expel it.[63]

Russian information manipulation has been another important though unnoticed element of Russia's soft power projection in the region.[64] Dmitry Kiselyov, a key Kremlin propagandist, once described journalism as a warfare tactic. His description encapsulated Moscow's interpretation of soft power: "If you can persuade a person, you don't need to kill him. Let's think about what's better: to kill or to persuade? Because if you aren't able to persuade, then you will have to kill."[65] The Middle East—a region with little history of a free press, inherently distrustful of the West, accustomed to government-controlled media and conspiracy theories—was arguably predisposed to Russian influence more so than democratic societies.

The two most visible Kremlin outlets in the region were *RT* Arabic and *Sputnik Arabic*. As mentioned in the earlier section, *RT* came out in Arabic after it was introduced in English, which shows the direction of the Kremlin's thinking early on. The *RT* and *Sputnik* objectives were to build legitimacy for the Kremlin and discredit the West. While the two outlets typically sowed confusion and played on conspiracy theories, their Middle East efforts emphasized building legitimacy through reporting local news such as human interest stories and sometimes coverage of Russia itself, all to boost Moscow's image. In its coverage of the situation in Syria, for example, *RT Russia* portrayed Syria as dysfunctional, a country that needed someone to come and fix things, and Russia as somewhat on the side, not directly involved.[66]

Another key feature of Moscow's efforts was an emphasis on social media targeting the region's large youth bulge. Moscow clearly invested significant resources in its Arabic propaganda, more so than in other regions. While it may not get as much bang for its buck in the Middle East as elsewhere, Russia's long-term investment in youth could pay off in the long run. Indeed, one recent Arab Youth Survey found that 64 percent of young Arabs saw Russia as an ally, while only 41 percent said the same about the United States. Moreover, the perception of the United States as the enemy had nearly doubled since 2016.[67]

In Turkey, *Sputnik* played a critical information operations role.[68] Furthermore, given the media environment in Turkey, some of the best Turkish journalists went to work for *Sputnik* radio; even pro-Western and anti-Recip Tayyip Erdogan analysts admitted that *Sputnik* produced quality work, even as they recognized its propaganda component. More to the point, many saw Russian media as the only independent alternative in President Erdogan's Turkey.

Lastly and more recently, *RT* and *Sputnik* increasingly partnered with local regional media outlets to enhance their legitimacy. Thus, in September 2018 Egypt's state-controlled Al Ahram entered a partnership with

Sputnik. Al-Ahram's history as the voice of the Arab nationalist movement had symbolic meaning. It embedded *Sputnik* deeply within the narrative of traditional Arabic-language media. *Morocco's News Agency* (*MAP*) and *Sputnik* signed an agreement "to strengthen bilateral cooperation" in December 2018; and in May 2020, *Sputnik* and Radio and the United Arab Emirates' *WAM* news agency signed a memorandum of understanding to exchange information.[69]

Moscow's Arabic propaganda remains an under-studied subject. More than anything, however, the Kremlin's inroads in the region's information space highlight Western own narrative problem in the Middle East and to the extent that the Kremlin's narrative resonates, the West has yet to put up an equally competitive alternative.

Conclusion

The Kremlin is committed to methodically building leverage throughout the Middle East. It uses all tools in its arsenal and intends them to reinforce each other, and while the Russian military matters, Moscow's soft power approach that supports its hard power efforts has been the most effective—within the confines of Moscow's own definition of soft power.

From a broader strategic perspective, the US is increasingly shifting toward great power competition. But policymakers and analysts disagree on whether the Middle East is a distraction from this competition, or an arena for it. Moscow for its part, however, unambiguously sees this region as crucial to its great power competition with the United States in particular, and the West more broadly.

Moscow's authoritarianism together with great power ambitions stand fundamentally at odds with those of liberal democracies, and thus their goals in terms of attraction, and means to attain them, also fundamentally differ from those of democratic governments and societies. The deeper underlying issue with Moscow's soft power projection is whether democratic or authoritarian values are ultimately more attractive—and how much sway Moscow's leverage holds. The answer to some extent depends on how well each side makes its case in the context of current global resurgence of authoritarianism. If the West doesn't compete for the Middle East, the relationships Moscow continues to cultivate on multiple levels throughout the Middle East and North Africa will over time pose an overall greater strategic challenge to American interests beyond this region.

Notes

1. Joseph S. Nye Jr., *Soft Power: The Means to Success in World Politics* (Public Affairs: New York, 2004), x.

2. G. John Ikenberry, "Review of *Soft Power: The Means to Success in World Politics*," *Foreign Affairs* (May/June 2004), https://www.foreignaffairs.com/reviews/capsule-review/2004-05-01/soft-power-means-success-world-politics.

3. In Russian, the phrase is: Ne umeesh, nauchim; ne khochesh, zastavim.

4. Joseph S. Nye Jr., "What China and Russia Don't Get about Soft Power," *Foreign Policy* (29 April 2013), http://www.foreignpolicy.com/articles/2013/04/29/what_china_and_russia_don_t_get_about_soft_power.

5. Nye.

6. Alexander Sergunin and Leonid Karabeshkin, "Understanding Russia's Soft Power Strategy," *Politics* 35 (4 March 2015): 353, https://doi.org/10.1111/1467-9256.12109.

7. Sergunin and Karabeshkin, 352.

8. Alexander Naumov, " 'Myagkaya sila' i vneshnepoliticheskii imidzh Rossiiskoi federatsii," *Perspektivy* (30 March 2015), http://www.perspektivy.info/misl/koncept/magkaja_sila_i_vneshnepoliticheskij_imidzh_rossijskoj_federacii_2015-03-30.htm; and Evgeniy Kuznetsov, "'Myagkaya sila' Rossii: chego ne khvataet?," *Russia in Global Affairs* (15 January 2018), https://globalaffairs.ru/global-processes/Myagkaya-sila-Rossii-chego-ne-khvataet-19290.

9. Innokentiy Adyasov, "Vozmozhna li rossiiskaya 'myagkaya sila'?," *Regnum* (30 May 2012), https://regnum.ru/news/1536886.html.

10. Mikhail Suslov, "Russian World: Russia's Policy Towards its Diaspora," *Russie.Nie.Visions* 103 (July 2017), https://www.ifri.org/sites/default/files/atoms/files/suslov_russian_world_2017.pdf.

11. Author email exchanges with Isabella Ginor and Gideon Remez, June 2019.

12. Leonid Vasiliev, "Rossiya, russkie, rossiyane," *Nezavisimaya Gazeta,* 23 January 2013, http://www.ng.ru/ideas/2013-01-23/5_russia.html.

13. Suslov, "Russian World."

14. Anders Aslund, "12 Ways in which Putin's Rhetoric Resembles Germany in the 1930s," *Kyiv Post,* 21 March 2014, https://www.kyivpost.com/article/opinion/op-ed/anders-aslund-12-ways-in-which-putins-rhetoric-resembles-germany-in-the-1930s-340335.html.

15. Fiona Hill, "Russia's Newly Found Soft Power," *Brookings* (26 August 2004), https://www.brookings.edu/articles/russias-newly-found-soft-power/.

16. Hill.

17. In more recent years, the number of Russian immigrants reportedly decreased to approximately 700,000, still a significant percentage of Israel's total population of approximately 8.5 million.

18. For example, Putin told Netanyahu in March 2016: "Russia and Israel have developed a special relationship primarily because one and a half million Israeli citizens come from the former Soviet Union, they speak the Russian lan-

guage, are the bearers of Russian culture, Russian mentality." From "Putin Says He Plans to Meet Israeli Prime Minister Soon," *TASS* (16 March 2016), http://tass.com/politics/862850. It is noteworthy that Putin exaggerated the number of Israeli citizens who came from the former Soviet Union; he also indicated that the number of Russian pilgrims going to Jerusalem to visit holy sites was growing.

19. Claire Provost, "The Rebirth of Russian Foreign Aid," *The Guardian*, 25 May 2011, https://www.theguardian.com/global-development/2011/may/25/russia-foreign-aid-report-influence-image; and Evgeniy Kuznetsov, "'Myagkaya sila' Rossii: chego ne khvataet?.," *Russia in Global Affairs* (15 January 2018), https://globalaffairs.ru/global-processes/Myagkaya-sila-Rossii-chego-ne-khvataet-19290.

20. "Putin Talks NSA, Syria, Iran, Drones in RT Interview," *RT*, 12 June 2013, https://www.rt.com/news/putin-rt-interviewfull-577/.

21. Vladimir Putin, "Speech and the Following Discussion at the Munich Conference on Security Policy," Kremlin.ru, 10 February 2007, http://en.kremlin.ru/events/president/transcripts/24034.

22. Russian Federation, "Russia's Participation in International Development Assistance Concept" (concept paper, 14 June 2007), https://www.minfin.ru/common/img/uploaded/library/2007/06/concept_eng.pdf.

23. Russian Federation, "The Foreign Policy Concept of the Russian Federation" (concept paper, 12 January 2008), http://en.kremlin.ru/supplement/4116.

24. "'Myagkaya sila' kak draiver prodvizheniya interesov Rossii za rubezhom," *Public Chamber of the Russian Federation* (3 November 2018), https://www.oprf.ru/press/news/2018/newsitem/47195.

25. Rossotrudnichesetvo official site, "About Rossotrudnichesetvo," accessed 6 June 2019, http://rs.gov.ru/ru/about.

26. Sergei Lavrov, "Myagkaya sila" Interview, *Rossiyskaya Gazeta*, 31 October 2008, https://rg.ru/2008/10/30/lavrov.html.

27. Examples include "Rossiya sosredotachivaetsya – vyzovy, na kotorye my dolzhny otvetit," *Izvestiya*, 16 January 2012, https://iz.ru/news/511884; "Rossiya: natsional'nyi vopros" *Nezavisimaya Gazeta*, 23 January 2012, http://www.ng.ru/politics/2012-01-23/1_national.html; "O nashikh ekonomicheskikh zadachakh," *Vedomosti*, 30 January 2012, https://www.vedomosti.ru/politics/articles/2012/01/30/o_nashih_ekonomicheskih_zadachah; "Demokratiya i kachestvo gosudarstva" *Kommersant*, 2 February 2012, https://www.kommersant.ru/doc/1866753; "Stroitel'stvo spravedlivosti. Sotsial'naya politika dlia Rossii." *Komsomolskaya Pravda*, 13 February 2012, kp.ru/daily/3759/2807793/; "Byt' sil'nymi: garantii natsional'noi bezopasnosti dlia Rossii." *Rossiiskaya Gazeta*, 20 February 2012, www.rg.ru/2012/02/20/putin-armiya.html; and "Rossiya i menyayushchiisya mir" *Moskovskiye Novosti*, 27 February 2012, www.mn.ru/politics/78738.

28. "Soveshchanie poslov i postayannyikh predstavitelei Rossii," *Kremlin.ru*, 9 July 2012, http://www.kremlin.ru/news/15902.

29. Russian Federation, "The Foreign Policy Concept of the Russian Federation" (concept paper, 18 February 2013), http://www.mid.ru/foreign_policy/official_documents/-/asset_publisher/CptICkB6BZ29/content/id/122186.

30. "Myagkaya sila. Sergei Lavrov rasskazal deputatam o napravleniyakh mezhdunarodnoi politiki," Embassy of the Russian Federation to Slovakia, 16 June 2016, https://slovakia.mid.ru/vnesnepoliticeskie-diskussii-i-analitika/-/asset_publisher/07ne8wRp5Mh2/content/id/22857956.

31. "Germany Rejects U.S. Proposal For Russia's Return To G7," *RFE/RL,* 27 July 2020, https://www.rferl.org/a/germany-rejects-russia-in-g7/30748671. htm; "A Year after Russia Reset, France Sees No Concrete Results: Minister," *Reuters,* 2 July 2020, https://www.reuters.com/article/us-france-russia/a-year-after-russia-reset-france-sees-no-concrete-results-minister-idUSKBN2431AI. On more voices calling for better relations with Russia, see, Rose Gottemoeller et. al, "It's Time to Rethink Our Russia Policy," *Politico,* 5 August 2020, https://www.politico.com/news/magazine/2020/08/05/open-letter-russia-policy-391434.

32. Russian Federation, "National Security Concept of the Russian Federation," approved by President Vladamir Putin, 28 June 2000, https://fas.org/nuke/guide/russia/doctrine/econcept.htm.

33. Russian Federation, "National Security Concept of the Russian Federation," Approved by Presidential Decree No. 24 of 10 January 2000 https://www.mid.ru/en/foreign_policy/official_documents/-/asset_publisher/CptICkB6BZ29/content/id/589768.

34. Russian Federation, "The Foreign Policy Concept of the Russian Federation" (concept paper, 30 November 2016), http://www.mid.ru/en/foreign_policy/official_documents/-/asset_publisher/CptICkB6BZ29/content/id/2542248.

35. Mark N. Katz, "Moscow and the Middle East: Repeat Performance?," *Russia in Global Affairs,* 7 October 2012, http://eng.globalaffairs.ru/number/Moscow-and-the-Middle-East-Repeat-Performance-15690, 8.

36. Jules Cretois, "Tunisie – Selma Elloumi Rekik: 'L'arrivée de touristes russes n'était pas qu'un phénomène passage,'" *Jeune Afrique,* 29 August 2018, https://www.jeuneafrique.com/621369/economie/tunisie-selma-elloumi-rekik-larrivee-de-touristes-russes-netait-pas-quun-phenomene-passager/.

37. "Le Royaume veut attirer 2 millions de touristes russes d'ici 2020," *Observatoire du Tourisme Maroc,* accessed 6 June 2019, http://www.observatoiredutourisme.ma/le-royaume-veut-attirer-2-millions-de-touristes-russes-dici-2020/.

38. Theodore Karasik, "Russia's Financial Tactics in the Middle East," The Jamestown Foundation (20 December 2017), https://jamestown.org/program/russias-financial-tactics-middle-east/; and Anna Borshchevskaya, "Russia's Moves in the Gulf and Africa have a Common Goal," The Washington Institute for Near East Policy (28 March 2019), https://www.washingtoninstitute.org/policy-analysis/view/russian-moves-in-the-gulf-and-africa-have-a-common-goal.

39. "Russia to Pay $83M to Israeli Pensioners in 2017," *The Moscow Times,* 8 June 2016, https://www.themoscowtimes.com/2016/06/08/russia-to-pay-to-

83m-to-israeli-pensioners-in-2017-a53205; "Medvedev's Awkward Crimea Moment: 'There's Just No Money. But You Take Care!'" *RFE/RL,* 24 May 2016, https://www.rferl.org/a/russia-medvedev-crimea-visit-no-money-social-media-pensioner/27754644.html; and Joshua Krasna, "Moscow on the Mediterranean: Russia and Israel's Relationship," *Russia Foreign Policy Papers*, Foreign Policy Research Institute (FPRI) (June 2018), 10, https://www.fpri.org/wp-content/uploads/2018/06/krasna2018.pdf.

40. Anna Borshchevskaya, "Putin's Self-Serving Israel Agenda," *Foreign Affairs,* 13 April 2017, www.foreignaffairs.com/articles/israel/2017-04-13/putins-self-serving-israel-agenda.

41. Robert O. Freedman, "From Khrushchev and Brezhnev to Putin: Has Moscow's Policy in the Middle East Come Full Circle?," *Contemporary Review of the Middle East* 5 (2018), https://journals.sagepub.com/doi/full/10.1177/2347798918762197.

42. Béchir Ben Yahmed, "[Édito] Au Moyen-Orient, la Russie remplace les États-Unis," *Jeune Afrique,* 29 May 2019, https://www.jeuneafrique.com/mag/779724/politique/edito-au-moyen-orient-la-russie-remplace-les-etats-unis/.

43. Hassam Ittani, "Exclusive - Russia and the Arabs: Ideology and Interests," *Asharq-Al-Awsat,* 28 May 2019, https://aawsat.com/english/home/article/1742956/exclusive-russia-and-arabs-ideology-and-interests.

44. Orlando Figes, *The Crimean War, A History* (New York: Metropolitan Books, 2012), 5.

45. President Putin Palestinian Organization for Culture and Economy website, accessed 6 June 2019, http://www.putin.org.ps/index.html; and Facebook page: https://www.facebook.com/PPPOCE/.

46. Giancarlo Elia Valori, "Between the Russian Orthodox Church and the Middle East Crisis," *Israel Defense,* 7 November 2017, https://www.israeldefense.co.il/en/node/30291; Valori; and Ksenia Svetlova, "To Russia with Love?," *Jerusalem Post,* 3 July 2008, https://www.jpost.com/Local-Israel/In-Jerusalem/To-Russia-with-love.

47. "Abbas yastaqbal raees al-Jamaa al-Imbratouria al-Orthodhaksia" (Abbas welcomes the president of the Imperial Orthodox Palestine Society), *RT,* 29 January 2019.

48. Benas Gerdziunas "The Kremlin's Tie-up with Lebanon's Greek Orthodox Community," *Deutsche Welle,* 7 July 2018, https://www.dw.com/en/the-kremlins-tie-up-with-lebanons-greek-orthodox-community/a-44539394.

49. Anna Borshchevskaya and Hanin Ghaddar, "How to Read Lebanon's Acceptance of Military Aid," *The Washington Institute for Near East Policy's Policy Watch* 3047, 7 December 2018, https://www.washingtoninstitute.org/policy-analysis/view/how-to-read-lebanons-acceptance-of-russian-military-aid; and Benas Gerdziunas, "Russia Uses Church, Far Right for Foothold in Lebanon," *Deutsch Welle,* 20 May 2018, https://www.dw.com/en/russia-uses-church-far-right-for-foothold-in-lebanon/a-43833438.

50. "Patriarch Kirill Urges Countries to Unite in 'Holy War' Against Terrorism," *RFE/RL,* 19 October 2016, https://www.rferl.org/a/russian-orthodox-pa-

triarch-kirill-returns-four-day-visit-britain-queen-elizabeth/28062173.html; and Fred Weir, "Is Russia's Intervention in Syria a 'Holy War'? Russian Orthodox Church: 'Yes,'" *The Christian Science Monitor,* 23 November 2015, https://www.csmonitor.com/World/Europe/2015/1123/Is-Russia-s-intervention-in-Syria-a-holy-war-Russian-Orthodox-Church-yes.

51. "Slovo svyateishego Patriarkha Kirilla v den' pamyati velikomychenika Georgii Pobedonostsa posle Liturgii v Georgievskom khrame na Poklonnoi Gore," Russian Orthodox Church, official site of the Moscow Patriarchate (6 May 2016), http://www.patriarchia.ru/db/text/4461534.html.

52. "Patriarch Kirill Meets Grand Mufti of Syria," The Russian Orthodox Church, Department for Church External Relations (18 September 2019), https://mospat.ru/en/2018/09/18/news163925/.

53. "Patriarch Kirill Meets with Children of Fallen Syrian Soldiers," *Orthodox Christianity,* 28 May 2018, http://orthochristian.com/113307.html.

54. Giancarlo Elia Valori, "Between the Russian Orthodox Church and the Middle East Crisis," *Israel Defense,* 7 November 2017, https://www.israeldefense.co.il/en/node/30291.

55. For example, see Russian culture center in Amman, Jordan, http://rs.gov.ru/en/locations/85/contact/card.

56. Caterina Lalovnovka, "Exclusif. Les Russes préparent une grande offensive culturelle à Agadir," *Maghreb Intelligence,* 16 May 2019, https://www.maghreb-intelligence.com/exclusif-les-russes-preparent-une-grande-offensive-culturelle-a-agadir/; and "12 étrangers, dont des personnalités, deviennent marocains par décret royal," *Telquel,* 24 May 2019, https://telquel.ma/2019/05/24/12-etrangers-dont-des-personnalites-deviennent-marocains-par-decret-royal_1639472/.

57. The Ministry of Defense of the Russian Federation, Syria page, accessed 6 June 2019, https://syria.mil.ru/en/index/syria/news/more.htm?id=12079277@egNews.

58. Anna Borshchevskaya, "Russia, Syrian Kurds, and the Assad Regime," in *Syrian Kurds as a U.S. Ally: Cooperation and Complications*, ed. Patrick Clawson (Washington, DC: The Washington Institute for Near East Policy, 2016), 46–51, https://www.washingtoninstitute.org/policy-analysis/view/syrian-kurds-as-a-u.s.-ally-cooperation-and-complications.

59. Anna Borshchevskaya, "While Mo Salah Sleeps in Grozny," *The Moscow Times,* 12 June 2018, https://www.themoscowtimes.com/2018/06/12/while-mo-salah-sleeps-in-grozny-op-ed-a61765; and "Kadyrov Makes Name for Himself in Horse Racing," *The Moscow Times,* 17 May 17 2011, https://www.themoscowtimes.com/2011/05/17/kadyrov-makes-name-for-himself-in-horse-racing-a7009.

60. "Muslim World League Makes History with Moscow Summit," *Arab News,* 30 March 2019, http://www.arabnews.com/node/1475061/saudi-arabia; "Moskva i Groznyi prinimayut konferentsiyu 'Islam-poslanie milosti I mira,'" *IslamNews,* 25 March 2019, https://islamnews.ru/news-moskva-i-groznyj-prinimayut-konferenciyu-«islam-poslanie-milosti-i-mira; and "Islamskaya konferen-

tsiya v Groznom proshla pri povyshennykh merakh bezopasnosti," *Kavkazskiy Uzel,* 31 March 2019, https://www.kavkaz-uzel.eu/articles/333666/.

61. "Kadyrovu prisvoili titul 'Geroi Islama' i vruchili orden 'Zvezda Ierusalima,'" *Regnum,* 1 April 2019, https://regnum.ru/news/society/2602556.html.

62. "Kadyrovu prisvoili titul 'Geroi Islama' i vruchili orden 'Zvezda Ierusalima.'"

63. Sarah Feuer, *Course Correction: The Muslim World League, Saudi Arabia's Export of Islam, and Implications for U.S. Policy* (Washington, DC: The Washington Institute for Near East Policy, 2019), 36–39, https://www.washingtoninstitute.org/policy-analysis/view/course-correction.

64. Anna Borshchevskaya and Catherine Cleveland, "Russia's Arabic Propaganda: What It Is, Why It Matters," *The Washington Institute for Near East Policy's Policy Notes* 57 (December 2018), https://www.washingtoninstitute.org/policy-analysis/view/russias-arabic-propaganda-what-it-is-why-it-matters.

65. Nick Schifrin, "Inside Russia's Propaganda Machine," *PBC News Hour* (11 July 2017), https://www.pbs.org/newshour/show/inside-russias-propaganda-machine.

66. Deena Dajani, Marie Gillespie, and Rhys Crilley, "Differentiated Visibilities in Russia's Role in the Syrian War: RT Arabic on Social Media," *Reframing Russia,* 10 June 2019, https://reframingrussia.com/2019/06/10/rt-arabic/.

67. ASDA'A, Arab Youth Survey, "A Call for Reform" (white paper, 11th Annual ASDA'A Youth Survey, 2019), 31 and 33, https://www.arabyouthsurvey.com/pdf/downloadwhitepaper/download-whitepaper.pdf.

68. H. Akin Unver, "Russia Has Won the Information War in Turkey," *Foreign Policy,* 21 April 2019, https://foreignpolicy.com/2019/04/21/russia-has-won-the-information-war-in-turkey-rt-sputnik-putin-erdogan-disinformation/; and "Sputnik, UAE Official News Agency Wam Sign a Memorandum of Understanding," *Sputnik,* 21 March 2019, https://sputniknews.com/agency_news/201903211073424082-sputnik-uae-news-agency-memorandum/.

69. "MAP, Sputnik Ink Agreement to Foster Cooperation," *MAP,* 28 January 2019, http://www.map.ma/en/Our-news/Map-sputnik-ink-agreement-to-foster-cooperation; and "Sputnik, UAE Official News Agency Wam Sign a Memorandum of Understanding."

Chapter 2

Evolution of the Russian Military since the Demise of the Union of Soviet Socialist Republics

Gregory J. Cook

Misha wore his usual mischievous grin when he walked into the office I shared with the chief of intelligence of the Russian Independent Airborne Brigade in Bosnia-Herzegovina that summer morning in 1997, but there was something different about his face. That difference was easy to spot—a bright, white gauze bandage on his suntanned cheek. "What happened to you?" As Misha strode to my desk, he explained he had been shot the previous year during the first Russian intervention in Chechnya and his protective vest had shattered the bullet. He pulled out his wallet, and dumped the fragments the medics had just removed from his cheek onto my desk. His wallet was empty except for the bullet fragments, and I thought, "What a perfect metaphor for the Russian military in the 1990s."

In June 1995, Shamil Basayev led a band of Chechen separatists into Budennovsk, just outside of Chechnya, and took a hospital with almost two thousand people hostage for five days. Russian forces, mainly comprised of Ministry of Interior troops, police, and counter-terrorism units, made three attempts to seize the hospital, and were unable to retake it. More than 160 civilians were killed, and more than 400 wounded, which spurred the negotiated end to the first Chechen War.[1] In 2006, I visited a Russian mechanized infantry brigade in Budennovsk, and while walking through the barracks area noticed an automated teller machine (ATM). I thought back to Misha; as a young, professional airborne officer deployed on a peacekeeping mission abroad, Misha was not getting paid—less than ten years earlier. Now draftees were paid regularly enough that the Russian military installed ATMs in the barracks. Shamil Basayev was killed within a matter of weeks of my Budennovsk visit in a special operation carried out by the Federal Security Service (FSB). Much had changed in the Russian military during the intervening nine years between Bosnia and Budennovsk. More changes lay ahead.

This chapter broadly examines the evolution of the Russian military since the 1991 collapse of the Soviet Union to help give the reader a better understanding of how events during that time affected the military and how it is used today. The discussion examines how the Soviet military was dissolved, the difficult times the Russian military endured during Boris Yeltsin's 1990s, and how the military has rebounded in the twenty-first century under President Vladimir Putin. Specifically, the chapter looks at Russia's foreign policy objectives and how the military is used in conjunction with other national instruments of power, the second Chechen conflict, the Five Day War with Georgia and military reforms that followed, and operations in Ukraine and Syria. The chapter concludes with a discussion focused on how effectively the Russian Federation uses its military to pursue national objectives and interests.

Before proceeding, it is useful to define exactly what the term *armed forces* means in contemporary Russia. The Armed Forces of the Russian Federation include: Strategic Rocket Forces, Ground Forces, Airborne Forces, Aerospace Forces, and the Navy. Russia also has a variety of paramilitary forces numbering almost half a million that can be used for operations within the borders of the Russian Federation, and occasionally outside its borders.[2] Paramilitary organizations should not be disregarded, and include Ministry of Interior (MVD), Ministry of Emergency Situations, FSB, border troops, Customs Service, and the National Guard, which was established in 2016 from special operations and riot control units of the MVD. The Main Directorate, formerly known as the Main Intelligence Directorate (GRU) of the Ministry of Defense, and the Foreign Intelligence Service (SVR) may participate in operations abroad as well. Special operations units, often called by the Russian abbreviation *Spetsnaz*, are not a specific branch or service of the military or paramilitaries but are units that can come from a variety of organizations, including the MVD, GRU, and SVR. As Bettina Renz pointed out, "Democratic states do not, as a rule, maintain an equivalent range of such quasi-military organizations."[3]

The Dissolution of the Soviet Military

Vladimir Putin famously remarked that "the collapse of the Soviet Union was indeed catastrophic for millions of people within the former Soviet Union."[4] The upheaval was not just political, but also had significant social and economic impacts. To compound all this chaos, the Union of Soviet Socialist Republics (USSR) military split into brand new militaries among the fifteen newly formed countries. Even in the best of times, this would not have been an easy feat, and would have challenged even the most efficient staff. But this was during the worst of times. These new militaries, and especially the Russian military, would not only have to split up the Soviet military machine into new organizations, but they would have to do so while significantly reducing manning levels and budgets, and redeploying hundreds of thousands of troops from abroad.

By the time the Soviet Union collapsed, it had already endured some significant setbacks and the resultant blows to confidence. After a couple of decades of stagnation under Leonid Brezhnev, and a series of short-lived leaders, Mikhail Gorbachev initiated social, political, and economic reforms under *glasnost* and *perestroika* that would eventually unleash forces that led to the demise of the USSR. These reforms and the resultant upheaval took place against a backdrop that included the unpopular and stagnating war in Afghanistan, the 1986 Chernobyl disaster, and—in an insulting revelation of the dysfunction of the Soviet military—a 1987 penetration of Soviet airspace by a German teenager who landed a plane on Red Square. Confidence certainly was not high in many parts of the Soviet and later Russian military.

The tasks were daunting. In 1985, the Soviet military numbered 5.3 million personnel. Gorbachev's reforms reduced that number to 4 million in the final year of the existence of the USSR, with 2.8 million of those personnel going into the Russian Federation's military when it was legally formed in May of 1992.[5] Not only did the military have to deal with reducing overall numbers of personnel, but it also had to recall and redeploy hundreds of thousands of troops and their families from the German Democratic Republic, Afghanistan, Mongolia, and other Eastern European countries of the Warsaw Pact. Many of these soldiers ended up without housing or bases.[6] These reductions and reshufflings might have been easier if there had been funding, but this all took place during times of great economic upheaval and distress. In addition, a single Soviet economy split into fifteen smaller national economies; and these economies all shifted from a centralized command system to a free market. Some of these economies collapsed, as inflation spiraled out of control, and defense funding suffered. The Soviet defense budget in 1988 was estimated to be more than $250 billion; only six years later, the Russian defense budget had fallen to $14 billion.[7]

Furthermore, the division of one military into fifteen was chaotic. For the most part, the newly independent states inherited whatever military units were stationed on their territory. There were a couple of exceptions to this rule, however. All agreed to surrender nuclear weapons to the Russian military, and the Black Sea Fleet, stationed on the Ukrainian peninsula of Crimea, was split between Ukraine and Russia. While not based on needs or threats, this methodology of dividing the Soviet military at least gave a logical framework for determining who got which units and equipment. This was not the case with manpower. Military personnel had the choice of serving in the Russian military, the military of the republic of their ethnicity, or the military of the republic in which they were stationed.[8] As an example, an ethnic Kazakh serving in Moldova had the choice of serving in the Russian forces, returning to Kazakhstan to serve in their armed forces, or staying in place and serving in the newly created Moldovan armed forces. This is the stuff of nightmares for a human resource manager.

Benign Neglect

The nineties were a period of benign neglect for the Russian military. Defense funding continued to be low, and given the economic turmoil of the times, there was no alternative as the Russian economy simply could not generate enough resources for the military, even if there had been the political will. Coinciding with the devolution of much of the Soviet military into the Armed Forces of the Russian Federation, the Russian military was called upon repeatedly to intervene at home and abroad. In the center of Moscow in October 1993, Russian tanks shelled the Russian Federation's Parliament building, known as the White House, as part of a constitutional crisis. Russian forces of all types played roles to varying degrees in conflicts within the borders of the former Soviet Union: Transnistria in Moldova, Nagorno-Karabakh, Abkhazia and South Ossetia in Georgia, and Tajikistan. The Russian military also deployed even further afield by sending contingents to Bosnia, and then Kosovo. The most revealing of Russia's operations during the 1990s, however, was Chechnya.

Chechnya, led by Dzhokhar Dudayev, declared its independence in November 1991, and lingered in a de facto autonomous status with minimal interference from the Russian Federation for three years. In November 1994, Russian-backed Chechen rebel forces attempted unsuccessfully to overthrow Dudayev's separatist government with disastrous results: forty tanks lost and more than 300 personnel killed. Russia made a second attempt to overthrow the separatist government with a *coup de main* the following month on New Year's Eve. Cobbling together four columns from thirteen different regiments and brigades, the Russian military believed a quick strike on the Chechen capital of Grozny could successfully overthrow the Dudayev government. The initial attempt was catastrophic. The Russians lost more than 200 armored vehicles, 1,400 personnel were killed in action, another 4,000 wounded, and 500 missing. One of the columns lost 105 of its 120 armored vehicles. An entire battalion of the 131st Motorized Rifle Brigade ceased to exist, and the 81st Motorized Rifle

Regiment took fifty percent casualties. The Russians regrouped, and using more deliberate tactics, were finally able to gain control of Grozny. For the next two years the Russian forces waged a counterinsurgency in Chechnya.[9] The seizure of the hospital in Budennovsk in June 1995 proved to be a turning point in Russian public opinion, however, and the rebel seizure of Grozny in August 1996 through a surprise attack proved to be the final straw. Yeltsin's national security advisor, Aleksandr Lebed, negotiated a ceasefire that again resulted in de facto autonomy for Chechnya. Russia demonstrated an inability to project power within its own borders to assert control over all its territory.

Throughout the nineties and the first decade of the twenty-first century, the effects of benign neglect were hard to ignore. Rather than patrolling silently under the world's oceans waiting to launch a retaliatory strike, Russian nuclear submarines performed their tasks as stationary targets tied to quays in dilapidated navy bases. When the submarine *Kursk* sank in August 1999, her skipper was getting paid $200 per month.[10] Hostage rescue operations during the Moscow Nord-Ost theater crisis in 2002 and the Beslan school crisis in 2004 revealed the level of ineptitude in the Russian military and other security services.

The Russian Military under Putin

Such was the dismal state of affairs in the Russian military when Vladimir Putin became the Russian prime minister in August 1999 and president the following year. Yeltsin promoted Putin from head of the FSB, a position Putin had assumed the previous year, to prime minister immediately following the start of Operation Allied Force, the North Atlantic Treaty Organization (NATO) aerial campaign against Serbia in protection of Kosovars. Russia was vehemently opposed to this operation, but completely impotent to stop it. Putin determined to change this situation and place Russia back in its rightful place as a leading power in the world. A series of September 1999 apartment building bombings throughout Russia—allegedly carried out by Chechen separatists—provided Putin with the pretext to turn things around and re-establish who was in control.

Overall since taking power, Putin has designed and executed Russia's foreign policy to regain what he sees as Russia's rightful place in the world, that is, a global power that must be reckoned with. He seeks to reverse the United States-dominated unipolar world order to a multipolar system.[11] Regionally, Putin seeks to establish Russian leadership of the non-NATO former Soviet Republics. It is important to recognize that the military is not *the* tool to achieve Russian foreign policy objective, but merely *a* tool. Indeed, Russia's conventional forces are dealing not from a position of relative strength vis-a-vis the West, but from a position of disadvantage. Therefore, the other instruments of national power—diplomatic, informational, economic, and, arguably in the case of Russia, criminal—are often used in combination in order to amplify and reinforce effects to achieve objectives and to compensate for relative military weakness. That should be kept in mind as this chapter examines the cases in which Putin used the military to further Russian interests. The military did not undertake these operations in a vacuum, and these operations were never purely military but always conducted in conjunction with the other instruments of national power.

The Second Chechen Campaign (1999–2009) differed greatly from the first, not the least of which is because it ended successfully. In no small part this was due to the lack of support from the local Chechen population who had already achieved de facto autonomy from Moscow for several years, and now viewed outside Islamist influences as starting an unnecessary second war against Russia. Another factor was that Putin would not allow failure to be an option this time around. Rather than trying to achieve a quick, cheap victory, the Russians deliberately and methodically set about subduing the rebellious province. First the Russians encircled the separatist capital of Grozny. Then they reduced it to rubble with direct and indirect fires and aerial bombardment. They then secured the capital and relentlessly pursued the fleeing rebels into the hills, while coopting other Chechen leaders who were willing to cooperate with Moscow. There were setbacks (e.g., Nord-Ost and Beslan), and it took a while, but Russia was able to re-establish control over its own territory and bring Chechnya back into its fold. Russia's military was gradually improving, benefitting from an improved economy literally fueled by increasing oil prices: oil was $28 per barrel in December 2001 and reached a high of $163 in June 2008.[12]

Having re-established sovereignty at home, Putin next sought to re-establish Russia as a force to be reckoned with abroad, especially the near abroad—the regions of the former Soviet and Russian empires that Russia no longer has under its political control, but saw as an area of "privileged interests," as then President Dimitry Medvedev put it in a 2008 television interview.[13] In fact, in this very interview, President Medvedev justified Russia's actions in Abkhazia and South Ossetia in Georgia just a few weeks earlier. After the NATO declaration concluding the Bucharest Summit in April 2008 stated that Georgia and Ukraine "will become members of NATO," Russia was determined not to let outside influences affect what it considered its regions of privileged interests, and set about derailing Ukraine's and Georgia's chances of ever joining NATO.[14] NATO membership for those two countries appeared to be a red line for Moscow, especially after almost universal Western recognition of Kosovo's independence declaration in February 2008.[15] Who exactly started the 2008 Russo-Georgian conflict and how is the subject of debate, which in and of itself is reflective of the Russian way of war where they deliberately made situations opaque and paralyzed potential adversaries with doubt and confusion.[16] But regardless of who started the conflict, Russian certainly took advantage of the situation to punish Georgia for trying to join NATO, and to further secure its grasp on South Ossetia and Abkhazia. Through these actions, Russia was also signaling that it would not tolerate Western international organizations encroaching on its regions of privileged interests.

Despite using sheer mass to inflict a fairly decisive defeat on the significantly smaller Georgian forces, the conflict highlighted Russia's military deficiencies to such an extent that the need for reform could no longer be denied. Defense Minister Anatoliy Serdyukov initiated a series of reforms, known as the New Look, to transform the Russian military from a legacy Soviet force designed for a Cold War with the United States and NATO to a modern, professional military capable of dealing with twenty-first century security challenges. And this time, with the economy recovering from the dislocation of the 1990s, and the leadership of Vladimir Putin, the financial resources and political will were available to carry out meaningful reforms.[17] Putin tripled the defense budget from less than $30 billion when he took over as Russian president in 2000 to more than $90 billion in 2015.[18] This dramatic increase in defense expenditures was not a result of increasing the portion of Gross Domestic Product (GDP) dedicated to defense. Indeed, spending as a percent of GDP remained roughly the same under Putin as under Yeltsin. The difference was a result of the economy growing.[19] The reforms reduced the military end-strength and reshaped personnel structures, eliminated mass mobilization in favor of increased readiness in smaller units, consolidated the professional military education system, and streamlined command and control structures, in addition to much-needed materiel modernization. One of the bedrock assumptions guiding the New Look reforms was that large-scale combat operations with peer competitors was not likely.[20] When viewed through the lens of the US Department of Defense's Joint Capabilities Integrated Development System's framework of DOTM-

LPF (doctrine, organization, training, materiel, leadership, personnel, and facilities), this had significant implications for a Russian military based on mass mobilization for centuries.

Although it was not possible to eliminate the military's reliance on conscription, Serdyukov initiated serious reforms in manning, cutting active duty military personnel by approximately ten percent to one million, significantly slashing the size of the officer corps while making it less top-heavy, and eliminating the warrant officer corps, which played a role similar to the noncommissioned officer corps in the United States military.

The base unit for the army's organization was changed from division to brigade, reflecting changes made in Western armies, and, hopefully, increasing readiness by facilitating higher manning levels, and capitalizing on the units' smaller size to increase strategic and operational mobility which was shown to be lacking during the war with Georgia. Russia executed the switch from division to brigade very quickly, replacing 203 divisions with low manning and readiness levels with 70 brigades that had better manning in 2009.[21] The intent was increased readiness, and, since Russia no longer relied on the mass mobilization system, cadre units could be removed from the force structure. Eliminating division headquarters had the added benefit of streamlining command and control by reducing the number of echelons that orders and reports had to pass through. The desire to increase command and control efficiency extended to the operational and strategic levels where six Soviet legacy military districts were eliminated and replaced with four Operational Strategic Commands, which increased joint coordination and synchronization across services and other power ministries.[22] Another piece of the defense reforms was consolidation of professional military education institutions to improve efficiency, reducing their number from 166 to 64.[23]

The final critical portion was modernization of equipment after decades of low acquisition levels by the post-Cold War Russian military. The State Armament Program 2011–20 envisioned replacing 70 percent of Russian military hardware with new kit by 2020. While impressive, the modernization efforts were not on pace to meet the goals the State Armament Program originally envisioned. And, furthermore, while the acquired equipment was certainly newer than what it replaced, it did not necessarily keep pace with the military technology of other nations.[24]

The progress made in Russia's military reforms would be showcased in Ukraine in 2014. Once again, a former Soviet republic crossed a line that provoked a Russian reaction. After pressure from Moscow, which wanted Ukraine to be a key member of the Russian-led Eurasian Economic Union, Ukrainian President Viktor Yanukovich changed his mind on signing an association agreement with the European Union toward the end of 2013. This change in position generated pro-Western demonstrations on Independence Square (Maidan Nezelezhnosti) in Kyiv. These demonstrations continued into the following year, and opposition to Yanukovich grew in strength, ultimately resulting in a vote from the Ukrainian parliament to remove him, after which Yanukovich fled to Russia.[25] Since the Russian-leaning Yanukovich had been ousted from power, presumably to be replaced with someone more Western-leaning, Russia once again reacted by punishing and preventing one of its neighbors from joining a Western international organization. Russia initiated actions to seize the Crimea Peninsula from Ukraine and, under the auspices of a referendum, Crimea separated from Ukraine and became part of the Russian Federation after the Russian Duma gave its approval in March 2014. Russia significantly upped the ante in this situation. While the Russian Federation had interfered in the internal affairs of its neighbors in the near abroad before, it had never seized territory from another country. After annexing Crimea, Russia backed separatist movements in the Ukrainian regions of Donetsk and Luhansk, a conflict that continued to simmer. Russia's actions and apparent success generated extensive discussion about how it is carrying out military operations, variously known as hybrid warfare, Russian New Generation Warfare, and tolerance warfare, among others. Whatever the name, this style of operating generated a great deal of consternation from Russia's other neighbors, especially NATO allies that border the Russian Federation. This, in turn, generated a flurry of activity as the United States and NATO sought to reassure allies and dissuade Russia from taking any other actions that might threaten alliance members' sovereignty.

Russia's operation in Crimea was carried out under unique circumstances that favored Russia's success. Despite Crimea being Ukrainian territory, the population of the peninsula was predominantly Russian ethnically, linguistically, and sympathetically. They were receptive to Russian messaging, and the military forces necessary to carry out the operation were already prepositioned as the Russian Black Sea Fleet was located on the peninsula. Furthermore, even a good portion of the Ukrainian military stationed on Crimea, particularly the Ukrainian Navy, was willing to go over to the Russian side without much resistance. This included the Ukrainian commander, who defected to Russia—taking roughly 75 percent of the Ukrainian service members stationed in Crimea with him—and became the deputy commander of the Russian Black Sea Fleet.[26] This allowed for a nearly bloodless takeover of the peninsula, its population, and Ukrainian military facilities. Reaction from outside of Ukraine to dissuade Russia from taking these actions was not strong, or at least not persuasive enough to prevent the hostile takeover. This was in part due to Ukraine not being a NATO member, and to the ambiguity and confusion sown by Russia, which disavowed any knowledge of the personnel carrying out the operation known variously as "little green men" and "polite people." The West was unable and unwilling to act decisively.

Russia decided to press on with similar actions to support separatists in the Don River Basin (Donbas), but did not achieve the same level of success as in Crimea. The circumstances were not as conducive. Most significantly, no Russian forces were stationed on the Ukrainian territory of this region. There were also fewer ethnic Russians, and the Ukrainian units were not as infiltrated with Russian sympathizers as the Ukrainian naval units in Crimea. That did not mean that Russia did not use a variety of forces, to include conventional units, special forces, contractors, volunteers, Cossacks, and other paramilitary organizations. But the conditions were not present to carry out the operation as swiftly as in Crimea, and the confrontation was bloodier and less decisive.

Conclusion: The Effective Use of an Effective Russian Military in Foreign Policy

The military operations in Syria reflected the resurgence of Russia's ability to project power even further abroad. While Russia's primary objective in Syria was to prop up the Assad regime and maintain its naval base in Tartus, Russia also challenged US influence in a region where there previously had been little or no competition since the end of the Cold War. Russian military action, which challenged the American influence in the Middle East, also forced the United States to cooperate with Russia, and recognize that Russia played a role in a strategically vital region.[27] This aligned with Russia's foreign policy ambition of being recognized as a global power. Russia's operations also sent a message to other potential and current international partners. Russia was a legitimate alternative to the United States. It could be a valuable partner or ally that would not judge despots on their human rights records or values, but on national interests. If you work with Russia, Russia will support you, regardless of transgressions against other countries or even your own people. Russia reinforced this message by using force in ways that demonstrated to the world that it could project power globally. There was no compelling reason why Russia had to deploy the aircraft carrier *Kuznetsov* around Europe into the Mediterranean, or launch cruise missiles from the Caspian Sea, or strategic bombers from Russian territory to strike targets in Syria when it already had forces in theater. Russia took these actions to demonstrate its re-emergence as a global power.

It has been quite a journey for the Russian Armed Forces since the collapse of the Soviet Union. Russia's political and military leaders dealt with dividing up the Soviet military into many different parts under some of the most challenging conditions imaginable. They fought conflicts and were used abroad in the 1990s while underfunded and undermanned. Once funding and solid national leadership were re-established, the Russian military was able to get its affairs in order, and eventually to carry out reforms that made it a more effective force reflective of its global and regional aspirations. This was especially true as the Russian government effectively used the military in conjunction with its other instruments of national power to pursue policy objectives. Certainly, there were setbacks along the way, and not everything went smoothly, but certain measures of effectiveness showed that the military had been a valuable tool in Russia's ability to achieve its policy objectives. The military re-established control over Russian territory by playing an essential role in subduing the separatist region of Chechnya. The use of military force in Georgia and Ukraine helped prevent those countries from becoming NATO members. Russian forces shocked many in the West with their ability to successfully carry out highly sophisticated and sensitive operations. And, while Russia's operations in the Donbas may not have had the success enjoyed in Crimea, they were successful enough to create a new frozen conflict that would provide another way of applying leverage over Ukraine since the potential of Crimean unrest could no longer be used. And finally, Russian operations in Syria kept Assad in place, and, moreover, provided a message that Russia was able to project power globally and should be considered as a viable alternative to the United States for those looking for leadership.

How far and how well the Russian military has recovered from the awful times it endured following the demise of the USSR inspires respect, but these accomplishments and the Russian military should not be overstated or overrated. In most cases, the Russian military faced some not insignificant issues. Even in the case of Crimea, where operations were extremely successful, some conditions were unique and would be difficult to replicate elsewhere.

Notes

1. Timothy J. Colton, *Russia: What Everyone Needs to Know* (New York: Oxford University Press, 2016), 117.

2. Bettina Renz, *Russssia's Military Revival* (Cambridge: Polity, 2018), 87.

3. Renz, 87–88.

4. Vladimir Putin, "Annual Address to the Federal Assembly of the Russian Federation," 25 April 2005, http://en.kremlin.ru/events/president/transcripts/22931.

5. Steven E. Miller, "Introduction: Moscow's Military Power," in *The Russian Military Revival*, ed. Steven E. Miller and Dmitri Trenin (Cambridge, MA: MIT Press, 2004), 4, 53, and 219.

6. Mark Galeotti, *The Modern Russian Army 1992–2016* (Oxford: Osprey, 2017), 6.

7. Miller, 4.

8. Miller, 5.

9. Gaelotti, *The Modern Russian Army*, 11–13.

10. Dave Majumdar, "Russia's Submarine Force is Back: How Worried Should America Be?," *The National Interest,* 5 July 2016, https://nationalinterest.org/blog/the-buzz/russias-submarine-force-back-how-worried-should-america-be-16858.

11. *Russia Military Power: Building a Military to Support Great Power Aspirations* (Washington, DC: Defense Intelligence Agency, 2017), 14–15.

12. Macrotrends, "Crude Oil Price – 70 Year Historical Chart," accessed 21 June 2019, https://www.macrotrends.net/1369/crude-oil-price-history-chart.

13. Dmitry Medvedev, interview by Channel One, Rossia, and NTV, 31 August 2008, http://en.kremlin.ru/events/president/transcripts/48301.

14. North Atlantic Treaty Organization, "Bucharest Summit Declaration Issued by the Heads of State and Government Participating in the Meeting of the North Atlantic Council in Bucharest on 3 April 2008," press release, 3 April 2008, https://www.nato.int/cps/en/natolive/official_texts_8443.htm.

15. Marcel H. Van Herpen, *Putin's Wars: The Rise of Russia's New Imperialism* (New York: Rowman & Littlefield, 2014), 233.

16. The volume of literature on the origins of the Georgian conflict is extensive. Van Herpen covers the topic in three chapters in his book, *Putin's Wars.* Timothy Thomas provides an excellent examination of the competing explanations but does not provide a solid conclusion in *Recasting the Red Star.*

17. Renz, *Russia's Military Revival,* 51.

18. Renz, 72.

19. Renz, 73.

20. Aleksey Gayday, "Reform of the Russian Army," in *Russia's New Army* (Moscow: Centre for Analysis of Strategies and Technologies, 2011), 20.

21. Mark Galeotti, "Reform of the Russian Military and Security Apparatus: An Investigator's Perspective," in *Can Russia Reform? Economic, Political*

and Military Perspectives, ed. Stephen J. Blank (Carlisle, PA: Strategic Studies Institute, 2012), 62.

22. Charles K. Bartles, "Defense Reforms of Russian Defense Minister Anatolii Serdyukov," *Journal of Slavic Military Studies* 24, no. 1 (2011).

23. Dale Herspring, *Military Reform, Putin's Russia: Past Imperfect, Future Unknown*, 6th ed. (New York: Rowman & Littlefield, 2016), 331.

24. Renz, *Russia's Military Revival,* 76–79.

25. Renz, 150.

26. Colton, *Russia,* 187–88.

27. Colton, 200–1.

Chapter 3
Culture under Construction: History and Identity as Instruments of Russian Policy[1]
Robert F. Baumann

It has long been axiomatic that there is a connection between any given country's domestic and foreign policies. In the case of Russia, culture—as much as objective interests—tends to drive both. A shared sense of culture, especially its subordinate elements of language, religion, and history, provides the foundation of national identity that profoundly influences aspirations for the future as well as the present moment. In 1806, the German idealist philosopher Johan Gotlieb Fichte penned what was arguably his most influential work, *Addresses to the German Nation*. In the aftermath of Prussia's shattering defeat by Napoleon, Fichte argued that only the unification of the German people—at the time still divided into many independent kingdoms—could forge a state strong enough to resist the tides of historical fortune. The problem demanded creating a sense of unity based on recognition of the shared elements of German culture. In *Addresses*, Fichte put forth an educational program that emphasized common elements of the "German experience," including everything from geography to language, and history to music. Fichte's concept offered a blueprint for other nations as well to construct binding identities. This chapter focuses on the state-sponsored interpretation of history to mold Russian identity and culture to support President Vladimir Putin's vision for the Russian Federation.

In the wake of the dissolution of the Soviet Union, Russia faced a problem like the one that confronted Germans two centuries earlier, but from an opposing perspective. The Russian Federation, shorn of the fourteen ethnically based republics that once constituted its empire, became smaller and more ethnically homogeneous. Even so, the federation urgently needed to re-establish its identity to move forward. The context was extremely challenging as Russians had lost simultaneously a guiding ideology (Marxism-Leninism) as well as a sense of where they stood on the global stage. Moreover, the transition from a socialist to capitalist economy was not going well, a situation compounded by second-order effects such as the impoverishment of pensioners, a collapse of support for public institutions such as universities and the military, rising crime, and general political disorientation. President Boris Yeltsin was not well-equipped by experience or education to manage the transition, which was why, incidentally, many citizens greeted the early years of Putin's presidency with a sense of relief. Amidst fears that Russia's experiment in Western democracy was not succeeding, identification with Europe began to decline. In response to deepening public malaise, Yeltsin recognized the need for a cohesive idea to help multi-ethnic Russia chart a course into the future. In 1996, therefore, he announced a project to create a Concept of State Nationalities Policy.[2]

The concept document focused on the structure of the federation and the degrees of autonomy accorded to various kinds of administrative jurisdictions that had been carved out on an ethnic basis. It only obliquely addressed the collective "who are we?" question for citizens of the Russian Federation. Scholar Peter Rutland noted that in 1990, Yeltsin invoked Russian national feeling as a political instrument against then-leader Mikhail Gorbachev prior to the Soviet break-up.[3] The idea was that the elevation of Russian national feeling would erode loyalty to the multinational Soviet Union. This subsequently left Yeltsin in the ironic position of having to come up with a Russian Federation nationalities policy in the absence of a clear definition of Russia itself. In the meantime, Yeltsin promoted the use of the somewhat archaic term *Rossiiane*—signifying all core subjects of the empire, with little regard for their ethnicity as long as they voluntarily accommodated themselves to Russian rule.[4] Since Soviet was no longer applicable as a descriptive term of reference for the population, Yeltsin turned to history for a useful precedent.

Fundamentally, the Soviet Union and, subsequently, the Russian Federation inherited the "nationalities policy" problem from the Russian Empire. The challenge they shared was to construct a cohesive country. During the late nineteenth century, imperial policy stressed Russification of politically conscious national minorities.[5] This meant, among other things, ensuring the instruction of Russian language and history in the schools. For empires, multinationality posed a common problem. Great powers, such as the British or French, that enjoyed a high degree of political success in establishing and sustaining their rule over many subject peoples, made the imperial language the medium of all official activity and a core element of all educational systems. The continuing influence of this model was long evident in the post-imperial British Commonwealth or across the Francophone countries of Africa. In addition, military institutions often served as an important instrument for constructing a common culture. Consequently, English remains the language of command in India and Pakistan. At the time that Russia established universal conscription in

1874, War Minister Dmitri Miliutin viewed military service as a means to instill a sense of citizenship and patriotism among soldiers of all ethnicities.[6] Integrating institutions, such as armies, indeed could do much to ground the population in a common experience and outlook. Still, by the time of the October 1917 Russian Revolution, nationality policy was still very much a work in progress.

As the Bolsheviks fought for power in Russia's Civil War from 1918 to 1921, they adopted what amounted to a "bait and switch" policy toward subject nationalities of the former empire. The Bolsheviks publicly supported the right to self-determination, thereby achieving an important political advantage over white counter-revolutionary forces, which failed to make a serious effort to win the support of non-Russians. However, as the Red Army consolidated its hold over minority regions of the country, the Bolsheviks rolled out the fine print in their self-determination promise. The Bolshevik leadership ultimately created an elaborate administrative structure establishing ethnic states in name that lacked real sovereignty in practice. At the top of the ethnic hierarchy were the constituent Soviet socialist republics, such as Ukraine, Estonia, Azerbaijan, Armenia, and Uzbekistan. In theory only, they were independent entities that voluntarily came together with Russia to form the Soviet Union. In practice, nearly all were coerced partly or wholly to join the union. In time, they more resembled American states like Texas or New York, which were fully subordinated to Washington on major policy questions while enjoying significant administrative autonomy on local matters. Beneath the constituent republics were additional territorial administrative layers: autonomous republics, autonomous regions, and so on. Each step on the administrative ladder carried real implications. Resource allocations and local decision-making autonomy corresponded to the position of each administrative unit in the overall hierarchy. For example, a full republic like Armenia would have the resources to build more factories, universities, and publishing houses than an autonomous republic like Tatarstan—even if the differences in the size of population or territory were not that great. The overarching result was that over decades, the Soviet Union fostered a common feeling of fledgling nationhood among populations of the republics that in some cases lacked any extensive history of independent statehood. The system dissolved with the end of the USSR. Russia found itself in need of "rebranding" without either a traditional or Soviet empire.

Returning to the main line of argument of this chapter, the Russian Federation inherited a complex administrative system for managing ethnic relations after 1991. Since the former constituent republics departed for full independence, former autonomous republics such as Bashkortostan, Tatarstan, and Chechnya formed the top rung of minority national administrative units in the federation. They initially announced serious claims to sovereignty and, in the case of Chechnya, even demanded full independence. Yeltsin, and Putin after him, waged war in Chechnya to thwart separatist aspirations. In the meantime, Putin steadily whittled away at the autonomy of Federation republics, reducing the prerogatives of republican leaders and, in most instances, selecting them from Moscow. In short, full reintegration into Russia was the focus of Putin's ethnicity policy. This was an important contextual factor in Russia's public dialog about national identity.

Particularly after his re-election in 2012, Putin emphasized in practice, if not in words, the centrality of Russian identity as an organizing principle for the Federation in the twenty-first century.[7] To better appreciate the importance of historical connections, it is useful to examine the Imperial Russian model. In 1833, Minister of Public Education for Tsar Nicholas I, Sergei Uvarov, authored a core ideology or identity for the regime. The formula he crafted consisted of three elements: Orthodoxy, autocracy, and nationality. The first designated the official religious orientation of the regime and the second the mode of government. The third, though partially dependent on the first two, is of particular interest to this study. Nationality, or *narodnost* in Russian, indicated a primarily civic and cultural sense of national identity based on use of the Russian language and a sense of belonging to Russia's empire.[8]

The formulation of Official Nationality was a product of Russia's distinct circumstances in the 1830s. It differed from what historians would later refer to as Romantic Nationalism, which simultaneously emphasized the distinctiveness and richness of national cultures. Presumed ethnic and linguistic homogeneity—along with shared historical experience, defined territory, and musical and literary traditions—constituted key ingredients.[9] Romantic Nationalism also assumed the existence of a community of nations that respected one another's sovereignty.

Neither did Official Nationality align well with another school of nineteenth-century ideology defined by historians, Integral Nationalism. This form accepted the features of Romantic Nationalism insofar as they described a given nationality but viewed the international environment much more threateningly. For integral nationalists, the world was Darwinian. Nations competed for resources and fought wars of expansion to secure a more privileged place in the food chain. What drove Integral Nationalism was a demand for completeness of the nation in question. In practice, this anticipated the subjugation and assimilation of other nations and their territories.[10]

For Uvarov, and by extension Nicholas I, Official Nationality offered a distinctively Russian approach serving to unify society and perpetuate the autocracy. The idea of nationality as an official instrument of Russian state policy reflected the interests of the empire. The regime could not accept Romantic Nationalism because to do so would be tantamount to recognizing that many of the subject populations of the empire could be legitimate candidates for separate nationhood. Conversely, the regime's problem with Integral Nationalism related to the behavior of the nationalists themselves. The drive to expand inherent in Integral Nationalism was bound to involve Russia in wars it could not afford. Besides, nationalism tended to stir populist movements that were most unwelcome in an autocratic state. For example, Russian Pan-Slavists envisioned a sprawling empire across the lands of East Central Europe and the Balkans, which were predominantly populated by fellow Slavic peoples such as the Bulgarians, Serbs, and Czechs. Pursuing this vision necessarily entailed collisions with the Ottoman and Austro-Hungarian Empires. Neither Nicholas nor his successors wanted nationalistic sentiments to hijack the state prerogative to make foreign policy.

Like most political movements, Pan-Slavism had a few prominent intellectuals in the vanguard. The foremost Russian Pan-Slav theorist was Nikolai Danilevsky, whose seminal work *Russia and Europe* was fraught with foreign policy implications. Republished in Russia in 1995, it became a popular seller for a second time.[11] In the Chapter Two title, Danilevsky asked rhetorically, "Why Is Europe Hostile to Russia?" He answered in his Chapter 5 explanation of the history of civilizations—following the theory of German history philosopher Johann Gottfried von Herder, or as Danilevsky described it, the theory of cultural-historical types.[12] Like Herder, Danilevsky viewed the rise and fall of diverse civilizations as an inevitable historical process. Each civilization had a life cycle and unique character born of the circumstances in which it emerged.[13] Danilevsky predicted an inevitable collision of the Slavic civilization with the West, or what he termed the Romano-Germanic civilization. Danilevsky is important not just for his influence in the nineteenth century, but due to his intellectual resurrection by twenty-first century Russian Eurasianists who defined Russia in civilizational terms as in opposition to the West.

Writing in 1999 about Danilevsky, B. P. Baluev argued that Europe tried to portray Russian Pan-Slavism as potentially menacing to the smaller Slavic nationalities that would be swallowed up by their enormous neighbor.[14] On the contrary, he contended, in fighting for the emancipation of the Bulgarians and Serbs from the Ottoman Empire, Pan-Slavists were liberators in Eastern Europe.[15] Thus, Baluev surmised, the Western narrative in this case really served to underline reflexive hostility toward Russia.

The theoretical militarization of Pan-Slavism owed much to the work of retired-general-turned-publicist Rostislav Fadeev in his work *The Eastern Question*. Fadeev posited a future Pan-Slav Empire led by Russia and including the Slavic territories of Eastern Europe with the possible exception of Poland.[16] Catholic and highly western in its cultural orientation, Poland did not fit the prescription for inclusion, although Fadeev was open to engagement with Poland. As if to make up for uncertainty about Poland, Fadeev's Pan-Slavist vision included Orthodox Greece as a suitable non-Slavic addition. Furthermore, the restoration of Constantinople to the world of Eastern Christendom would fulfill Russia's historical destiny. The closest Russia came to making that a reality was in the closing months of the 1877 Russo-Turkish War when Russian forces halted not far from Istanbul. They did not proceed farther because Alexander II did not wish a repeat of the Crimean War when Britain and France combined forces to win a small expeditionary war on Russian soil. Russia lost little but pride in the end, but came to a painful realization of its economic and military limitations. Russia's expansionist aspirations never faded entirely from view, however. Subsequently during World War I, the allies induced an exhausted Russia to stay in the fight with the prospect of future control of the straits affording access to the Black Sea.

Following the war and revolution, Russian culture split into two streams, one emanating from the Bolshevik Revolution and the other from the consequent émigré diaspora. While the Bolsheviks undertook the territorial organization of the country in administrative units based in principle on the establishment of ethnic homelands, fugitives of the revolution sought to construct imaginary empires of the intellect. One such construction was Eurasianism. Figures like Ivan Ilyin imagined a Russian civilization that would emerge after the inevitable collapse of the Soviet Union. As a leading scholar on the subject, Marlene Maruelle, puts it, "Eurasianism was less an ideological platform than an atmosphere, a conception of the world."[17] Ilyin vigorously argued that Russian civilization was Eurasian, not European as had been thought by most Russian intellectuals of the late imperial era. For Ilyin, as for other Eurasianists in emigration like Nikolai Trubetskoy, the European mode of development was separate and distinct. Russia, with its deep connection to the Orient, faced a destiny of its own.[18] Ilyin's deep dive into Russian history and philosophy proved almost unreadably convoluted and created few ripples at the time.

Another who brought the concept forward was historian George Vernadsky, who eventually emigrated to the United States and taught Russian history at Yale University.[19] As he explained in the introductory chapter of his standard one-volume history, "The Russia that we are to consider is a single geographical unit, Eurasia. . . . Eurasia refers not to a vague socio-historical combination of Europe and Asia but rather to a specific geographical area of the great central continental land mass. . . . All the vast expanses of this Eurasian area have been occupied by the Russians in the course of a long historical process."[20] In a separate volume devoted to Russia's relationship to the Mongols, Vernadsky based his argument for Eurasianism on the theory that not only was the Mongol invasion of Russia's ancestral Kievan civilization a watershed moment, but the two centuries of occupation by an Asian power left an indelible imprint on Russian culture. The principles of Russian autocracy, he argued, flowed from the influence of the khans.[21] This perspective, according to some scholars, constitutes an original contribution of Eurasianism to the historiography of Russia.[22]

Eurasianism bubbled up again in the 1990s when Russia was searching for a post-Soviet identity. According to Dmitry Trenin, centuries of empire followed by seven decades as the central piece of the Soviet Union constrained the development of a Russian nation.[23] Multiple variations on the Eurasian theme co-exist in Putin's Russia in more recent years, but the best-known early twenty-first century proponent of the idea is Alexander Dugin. An ideological vagabond over the years, Dugin seems to possess the right mix of charisma, gravitas, and audacity to remain relevant, though probably not central, in Russian political discourse.[24] Dugin's ideas resonate with some of the so-called *siloviki*, Russian powerbrokers, among whom the general proposition of a Eurasian civilization centered on Russia was broadly appealing. Thus, Eurasianism provides a satisfying blend of historical mission, cultural distinctiveness, and intellectual veneer to assume the ideological space once occupied by Marxism-Leninism. Perhaps above all, it is sufficiently ambiguous to accommodate a wide variety of perspectives

Eurasianism also harmonizes with aspects of Orthodox Christianity, which has managed to restore itself in part to its former place in pre-revolutionary Russian society. Vernadsky, among others, argued that Orthodoxy was the critical element of Russian culture that spanned history from the Kievan civilization through the Mongol occupation to the revolution. Its limited renaissance in the twenty-first century provided a vital sense of continuity to the cultural past.[25] The church also became an important pillar of the Putin regime and received generous moral and financial support in exchange. This altered the constitutionally established relationship between church and state. The Russian Orthodox Church received permission to establish a footprint within the national educational system and the military, even launching a grand new cathedral specifically for the latter. As explained by legal scholar Robert Blitt, "The breakdown in the constitutional principle of secularism so evident in domestic affairs has spilled over into Russia's foreign policy, leading to the bizarre reality whereby a secular state is advocating on behalf of religious Orthodoxy and 'traditional' values abroad."[26]

Both church leadership and the Russian government hoped that Orthodox spirituality would serve as an instrument of outreach to the diaspora of Russians around the world in addition to fellow Orthodox communities in Eastern and Southern Europe. Neither line of effort proved extremely effective, in part due to the controversy with the Orthodox Church of Ukraine; this controversy, in turn, led to a dispute between Moscow and the Greek Orthodox Patriarchate of Constantinople, the historic center of the faith. Meanwhile, the Russian Orthodox Church of the Moscow Patriarchate initiated a global construction campaign, funding new churches in such disparate locations as Argentina, China, Japan Thailand, Cuba, and Africa.[27] The effort not only created a support network for Russians traveling or living abroad, but also provided visible cultural symbols that advertised a Russian presence and values.

Still, many in the diaspora feel a bit conflicted about Russia today. While a strong cultural affinity remains, such as in the form of online discussion groups, there is often less conviction about the current government. Russians living abroad are welcomed to return, but have not done so in large numbers as this book is written. Still taking advantage of the internet, Moscow's use of important cultural symbols, the preservation of heritage, and the promotion of the Russian language help to preserve communal ties. Thus, Russia's reliance on Orthodoxy in foreign policy aligns well with the proposition that Russians belong to a distinctive civilizational tradition expressed in Eurasianism.

Eurasianism and Orthodoxy have been utilized since 1991 to propel public discussion about the identity of the Russian state and the people within it. At the moment when the USSR disintegrated, another more Western-leaning vision seemed possible. Given the impetus of Gorbachev's reforms and Yeltsin's cooperative attitude, the emergence of a stable Russia that identified itself as European, open, and democratic competed for primacy. However, the economic and social turbulence of the Russian Federation's first decade as a separate regime helped impel popular opinion to retreat to a more nativist outlook.

From the start of his presidency, Putin took an interest in shaping the national dialogue, but—other than promoting Russian nationalism in a broad way—stayed out of most of the details. This was almost certainly a prudent posture. He let others test new ideas in the realm of popular debate without wasting his own political capital. Broadly, he strongly encouraged exploration of Russian history by academics and amateurs alike, but did not prescribe a specific interpretation. Early in his presidency, Putin spoke of the "Russian world," an inclusive category embracing those who identify with Russia.[28] Scholars were free to work on the details. As scholar Stephen Cohen explained: "There is almost no historical censorship in Russia today."[29] Putin perhaps understood from the Soviet past that it does not pay to be pinned down to a single explanation of history. Even the official Marxist-Leninist narrative of history required regular revision based on the exigencies of the moment. Hence the often-repeated Soviet joke: "The only thing harder to predict than the future is the past."[30] When the truth changes, it sows doubt and confusion. In contrast, by maintaining a broad discussion that encompasses a variety of interpretations which still broadly adhere to a basic common narrative, shifts in emphasis do not create such a high degree of cognitive dissonance.

The same general principle seemed to apply to the question of identity. The 2012 official use of the expression "Russian civic nation" (*rossiiskaia grazhdanskaia natsiia*) offered an appropriately fuzzy compromise position on the question of nationality. In any case, the strong implication in official rhetoric was that Russians as an ethnic and historical group were at the center of the narrative, but that many others were included as well. Some were also excluded. Among those peoples not implicitly embraced by the widely shared sense of the civic nation were migrants from the North Caucasus or Central Asia.[31] Some of the ambiguity stemmed from official inconsistency in terms of reference. Pal Kolsto noted that in an 18 March 2014 speech to the Russian Federal Assembly, President Putin referred to the *russkii narod*, normally taken to be an explicitly ethnic expression.[32]

During the imperial period, the term *inorodtsy* captured the sense of those who did not belong to the core population of the empire. This generally referred to the non-Slavic, or sometimes non-European, segment of the population. In many instances, this distinction had practical implications. When Russia implemented universal military conscriptions in 1874, the new legislation excluded many *inorodtsy* living along the fringes of the empire. The common explanation was that many were not culturally ready for the regimentation of military life, although in some instances their loyalty was in doubt as well.[33] One purpose of conscription reform was to cultivate within the multiethnic citizenry a shared sense of belonging and obligation to the Russian empire.

Even as it seeks to instill a collective identity by means of an ideological narrative, Russia since 1991 has encouraged a revival of interest in individuals who have been important in the national history. Acclaim for individuals who personify national character and virtues is typically a vital element in cementing a sense of collective identity. For instance, in 2016, Russia placed a monumental statue to Vladimir the Great in Moscow, an event that continues to rankle Ukrainian nationalists who claim the historic Grand Prince of Kyiv as a seminal figure in their own history.[34] As the officially recognized Christianizer of the ancient Rus' civilization, Vladimir was integral to both histories. In the eyes of Ukrainians, Russia's claim to Vladimir as a forefather of modern Russian civilization implied pretensions to broader political and cultural hegemony. This would not be far out of step with some interpretations of Eurasianism.

Another figure long associated with Russian civilization was Mikhail Lomonosov, whose name is borne by Moscow State University. Though Lomonosov was certainly an important contributor to the arts and sciences in Russia, he achieved near-mythical proportions as a result of Soviet efforts to promote his legacy. Soviet biographers made a particular point of depicting Lomonosov as the standard-bearer of a distinctly Russian scientific tradition, valiantly struggling to advance the frontiers of knowledge in the face of criticism by foreign antagonists. Two films, one in 1955 and a second serialized for television in the 1980s, reinforced the same messages. The former, directed by Mikhail Shapiro, portrayed foreign academicians as "villainous," while the latter made the same point in a slightly more understated fashion.[35] Scholar Steven Usitalo observed, "What Soviet-era hagiographers attempted was to subsume representations of Lomonosov into an all-embracing cultural mission aimed at creating a 'New Soviet Man.'"[36] Thus, for Soviet image-makers, Lomonosov was more an instrument of ideological purpose than a pillar of Russian national identity.

Lomonosov also received reverential treatment in the post-Soviet era. For example, a 2011 exhibition and academic symposium at the Hermitage Museum in St. Petersburg generated several new publications as well as new editions of old works. Usitalo described Lomonosov's continuing significance: "But with Russia undergoing many of the same trials of trying to catch up, or at least perceiving the need to draw nearer with the 'West' which have marked its development since Peter the Great's time, it is plausible that Lomonosov might again serve as an exemplar."[37] For Putin, the past would always serve as prelude to the future.

Certain individuals and moments in Russian military history have remained iconic since the Napoleonic Wars. The most enduring moment of the nineteenth century was the 1812 Battle of Borodino at which a Russian army under the command of Marshal Mikhail Kutuzov fought Napoleon's forces essentially to a draw. To be sure, Russian historians tended to claim victory, although the subsequent withdrawal of Kutuzov's army to the east of Moscow suggested otherwise. In fact, Borodino came to stand for final Russian victory in the war with France, marked beyond dispute by the triumphant 1814 parade of Russian forces in Paris with Tsar Alexander I at their head. The great ordeal of the war was best captured in Leo Tolstoy's classic novel *War and Peace*. Thus, Russian heroism at Borodino was widely commemorated in history, literature, and poetry; in a way, it came to stand for everything that was good about the Russian Empire itself.[38]

Historian Marc Raeff viewed the Napoleonic Wars as fundamental to the rise of Russian national consciousness. Indeed, he contended that modern nationalism more broadly "is a phenomenon whose birth can be pretty exactly traced to the time of the French Revolution and Napoleonic Wars."[39] More recent events provide a historical echo that tends to affirm Raeff's claim. Re-enactments of the Battle of Borodino became popular and colorful fare, as well as reminders of one of Russia's greatest victories over a Western invader.

Also striking in the treatment of history after 1991 was that certain moments of imperial history which received tremendous acclaim during the Soviet period were later pushed to the margins. For example, the Pugachev Rebellion (1773–75) and the Decembrist Revolt (1825) previously enjoyed prominent places in the official Soviet narrative about Russia's revolutionary tradition. However, under Putin, the October Revolution itself was no longer seen in the same light, as evidenced by the tepid commemoration in 2017. It would be reasonable to speculate that Putin's regime does not want to advertise the role of social movements in shaping the course of history and politics. Thus, the Decembrists in particular, as bearers of Western political values, have received far less attention in more recent years.

As for remembering the Soviet period, numerous controversies remained. There was, above all, the looming role of Joseph Stalin, who continued to enjoy favorable approval ratings in Russian polls. According to a 2018 Levada survey, 57 percent fully or mostly agreed with the proposition that Stalin "was a wise leader who led the Soviet Union to might and prosperity;" only 18 percent fully or mostly disagreed.[40] Of course, Stalin's role as war leader was a central factor in the assessment of his career. Yet, it is possible for many Russians to feel conflicted about Stalin. The same poll found that 44 percent fully or mostly agreed that he was "a cruel, inhuman tyrant responsible for the deaths of millions of innocent people."[41]

Remembrance of victory in the Great Patriotic War and the Soviet Union's place as a great power have continuously resonated across Russia since 1945. This is true even as the generation that fought and survived World War II is quickly diminishing numerically in the twenty-first century. That loss of living memory is in some respect convenient for the regime, which enjoys greater latitude to influence national memory about the war. This facilitated, for example, focusing on the successful elements of Stalin's record such as his role as strategist. Russians clearly held on to these memories as part of their core identity. This aligned with the Putin administration's aim to foster patriotic feelings by selectively highlighting politically useful features of Russian history in the public narrative. Accordingly, religious scholars, with official encouragement, drew explicit links between Russia's history as an Orthodox nation and its sense of patriotism.[42] Increasingly, seeing the West as a civilizational adversary was an integral part of the story which, in turn, made Russians more receptive to claims of imminent threat from NATO.[43]

From the start of his presidency in 2000, history and identity served Putin as navigational aids for action. He wanted Russians to participate in forming a defining national narrative that in turn would shape their future and facilitate Russia's restoration as a great power. The challenge was to weave several often-contradictory histories into a common narrative of a shared past even as it pointed the way forward. Meanwhile, the concept of what it means to be Russian would continuously evolve. Changing demographics alone dictated some accommodation to a new reality. Russia's challenge remains to forge a twentieth-first-century culture that can incorporate change while retaining crucial elements of continuity.

Notes

1. The author wishes to acknowledge Scott Gorman of the School of Advanced Military Studies, US Army Command and General Staff College, who read and commented on a previous draft of this chapter.

2. Helge Blakkisrud, "Blurring the Boundary between Civic and Ethnic: The Kremlin's New Approach to National Identity under Putin's Third Term," in *The New Russian Nationalism: Imperialism, Ethnicity and authoritarianism 2000–2015*, ed. Pal Kolsto and Helge Blakkisrud (Edinburgh: Edinburgh University, 2016), 261, https://www.jstor.org/stable/10.3366/j.ctt1bh2kk5.16. For an overview of literature on the development of Russian identity, see Peter Duncan, "Contemporary Russian Identity between East and West," *The Historical Journal* 48, no. 1 (March 2005): 277–94. A concise theoretical explanation of the Soviet system of federalism is available in A. M. Iusupovskii, *Poiski novykh podkhodov k resheniiu natsional'nykh problem: uroki istorii* [An investigation of new approaches to resolution of nationalities problems: lessons of history] (Moscow: 1990): 37–38.

3. Peter Rutland, "The Presence of Absence: Nationality Policy in Russia," accessed 14 June 2019, http://prutland.faculty.wesleyan.edu/files/2015/08/Ethnicity-policy.pdf.

4. Dmitri Trenin, *Post-Imperium: A Eurasian Story* (Washington, DC: Carnegie Endowment for International Peace, 2011), 60–61. Trenin argued that Russian ethnic consciousness remained low even in the twenty-first century. This chapter generally adhered to the Library of Congress system of transliteration from Cyrillic to English, but made exceptions in instances where contrary spellings have become the de facto standard in English. Thus, the term Rossiiane can also sometimes be rendered as Rossiyane.

5. For a good discussion of the challenge, see Alfred Rieber, *The Struggle for the Eurasian Borderlands: From the Rise of Modern Empires to the End of the First World War* (Cambridge: Cambridge University, 2014).

6. Robert F. Baumann, "Subject Nationalities in the Military Service of the Tsar: The Case of the Bashkirs," *Slavic Review* 46, no. 3–4 (Fall/Winter 1987): 489–500, and "Imperial Service Reform and Russia's Imperial Dilemma," *War & Society* 4, no. 2 (September 1986): 31–49. See also Teresa Rakowska-Harmstone, "'Brotherhood in Arms': The Ethnic Factor in the Soviet Armed Forces," in *Ethnic Armies: Polyethnic Armed Forces From the Time of the Habsburgs to the Age of the Superpowers*, ed. N. F. Dreiszige (Waterloo, Ontario: 1990), 123–57.

7. For a useful contextual discussion, see Andrei Tsygankov, *Russia's Foreign Policy: Change and Continuity in National Identity* (Lanham, MD: Rowan and Littlefield, 2016), 63–67 and 237–38. Tsygankov constructed a theoretical argument explaining how Russia's identity in international affairs was conflicted between those who wanted to be part of the West and those who viewed Russia as a distinct civilization in opposition to the West. He argued for continued Western engagement that respected Russian concerns. See also Igor Zevelev,

Russian National Identity and Foreign Policy (Washington, DC: 2016). Zevelev notes the role of Foreign Minister Sergei Lavrov in this process.

8. For a good, concise discussion, see Nicholas Riasanovsky, "'Nationality' in the State Ideology during the Reign of Nicholas I," *The Russian Review* 19, no. 1 (January 1960): 38–46. For a more detailed analysis, see Riasanovsky's *Nicholas I and Official Nationality in Russia* (Los Angeles: University of California Press, 1959). For useful commentary on Uvarov views on the question of Slavic identity, see M. M. Shevchenko, "Slavianskii vopros glazami russkogo pravitel'stva v 1842 godu: S. S. Uvarov i K. V. Nesselrode" [The Slavic question through the eyes of the Russian government in 1842: S. S. Uvarov and K. V. Nesselrode]," *Russkii sbornik* [Russian Collection], T. I (Moscow: 2004), 29–39. For a look at the way Russian national identity, and official nationality in particular, have shaped modern foreign policy, see Zevelev, 6.

9. Ivo Banac, *The National Question in Yugoslavia: Origins, History, Politics* (Ithaca, NY: Cornell University, 1984), 27–29.

10. Banac, 28.

11. Trenin, *Post-Imperium*, 104.

12. Nikolai Danilevsky, *Rossiia I evropa* [Russia and Europe] (St. Petersburg: 1871), 23; see chapters two (23–53) and five (91–113).

13. Johann Gottfried von Herder, *Reflections on the Philosophy of the History of Mankind* (Chicago: University of Chicago, 1968), 3–78.

14. B. P. Baluev, *Spory o sud'bakh Rossii: N. Ia. Danilevskii I ego kniga 'Rossiia I Evropa* [Arguments on the Fate of Russia: N. Ia. Danilevsky and His Book 'Russia and Europe'] (Moscow: Editorial, 1999), 235.

15. Baluev, 235. See also V. A. Shnirel'man, "Tsivilizatsionyi podkhod kak natsional'naia ideia: tsivilizatsiia vmesto natsii [A Civilizational Approach as a National Idea: Civilization Instead of Nation]," in *Natsionalizm v mirovoi istorii* [Nationalism in World History], ed. V. A. Tishkov and V. A. Shnirel'man (Moscow: Nauka, 2007), 82–105. Shnirel'man made the point that Russians have a lengthy history of thinking of themselves as part of a distinct civilization.

16. See Rostislav A. Fadeev, *Opinion on the Eastern Question* (London: E. Stanford, 1871).

17. Marlene Laruelle, "Les ideologies de la 'Troisieme voie' dans les annees 1920: Le movement Eurasia russe," *Vingtieme Siecle Revue d'histoire* 70 (April–June 2001): 34–36, https://www.jstor.org/stable/3771702. Also of interest on Ilyin's popularity in the Putin era is Anton Barbashin and Hannah Thoburn, "Ivan Ilyin and the Ideology of Moscow's Rule," *Foreign Affairs*, 20 September 2015, https://www.foreignaffairs.com/articles/russian-federation/2015-09-20/putins-philosopher.

18. Laruelle, 34–36. For a deeper look at Laruelle's thesis about Eurasianist historiography, see her book *Ideologiya russkogo evraziistva ili Mysli o velichii imperii,* trans. Tat'iana Grigor'eva (Moscow: Natalis, 2004). Linguist Nikolay Trubetskoi, who also became a founder of Eurasianism, wrote *Nasledie Chingiz khana: vzgliad na russkuiu istoriiu ne s zapada, a s vostoka* [Chingiz Khan's Legacy: A View of Russian History not from the West, but from the East] (Ber-

lin: 1925) This work was republished in Moscow in 1999 as part of the popular rediscovery of Trubetskoy's works.

19. Vernadsky departed Russia due to the revolution but as an established scholar was able to land a teaching position in the United States, where he became a foundational figure in the scholarship on Russian history.

20. George Vernadsky, *A History of Russia*, 3rd rev. edition (New Haven, CT: Yale University Press, 1951), 5.

21. See George Vernadsky, *Russia and the Mongols* (New Haven, CT: Yale University Press, 1953). Vernadsky also produced *Kievan Russia* (Yale University Press: New Haven, CT: 1948), in which he cemented the idea that Kievan civilization was the direct ancestor of the Russian Empire.

22. Charles Halperin, "George Vernadsky, Eurasianism, the Mongols, and Russia," *Slavic Review* 41, no. 3 (Autumn 1982): 477, https://www.jstor.org/stable/2497020.

23. Trenin, *Post Imperium*, 60–61.

24. Charles Clover, *Black Wind, White Snow: The Rise of Russia's New Nationalism* (New Haven, CT: Yale University Press, 2016), 186–90.

25. Halperin, "George Vernadsky, Eurasianism, the Mongols, and Russia," 477–93.

26. Robert C. Blitt, "Russia's Orthodox Foreign Policy: The Growing Influence of the Russian Orthodox Church in Shaping Russia's Policies Abroad," *University of Pennsylvania Journal of International Law* 33-2 (2011): 365.

27. Blitt, 414–15.

28. Igor Zevelev, "The Russian World in Moscow's Strategy," Center for Strategic and International Studies, 22 August 2016, https://www.csis.org/analysis/russian-world-moscows-strategy.

29. Stephen A. Cohen, "Historical Monuments, From Moscow to Charlottesville: August 17," in *War with Russia? From Putin and Ukraine to Trump and Russiagate* (New York: Hot Books, 2019), Kindle.

30. The author heard this Soviet joke on many occasions in various versions while researching in the USSR and Russia between 1979 and 2014. For one rendering of the story, see Rachel Donadio, "The Iron Archives," *New York Times,* 22 April 2007, https://www.nytimes.com/2007/04/22/books/review/Donadio.t.html.

31. Blakkisrud, "Blurring the Boundary," 264.

32. Pal Kolsto, "The Ethnification of Russian Nationalism," in *The New Russian Nationalism: Imperialism, Ethnicity and Authoritarianism 2000–2015*, ed. Pal Kolsto and Helge Blakkisrud (Edinburgh: Edinburgh University, 2016), 18–19.

33. Baumann, "Imperial Service Reform," 31–49.

34. The place that Russians refer to as Kiev is Kyiv to Ukrainians. To both sides, the choice of spellings has political implications.

35. Steven Usitalo, *The Invention of Mikhail Lomonosov: A Russian National Myth* (Boston: Academic Studies Press: 2013), 250–53.

36. Usitalo, 251.

37. Usitalo, 259–60.

38. For a good discussion, see Elisabeth Cheaure and R. D. Keil, "'Adler im Kopf, Schlangen im Herzen' Napleon, Borodino und nationale Identitat in Russland," *Osteuropa* 63, no. 1, Mythos Erinnerung: Russland und das Jahr 1812 (January 2013): 29–50, https://www.jstor.org/stable/44934551.

39. Raeff, "At the Origins of a Russian National Consciousness: Eighteenth Century Roots and Napoleonic Wars," *The History Teacher* 25, no. 1 (November 1991): 7.

40. "Positive Views of Stalin on the Rise," *RadioFreeEurope/RadioLiberty* (11 April 2018), https://www.rferl.org/a/positive-views-of-stalin/29159116.html.

41. "Positive Views of Stalin on the Rise."

42. A. N. Shvechnikov, ed., *Pravoslavie I patriotizm* [Orthodoxy and patriotism] (St. Petersburg: 2005), 6–7. This work is the collected proceedings of a conference on Orthodoxy in 2004. A central theme addressed the oppositional relationship of the Orthodox Christian world with the West.

43. A notable example of this trend was Nikolai Starikov's *Kak predavali Rossiiu* [Ilow Thcy Bctraycd Russia] (St. Petersburg: 2018), which discussed fifteen historical cases in which Western governments took advantage of Russia. Slightly older but also of interest is Viktor Starodubov's *Ot razoruzheniia k kapituliatsii* [From Disarmament to Capitulation] (Moscow: 2007). Starodubov, a retired lieutenant general, traced Russia's military relationship with the West from the era of disarmament to what he described as submission. Again, the point is that Russia was treated unjustly.

Chapter 4

Managing the Agenda: The Moscow Conference
on International Security (MCIS)

Mark R. Wilcox

In late April 2019, the Russian Ministry of Defense (MOD) hosted the eighth annual Moscow Conference on International Security (MCIS). This conference was the latest step in the evolutionary development of an annual event that began in 2012. Russia's minister of defense, Army General Sergey Shoygu, observed that since its origin in 2012, the MCIS had "recommended itself as an authoritative and open area for discussion of the most current issues of global and regional security." The growing demand for the conference was demonstrated by the attendance in 2018 by over 850 delegates from ninety-five countries, including more than 40 senior defense officials and representatives of seventy academic and non-governmental organizations.[1]

From a single topic in 2012, missile defense, the ambit of the MCIS has expanded to cover issues that range well beyond European security (see Figure 4.1). The conference provided Moscow the opportunity to showcase its security concerns with the aim to shape European and broader global security agendas.

The purpose of this chapter is to examine the phenomenon of the MCIS from its inception in 2012 through 2019. In its simplest form, the agenda of the MCIS can be seen as an annual catalog of the threats, challenges, and opportunities Russia faces in guaranteeing its security. The MCIS may be Moscow's answer to the Munich Security Conference. Given that the history of the MCIS correlated to President Vladimir Putin's return to the presidency and Sergey Shoygu's assumption of the role of defense minister in November 2012, the MCIS reflected their leadership of the Russian security apparatus, which is characterized, *inter alia*, by the ascendancy of the armed forces in Russian foreign and security policy and the diminished role of the Ministry of Foreign Affairs (MFA). The expansion of the Ministry of Defense-sponsored MCIS agenda from a narrow focus on a single military issue—missile defense—to a *tour d'horizon* of global security issues offers validation of Russian analyst Alexandr Golts's claim: "The Armed Forces have . . . become the Kremlin's main if not sole foreign policy tool."[2]

This chapter examines each iteration of the MCIS in turn. Based on this examination, the chapter offers conclusions about the MCIS as a tool

Dates	Topic(s)
3–4 May 2012	The Factor of Anti-Missile Defense in the Formation of a New Security Space
23–24 May 2013	Military and Political Aspects of European Security
16–17 April 2014	Global Security and Regional Security
16–17 April 2015	Global Security: Challenges and Perspectives
27–28 April 2016	**V Moscow Conference on International Security** (Terrorism, Asia-Pacific, Middle East, Emerging Security Challenges, Color Revolutions and Military Role in Security, Central Asia, Global Security and Military Cooperation, Problems of War and Peace in Europe)
26–27 April 2017	**VI Moscow Conference on International Security** (Global Security, European Security, Middle East, Ballistic Missile Defense, Security of Information Space, Asia-Pacific, Central Asia, Military-to-Military Engagement)
4–5 April 2018	**VII Moscow Conference on International Security** (Defeat of ISIL in Syria, Global Security in a Polycentric World, European Security, Regional Security in the Middle East and North Africa, "Soft Power" as a Tool to Pursue Military-Political Objectives, Asia: Regional Security Aspects, Regional Specifics of Defense Agencies' Response to National Threats and Challenges)
23–25 April 2019	**VIII Moscow Conference on International Security** (Military Dangers and Threats in the Modern World, Security in the Modern World: Regional and Global Factors and Trends, Outcomes of Defeat of ISIS in Syria and Iraq, "Color" Revolutions and "Hybrid" Warfare, Ballistic Missile Defense and Placement of Weapons in Space, Military-to-Military Peacekeeping Engagement, Northern Africa: Terrorism and Illegal Migration, Reconstruction and Economic Development of Syria and Iraq—Return of Refugees, Military Cooperation and Regional Security, International Peacekeeping Effort: New Perceptions and Military Cooperation, Regional Security Aspects: Asia, Africa, and Latin America)

Figure 4.1. Iterations of the Moscow Conference on International Security, 2012–19. Compiled by the author.

for Russia's strategic messaging, a means to highlight the role of the armed forces—and in particular Defense Minister Shoygu—in national security, and an indicator of the Russian leadership's turn away from the West and toward non-western countries. The starting point for this study of the MCIS is the conference on missile defense held in Moscow in May 2012. Although its title as the Moscow Conference on International Security was introduced in 2014, the Russian MOD regarded the meetings held in 2012 and 2013 as iterations of the MCIS, notwithstanding their limited programs.

The topic of the conference held 3–4 May 2012 was "The Factor of Anti-Missile Defense in the Formation of a New Security Space." The items for discussion ranged from assessment of the threat of proliferation of missile technologies to determination of directions of cooperation in the sphere of anti-missile defense toward the goals of support of strategic stability and equality of rights in strategic partnership. The MOD reported that around 200 political figures, military specialists, and experts from fifty countries, including Russia, European and Asian countries, and the United States and Canada, were invited.[3] A delegation of eight officials from the United States government, including Ellen O. Tauscher, undersecretary of state for Arms Control and International Security, and Madelyn R. Creedon, assistant secretary of defense for Global Strategic Affairs, participated. Speaking optimistically given the ongoing clash between the United States and Russia over missile defense in Europe, Tauscher opined that "cooperation on missile defense could be a game-changer" in the relationship and hoped that the meeting would "revitalize the spirit of cooperation" on the issue.[4]

The 2012 conference on missile defense was an orchestrated opportunity to convey Moscow's message on the issue. A month before the conference, the Russian newspaper *Kommersant* reported that the conference would be part of "an offensive on the information front" at which the MOD would make its case for the danger that the European missile defense system presented to Russian nuclear forces. As a result of this "international military conference organized by the military department to which military persons and experts from all over the world will be invited," the United States felt pressure to further justify plans for the European system. Russian Deputy Defense Minister Anatoly Antonov explained the uniqueness of the conference: "Never before has any security problem been discussed in the Defense Ministry so openly. . . . We intend to convey our assessments of the influence of missile defense on global and regional security, and we are prepared to discuss all points of view. Let them show us we are wrong using facts."[5]

The assessments of the Russian side remain readily available on the MOD website. The 2012 conference website provides articles by Russian academics, official statements, and fact sheets, as well as speeches by senior Russian defense officials at the conference, include Russian- and English-language texts. The overall themes of the Russian narrative were the challenge posed by missile defense in Europe and, globally, Russia's efforts to maintain defense capabilities in the face of this threat and to work cooperatively with the North Atlantic Treaty Organization (NATO) to address the challenges of missile proliferation and missile defense. In support of this narrative, at the conclusion of the conference, the Russian MOD invited attendees to visit a radar tracking station at Sofrino outside Moscow "to show them that Russia has all that is needed for international missile defense cooperation."[6]

Rather than focus on a single issue like missile defense, the MOD and Defense Minister Shoygu expanded the scope of the 23–24 May 2013 conference program to encompass a host of issues related toEuropean security. The conference organizers took note of positive developments in European security, yet identified the need to address contemporary threats and challenges and overcome factors that threatened undivided security in Europe. The goal of the International Conference "Military and Political Aspects of European Security" was open discussion of these problems and "formulation of proposals toward the search for mutually acceptable solutions."[7]

The desired level of participation for the conference was ministers of defense (along with experts and academics in the field). Aside from Shoygu, however, no other defense ministers attended. Shoygu specifically invited United States Defense Secretary Chuck Hagel, but he demurred, sending Deputy Assistant Secretary of Defense for Russia, Ukraine, and Eurasia Evelyn Farkas in his stead.[8] Others who sent lower-ranking officials included NATO and Finland. The highest-ranking attendee outside the Russian government appears to have been Nikolay Bordyuzha, the secretary general of the Collective Security Treaty Organization.[9]

Changes to the conference in 2013 appear to have been based on Shoygu's desire to raise the profile of an event that he had initiated and President Putin supported.[10] Shoygu even proposed holding a meeting of the NATO-Russia Council (NRC) at the level of defense ministers on the margins of the conference. The Russians dangled the prospect of a briefing on the upcoming exercise West (Zapad) 2013, "about which NATO partners are concerned," as a sweetener for NATO defense ministers, albeit without success.[11] Notwithstanding the dearth of ministerial-level attendees from outside Moscow, a significant change from the 2012 conference was the contribution of high-level Russian officials from outside the MOD: President Putin offered greetings to the conference, Head of the Presidential Administration Sergey Ivanov attended, and Minister of Foreign Affairs Sergey Lavrov addressed the conference. The visit of "defense officials and military experts from Armenia, Germany, Hungary, Latvia, Norway, South Africa, Sweden, Turkmenistan, Ukraine, the United States, and Zimbabwe" to the base of the Taman Division at Alabino in the Moscow region was also a novel event for the conference.[12] While the visit to the missile defense radar at Sofrino at the end of the 2012 conference appeared not to have been planned beforehand, the visit to this unit was a part of the conference program. The substantive change from the 2012 conference to that of 2013 was the expansion of the agenda, a change that was linked to the Russians' messaging effort.

The expansion of the conference agenda in 2013 served several narratives. First, the Russians could communicate their concern over developments in the European security environment and their desire for a formal European security treaty. Missile defense, however, remained a dominant theme for the Russians. Having observed that the head of the Russian presidential administration Ivanov, Deputy Defense Minister Antonov, and Chief of the General Staff General Valery Gerasimov all succeeded in continuing to obstruct progress toward agreement with the United States on missile defense, veteran Russian defense commentator Aleksandr Golts noted: "The focus of Moscow's conference on European security, it would seem, was to give the Defense Ministry another chance to rebuff the West."[13] Another theme for Moscow was conventional armed forces. Part of the context for the meeting, from the Russian MOD perspective, was the ongoing transformation of the armed forces of Russia and other countries in Europe, according to Sergey Koshelev, director of the Russian MOD Department for International Military Cooperation, and Aleksandr Grushko, Russia's ambassador to NATO.[14] Finally, the Russians planned to use the meeting to raise issues about security in Central Asia in the context of a possible withdrawal by the United States and NATO from Afghanistan.[15]

It also appears that part of the Russians' messaging at the 2013 conference was to raise the prestige of the event itself, partly by linking it to the well-established and respected Munich Security Conference. Two pieces of evidence point in this direction. First, Antonov's speech to the 2013 Munich Security Conference was included as one of the supplemental materials on the web site of the 2103 Moscow conference.[16] Second, Antonov officially announced the 2013 Moscow conference while he was at the meeting in Munich.[17]

By 2014, the third year of the conference and the first year it would be called The Moscow Conference on International Security (MCIS); the MOD's annual gathering was, Shoygu proudly said, "already a tradition."[18] The agenda of the MCIS in 2014 shifted further afield from that of the preceding two conferences, encompassing issues beyond Europe. The MOD organizers made a conscious effort to move the conversation on security away from what had taken place earlier in the year at the Munich Security Conference, at which Ukraine featured prominently, and toward issues like color revolutions that better fit Moscow's narrative.

The announced topics of the MCIS, which took place 23–24 May 2014, were Global Security and Regional Stability, The Search for Paths to Stabilization of the Situation in the Near East and North Africa, and Afghanistan and Regional Security.[19] In reality, according to an MOD press release, the agenda would be "dominated by the problem of the spreading 'coloured [sic] revolutions,' which are destabilizing the situation in many regions of the world."[20] Discussions also centered on the consequences of the Arab Spring and the prospects for stability in Afghanistan after the end of NATO's International Security Assistance Force mission.

The MCIS 2014 was another step forward in Russian MOD efforts to spread conference messages and demonstrate the importance of the military in Russia's security policy. The website for the conference played a key role in portraying the MCIS as a major international event. The site included links to the texts and, for the first time, videos of speeches by the major participants from Russia, and an eighty-six-page document on the results of the conference that contained the text of welcoming remarks by President Putin and UN Secretary General Ban Ki Moon, as well as those of all participants in the three sessions of the conference.[21] The site also listed attendees from the thirty-six countries and five international organizations that sent representatives to the conference. The military's role in international affairs was apparent in the number of bilateral meetings that Defense Minister Shoygu held with his counterparts on the margins of the conference. The MOD announced that he planned to meet with the defense ministers of Iran, Pakistan, Azerbaijan, Serbia, and Armenia. The MCIS also provided the venue for a bilateral meeting between the Azerbaijani and Iranian defense ministers, at which they agreed to develop cooperation between their armed forces.[22]

The situation in Ukraine turned out to be the elephant in the room at the MCIS, notwithstanding Russian MOD Director for International Military Cooperation Koshelev's expectation that the conference would not address it. In the weeks before the MCIS, he noted, "we are troubled by Ukraine's future. That is why, although issues concerning stabilization in Ukraine have not been included on the agenda for the conference, we will be ready to discuss them."[23] And discuss them, they did. For example, General Gerasimov and Minister of Defense of Belarus General-Lieutenant Zhadobin discussed Ukraine in their speeches. Collective Security Treaty Organization Secretary General Bordyuzha stated, "Ukraine is now the main theater of the fight to push Russia to the periphery of European civilization. The events taking place in this country fit very well in the logic of the plans implemented by the West, and their connection with the events in Yugoslavia in 1999 and the 2008 Georgia-Ossetian conflict is evident."[24] A political officer from the Chinese People's Liberation Army noted Beijing's concern over the situation and its "very complicated historical roots."[25]

Perhaps most vocal about the influence of the situation in Ukraine was Deputy Defense Minister Antonov. In comments preceding the conference, he lamented the decision by certain Western (NATO) states, like the United States, not to send official delegations, let alone their ministers of defense. He affirmed that the conference would take place despite these absences and opined that the decision by NATO countries placed them "in an awkward position."[26] In a separate interview, Antonov appeared to take a swipe at the NRC and, arguably, the Munich Security Conference, which had featured debate about Ukraine several months earlier: "We will hold this conference in any case. Let me remind you that the Russian Defense Ministry annually invites senior officials of foreign defense departments and international organizations, as well as non-governmental experts to an open debate on international security issues. *This is a crucial task now that many debate platforms have sunk, so to say.*"[27]

As had been the case in 2013, the Russians proposed a meeting of the NRC in conjunction with—or, at least, in close proximity to—the MCIS. Whereas Shoygu had sought a meeting in Moscow the preceding year, in 2014 Koshelev told a Russian news agency the MOD suggested a meeting in Brussels sometime before the last day of the 2013 conference. According to Koshelev, NATO Secretary General Anders Fogh Rasmussen had the same idea and "NATO took over the initiative," but proposed a date after the conclusion of the MCIS. Although Moscow could not agree to the date, according to Koshelev the proposal remained alive. Most importantly, "it was a Russian idea first."[28]

The IV MCIS took place 16–17 April 2015, on the eve of the commemoration of the seventieth anniversary of the victory over Nazi Germany (i.e., victory in the Great Patriotic War of 1941–45), timing "that allowed participants to address the Second World War lessons which are timely for global modern policy and international relations."[29] This theme played well into the Russian narrative that the cooperation among the Allies during the Second World War/Great Patriotic War had been a high point in relations between them, a time worthy of emulation. The two topics of the conference's program also supported this narrative. The first, the Islamic State and combating terrorism, dealt with a foe common to all, like Nazi Germany in the 1940s. The second topic, international legal mechanisms in the field of security, could be seen as a reminder of the norms of cooperation and international conduct during the war and the post-war era.

Although the program retained, in part, a focus on European security, the situation in Ukraine was not on the agenda, nor were Ukrainian representatives invited. Deputy Defense Minister Antonov explained after the MCIS that Ukraine had not been invited because officials in Kyiv would have been focused on cease-fire negotiations. "The peaceful resolution of this conflict is much more important. We did not want to make our Ukrainian colleagues dependent on our event."[30] It seems though, the real reason behind keeping the Ukrainians away was to minimize threats to Moscow's control of the narrative at the conference. Speaking on the eve of the conference, former chief of the Russian General Staff Yuri Baluyevskiy opined that "well-known thoughts about notorious developments" would be expressed and Ukraine would come up "between the lines" at the MCIS.[31] Antonov took a similar line in early March 2015, when he explained, "in view of a most severe information battle around the crisis in the southeast of Ukraine, we decided not to exacerbate the situation at the conference to the limit, and at this stage decided not to invite our Ukrainian colleagues to the event."[32]

The 2015 MCIS also featured a rigorous schedule of bilateral meetings on the margins of the conference between Shoygu and his counterparts. He met with the Greek defense minister, the only one from a NATO country to attend, the day before the MCIS. Shoygu highlighted the "rich history and long-standing defense and military technical relations" between the countries and expressed gratitude for "the Greek government's memory of the feat of the Soviet people in the Great Patriotic War."[33] In his meeting with the Serbian defense minister, Shoygu praised Serbia as a "reliable partner in the military and military-technical sphere."[34] Shoygu also met with several non-European defense ministers, an indication that the MCIS was beginning to shift away from the West and toward "the rest." In the cases of India and Egypt, Shoygu's invitations included offers to participate in some of his other pet projects, the international army games, the tank biathlon, and the Aviadarts flying competition.

Among Shoygu's other interlocutors were senior defense officials of countries that were hostile to the United States or in strained relations with Washington. During his meeting with Iranian Defense Minister Dehqan, Shoygu "agreed to discuss all the technical aspects of the S-300 air defense system and arrange for the delivery of the weapons to Iran" by the end of the year (which did not happen). Dehqan, speaking of the MCIS, suggested that a permanent secretariat be established to follow up on agreements concluded at the meeting.[35] Shoygu met with North Korean Minister of Defense General Hyong Yong Chol in Moscow immediately prior to the MCIS and invoked the celebration of the seventieth anniversary of the end of World War II as a means of further solidifying cooperation between the two countries. He thanked the North Koreans for the "caring attitude towards the memory for the Soviet soldiers who took part in fighting for Korea's liberation." In an apparent swipe at those whom he saw as attempting to falsify history about the Great Patriotic War, Shoygu added, "This is particularly important today when the tragic events of the Second World War are becoming a subject of political speculations."[36] He affirmed the permanence of Russia's military cooperation with North Korea and pledged that "Moscow will only increase its cooperation with Pyongyang."[37] Pakistani Minister of Defense Khawaja Muhammed Asif conducted bilateral meetings with Shoygu and his Iranian counterpart while attending the MCIS.[38]

In addition to greater international participation, the IV MCIS included more voices from the Russian MOD. According to a MOD official, "a special thing about the upcoming conference will be that high-ranking officials from the Russian Defense Ministry" will have the chance to offer their views. These views "sometimes [differ] from the materials and estimations that exist in the press and are sometimes called [those] of the Defense Ministry. That is, the officials will give their estimations and will make it clear what the Russian Federation thinks, plans and how it will react to specific threats and challenges to national security."[39] In other words, the MOD would have more opportunities to propagate its narrative.

By 2016, the MCIS had evolved from a single-issue conference conducted under the sole auspices of the MOD to one with a broader agenda that enjoyed the imprimatur of the government writ large. A Russian government resolution published on 12 February 2016 tasked the defense ministry to form an organizing committee under the chairmanship of Antonov and to prepare and organize the conference and its program. The foreign ministry's role was limited to providing "the issue of visas to conference participants, guests and the media, in line with the established procedures and without visa fees."[40] The foreign ministry's secondary and, in fact, technical support role to the MOD for the conference, was now codified.

The program's agenda and participants showed the continuing evolution of the focus of the MCIS away from Europe and the West and toward other regions such as the Middle East, Asia-Pacific, Central Asia, and Latin America. As for specific issues, in contrast with Defense Minister Shoygu's warm comments about North Korea at the 2015 MCIS, the Russian line at the 2016 meeting was more cautious. Russia's permanent representative to the International Atomic Energy Agency, Vladimir Voronkov, told reporters on the margins of the MCIS that a possible fifth test of a nuclear weapon by North Korea would increase tensions. In the event of a test, the international community should react strongly and "I am absolutely positive that [Russia] will condemn it, as we did before."[41] The Russian intelligence apparatus delivered a coordinated message about the threat of the spread of Islamist terrorism. The deputy chief of the Russian General Staff Main Intelligence Directorate warned of the spread of the Islamic State and associated groups like Boko Haram throughout Africa to create a "Terrorist Internationale" on the continent. Aleksandr Bortnikov, the director of the Federal Security Service highlighted the use by "Islamic extremist elements" of the "newest information technologies, primarily the opportunities provided by the Internet, to advocate terrorism as the only method of a global war on the infidels."[42]

The Russians also used the 2016 MCIS to attempt to drive wedges between western allies and partners. The attendance, once again, of the Greek defense minister at the MCIS—the only such attendance by a western official—and his claim that EU sanctions against Russia "had been a disaster both for Russia and the EU," were a source of concern for NATO, but must have been satisfying for Moscow. Former Afghan President Hamid Karzai called for increased cooperation between Russia, the United States, China, and India on the path to success in stabilizing Afghanistan, noting "When the U.S. acted on its own, it didn't achieve success with its allies, and Russia's assistance was needed."[43]

In a post-conference assessment, Defense Minister Shoygu rattled off a list of statistics about attendees—defense ministries represented, defense, international organizations, and media representatives—to tout the success of the V MCIS. In keeping up appearances for this project of Shoygu's, the conference featured both a live webcast on the website of the MOD and extensive coverage by Russian and international media. Most notably, however, was Shoygu's use of the MCIS to support Russia's broader security agenda by laying the groundwork for additional events (that would, of course, feature him). For example, Shoygu hosted an informal meeting with defense ministers of the member countries of the Association of Southeast Asian Nations (ASEAN) immediately before the conference. According to Shoygu, this meeting "made an important contribution to preparations for the Russia-ASEAN Summit" which took place in Sochi shortly thereafter and was "timed to coincide with the twentieth anniversary of the dialogue partnership between [Russia] and Association member states."[44]

The VI MCIS, in 2017, was marked by a "harsh anti-American and anti-Western tone," which was reflected in speeches by Foreign Minister Lavrov ("condemned US 'aggression' in Syria and NATO's unilateral actions"), Russian Security Council Secretary Nikolai Patrushev ("accused the West of 'fact manipulation and information falsification'") and Foreign Intelligence Service Chief Sergey Naryshkin ("claimed that the West was stoking an ideological confrontation of Cold War intensity").[45] A former senior US official with extensive experience in Russia observed during his trip to attend the VI MCIS "a deep-rooted distrust toward the U.S. and NATO" at a level he had not seen in his twenty-five-plus years of travel in the USSR and Russia.[46]

Among the approximately 800 participants from 86 countries were 22 ministers of defense, 14 chiefs of defense staff or deputies, and 35 national delegations. The "most representative delegations were represented by countries of Asia, the Near and Middle East, Europe and Latin America." In addition to the participants, more than 400 journalists from 32 countries attended the VI MCIS.[47]

For the third year, the MOD organized an information session about the upcoming Army-2017 military-technical forum—one of Shoygu's major initiatives—for the VI MCIS. The MOD reported that both participants and guests of the MCIS showed great interest in the materials and presentations about Army-2017, and information booklets were available to participants in six languages.[48] The major public relations innovation of the VI MCIS was the startup of a YouTube channel, which enabled viewers to catch their favorite MCIS speeches and discussions either live or after the fact.

The leadership of the Russian MOD and armed forces conducted more than forty bilateral meetings on the margins of the VI MCIS. Defense Minister Shoygu told the Iranian defense minister, who was at the MCIS for the fourth time, that he was "satisfied with the level of coordination with Iran on Syria" and noted that their cooperation in the battle against terrorism was bearing fruit.[49] In a meeting with his Brazilian counterpart,

Shoygu spoke of the "intensity" of Russo-Brazilian dialogue, including "military-technical cooperation," and proposed military exchanges for training.[50] At a meeting with his Pakistani counterpart, Shoygu praised the development of ties between his and Pakistan's general staffs. Declaring solidarity with Pakistan over their shared experiences with terrorist attacks, Shoygu noted that the world was becoming "neither calm nor stable" so the battle against terrorism called for a "consolidation of all interested in this effort."[51] Besides Shoygu, Deputy Defense Minister for International Cooperation Aleksandr Fomin met with senior defense officials of Venezuela, Brunei, Cameroon, and Paraguay. Chief of the General Staff Gerasimov met with his Jordanian counterpart and noted the "traditionally . . . friendly character" of relations between the two countries' armed forces.[52] He also received the Nicaraguan chief of defense staff, whom he thanked for that country's support for Russia in the UN General Assembly on Crimea, Ukraine, and Syria, which Moscow viewed as a strong confirmation that "Nicaragua is a dependable political ally."[53]

The emphasis of the VII MCIS in 2018 was not on events in the West. The main theme was the Near East after the fall of the Islamic State, and plenary sessions were also dedicated to regional security issues in Europe, Asia, Africa, and Latin America. On 3 April, before the formal opening of the conference, participants had the opportunity to visit "Park Patriot" (officially the "Military-Patriotic Park of Culture and Relaxation of the Armed Forces of the Russian Federation 'Patriot'"), located in Kubinka in the Moscow region. There they had the opportunity to view an exhibition oriented on Russia's operations in Syria, to include the various weapons and equipment used by the Russian navy, air forces, and engineering forces in the conflict. Also on display were weapons and equipment of terrorist forces.[54] Commanders of the Russian National Guard (Rosgvardiya) and the Deputy Minister of Internal Affairs participated for the first time. The upcoming Army-2018 military-technical exposition and National Security Week were both featured at side events during the VII MCIS, as the former had been in 2017. In 2018, the booklets about the upcoming forums were made available to participants in only four languages (Russian, English, Arabic, Chinese), as opposed to six in 2017.[55]

Once again, the MCIS provided opportunities for a robust schedule of bilateral meetings on the margins between Russian officials and their international counterparts. The Ministry of Foreign Affairs was even able to tag along with the MOD, as Foreign Minister Sergey Lavrov used the occasion of the VII MCIS to carry out a bilateral meeting on 5 April with

Thomas Greminger, the secretary general of the Organization for Security and Cooperation in Europe, who was in Moscow to attend the conference.

Defense Minister Shoygu met with the Pakistani Defense Minister and cited the "new level" of bilateral relations "in all areas," while his Pakistani counterpart noted a "strategic convergence of our interactions [that] covers Afghanistan, Central Asia and the situation in all the Near East."[56] Shoygu also met with senior defense officials from South Africa, Ethiopia, and Guinea for discussions on military cooperation in Africa and, in some cases, signing of defense agreements. In a meeting with his Laotian counterpart, Shoygu praised Laos as a "reliable partner of Russia."[57] Deputy Defense Minister Fomin met with military leaders from the Republic of Congo, Uruguay, and Mali, and senior defense officials of Sri Lanka and Singapore.

The VIII MCIS, held in April 2019, maintained what had become a decidedly more overt anti-American and anti-western tone for the annual gathering. NATO declined to participate, consistent with established practice after the Russian intervention in Ukraine. A source in NATO took issue with the conference, itself, citing experience with previous iterations of the conference, which had "not been constructive and had not facilitated the furtherance of our [NATO and Russia] dialogue."[58]

In his opening remarks to attendees, Defense Minister Shoygu asserted that the potential for conflict was increasing in various regions of the world. New points of potential military conflict are appearing, and many of these possible conflicts "are being initiated from outside," a completely unsubtle jab at the United States. He highlighted ongoing conflicts and tensions in Yemen, Libya, Syria, Iraq, and Africa. Within this context, "more and more often steps are being taken towards neocolonial interference in the internal affairs of sovereign states." In Southeast Asia, "under the aegis of the formation of a new security system in the so-called Indo-Pacific region, attempts are being undertaken to deter interactions between countries in the interests of creating new dividing lines." Shoygu "devoted special attention . . . to the conduct of the USA in the international arena."[59]

Chief of the General Staff Gerasimov was more blunt—and hyperbolic—in his remarks, in which he stated that relations between the United States and Russia were at "the lowest level in all history." The internal political situation in the United States was precluding improvement in the relationship. He warned that the possible withdrawal of the United States from the New START treaty would eliminate the one remaining agreement to control nuclear weapons, a situation that would cause Russia to assume the worst case for developments in the US arsenal. The "aggressive direction of the policy of the United States of America and its allies" constituted the greatest influence on global and regional security. The end result of this approach would be "the destruction of the entire system of strategic stability in the world."[60]

Once again, participants in the conference had the opportunity to visit Park Patriot on 23 April before the formal start of the conference and the leadership of the MOD used the occasion to host senior defense officials from non-NATO countries. Deputy Defense Minister Fomin and Gerasimov met with counterparts from the Congo, Kazakhstan, Argentina, Iraq, Bolivia, Namibia, India, Vietnam, South Africa, Pakistan, Sudan, Philippines, Cameroon, and Finland. The Nigerian Defense Minister, in remarks to the conference, specifically requested Russian assistance in his country's battle against Boko Haram.[61]

Conclusion

The MCIS grew from its humble origins as a one-off meeting that only featured speakers from the Russian Federation to an internationally attended confab that affords Moscow an opportunity to shape the narrative about a wide range of security issues. The MCIS has come to be an instrument of soft power, employed by the Ministry of Defense, and Defense Minister Shoygu, in particular, in pursuit of Moscow's national security goals. Perhaps having failed to resolve issues in the near abroad using soft power, as Paul Goble argued in 2017, Shoygu and the armed forces are seeking to use it outside Europe and the former Soviet space.[62] Given the expansion of participation in the MCIS over the years and the number of bilateral meetings Shoygu and other Russian defense leaders have conducted in conjunction with recent conferences, it appears that the Russian Ministry of Defense used the MCIS as a soft power tool to further Russian influence among a broader audience than just the near abroad.

The value of the MCIS as a means to spread Moscow's message owes much to Defense Minister Shoygu's promotional skills. Events such as the MCIS raise the prestige of the armed forces and solidify their role in Russian security affairs. They also raise the profile of Shoygu himself, who, as Aleksandr Golts observed, "is very good at PR [public relations] and understands that he continually has to be in the limelight."[63] Deputy Defense Minister Fomin, in an interview with *Krasnaya Zvezda* in March 2018, placed the MCIS in the same context as other outreach efforts of the MOD, such as the Army International Games and the "Army" International Military-Technical Forum. He noted that foreign attendance at the

2012	2013	2014	2015	2016	2017	2018	2019
Speakers and Panelists (Countries)							
Russian Federation	Russian Federation	Russian Federation	Russian Federation	Russian Federation	Russian Federation	Russian Federation	Russian Federation
NATO/EU	NATO/EU	NATO/EU	NATO	NATO	NATO	NATO	NATO
			Greece	Croatia	Belgium	Slovakia	Bulgaria
				FRG	Croatia	USA	Czech Rep.
				Italy	Czech Rep.		
				UK	FRG		
				USA	France		
					Greece		
					USA		
CIS/CSTO	CIS/CSTO	CIS/CSTO	CIS/CSTO	CIS/CSTO	CIS/CSTO	CIS/CSTO	CIS/CSTO
			Belarus	Belarus	Armenia	Armenia	Armenia
				Kyrgyzstan	Belarus	Belarus	Belarus
				Tajikistan	Kazakhstan	Kazakhstan	
					Uzbekistan	Tajikistan	
EUROPE	EUROPE	EUROPE	EUROPE	EUROPE	EUROPE	EUROPE	EUROPE
				Serbia	Austria	Serbia	Serbia
				Switzerland	Finland		
					Serbia		
ASIA	ASIA	ASIA	ASIA	ASIA	ASIA	ASIA	ASIA
			Afghanistan	Afghanistan	Afghanistan	Afghanistan	Cambodia
			China	Bahrain	Bangladesh	China	Egypt
			India	Bangladesh	Egypt	Egypt	Iran
			Indonesia	Egypt	India	India	Iraq
			Iran	India	Iran	Indonesia	Malaysia
			Mongolia	Indonesia	Israel	Iran	Mongolia
			Pakistan	Laos	Jordan	Israel	Myanmar
				Lebanon	Laos	Mongolia	Pakistan
				Mongolia	Pakistan	Pakistan	Saudi Arabia
				N. Korea	Philippines	Singapore	Syria
				Saudi Arabia	Saudi Arabia	Sri Lanka	
				Singapore	Singapore	Syria	
				Vietnam	UAE	UAE	
					Vietnam	Vietnam	
AFRICA	AFRICA	AFRICA	AFRICA	AFRICA	AFRICA	AFRICA	AFRICA
			South Africa	Cameroon	Cameroon	Cameroon	
				Namibia		Guinea	
				South Africa		Rep. Congo	
LATIN AMERICA	LATIN AMERICA	LATIN AMERICA	LATIN AMERICA	LATIN AMERICA	LATIN AMERICA	LATIN AMERICA	LATIN AMERICA
				Argentina	Brazil	Argentina	
				Chile	Venezuela	Nicaragua	
				Uruguay		Uruguay	
				Venezuela		Venezuela	
Speakers and Panelists (International Organizations)							
				CSTO	CSTO	CSTO	
				OSCE	OSCE	OSCE	OSCE
					SCO	SCO	SCO
					UN	UN	UN
						CIS	CIS
						ICRC	ICRC

Figure 4.2. Speakers and Panelists at the MCIS, 2012–19. Compiled by the author.

MCIS and the Army International Games had shown substantial growth and concluded:

> All of this attests, above all, to the activeness with which the Russian Defense Ministry is developing contacts with other countries' military departments, Despite pressure being brought upon them, many states understand that it is impossible to maintain international security without Russia's participation.[64]

Analyst Roger McDermott's observation in 2015 that the MCIS had "become an intrinsic part of Russia's information warfare tools being used against Washington and NATO" retains its validity today. The "unmistakable" message the MOD conveyed through the MCIS has become: "the Kremlin considers the United States and NATO to be far greater threats to Russian security than international terrorism or other transnational security threats."[65]

Consistent with this message and the Kremlin's policy, the MOD has used the MCIS as a venue to move away from the West and cultivate relationships with the armed forces and governments of states in Asia, Africa, and Latin America. This tendency became apparent after Russian interventions in Ukraine and Syria. Indicators of this shift can be seen in the bilateral meetings Shoygu and other military leaders have conducted on the margins of the MCIS and the participation of speakers and panelists from outside the West in the MCIS.

As Angela Stent, one of the leading experts on Russia, observed:

> Russia and the West view each other as competitors, adversaries, and occasional partners. . . . As far as the rest of the world is concerned, Russia is a large authoritarian state ruled by a leader with whom one can do business. Other countries might be wary of the methods Moscow employs to achieve its goals, but they are unconcerned about its domestic situation, recognize that it seeks a sphere of influence in its neighborhood, and are content to pursue engagement without containment.[66]

The evolution of the MCIS has made it a symbol of "Putin's World" and the hardening of its position in opposition to the United States and the West in general. As a part of the narrative being propagated by Defense Minister Shoygu and the MOD, it will continue to play a role in attracting other states, through their armed forces, in Moscow's direction.

Notes

1. "Obrashchenie Ministra oborony Rossiiskoy Federatsii Generala Armii Sergeya Shoygu k uchastnikam VIII Moskovskoy konferentsii no mezhdunarodnoy bezopasnosti [Message of the Minister of Defense of the Russian Federation Sergey Shoygu to Participants of the VIII Moscow Conference on International Security]," accessed 27 May 2019, https://stat.mil.ru/mcis/minister.htm.

2. Aleksandr Golts, "New Divisions May Reduce Army's Combat Readiness," *Eurasia Daily Monitor* 13, no. 97 (18 May 2016): https://jamestown.org/program/new-divisions-may-reduce-russian-armys-combat-readiness/.

3. "Konferentsiya po PRO – O konferentsiy [Conference on BMD – About the Conference]," Ministry of Defense of the Russian Federation, accessed 24 September 2017, http://mil.ru/conference_of_pro/greeting.htm.

4. "Ellen O. Tauscher, Undersecretary of State for Arms Control and International Security, Holds a News Briefing via Teleconference on the Russian Ministry of Defense Conference on Missile Defense in Moscow," *Political Transcript Wire* (Lanham), 3 May 2012, http://search.proquest.com/docview/1010771149/6639693658C74BC0PQ/277?accountid=28992.

5. "Russia to Argue Against US Missile Defense System at International Conference," *BBC Monitoring*, 22 March 2012, http:// search.proquest.com/docview/929708941/6639693658C74BC0PQ/129?accountid=28992.

6. "Russia Can Protect Europe Against Missile Strikes from South – Ministry," *Interfax*, 4 May 2012, search.proquest.com/docview/1011054910/6639693658C74BC0PQ/199?accountid=28992.

7. "Moskovskaya konferentsiya po Evropeiskoy bezopasnosti – o konferentsiy [The Moscow Conference on European Security – About the Conference]," Ministry of Defense of the Russian Federation, accessed 24 September 2017, http://mil.ru/konf_evrodefence/konferencia.htm.

8. "Russian Dropout from CFE Treaty Harms European Security – Washington," *Daily News Bulletin* (Moscow), 23 May 2013, search.proquest.com/docview/1354971921/C43326F52CDE4DF4PQ/184?accountid=28992.

9. "CSTO Gives Negative Forecast for Afghan Situation," *Interfax,* 23 May 2013, search.proquest.com/docview/13547664458/6639693658C74BC0PQ/228?accountid=28992.

10. "European Missile Shield, Afghanistan to Be Discussed at Intl Security Conference in Moscow," *Interfax*, 27 March 2013, search.proquest.com/docview/1320144009/5B2424424CBD4319PQ/98?accountid=28992.

11. "Russian, US Defense Chiefs Discuss Need for 'Resumption of Dialogue" by Phone," *BBC Monitoring*, 25 March 2013, search.proquest.com/docview/1319244243/4D37E127415548A8PQ/538?accountid=28992.

12. "Foreign Defense Officials Visit Russian Military Base," *IANS* (New Delhi), 25 May 2013, search.proquest.com/docview/1418428981/6639693658C-74BC0PQ/358?accountid=28992.

13. "Russian Paper Says Brass Determined to 'Obstruct' West," *BBC Monitoring*, 28 May 2013, search.proquest.com/docview/1355654939/C43326F52C-DE4DF4PQ/227?accountid=28992.

14. For Koshelev, see "Russia Invites Its NATO Partners to Attend Security Conference in Moscow," *Interfax*, 19 March 2013, search.proquest.com/docview/1318003052/5B2424424CBD4319PQ?105?accountid=28992. For Grushko, see "Moscow Security Conference Will Be of Euroatlantic Scope – Grushko," *Interfax*, 22 April 2013, search.proquest.com/docview/1335076493/5B2424424CBD4319PQ/90?acountid=28992.

15. "CSTO Gives Negative Forecast for Afghan Situation – Bordyuzha," *Interfax*, 23 May 2013, search.proquest.com/docview/1354764458/6639693658C-74BC0PQ/228?accountid-28992.

16. "Tesisy vystupleniya zamestiteliya ministra obrony Rossiiskoy Federatsii A.I. Antonova na Myukhenskoy konferentsii po voprosam bezopasnosti [Theses of the Speech of the Deputy Minister of Defense of the Russian Federation A.I. Antonov at the Munich Security Conference]," Ministry of Defense of the Russian Federation, accessed 24 September 2017, http://mil.ru/konf_evrodefence/materials/more.htm?id=11745803@cmsArticle.

17. "Moscow Expected to Host Conference on Security in Euro-Atlantic Area in May – Newspaper," *Interfax*, 2 February 2013, search.proquest.com/docview/1283529521/5B2424424CBD4319PQ/95?accountid=28992.

18. "Shoygu Hopes NATO Colleagues Participate in Int'l Security Conference," *Daily News Bulletin* (Moscow), 23 October 2013, search.proquest.com/docview/1444578056/5B2424424CBD4319PQ/123?accountid=28992.

19. *MCIS – III Moskovskaya Konferentsiya no mezhdunarodnoy bezopasnosti: Materialy konferentsii* [*MCIS – III Moscow Conference on International Security – Conference Materials*] (conference proceedings, 3rd Moscow Conference on International Security, Moscow, Russia, 23–34 March 2014), http://mil.ru/files/morf/MCIS_report_catalogue_final_RUS_21_10_preview.pdf.

20. "International Security Conference Set to Open in Moscow," *Interfax*, 23 May 2014, http://search.proquest.com/docview/1527835927/2D788B1EC-92941CBPQ/12?accountid=28992.

21. These participants were: Minister of Defense Shoygu, Chief of the General Staff Army General Gerasimov, Chief of the Main Operational Directorate of the General Staff Colonel-General Zarudnitskoy, and General-Lieutenant Sergun, also of the Main Operational Directorate of the General Staff.

22. "Azerbaijan, Iran to Develop Military Cooperation – Minister," *BBC Monitoring*, 23 May 2014. http://search.proquest.com/docview/1527434910/C43326F52CDE4DF4PQ/233?accountid=28992.

23. *MCIS – III Moskovskaya Konferentsiya no mezhdunarodnoy bezopasnosti: Materialy konferentsii*, 14–25.

24. "CSTO General Secretary Accuses West of Trying to Push Russia to Periphery of European Civilization," *Interfax*, 23 May 2014, http://search.proquest.com/docview/1527992055/4D37E127415548A8PQ/474?accountid=28992.

25. "Chinese Military Officials Troubled by Ukraine Situation," *Interfax,* 23 May 2014, http://search.proquest.com/docview/1527963645/4D37E127415548 A8PQ/392?accountid=28992.

26. "Defense Ministry: Moscow Security Conference Representative even without Some Western States," *Interfax*, 23 May 2014, http://search.proquest. com/docview/1527931372/2D788B1EC92941CBPQ/22?accountid=28992; and "NATO Put Itself in Awkward Position by Refusing to Attend Moscow Security Conference – Antonov," *Interfax,* 19 May 2014, http://search.proquest.com/ docview/1525976913/5B2424424CBD4319PQ/84?accountid=28992. Emphasis added by chapter author.

27. "Deputy Defense Minister: Moscow Intl Security Conference to Be Held in Any Case," *Interfax*, 30 October 2014, http://search.proquest.com/ docview/1618905923/5B2424424CBD4319PQ/92?accountid=28992.

28. "Russia Puts Forth Idea to Hold Russia-NATO Council in Brussels – Defense Ministry," *The Philippines News Agency*, 23 May 2014, http://search. proquest.com/docview/1527353653/C43326F52CDE4DF4PQ/307?accountid=28992.

29. *VI Moscow Conference on International Security* (conference proceedings, Moscow, Russia, 26–27 April 2017), http://mil.ru/files/morf/6_MCIS_ booklet.pdf.

30. "No Way Russia Will Fight Ukraine – Deputy Defense Minister," *Interfax*, 30 April 2015, http://search.proquest.com/docview/1677304226/4D37E127 415548A8PQ/433?accountid=28992.

31. "International Security Conference Opens in Moscow," *The Philippines News Agency*, 16 April 2015, http://search.proquest.com/ docview/1673304831/2D788B1EC92941CBPQ/27?accountid=28992.

32. "Ukraine Not Asked to Moscow Conference 'Not to Exacerbate' Relations – Official," *BBC Monitoring*, 5 March 2015, http://search.proquest.com/ docview/1660618244/6639693658C74BC0PQ/135?accountid=28992.

33. "Russian, Greek Defense Ministers Discussing European Regional Security Issues," *Interfax*, 15 April 2015, http://search.proquest.com/ docview/1673351637/2D788B1EC92941CBPQ/16?accountid=28992.

34. "Serbia Is a Reliable Partner in Russia's Military Sphere – Shoygu," *Interfax*, 15 April 2015, http://search.proquest.com/docview/1673466190/ C43326F52CDE4DF4PQ/317?accountid=28992.

35. "Iran, Russia Agree on Delivery of S-300 System by End of 2015," *BBC Monitoring*, 16 April 2015, http://search.proquest.com/docview/1673539589/4D 37E127415548A8PQ/476?accountid=28992.

36. "Shoygu Thanks North Korean Counterpart for Looking after Soviet Soldiers' Graves," *Interfax*, 15 April 2015, http://search.proquest.com/docview/1 673385945/4D37E127415548A8PQ/477?accountid=28992.

37. Russia to Increase Ties with North Korea – Russian Defence Minister," *BBC Monitoring*, 15 April 2015, http://search.proquest.com/ docview/1673117910/C43326F52CDE4DF4PQ/239?accountid=28992.

38. "Russia, Pakistan to Broaden Defense Cooperation," *Interfax*, 16 April 2015, http://search.proquest.com/docview/1673798789/C43326F52CDE4DF-4PQ/204?accountid=28992; and "Iranian, Pakistani Defence Ministers Discuss Border Security," *BBC Monitoring*, 17 April 2015, http://search.proquest.com/docview/1673800060/5B2424424CBD4319PQ/93?accountid=28992.

39. "Head of General Staff GRU to Assess Threats, Challenges to Russia's Security at Press Conference in Moscow," *Interfax*, 9 April 2015, http://search.proquest.com/docview/1672100114/2D788B1EC92941CBPQ/36?accountid=28992

40. "Moscow to Host Security Conference in Late April," *Interfax*, 12 February 2016, http://search.proquest.com/docview/1764832094/5B2424424CBD-4319PQ/67?accountid=28992.

41. "Fifth Nuclear Test in DPRK May Further Escalate Tensions – Russian Envoy to IAEA," *Interfax*, 27 April 2016, http://search.proquest.com/docview/1784664254/4D37E127415548A8PQ/385?accountid=28992.

42. "Russian Military Intelligence Warns against Threat of 'Terrorist Internationale' Rise in Africa," *Interfax*, 27 April 2016, http://search.proquest.com/docview/1784774032/4D37E127415548A8PQ/428?accountid=28992; and "ISIL Leaders, Recruiter Trying to Mobilize Youngsters Online – Bortnikov," *Interfax*, 27 April 2016, http://search.proquest.com/docview/1784692278/4D37E127415548A8PQ/429?accountid=28992.

43. Con Coughlin, "NATO's United Front under Threat after Greece Signs Arms Deal with Russia," *The Telegraph*, 8 July 2016, https://www.telegraph.co.uk/news/0/natos-united-front-under-threat-after-greece-signs-arms-deal-wit/; and "Ex-Afghan President Favors U.S.-Russian-Chinese-Indian Cooperation to Promote Security in Southwest Asia," *Interfax*, 27 April 2016, http://search.proquest.com/docview/1784719389/C43326F52CDE4DF4PQ/312?accountid=28992.

44. "Moscow Conference on Int'l Security Draws Approx. 700 Delegates from Over 80 Countries," *Interfax*, 4 May 2016, http://search.proquest.com/docview/1786770030/fulltext/5B2424424CBD4319PQ/80?accountid=28992.

45. "Russian Defense Ministry's Sixth Conference on International Security – Part I," The Middle East Media Research Institute, Special Dispatch No. 6904, 4 May 2017, https://www.memri.org/reports/russian-defense-ministrys-sixth-conference-international-security--part-i.

46. "Trip to Complex, Troubled Russia," unpublished report, June 2017.

47. "Minoborony Rossii obobshchit predlozheniya po bor'be s mirovoym terrorizom, pozbychavshie na VI Mosckovskoy konferentsii po mezhdunarodnoy bezopasnosti, i izdast itogovyi sbornik [The Ministry of Defense of Russia Will Summarize the Proposals on Combatting World Terrorism, Sounded at the VI Moscow Conference on International Security and Will Publish a Summary Document]," Ministry of Defense of the Russian Federation, 28 April 2017, https://function.mil.ru/news_page/country/more.htm?id=12121131@egNews.

48. "Na VI konferentsii MCIS GUNID MO RF organizovalo prezentatsiyu Mezhdunarodnogo voenno-tekhnicheskovo foruma 'Armiya-2017' [At the VI

MCIS Conference the GUNID of the Ministry of Defense of the Russian Federation Organized a Presentation on the International Military-Technical Forum 'Army-2017']," Ministry of Defense of the Russian Federation, 27 April 2017, https://function.mil.ru/news_page/country/more.htm?id=12120821@egNews.

49. "V Minoborony Rossii udovletvoreny urovnem koordinatsii s Iranom po Sirii [In the Ministry of Defense of Russia There Is Satisfaction with the Level of Coordination with Iran on Syria]," Ministry of Defense of the Russian Federation, 27 April 2017, https://function.mil.ru/news_page/country/more. htm?id=12120813@egNews.

50. "Ministr oborony Rossii general armii Sergei Shoygu provel vstrechu so svoim brazil'skim kollegoi [The Minister of Defense of Russia Army General Sergey Shoygu Conducted a Meeting with his Brazilian Colleague]," Ministry of Defense of the Russian Federation, 26 April 2017, https://function.mil.ru/ news_page/country/more.htm?id=12120810@egNews.

51. "Sotrudnichestvo Rossii i Pakistana v boenoi sfere spocobstvuyet ukrepleniyu stabil'nosti v regione [Cooperation between Russia and Pakistan in the Military Sphere Facilitates Strengthening of Stability in the Region]," Ministry of Defense of the Russian Federation, 26 April 2017, https://function.mil.ru/ news_page/country/more.htm?id=12120803@egNews.

52. "Rossiya I Uordaniya namereny usilit' dvustoronee voennoe sotrudnichestvo [Russia and Jordan Intend to Strengthen Bilateral Military Cooperation]," Ministry of Defense of the Russian Federation, 26 April 2017, https://function. mil.ru/news_page/country/more.htm?id=12120781@egNews.

53. "Nachal'nik Genshtaba VS RF general armii Valeriy Gerasimov provel vstrechu s kollegoi iz Nikaraguya [The Chief of the General Staff of the VS RF Army General Valeriy Gerasimov Conducted a Meeting with a Colleague from Nicaragua]," Ministry of Defense of the Russian Federation, 26 April 2017, https://function.mil.ru/news_page/country/more.htm?id=12120760@egNews.

54. "Uchastniki VII Moskovskoi konferentsii po mezhdunarodnoi bezopasnosti posetili park 'Patriot' [Participants of the VII Moscow Conference on International Security Visited Park 'Patriot']," Ministry of Defense of the Russian Federation, 3 April 2018, https://function.mil.ru/news_page/country/more. htm?id=12169735@egNews.

55. "Presentatsiya Mezhdunarodnykh forumov 'ARMIYA-2018' i 'Nedeliya national'noi bezopasnosti' budet predstavlena na VII Moskovskoi konferentsii po mezhdunarodnoi bezopasnosti MCIS-2018 [A Presentation of the International Forums 'Army-2018' and 'National Security Week' will be Made at the VII Moscow Conference on International Security]," Ministry of Defense of the Russian Federation, 4 April 2018, https://function.mil.ru/news_page/country/ more.htm?id=12169938@egNews.

56. "Rossiisko-pakistanskie otnoshenie vyshli na kachestvenno novy uroven [Russo-Pakistani Relations Reached a Qualitatively New Level]," Ministry of Defense of the Russian Federation, 4 April 2018, https://function.mil.ru/news_ page/country/more.htm?id=12169934@egNews.

57. "Rossiya natselena na usilenie vzaimodeistviya s Laosom v voennoi i boenno-tekhnicheskoi sfere [Russia Is Inclined toward Strengthening Interaction with Laos in the Military and Military-Technical Sphere]," Ministry of Defense of the Russian Federation, 4 April 2018, https://function.mil.ru/news_page/country/more.htm?id=12169890@egNews.

58. "NATO otkazalas' uchastvovat' v Moskovskoi konferentsii po bezopasnosti [NATO Refused to Participate in the Moscow Security Conference]," *RIA Novosti*, 10 April 2019, https://ria.ru/20190410/1552558970.html.

59. "Ministr oborony Rossii otmechaet nakoplenie konfliktnogo potentsiala v pazlichnykh regionakh mira [The Minister of Defense of Russia Notes the Accumulation of Conflict Potential in Various Regions of the World]," Ministry of Defense of the Russian Federation, 24 April 2019, https://function.mil.ru/news_page/country/more.htm?id=12227560@egNews.

60. "Po otsenke nachal'nika rossiiskogo Genshtaba, otnosheniya Rossii s SShA i NATO nakhodyatsya na samom nizkom urovne za vsyu istoriyu [According to the Assessment of the Chief of the Russian General Staff, Russia's Relations with the USA and NATO Are at the Lowest Level in All History]," Ministry of Defense of the Russian Federation, 24 April 2019, https://function.mil.ru/news_page/country/more.htm?id=12227566@egNews.

61. Andrew McGregor, "Nigeria Seeks Russian Military Aid in its War on Boko Haram," *Eurasia Daily Monitor* 16, no. 67 (8 May 2019): https://jamestown.org/program/nigeria-seeks-russian-military-aid-in-its-war-on-boko-haram/.

62. Paul Goble, "Having Lost 'Soft' Power in Post-Soviet Space, Moscow Increasingly Using 'Hard,'" *Eurasia Daily Monitor* 14, no. 78 (13 June 2017): https://jamestown.org/program/lost-soft-power-post-soviet-space-moscow-increasingly-using-hard/.

63. Aleksandr Golts, *Military Reform and Militarism in Russia* (Washington, DC: The Jamestown Foundation, 2018), 202.

64. "Russian Deputy Defense Minister Fomin Interviewed on Putin's Annual Message to Federal Assembly," *Krasnaya Zvezda Online*, 12 March 2018, http://redstar.ru/wp-content/uploads/2018/03/025-12-03-2018-1.pdf.

65. Roger McDermott, "Russia's Information Warfare Targets Washington and NATO," *Eurasia Daily Monitor* 12, no. 74 (21 April 2015): https://jamestown.org/program/russias-information-warfare-targets-washington-and-nato/.

66. Angela Stent, *Putin's World: Russia Against the West and with the Rest* (New York: Hatchette Book Group, 2019), 6.

Chapter 5
Contemporary Russian Power in Nicaragua[1]
Maj. Nicole L. Hash

Russia "broke a window" into Central America in February 2010 with a peace offensive led by Foreign Minister Sergei Lavrov. Lavrov visited Cuba, Nicaragua, Guatemala, and Mexico to popularize the Russian language and culture. In Nicaragua, this window meant a "soft expansion"—establishing a Russian Center at the Central American University under the auspice of the Russkiy Mir Foundation, established by President Vladimir Putin in 2007.[2] Its mission is to encourage the "appreciation of Russian language, heritage, and culture" abroad.[3] Russkiy Mir is a nation-branding tool designed to cultivate a positive image of Russia.

Russia's Russkiy Mir engagement in Nicaragua is a small component of a much larger effort to expand Russia's global power—to establish a "new normal." According to Vladimir Davidov and Violetta Tayar, Russian specialists on Latin America, "the 'new normal' accounts for increasing inequality, especially social inequality. . . . Note that this trend started after the removal of the Soviet Union antipode. It seems that the West does not feel the necessity to demonstrate its social competitiveness."[4] Russia, therefore, seeks to demonstrate its ability to provide an alternative to the West.

Russia's Foreign Policy Concept (FPC) and National Security Strategy (NSS) both contain "Russia and the World" sections.[5] The two most-cited themes in the works are "preventing color revolutions" or regime changes and generating alternatives to the world order.[6] First, the Russian Federation works to preserve international order, follow international laws, create stability in lieu of instability, and protect their own and others' sovereignty as supreme over values espoused by the United Nations and the international order. Essentially, Russia seeks enforcement of the status quo of 2016 borders except where interrupted by terrorism and state leadership and when it perceives an external state has meddled with that state. Color revolutions were the early 2000s series of peaceful, democratic revolutions to remove one-party rule, reduce corruption, and decrease authoritarianism along Russia's border, or in states with historical ties to Russia. These included the 2004 Ukrainian Orange Revolution, Georgia's 2003 Rose Revolution, and Kyrgyzstan's 2005 Tulip Revolution. Generally, from the Russian perspective, the Arab Spring is seen as a continuation of these revolutions. Second, Russia seeks to participate in an alternate world order—or rather, alternate organizations, structures, treaties, and relationships outside of the traditional western-dominated ones. Where economic, political, and security organizations do not represent Russia's national interests, Russia endeavors to align itself with organizations that do support it.[7]

Although Russian Federation President Vladimir Putin and Russian Ambassador to Nicaragua Andrei Budayev both describe Russia's actions in Latin America, and specifically Nicaragua, as "soft power," the terminology does not adequately describe the intent, purpose, and methods of Russia's expression of power in Nicaragua. This chapter discusses how Russia seeks to use and expand soft, smart, and sharp power within Nicaragua to achieve its foreign policy goals of generating alternatives to the West and curtailing the potential for color revolutions.

Historic Comrades, Historic Competitors

Russia and Nicaragua share a Cold War past and a common competitive relationship with the United States. Until the Communist struggle in Nicaragua took root in 1979, Nicaragua served as a staging ground for US activities, including pro-US efforts in other Central American states. From 1912 to 1933, US Marines were stationed in Nicaragua, supporting the conservative government, which in turn favored US industry access to Nicaraguan timber. In the 1961 US invasion of Cuba, Nicaragua provided launch sites for the Bay of Pigs Invasion. The United States supported the Somoza political dynasty.[8] At each turn until 1979, whenever a rebellion or revolution occurred, the US revoked diplomatic relations with Nicaragua and re-instituted them after a year.[9] The US did provide aid to the Sandinista government until 1981, when President Ronald Reagan cut off aid and increased US covert action in the region.[10] Later, the United States clandestinely and then infamously backed the Contras—groups opposed to the Sandinista government formed by former national guardsmen and Sandinista soldiers, peasants, and farmers unsatisfied with the Sandinista land policy.[11] José Daniel Ortega Saavedra, who led the Sandinista's urban campaign, was elected president in 1985, defeated by his US-backed former colleague Violeta Barrios de Chamorro in 1990, and returned to the presidency of Nicaragua in 2006.[12]

The Soviet Union began its fiscal support for the Sandinista Party (FSLN) after the United States withdrew funding for the Sandinista government in 1981. By 1984, the Soviet Union was providing Nicaragua with military equipment at an estimated $100 to 150 million annually. The two countries signed formal trade and cooperation treaties.[13] Soviet economic aid consisted of oil, wheat, and the construction and staffing of the Soviet-Nicaraguan Friendship Hospital. When the US began funding the Contras, Soviet military aid changed from minimal to T-54 and T-55 tanks, SA-7 surface-to-air missiles, ZPU light antiaircraft guns, and RPG-7 anti-tank grenades. The Nicaraguan Army became the largest military force in Central America, larger than all other Central American armies combined.

Russia understands that Soviet actions to support the Sandinistas in the 1980s achieved the objective—a friendly regime. Contemporary support for the Ortega-Murrillo government seeks a similar end state—a friendly regime in Nicaragua. The relationship between Nicaragua and Russia also serves Russia's foreign policy goals—preventing a democratic color revolution and providing Nicaragua an alternate to western-dominated structures.

Contemporary Cooperation

Russia's first attempts to continue the Soviet Union's strong relationship with Nicaragua failed, mostly along economic lines. Russia's economy struggled to succeed domestically in the decade following the end of the Cold War and lacked the capacity to extend financial support to traditional client states like Cuba and Nicaragua. After the Nicaraguans re-elected Ortega in 2006, Russia renewed its relationship with Nicaragua, citing a "short break" in a decades-long friendship.[14] Economically, Russia in the early 2000s benefitted from high oil prices that reignited a relationship with Ortega's government.

Presently, Russia is reinvigorating military, development, and social support programs in Nicaragua. Russia stepped up military cooperation, from training Nicaraguan cadets in Russian academies to joint military exercises, weapons sales, an agreement to use naval port facilities, and the establishment of a Russian Global Navigation Satellite System (GLONASS)—a GPS alternative—facility in Nicaragua. Further, Russia built a vaccine production facility in 2016 (although as of May 2019, it had yet produced a single vaccine). Other projects, such as literary and food programs, seek to increase Russia's soft power in Nicaragua.[15]

The only Russia-related project opposed by Nicaraguans was the planned trans-isthmus Nicaraguan canal. A Chinese investor signed a contract to build the canal; Russia had hoped to provide the heavy machinery and expertise for its construction. In 2013, 2014, and 2015, construction was interrupted by protests of indigenous people who would be displaced by the canal. These protests and Chinese investor Wang Jing's financial downfall stopped progress on the canal. Contemporary Russian efforts in Nicaragua are more likely to meet with success than not.

Hard, Soft, Smart, and Sharp

Renowned scholar Joseph S. Nye Jr. commented that power is the "ability to do things and control others, to get others to do what they otherwise would not" and "the ability to change the behavior of states."[16] Political scientists describe power as having three relational aspects. First, power can command or dictate choice. In its second aspect, power frames and sets agendas—using existing societal structures, ideas, and institutions to "shape others' preferences by affecting their expectations of what is legitimate or feasible."[17] Powerful actors set the table; others may only choose to eat what is already at the table. For example, in 2005 the United Nations endorsed the concept of "responsibility to protect," meaning that states only maintain sovereignty if they protect their citizenry. This clearly limits a state's choices; a state may not choose to violate crimes against humanity, although the definition of crimes against humanity is impermanent and interpretable.[18] These options, therefore, are not included as potential choices even though these options do exist. In the third aspect, power shapes ideas and beliefs that shape the initial preferences of others. A state's preference to add "responsibility to protect" was likely shaped by decades of messaging following World War II. This discourse suggests that avoiding crimes against humanity like the Holocaust and Holodomor is a desirable trait that describes a just state, and a just state believes other states should not be allowed to commit these same crimes. Power commands, frames, and sets agendas—and shapes basic beliefs and perceptions.[19] Nye divided power into three variants—hard, soft, and smart. Hard power consists of sticks and carrots. Military might and economic punishment—or sanctions—are sticks. Forming alliances and providing economic aid are carrots.

According to Nye, Russkiy Mir was an example of soft power, which he said involved "intangible power resources such as culture, ideology and institutions," as the method of setting international norms.[20] Nye further described that soft power shunned "the traditional foreign policy tools of carrot and stick, seeking instead to achieve influence by building networks, communicating compelling narratives, establishing international rules, and drawing on the resources that make a country naturally attractive to the world."[21] The three pillars of soft power are political values, culture, and foreign policy. In Vladimir Putin's words:

> "Soft power" is all about promoting one's interests and policies through persuasion and creating a positive perception of one's country, based not just on its material achievements but also its spiritual and intellectual heritage.[22]

Smart power combines soft and hard power to enhance a state's attractiveness by backing soft power with hard power. For example, Russia's naval presence in Nicaragua supports the attractiveness of its soft power narrative to Nicaragua—Russia will support Nicaragua's sovereignty and provide an alternative to the Western-dominated table—but is also clearly a hard power measure.

Scholars Peter Rutland and Andrei Kazantsev described Russia's use of soft power as a failure to achieve soft power wins in the manner that Nye prescribed. Russia did not generate soft power "attractiveness" through manipulation of the press, state-sponsored news, fake news generation, and crackpot ideas and viral conspiracy theories produced by the Russian Internet Research Agency. Rather, these messages provided a seeming repudiation of Russian soft power messaging, according to Rutland and Kazantsev.[23] Russia continues to fund and expand soft power endeavors like Russkiy Mir and international news media sources like *Sputnik* and *RT*. If these measures are not effective soft power measures, then to what end does the Russian Federation expend funds?

In a National Endowment for Democracy study, Christopher Walker and Jessica Ludwig described this phenomenon as "sharp power." Sharp power is authoritarian soft power. Specifically, sharp power involves turning authoritarian influence externally and "centers on distraction and manipulation."[24] Instead of a "charm offensive," authoritarian initiatives seek to "correct" facts, narratives, and images of a state through media, culture, think tanks, and academia.[25] If this definition seems similar to the principles of information use in the Russian "hybrid" war—or of disinformation campaigns, active measures, and information operations—that should not be a surprise as they are essentially the same practice. Putin, for his part, insisted that a state manage its image abroad and repair "distortion."[26] This concept also explains why Russia would fund seemingly inept soft power measures. These measures were not ineffective soft power measures—but actually sharp power measures.

Sharp power directs the "unattractiveness" of authoritarianism outside of the authoritarian regime.[27] Walker and Ludwig described the Russian application of sharp power as a result of the Russian ruling elite's belief "they did not need to convince the world that their autocratic system was appealing in its own right. Instead, they realized that they could achieve their objectives by making democracy appear to be relatively less attractive."[28] These sharp power efforts focus on the United States and Europe. Further, these efforts threaten Latin America and Central Europe because of their recent and relatively weak democratization and proximity to the United States and Europe. Russian disinformation campaigns and active measures seek to dismantle the philosophical underpinnings of the Western democratic systems as well as diminish their credibility. In lieu of building attractiveness, Russian sharp power seeks to diminish Western soft power.[29] Walker and Ludwig commented that Russian sharp power "manipulates, confuses, divides and represses."[30] Russia conveys this power through the managing or manipulation of discourse through media.

Media, Discourse, and Power Transmission

In sociology, discourse is how one thinks about people, things, and society and the relationship between them.[31] Discourse refers to the transmission of power and ideology through cognitive processing of information that produces mental models and societal interpretations.[32] Discourse is processed socio-cognitively, in that how a person thinks about a topic is influenced by inputs—by one's own thoughts—and produces an output that has been affected by both inputs and the cognition process. Recall the second and third aspects of Nye's soft power; these aspects express power because they set the frame of how an institution, structure, or relationship works, and influences initial beliefs. Power relations are discursive, meaning that the study of discourse can reveal how power relations are exercised.[33] Social theorist Michel Foucault posited that institutions can create the structure or framework that determines how discourse is reproduced in society. [34] For example, President George W. Bush's definition of the Axis of Evil as Iran, Iraq, and the Democratic People's Republic of Korea influenced how society interpreted the behavior of those three states and assisted in gaining society's acceptance for Operation Iraqi Freedom. Foucault saw institutions as the entities that framed ideology, shaped discourse, and distributed that discourse. Discourse—or how we talk about what we talk about—shapes ideology, or how we think or cogitate about a subject. There is a relationship between institutions, ideology, and society and discourse.[35] Political leaders and governments use discourse to convey power, structure, themes, and ideology. In short, discourse—words, text, images, and dialogue—transmits power.

Noam Chomsky described the role of intelligentsia—a term that includes historians, scholars, journalists, and political commentators—as undertaking "to analyze and present some picture of social reality. By virtue of their analyses and interpretations, they serve as mediators between the social facts and the mass of the population: they create the ideological justification for social practice."[36] Anne O'Keeffe described media as an "institution that shapes discourse."[37] Institutions govern behavior and set customs and norms. Media meets all the requirements of an institution. It is almost universal and outlives its audience, and its primary function is "socialization and social control."[38] Further, mass media's unique function "is to provide both to the individual and to society a coherence, a synthesis of experience, an awareness of the whole which does not undermine the specialization which reality requires."[39] Mass media, then, is a social institution created by the demands of a society. This is in contrast with media's oft-stated ideological goal—to speak truth to power. Media is a form of discourse as well as an institution. Media discourse "refers to interactions that take place through a broadcast platform, whether spoken or written, in which the discourse is oriented to a non-present reader, listener, or viewer. . . . Media discourse is a public, manufactured, on-record, form of interaction."[40] Media, then, is an institution that transmits power by shaping public discourse and society.

Power cascades through discourse from one level to another.[41] At the top of Robert Entman's original Cascade Model for Network Activation, strategic or elite leaders set the narrative at the national level. This narrative gives issues their initial discursive frame. Then, at the second tier, strategic documents and foreign policy staff reproduce these issues, altering the frame of the issues in the process. On the third tier down, the already twice-framed issues are released to the media, which frames the topic for the public. Public opinion informs the media, and news frames used by the media to describe an issue inform discourse about an issue and re-frame an issue at the elite level. Framing bundles certain elements together and prioritizes the selection or inclusion of some facts, narratives, or events over others. This promotes one view or interpretation of an event over another.[42] Framing traditionally attempts to explain and understand agenda-setting in political discourse and media discourse. Robert Entman stated that "framing entails selecting and highlighting some facets of events or issues and making connections among them so as to promote a particular interpretation, evaluation, and/or solution."[43] Essentially, how a president communicates a topic, how the administration enacts a policy, and how journalists discuss the topic in media promote a frame, or as Entman described it, a "particular interpretation, evaluation, and/or solution" to an issue.[44] Further, this discourse or communication provides the inputs that the public has available to help form opinions and think about a topic. Again, Nye's second and third aspects of soft power apply—setting the agenda or frames and impacting initial beliefs.

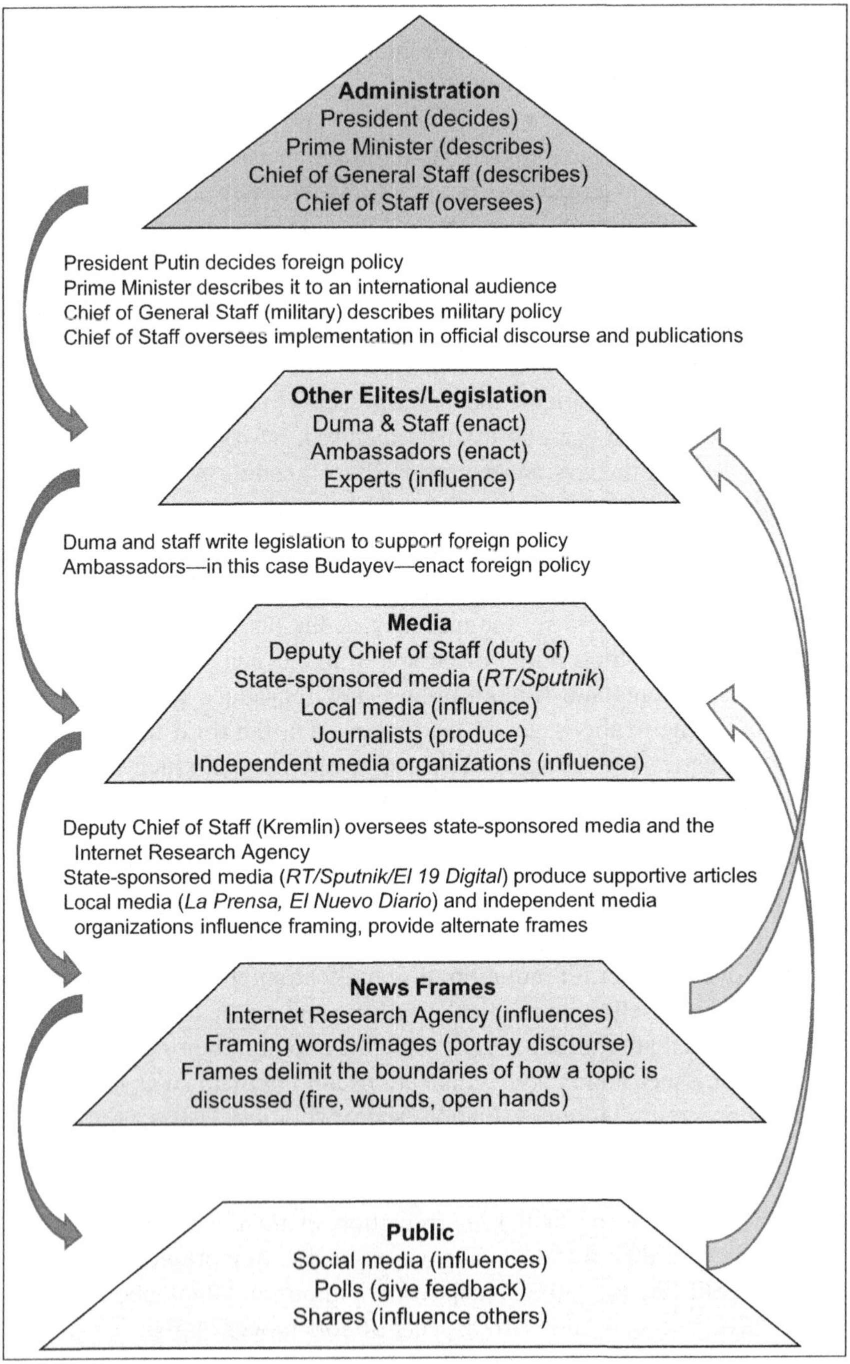

Figure 5.1. Russian Foreign Policy Cascading Model for Network Activation—
Nicaragua. Created by the author.

Both Russian and Nicaraguan media are dominated by state-run institutions. In Russia, the most popular television stations are state-owned or owned by a state business. Further, the November 2019 Sovereign Internet Law required Russian servers to have technology installed by 2021 that would allow Roskomnadzor, the federal executive body that provides media control—supervision censorship—to counter threats should Russian internet be attacked from outside its borders.[45] In Nicaragua, 80 percent of the press is considered state-run. In 2018, Reporters Without Borders assigned a Freedom Score of 90 out of 180 on its Press Freedom Index; by 2019, the score had fallen to 114.[46] Russia's Freedom Score was 149. Likewise, the Nicaraguan constitution only allowed "constructive criticism" by the media.[47] In a 2016 Latin American Public Opinion Project (LAPOP) Barometer of the Americas media study, 63 percent of Nicaraguan respondents believed one needed to be careful when speaking about politics, 74 percent felt one must be careful when talking about the president, and 47 percent indicated there was little freedom of the press.[48] These beliefs originate in the reality in which the Nicaraguan media works. Journalists from Nicaraguan media source *Canal 100% Noticias*, an anti-Sandinista media-source, faced imprisonment and some fled Nicaragua. Russia's media for export to Spanish-speaking countries is *RT en Español (RT)*, formerly *Russia Today*; this state-run organization's explicit mission is to conduct soft power operations to enhance Russia's image abroad. Likewise, *Sputnik* provides "alternative" news in a propaganda-like fashion.

The Ambassador's Plan

Critical Discourse Analysis is a multidisciplinary tool for assessing how language via discourse is used to transmit power. In my critical discourse analysis, I identified the two dominant discursive themes in Russia's Foreign Policy Concept and National Security Strategy to be "preventing a color revolution" and "establishing alternatives" to the West and Western influence.[49] Additionally, these themes correlate with much existing scholarship. Preventing a color revolution means preserving the existing government, preventing coup d'états, and maintaining sovereignty above other international values. Russian elites view these revolutions as externally fueled and dangerous to stability in the region where they believe they retain direct influence.[50] The Arab Spring further kindled Russian fears that their own government might not be safe from a color revolution. "Establishing alternatives" refers to forming alliances and relationships outside of Western-dominated organizations, as well as forming alternate banking and financial options and alternative information sources like the Shanghai Cooperation Organization (banking), Eurasian Economic Union (trade), the Collective Security Treaty Organization (defense), controlled internet services, and numerous media platforms. These themes are the elite level of Entman's Cascading Model for Network Activation. The Russian ambassador for Nicaragua represents the administrative level.

Russian Ambassador to Nicaragua Andrei Budayev focused on developing Russian soft power in Nicaragua. In 2017, Budayev penned an article outlining measures that Russia planned to take to augment its soft power in Nicaragua. Most of these are true soft power measures to attract attention to Russia's cultural, scientific, and spiritual accomplishments. In Nicaragua, this includes the establishment of GLONASS, fostering the Nicaraguan Congressional "Friends of Russia" group, and continuing programs that send high numbers of Nicaraguan students to Russian civilian higher education. Events celebrating famous poet Alexander Pushkin, the Russian language recitation event known as *Totalalniy Diktant*, and the 2018 World Cup in Russia round out this list.

However, Budayev's endeavors also include "smart power" events, such as signing an agreement for Russia to use Nicaraguan ports for its navy and joint counter-narcotics and military training events. Smart power includes the carrots of hard power's sticks and carrots, as well as soft power attractiveness.[51] Russia's counter-narcotics police training links the attractiveness of Russian training and competence with the fact that joint training further connects the two states' government functionaries. Russia specifically avoids hard power in Nicaragua and accomplishes what it needed to without force—establishing an alternative to Western-dominated military alliances and training events sponsored by US Southern Command and Army South.

Budayev's soft power involves information-related endeavors. First, the embassy uses digital diplomacy and information technology to disperse Russia-positive narratives. Secondly, the embassy sponsors events with the specific intent of being featured in news media. Budayev himself described Russian soft power as "intensive work to counteract information campaigns by Nicaraguan right-wing liberal media, which make biased and one-sided coverage of events in Russia and individual aspects of its foreign policy and misrepresent Russian-Nicaraguan cooperation. The embassy's efforts have resulted in a much larger amount of content with objective assessments."[52] The content that Budayev created, however, centered on the World Cup (baseball is Nicaragua's most beloved sport), Puskin poetry recitals, and the Soviet tradition of dictation.

Budayev's final endeavor of counteracting one-sided news is concerning. When taken into consideration with Russia's *Sputnik* and *RT* Spanish-language media sources, this endeavor takes on an authoritarian cant to soft power—controlling information. The use of narratives as power is incorporated into the Russian lexicon of national security and foreign policy as a component of *aktivnye meropriyatiya*, or active measures. Active measures exploit gaps in Western alliances, create discord among allies, and weaken the global perception of the US to the world.[53] The US Intelligence Community's declassified assessment of Russian activities and intentions in the 2016 US presidential elections named *Sputnik* and *RT* as components of "Russia's state-run propaganda machine." Other components of this machine were domestic media and trolls. All "serve as a platform for Kremlin messaging to Russian and international audiences," the report noted.[54] This type of power over information, narrative, and discourse falls into Walker and Ludwig's category of sharp power.[55]

Correcting One-Sided Narratives

How did Budayev "correct" one-sided news? To answer this, I examined three news sources: *El 19 Digital*, which favors Ortega's government and is run by his party; *La Prensa*, a right-wing liberal media venue that typically favors Western powers; and *El Nuevo Diario*, which is considered a more neutral platform for news. *El Nuevo Diario* is the target of Budayev's influence and the venue through which his embassy attempted to influence discourse about Russia.

In "Russian Presence in Nicaragua: The Role and Main Characteristics of Soft Power in Russian-Nicaraguan Relations," Budayev cited five articles from independent observers—basically two sources—that counter one-sided reporting about Russia. The first source is the Universidad Nacional Autónoma de Nicaragua, Managua (UNAN-Managua). Budayev mentioned that these articles countered one-sided reporting to mirror the role of a university. One can logically expect a university to celebrate the annual Russian-language dictation contest *Totalniy Diktant*, support professorial and student exchanges, and embrace an independent viewpoint.[56]

The second source is a foreign policy journalist who writes for *El Nuevo Diario*, Miguel Carranza Mena. The evolution of Mena's articles about Russia and the US achieved Budayev's goal to gain influence in a respected, neutral media source like *El Nuevo Diario*. Mena's articles from 2013 were generally neutral. By 2015 and continuing to the present, Mena's opinions echo *Sputnik*'s opinions as presented in the Latin American edition.

An example of Mena's transformation was the installation of the GLONASS satellite station in Nicaragua. On 10 April 2017, *Sputnik* published an article titled, "Is the Russian Satellite Station in Nicaragua a Spy Center? The US Thinks It Is."[57] Mena followed with a 24 April opinion article in *El Nuevo Diario* titled, "Then Is the GPS also a Spy System?"[58] The *Sputnik* article alleged that in addition to the US believing it is a spy center, the US had begun spying on Russia in Nicaragua because some of its diplomats spoke Russian. Mena concluded that the GLONASS system was innocuous and simply the Pepsi to GPS's Coke. However, he used the word "gringo" to describe the US. Outside of friendly conversations, this term has derogatory connotations.

In a similar pairing of articles, Mena described how the West generated Russophobia about the 2018 World Cup like it did to prevent Russian participation in the 2016 Summer Olympic Games.[59] Russia hosted the 2014 Winter Olympics, but the Olympic Committee banned Russia from the 2016 Olympics for illegal doping of its athletes. *Sputnik* stated that the World Cup would improve Russia's image in the world, and later stated that it dispelled "horror stories" about Russia.[60]

Budayev's ability to gain an ally in a neutral media format has been a success, but with a limited shelf-life. Mena's anti-western rhetoric amplified dramatically after January 2019, with several Twitter references to "genocidal gringos."[61] No longer employed at the adamantly neutral *El Nuevo Diario*, he now reports for the Nicaraguan National Assembly.[62] Although temporarily effective, Budayev's sharp power lacked staying power.

A Sharp, Ready Narrative

The transmission of Russian Foreign Policy and National Security Strategy discursive themes of preventing a color revolution and establishing alternatives have far more staying power than Budayev's endeavors. To identify how these discursive themes manifested in Russian media and how Nicaraguan media presented these themes to the public, this chapter's analysis looks at discourse in Nicaraguan media articles about Russia as well as Russian media articles about Nicaragua from the period of 15 March 2018 to 30 May 2018. I examined articles from Russia's two externally focused state-owned media sources, *RT* and *Sputnik*. *RT en Español* states that its purpose is to serve as a "primary source of alternative information in the West, focusing on covering themes ignored by mainstream media."[63] *Sputnik* indicates its purpose is to provide information oriented to an international audience.[64] My analysis is based on forty-four articles from *RT* and ninety from *Sputnik*.[65] The discursive theme of preventing a color revolution appeared seventeen times in *RT* and twenty in *Sputnik*. The term "alternatives" was featured eight times in *RT* and seventeen times in *Sputnik*.

The *RT* articles depicted these national interests by demonstrating US incompetence, and stating that the US is a legitimate threat and has unfair policies. Russia, on the other hand, is described as having strong military capabilities and values dialogue as well as preserving order and offering a better economic solution. Like *RT,* the *Sputnik* discourse maligns the US, stating that the country caused Argentina, Brazil, Chile, Colombia, Paraguay, and Peru to suspend their participation in Unión de Naciones Suramericana (UNASUR).[66] One article indicated: "Remember that up until now, Nicaragua had a high growth rate of 2.5 percent to 5 percent, and up until April, it was the safest country in Central America. . . . And this was the spark waiting for an international conspiracy."[67] Additionally, *Sputnik* cited the anti-Western site *Nicaleaks*, declaring that protests like these were "one of the basic principles of non-conventional war, perfected by Washington to defeat governments that don't agree with them and get society to confront the government with whatever excuse, strengthen the conflict from abroad, and complete the 'siege' at the diplomatic level."[68] Conspiracy theories, sowing discord by pointing out how they negatively influenced UNASUR, and generating a bad image of the US are all active measures meant to weaken the United States. Russia's message to Latin America is clear: Washington does not support choice and is conducting a war; Russia is a better option.

The period of 18 to 23 April 2018 coincided with violent protests in Managua. Protesters filled the streets to oppose social security and pension reform. President Ortega announced reforms on 16 April 2018. The changes required employees to contribute 7 percent of their salaries instead of 6.25 percent and employers to contribute 22.5 percent of employee salaries to social security, up from 19 percent. Additionally, pensioners would contribute 5 percent of their pensions for medical costs.[69] Widespread protests turned violent. Estimates vary but between 30 and 317 protesters, as well as 21 police officers and 23 children, died during the protests; hundreds more were wounded.[70] The violence that occurred during these protests generated discourse globally. Canada and the United States condemned the violence, Guatemala mourned, and Russia declared soliZdarity with the government of Nicaragua.[71] This event generated sufficient discourse on a global scale to involve the national interests of several states—most notably, the United States and the Russian Federation.

"The Wound in Nicaragua: What to Expect from the Dialogue between Government and Opposition?" is a good example of how *RT* projects sharp power to support Russian national interests. The 18 May 2018 article opened with an image of a distressed Vice President Rosario Murillo, with her hands on her head in a position that was almost surrender and almost frustration. Her bottle of water tipped over on the table, she had set aside the microphone and had nothing to say. President Daniel Ortega was dressed in a graveyard black coat, looking concerned and staring into the distance. His hands were on the table, as if showing he was unarmed and had played his cards. He appeared resolute, but sad; the glass on the table was almost empty. The image was clearly from a government building, and a headless police officer stood behind the two, who were seated, giving the impression that they had no option to retreat. The two were forced to face what was in front of them. The image conveyed a message that correlated to the article: Nicaragua and its governing team were gravely wounded.

The article first characterized the protests as a wounding event, with the mental image of a woman reading the names of the dead. Then, it posited the threat to Ortega through the voice of a student: "This is not a dialogue table, it is negotiating table for your exit," which implied a color revolution.[72] The article placed blame directly on the "sectors that oppose the Ortega government," implying instability and color revolution.[73] It then noted that the Ortega government had made progress; but the violence had stopped it—the threat of an alternate world order was paralyzing the country. The article blamed the media, specifically *La Prensa* and *Confidencial*, for advancing the protests and followed with a picture of police carrying the coffin of a fellow police officer. Fake news and information dominance were responsible for the deaths. What made this article so exemplary of Russian informational soft power was that it not only identified discursive elements and phrases supportive of Russian strategic messages projected through a Nicaraguan lens; it also painted the US as an existential threat and assessed who gained soft power in the interchange.

The author, Nathalie Balbás, indicated the root causes of the protests, deaths, and violence were US Congress approval of the NICA Act (Nicaraguan Investment Conditionality Act of 2016) and Ortega's request for the US to pay reparations. In 1991, the Chamorro government had renounced the collection of reparations that the United States owed Nicaragua because of US support for the Contras in the 1970s; this followed the International Court of Justice in The Hague judgement that the US owed Nicaragua $17 million. In 2017, Ortega requested the US to pay the reparation, disavowing the reprieve Chamorro had granted.[74]

The US Congress approved the NICA Act, which would block loans from international financial institutions like the World Bank and International Monetary Fund unless Nicaragua became more transparent, fair, and free. Essentially, this implied significant weakening of the executive branch in Nicaragua, and a crackdown on corruption. Congress considered the NICA Act in early 2018 but did not pass it until December 2018.[75] Balbás implied that the United States' refusal to pay reparations, coupled with its blocking of financial transactions, generated the anger that resulted in protests and violence.

Balbás, in her *RT* article, assessed that the student movement and Catholic Church gained soft power in this interchange. The students agreed to a dialogue if the Catholic Church, specifically Managua's auxiliary bishop—Silvio José Báez, who was injured in the protests—negotiated.[76] Further, she called this a "classic mutation of color revolution," because the state's position had weakened as a result of the protests.[77] She maligned USAID (United States Agency for International Development) money, stating that it had fomented these political groups and led to violence. The article closed with an allegation of a western-sponsored coup d'état, or color revolution, demonstrating Balbás' ideological alignment with both Ortega and Putin rhetoric.

Although the *RT* article clearly depicted a Nicaraguan problem set, it demonstrated the discourse that Russian state-sponsored media used to project sharp power through Nicaraguan media. Further, the discursive elements Balbás used to describe the Nicaraguan protests mirrored how the Russian National Security Strategy described its threats and world view. In this article, the lack of an alternate world in which international institutions like the International Monetary Fund and World Bank would support Ortega, and the presence of a violently disruptive force (the protests) which received money from the West (USAID) demonstrated how critical preventing color revolutions and generating an alternate world was to both Russia and Nicaragua.

Likewise, narratives in *Sputnik* projected Russian national interests through sharp power. A short summary of an opinion interview demonstrated how the messages of building an alternate world order and preventing color revolutions cascaded through *Sputnik*. The title of Victor Ternovsky's May 2018 article, "The US Is Going for Nicaragua," referenced fake news, instability (promoted by America), intervention, a desire for nonintervention in sovereign states, and preservation of the existing world order.

Moscow-based journalist Victor Ternovsky began his article with what he implied was a grossly simplified and false statement, "In Nicaragua, there is a bad government. It is so bad that it does not even have the slightest bit of popular support. The people couldn't take it anymore, so they took to the street, where they encountered very aggressive police."[78] His article then refuted each assertion by the western media, labeling them as fake news. The protestors burned a bus and two police officers died, but the Western media says they were peaceful. The article made no mention of the dozens of protesters who were killed. Ortega's government, on the other hand, planned a Song of Peace and Love protest march for dialogue in its effort to build information dominance. In a series of false dichotomies, Ternovsky matched fake Western news with fake or deliberately misleading Russian news at every turn.[79] The message was clear: US democratic institutions like the media are not credible.

Ternovsky concluded, like Balbás, that the ongoing instability in Nicaragua was "promoted by the Americans;" non-governmental organizations were tools of aggression and intervened in states' affairs.[80] Finally, Ternovsky asserted that US strategy in Nicaragua would fail, partly thanks to Managua's strong relationship with Moscow. The US was the villain, and Russia the savior and viable world alternative to Western values. Essentially, Ternovsky concluded that a color revolution had to be prevented and to do so, Nicaragua needed an alternate world order—Russia's.[81]

For When Western Power Fails

El 19 Digital's special role in Nicaraguan media deserves further description. *El 19 Digital's* motto is "*El 19*—for more victories!" and its website splashes the banner "United Nicaragua Triumphs" and "We want to live in peace." Among its sections are national news, local news, the economy, sports, international news, innovation, training, specials, and "Discourses of Daniel and Rosario," Nicaragua's president and vice president. Unlike *El 19 Digital's* jailed competitors, the media site owned by the FSLN projects the party platform. Further, Vice President Rosario Murillo is the curator and editor of the news source's content. While Russia has some state-sponsored media, neither the Russian Federation president nor its prime minister personally curate the content. Any article published in *El 19 Digital* has the approval of the Nicaraguan executive branch.

Above all else, *El 19 Digital* projects Nicaragua's own national interests. Foremost among these is to maintain the credibility of Nicaragua's government. For example, when organic Nicaraguan firefighting forces had difficulty containing a large April 2018 forest fire in the biological reserve in Indio Maíz, *El 19 Digital* lauded the assistance of an expert from the US Forestry Service.[82] The next day, *El 19 Digital* highlighted Buda-yev's World Cup event in which the Russian embassy gave away soccer balls.[83] In this way, *El 19 Digital*'s narrative supported Nicaraguan national interests. With the nebulous West as a common antagonist and competitor, Russian strategic messages and Nicaraguan messages frequently align.

Between 15 March and 16 April 2018, *El 19 Digital* did not publish any anti-US articles. It published exactly two articles about the US and Nicaragua. One concerned an official agreement to simplify travel procedures between the two countries, with both US and Nicaraguan officials lauding the endeavor.[84] The second article concerned the visit of the US Forestry Service expert who consulted on stopping fires in the Indio Maíz biological reserve.[85] Prior to the protests, Nicaraguan state media did not adopt Russia's framing of its strategic messages.

However, this changed when the US-positive narrative no longer served Nicaraguan interests. On 1 May 2018, *El 19 Digital* published "Sandinista Peace Offensive." The article provided evidence of Russia's sharp power narrative. The initial image showed a huge, peaceful crowd with Nicaraguan and FSLN flags; the crowd was coincidentally red, white, and blue. Fabrizio Casaria, the author and a Marxist writer, reminded the reader that the FSLN was powerful and that it encouraged and preserved peace against the "soft coup" and interventionist strategy of the United States. Casari blamed the protestors for subsequent violence and stated that it delegitimized them. He noted that the FSLN was unified, broad-based, and disposed for peace and that Nicaragua would not be colonized and the "right" opposition would be financially dependent on Washington, DC.[86] Finally, Casari stated that Nicaragua would not return to being a US "backyard colony."[87]

On 8 May 2018, Russia and Nicaragua signed an agreement for tighter political cooperation, distancing Nicaragua from the US in an alternate arrangement. In the agreement, Russia lauded Nicaragua's recognition of Russian actions in Crimea, Ukraine, Georgia, and Chechnya.[88] That same day an article titled "Nicaragua under Enemy Fire" described how Russian and Nicaraguan foreign policy narrative frameworks were aligned. The article's author opened with a red and orange-tinted image of a street in Nicaragua on fire, as if to give the impression that Nicaragua was under real enemy fire from the United States.

This fire was the NICA Act. The article's author, Luis Varese, de-scribed the US financial limitations placed on the Sandinista regime as an "offensive" attack; he cited *From Dictatorship to Democracy: A Conceptual Framework for Liberation* by the CIA's Gene Sharp as the US playbook.[89] Likely, Varese referred to Sharp's conception of a subversive, nonviolent struggle that would require external assistance—from the US or elsewhere—to conduct a successful color revolution or coup d'état.[90] The article commended the police, and attacked the media for obfuscating their good work during the protests by generating fake news. Varese described the current world order as the Western Goliath against the Nicaraguan David, and that this order did not support the Nicaraguan people.[91] UNASUR weakened when US-friendly states left the organization, destroying an alternate world option. Finally, Varese reminded the reader that the US was the main enemy dividing Nicaraguans.

Two weeks after the protests began, *El 19 Digital*'s treatment of the US transitioned from neutral to mimic many of the frames in Russia's National Security Strategy and Foreign Policy Concept. For survival, the Ortega government signaled to the Russian Federation through an agreement, parallel discourse, and similar narrative framing that the government of Nicaragua had definitively chosen a side. In this case, Russia's sharp power succeeded. First, it weakened how the Nicaraguan government perceived the US and created an alternate narrative that Russia had all the capabilities and values Nicaragua needed. In keeping with Nye's second aspect of soft power, Russia set a second agenda with different possible options. In the third aspect, Russia's messaging through *RT* and *Sputnik* created the belief that what Nicaragua truly wanted was what Russia wanted for it—alignment with Russia. Finally, Russia's manipulation of the news media, maligning of the West and the US, and professed belief in regime stability in the face of violent interventions like the protests generated support for Russia's national interests through discrediting American democratic institutions and values.

Conclusion

The idea of sharp power helps explain how Russia applies "soft power." Ambassador Budayev's counteraction of "one-sided narratives" is a provision of sharp power. Instead of generating attractiveness, a state seeks to force a proper opinion and compel through arguments laced with logical fallacies and deliberate inaccuracies, or by eliminating contrary facts. Further, critical discourse analysis identified that Russia projects its foreign policy principles and national interests through state-sponsored media sources *Sputnik* and *RT*. When the ideas of preventing color revolutions and generating alternatives to the West became lucrative, this discourse directly influenced Nicaragua's state-run *El 19 Digital*. Russian-positive discourse found a home in *El 19 Digital* once Vice President Rosario Murillo, the editor, realized that positive relations with the US were unlikely. Moreover, following the violent April 2018 protests, Nicaragua's national interest became to prevent a color revolution. Doing so would require alternate organizations, structures, and relationships like those provided through Russia's alternatives, which were outside of the traditional Western-dominated ones. Once interests aligned, Nicaraguan discourse in *El 19 Digital* resembled Russia's foreign policy objectives.

Russia's sharp power proved extremely powerful in this case. When a significant event in another state required a new discourse, it was only a matter of weeks before Russia's foreign policy objectives cascaded into Nicaragua's national discourse and onto the global stage. In this case, Russian discourse in media was *potential* power until a catalyst made it *actual* power.

Discursive practice is part of social practice. Under the reinforcing influence of Russian media, those who ascribe to Ortega's tenets will further ideologically align with Russia. Like the results of Russia's interference in the 2016 US campaigns, Nicaraguan society will likely become further divided as this discursive practice imbeds itself into socio-cognition. Further, as this book is published, Russian narrative frameworks are beneficial to the Nicaraguan government's policies.

Strategists should consider Russian information activities, even when they seem ineffective on the surface, as potential power. Further, they should analyze Russia's intentions to manipulate, confuse, divide, and repress as "sharp power" initiatives vice "soft power."[92] Conspiracy theories, discrediting of alliances, and weakening of the United States' image abroad are tools that add to this potential. Russian foreign policy discourse—building an alternate world and preventing color revolutions—is attractive and desirable to states out of favor with the West. Where there is a gap in US support for a state, the subsequent sense of alienation creates a void that the Russian foreign policy narrative framework can fill and Russian sharp power can fully exploit. Its sharp power through information activities sets the conditions for Russia to serve as the best alternative to the negotiated agreement of the liberal world order.

Notes

1. This chapter includes excerpts from the author's previous work: Maj. Nicole L. Hash, "Evaluating Russian Soft Power in Nicaragua," a Military Art and Science thesis, US Army Command and General Staff College, Fort Leavenworth, Kansas, 2019.

2. Evgeniy Vasiliev, "Latin American Russian World," *Russkiy Mir,* 1 March 2010, https://rusmir.media/2010/03/01/fond.

3. "About Russkiy Mir Foundation," *Russkiy Mir,* accessed 5 May 2019, https://russkiymir.ru/en/fund/.

4. Vladimir Davydov, "Latin American Region in an Environment of a 'New Normal' and our Positions in this Context," *International Affairs,* 15 November 2018, https://interaffairs.ru/news/show/20992.

5. Vladimir Putin, "Russian National Security Strategy: Presidential Edict 683," Russian Federation, 31 December 2015.

6. Vladimir Putin, "Foreign Policy Concept of the Russian Federation," Ministry of Foreign Affairs of the Russian Federation, 30 November 2016, http://www.mid.ru/foreign_policy/official_documents/-/asset_publisher/CptICkB6BZ29/content/id/2542248.

7. Hash, "Evaluating Russian Soft Power in Nicaragua," 46–47.

8. Carlos M. Vilas, "Revolutionary Attempts in Late Cold War Settings: Nicaragua in the 1980s," *Journal of Third World Studies* 21, no. 2 (23 October 2004): 49.

9. Office of the Historian, "A Guide to the United States' History of Recognition, Diplomatic, and Consular Relations, by Country, since 1776: Nicaragua," Office of the Historian, United States Department of State, accessed 30 November 2018, https://history.state.gov/countries/nicaragua.

10. Marc Edelman, "Soviet-Nicaraguan Relations and the Contra War," *International Journal on World Peace* 5, no. 3 (1988): 54.

11. Brown University, "Understanding the Iran-Contra Affairs - The Iran-Contra Affairs," accessed 30 November 2018, https://www.brown.edu/Research/Understanding_the_Iran_Contra_Affair/n-contras.php.

12. *Encyclopedia Britannica*, "Daniel Ortega: Biography & Facts," accessed 30 November 2018, https://www.britannica.com/biography/Daniel-Ortega.

13. Stephen Kinzer, "Soviet Help to Sandinistas: No Blank Check," *The New York Times,* 28 March 1984, https://www.nytimes.com/1984/03/28/world/soviet-help-to-sandinistas-no-blank-check.html.

14. V. E. Travkin, "Daniel Ortega: Glavnoe Sobytie v Nikaragua i v Mire – Proval Neoliberlizma," *Latinskaya Amerika* 1 (2009): 5.

15. Vika Evreba, "Ufimka planiruet stroit kliniku v glukhoi derevne v Nikaragua" *MKRU,* 9 September 2018, https://ufa.mk.ru/social/2018/09/12/ufimka-planiruet-stroit-kliniku-v-glukhoy-derevne-v-nikaragua.html.

16. Joseph S. Nye Jr., "Soft Power," *Foreign Policy* 80 (1990): 154–55, https://doi.org/10.2307/1148580.

17. Joseph S. Nye Jr., *The Future of Power* (Philadelphia: PublicAffairs, 2011), 13–16.

18. United Nations Office on Genocide Prevention and the Responsibility to Protect, "Responsibility to Protect," *United Nations,* accessed 14 May 2019, https://www.un.org/en/genocideprevention/about-responsibility-to-protect.shtml; and Gerald L. Neuman, "What Counts as a Crime Against Humanity?," *Harvard International Law Journal,* accessed 28 May 2019, https://harvardilj.org/2019/01/what-counts-as-a-crime-against-humanity/.

19. Nye, *The Future of Power*, 13–16.

20. Nye, "Soft Power," 167.

21. Nye, 167–68.

22. Vladimir Putin, "Russia in a Changing World: Stable Priorities and New Opportunities," 9 July 2012, http://en.kremlin.ru/events/president/news/15902.

23. Peter Rutland and Andrei Kazantsev, "The Limits of Russia's 'Soft Power,'" *Journal of Political Power* 9, no. 3 (September 2016): 398.

24. Christopher Walker and Jessica Ludwig, "From 'Soft Power' to 'Sharp Power': Rising Authoritarian Influence in the Democratic World," in *Sharp Power: Rising Authoritarian Influence* (Washington, DC: National Endowment for Democracy, 2018), 6.

25. Walker and Ludwig, "From 'Soft Power' to 'Sharp Power,'" 6

26. Rutland and Kazantsev, "The Limits of Russia's 'Soft Power,'" 395–413.

27. Walker and Ludwig, "From 'Soft Power' to 'Sharp Power,'" 6.

28. Walker and Ludwig, 9.

29. Walker and Ludwig, 12.

30. Walker and Ludwig, 12.

31. Nicki Lisa Cole et al., "What Is Discourse?," ThoughtCo, accessed 3 December 2018, https://www.thoughtco.com/discourse-definition-3026070.

32. Ruth Wodak, Norman Fairclough, and Teun A. van Dijk, "Discourse as Social Interaction," in *Discourse as Social Interaction*, ed. Teun A. van Dijk (SAGE Publications, 1997), 258–84.

33. Wodak, Fairclough, and van Dijk, 258–84.

34. Teun A. van Dijk, "Sociocognitive Discourse Studies" (unpublished manuscript, February 2016), 2, http://www.discourses.org/OldArticles/Sociocognitive%20Discourse%20Studies.pdf.

35. Wodak, Fairclough, and van Dijk, "Discourse as Social Interaction," 272.

36. Noam Chomsky, *On Language* (New York: The New Press, 1990), 4.

37. Anne O'Keeffe, "Media and Discourse Analysis," *The Routledge Handbook of Discourse Analysis* (London: Routledge, 2010), 441.

38. Thelma McCormack, "Social Theory and the Mass Media," in *The Canadian Journal of Economics and Political Science/Revue Canadienne d'Economique et de Science Politique* 27, no. 4 (1961): 487.

39. McCormack, 488.

40. O'Keeffe, "Media Discourse Analysis," 441.

41. O'Keeffe, 441.

42. Pippa Norris, Montague Kern, and Marion Just, *Framing Terrorism: The News Media, the Government and the Public* (New York: Routledge, 2003), 11.

43. Robert M. Entman, "Cascading Activation: Contesting the White House's Frame After 9/11," *Political Communication* 20, no. 4 (24 June 2010): 415–32.

44. Robert M Entman, "Framing: Toward Clarification of a Fractured Paradigm," *Journal of Communication* 43, no. 4 (1 December 1993): 51–58.

45. Alena Epifanova, "Deciphering Russia's 'Sovereign Internet Law:' Tightening Control and Accelerating the Splinternet," *The German Council on Foreign Relations* 2 (January 2020): 1–11, https://dgap.org/sites/default/files/article_pdfs/dgap-analyse_2-2020_epifanova_0.pdf.

46. "2019 RSF Index: Authoritarianism and Disinformation Worsen the Situation in Latin America," Reporters without Borders, accessed 26 April 2020, https://rsf.org/en/2019-rsf-index-authoritarianism-and-disinformation-worsen-situation-latin-america.

47. "Alarming Decline in Press Freedom and Free Speech in Nicaragua," Reporters without Borders, 22 August 2018, accessed 14 November 2018, https://rsf.org/en/news/alarming-decline-press-freedom-and-free-speech-nicaragua.

48. Jose Miguel Cruz, "Análisis Preliminar del Barómetro de las Américas de LAPOP" (presentation, Vanderbilt University, Nashville, TN, December 2016), accessed 2 December 2018, https://www.vanderbilt.edu/lapop/nicaragua/RRR_Nicaragua_AB2016_v10_public_W_12.15.17.pdf.

49. Hash, "Evaluating Russian Soft Power in Nicaragua."

50. "Putin: We Will Not Allow Color Revolutions in Russia and the CSTO," *Vesti.ru,* 12 April 2017.

51. Nye, *The Future of Power*, xvi.

52. A. Budayev, "Russian Presence in Nicaragua: The Role and Main Characteristics of 'Soft Power' in Russian-Nicaraguan Relations," *International Affairs: A Russian Journal of World Politics, Diplomacy & International Relations* 63, no. 5 (September 2017): 204–13.

53. Michael Weiss, "'Aktyvnye Meropriyatiya' Rossiiskikh Spetssluzhb," *InoSMI.Ru,* 28 July 2016, https://inosmi.ru/politic/20160728/237359416.html.

54. Office of the Director of National Intelligence, *Intelligence Community Assessment: Assessing Russian Activities and Intentions in Recent US Elections* (Washington, DC: Director of National Intelligence, 2017), 3, https://www.dni.gov/files/documents/ICA_2017_01.pdf.

55. Walker and Ludwig, "From 'Soft Power' to 'Sharp Power,'" 18.

56. Budayev, "Russian Presence in Nicaragua."

57. "¿Es La Estación Satelital Rusa En Nicaragua Un Centro de Espionaje? En EEUU Creen Que Sí - Sputnik Mundo," *Sputnik,* 10 April 2017,), https://mundo.sputniknews.com/america_del_norte/201704101068273807-washington-post-glonass-america-latina/. Note: Other installations included Vietnam, Iran, Indonesia, Spain, Antarctica, Brazil, and Cuba; in December 2018, Venezuela's station was completed.

58. Miguel Carranza Mena, "¿Entonces el GPS también es un sistema de espionaje?," *El Nuevo Diario,* 28 April 2017, http://www.elnuevodiario.com.ni/opinion/426061-gps-es-sistema-espionaje/.

59. Miguel Carranza Mena, "La Rusofobia Quiere Desacreditar El Mundial de Futbol," *El Nuevo Diario,* 26 March 2017, https://www.elnuevodiario.com.ni/opinion/422864-rusofobia-quiere-desacreditar-mundial-futbol/. Note: Shortly after the 2014 Olympics, Russia invaded Crimea.

60. "El Mundial 2018 demostró la falsedad de las 'historietas de horror' sobre Rusia," *Sputnik,* 20 July 2018, https://mundo.sputniknews.com/world-cup-2018-archive/201807201080575414-mundial-rusia-rompe-estereotipos/.

61. Miguel Carranza Mena, Twitter post, 13 March 2019, https://twitter.com/carranzamena84/status/1105967156615933952.

62. Miguel Carranza Mena, Twitter post, 4 March 2019, https://twitter.com/carranzamena84/status/1102575877060288513; Hash, "Evaluating Russian Soft Power in Nicaragua," 63.

63. "Quienes somos," *RT en Español,* accessed 17 April 2019, https://actualidad.rt.com/acerca/quienes_somos. Note: In Spanish, "una de las principales fuentes de información alternativas en Occidente, dado que a menudo cubre temas ignorados por los medios de comunicación de masas del 'mainstream.'"

64. "Quienes Somos," *Sputnik,* accessed 16 April 2019, https://mundo.sputniknews.com/docs/about/quienes_somos.html.

65. Hash, "Evaluating Russian Soft Power in Nicaragua," 57–62.

66. Fabian Cardozo, "Que hay detrás del debilitamiento de la Unasur?' *Sputnik,* 25 April 2018, https://mundo.sputniknews.com/radio_gps_internacional/201804251078187657-unasur-necesita-doctrina-de-seguridad/.

67. "¿Qué tiene que ver el FMI en las violentas protestas en Nicaragua?," *Sputnik,* 17 May 2018, https://mundo.sputniknews.com/radio_telescopio/201805171078750593-protestas-dialogo-crisis/.

68. Vicky Pelaez, "Guarimbas nicaragüenses quieren glope a Daniel Ortega," *Sputnik,* 25 April 2018, https://mundo.sputniknews.com/firmas/201804251078204199-nicaragua-protestas-violencia/.

69. Oswaldo Rivas, "Nicaraguans Take to Streets in Protest over Social Security Changes," *Reuters,* 19 April 2018, https://www.reuters.com/article/us-nicaragua-protests/nicaraguans-take-to-streets-in-protest-over-social-security-changes-idUSKBN1HR02A.

70. Natalie Gallon, "At Least 317 Killed in Ongoing Protests in Nicaragua, Rights Group Says," *CNN World News,* 5 August 2018, https://edition.cnn.com/2018/08/05/americas/nicaragua-violent-protests/index.html.

71. "Preocupación mundial por represión en Nicaragua," *El Nuevo Diario,* 24 April 2018, https://www.elnuevodiario.com.ni/nacionales/461959-preocupacion-mundial-represion-nicaragua/.

72. Nazareth Balbás, "La herida de Nicaragua: ¿Qué esperar del diálogo entre gobierno y oposición?," *RT en Espanol,* 18 May 2018, https://actualidad.rt.com/actualidad/272022-herida-nicaragua-esperar-dialogo-gobierno-oposicion.

73. Balbás.

74. Balbás.

75. Nicaragua Human Rights and Anticorruption Act of 2018, H.R.1918, 115th Congress, *Congressional Record* (20 December 2018), https://www.congress.gov/bill/115th-congress/house-bill/1918/actions.

76. Elisabeth Malikin and Frances Robles, "Nicaragua Clergy, Siding with Protestors, Becomes 'Terrible Enemy' of Ortega," *The New York Times,* 22 July 2018, https://www.nytimes.com/2018/07/22/world/americas/nicaragua-protests-catholic-church.html.

77. Nazareth Balbás, "La herida de Nicaragua: ¿Qué esperar del diálogo entre gobierno y oposición?," *RT en Espanol,* 18 May 2018, https://actualidad.rt.com/actualidad/272022-herida-nicaragua-esperar-dialogo-gobierno-oposicion.

78. Victor Ternovsky, "EEUU va a por Nicaragua," *Sputnik,* 12 May 2018, https://mundo.sputniknews.com/radio_que_pasa/201805121078633913-protestas-nicaragua-eeuu/.

79. Ternovsky.

80. Ternovsky.

81. Ternovsky.

82. Pedro Ortega Ramírez, "Experto del Servicio Forestal de EE.UU. asesora a Defensa Civil," *El 19 Digital,* 11 April 2018, https://www.el19digital.com/articulos/ver/titulo:75797-experto-del-servicio-forestal-de-eeuu-asesora-a-defensa-civil.

83. Carlo Fernando Álvarez, "Embajada de Rusia presenta detalles sobre la Copa Mundial de Fútbol 2018," *El 19 Digital,* 13 April 2018, https://www.el-19digital.com/articulos/ver/titulo:75884-embajada-de-rusia-presenta-detalles-sobre-la-copa-mundial-de-futbol-2018.

84. Tania Cerón Méndez, "Nicaragua y Estados Unidos buscan facilitar tramites migratorios a connacionales," *El 19 Digital,* 5 April 2018, https://www.el19digital.com/articulos/ver/titulo:75634-nicaragua-y-estados-unidos-buscan-facilitar-tramites-migratorios-a-connacionales.

85. Pedro Ortega Ramírez, "Experto del Servicio Forestal de EE.UU. asesora a Defensa Civil, *El 19 Digital,* 11 April 2018.

86. Fabrizio Casari, "Sandinistas, ofensiva de paz," *El 19 Digital,* 1 May 2018, https://www.el19digital.com/articulos/ver/titulo:76493-sandinistas-ofensiva-de-paz.

87. Casari. Note: The word "backyard" is highly offensive to Nicaraguans. Backyards are where pets relieve themselves, families hide their mess, and the lawn might be unattended. The neighbors should not see a family's backyard.

88. "Rusia y Nicaragua fortalecerán la coordinación en materia de política internacional." *Sputnik,* 8 May 2018, https://mundo.sputniknews.com/politica/201805081078501719-moscu-america-latina-managua-relaciones/.

89. Luis Varese, "Nicaragua bajo fuego enemigo," *El 19 Digital,* 8 May 2018, https://www.el19digital.com/articulos/ver/titulo:76791-nicaragua-bajo-fuego-enemigo.

90. Gene Sharp, *From Dictatorship to Democracy: A Conceptual Framework for Liberation*, 4th ed. (Boston: The Albert Einstein Institution, 2010).

91. Varese, "Nicaragua bajo fuego enemigo."

92. Walker and Ludwig, "From 'Soft Power' to 'Sharp Power,'" 12.

Chapter 6
Great Power Engagement in Africa:
From "Object" to Partner?
Roderic C. Jackson

In the second decade of the twenty-first century, Africa is a continent on the move. This chapter advances the idea that the great powers involved in Africa have always focused primarily on their own interests, which inevitably fueled competition; such involvement only marginally improved the average African nation's ability to integrate and profit in the globalized world of the late twentieth and early twenty-first century. In the first quarter of the twenty-first century, increased great power engagement in Africa from Russia, China, and the United States occurred from an advantageous position of power that views Africa as an object. This viewpoint impedes developing mutually beneficial relations with African states.

Africa is an attractive continent. It logged more than 5 percent gross domestic product growth from 2000 to 2010.[1] Since then growth has slowed to a anticipated 3.6 percent growth rate from 2019 to 2020.[2] With an increasing youth population (aged 14–24) projected to double in size from 226 million in 2015 to 452 million in 2055, human capital exists to continue fueling growth.[3] The combination of natural resources, human capital, and huge potential economic markets makes Africa an unavoidable destination for international engagement in the globalized world. Since the early 2000s, Africa has attracted not only interest from Russia, China, and the United States, but also sustained engagement from France, and other lesser powers including Turkey, United Arab Emirates, Qatar, Saudi Arabia, India, and Brazil. Renewed interest, especially from Russia and China, encroaches upon America's dominant engagement, which has been minimally contested since the end of the Cold War. The rise of the continent has continued despite numerous structural issues during the post-colonial period. The uptick in competition in Africa is nothing new; it has existed with different powers since the Berlin Conference of 1884–85.[4]

This conference marked the beginning of what is known as the first scramble for Africa, a term describing how great powers have operated in Africa for selfish strategic gain in a competitive manner. Access to resources and influence ultimately increased a great power's ability to exercise power. Engagement has evolved over four distinct periods: the initial scramble; Cold War and independence; post-Cold War; and transition to a multipolar world.[5] Throughout these periods, Africans gained independence, struggled to provide goods and services (often these problems are self-inflicted through poor governance), and forcibly made choices about international partnership based on ideologies that did not significantly advance the average African leader's ability to secure and develop his country.

This chapter explores great power engagement in Africa over four periods. The first period provides a foundation for understanding the long-standing inferior relationship that Africa has endured and which inhibited African sovereign nations from equally participating and optimizing rewards in the international system. The second period is defined by relations during decolonization and the Cold War. The third period looks at how great power influence decreased after the Cold War and at the turn of the century reemerged as a strategic resource for the great powers. Finally, the fourth period, which is ongoing, explores Africa in the multipolar world and two possible futures for the continent. The conclusion briefly assesses the future and suggests the best route for Africa to escape great power dominance in the new multipolar world.

Possession Prized over Freedom: First Scramble Period

The first period of foreign power engagement in Africa begins with the Berlin Conference from 1884–85.[6] Led by the German Chancellor Otto von Bismarck, the conference hosted every European state, except Switzerland. The key objective of the conference was to establish guidelines for how participating countries would divide and manage the African continent. Leaders felt prior coordination would minimize future conflict as each power instituted a system of domination and exploitation. This initial period of European domination was characterized in contemporary scholarship as the African colonial period. The United States also participated in this conference; however, its participation did not lead to any colonial possession. Further, the United States did not object to or ratify conclusions about dividing the Africa continent.[7]

Major participants in the initial scramble to possess Africa included the United Kingdom, France, Germany, and Belgium. Complete possession characterized this period. The first—and likely most important—task for colonializing powers was to take possession of Africa and dominate the future direction of the continent. Each country had to take control of existing populations. Using justifications indicative of what John Stuart Mill suggested in *On Liberty*—"despotism is a legitimate mode of government in dealing with barbarians provided that the end be their improvement and the means justified by actually effecting that end"—the great powers began their efforts to institute control over their new conquests.[8] Colonial powers used military technologies and logistics to their advantage to exert control over Africans.[9]

Taking control in African colonies required disruption or lessening of pre-colonial systems including political, social, economic, and security structures.[10] Colonizers began to optimize operations from around 1920 forward, other than the Belgium Congo where King Leopold II optimized operations in 1909—declaring himself an absolute ruler of the Congo and associated riches.[11] Although various methods were used to control Africans, every instance can be characterized as either indirect or direct rule.[12] The United Kingdom tended to employ indirect rule based on its experiences in India that leveraged existing structures to support imperialist orders. France relied on direct rule, which eroded traditional structures of influence and delegitimized former leaders.[13] Initially, Africans had to work for European masters to avoid adverse consequences. From 1920 on, many African men were forced to pay a tax to the colonial administration—paid with money earned independently or by working for the colonial administration. This change detached men from families and all but foreclosed on any thought of Africans returning to pre-colonialization governing structures.[14]

Period	Powers	Objective(s)	Effect(s)	Dates
I. Possession	European	Objective possession, domination Major participants: UK, FR, DE, BE	Destroyed existing political/social/economic pre-colonialization structures	1884–1945 End of WW II
II. Leverage	Limited	Ideological proxy struggle Major participants: US, RU, CN, FR	Superimposed ideological struggle between communism and capitalism, entrenched autocratic rule	1947–1991 End of the Cold War
III. Neglect-Rediscovery	Unipolar	Hegemonic unipolar world Major participants: US (France enduring)	Established US as the only superpower; Africa lost strategic relevance and China operationalized its Africa policy	1991–2010 End of financial crisis
IV. Necessity	Multipolar	Multipolar competitive world Major participants: US, RU, CN, FR + many others	Increased competition among great powers and other powers reducing US hegemonic power as international system moves toward multipolarity	~2010–Present

Figure 6.1. Analysis of scramble periods. Created by the author.

African males not only endured taxation; they also participated in two of the most destructive wars in history: World War I and World War II. The United Kingdom, France, and Germany recruited and coaxed Africans into the fight, ironically to support their free colonial masters. Considering only the French example, close to 500,000 Africa soldiers participated in WWI.[15] Records indicate that 200,000 Africans fought for France during WWII.[16] Over three decades, more than 700,000 African soldiers participated in two world wars to secure rights for their French colonial masters.

Participation in the world wars awakened African desires for freedom. The European powers had also grown tired and poorer from war debts and the political and economic costs of maintaining colonies.[17] African soldiers themselves returned home from a war whose objective was to maintain freedom and liberty for their colonial masters in Europe. Not surprisingly, they advocated for freedom from colonial rule. Soldier experiences along with scholars and Pan Africanists worldwide kept decolonization on the global agenda until colonial powers gradually agreed to begin relinquishing power in the 1950s. Increased pressures from citizens, mounting costs of maintaining the colonies, and continued cries for freedom from the colonies all exerted influence on European countries relinquishing power over their colonies.[18]

Leveraged but Independent: Second Scramble Period

This second period of scrambling for influence and resources was initiated by a major period of decolonization—the process of European powers ceding independence to African authorities. Great power relationships adjusted on the continent during this period. Europeans, exhausted after the war, ceded their dominance to the two powers engaged in a new conflict that enveloped the world. This new conflict, the Cold War, embodied a forty-year rivalry between the Soviet Union and the United States over the supremacy of capitalism versus communism. The fall of the Berlin Wall in 1989 and the collapse of the Soviet Union in 1991 marked the end of this war.[19] The 1950s marked the emergence of a new group of powers on the African continent, albeit with limited engagement from the US and Soviet Union during the first decade of the Cold War.

The wave of decolonization during the 1950s started with Libya in 1951. As of 1970, all but a handful of countries had gained independence.[20] Independence conferred statehood and various forms of sovereignty, including Robert H. Jackson's quasi-state labeling that asserted some African states were legally sovereign but unable to execute the requirements of a sovereign state, namely to control its borders.[21] State projects suffered internally from inadequate institutions and a lack of trained personnel to build institutions with strong governance principles and the capacity to provide desperately needed goods and services.[22]

Lack of resources and functional institutions and an inability to reconcile state- and nation-building imperatives influenced new leaders to reduce liberal expression of political will. These cumulative effects encouraged new leaders to adopt authoritarian rule as a solution and, in many cases, the worst possible form emerged: personal rule.[23] One explanation for adoption of authoritarian rule is how imperial powers divided Africa in terms of map squares with little regard to ethnicity. At independence, trans-border and internal ethnic issues overwhelmed new states and added to the difficult task of providing goods and services.[24] Former colonial powers in some cases attempted to maintain relationships that allowed penetration into all aspects of new African states.[25] France and the United Kingdom codified these neocolonial relationships by leveraging Francophone and Commonwealth communities. These arrangements allegedly entitled members to "affinity club" benefits that really served to maintain influence over former colonies.[26]

As newly formed states began experimenting with independence and state power in the 1950s, the Soviet Union and the United States slowly began superimposing opposing ideologies and assuming the vacuum left by European powers. New leaders fearing regime instability turned to the United States and the Soviet Union, now considered superpowers, to secure their respective regimes.[27] During this period, superpowers just did not walk into African states; they were often invited by sovereign nations to engage in state affairs, even if support improved security in autocratic regimes.

Regardless of how relationships to African states began, the two superpowers leveraged internal and external regime challenges to wage proxy wars. The Democratic Republic of the Congo, Ethiopia, and Angola were key battlegrounds during the Cold War where combatants were aided with equipment and advisors. In fact, ideological positioning was so important during the Cold War that the United States and the Soviet Union switched alliances between Ethiopia and Somalia during the conflict.[28]

Through the 1970s, Cold War ideological positioning and alliances forced sovereign leaders to choose between the two superpowers, and China to a limited extent. The diplomatic, information, military, and economic paradigm helped provide a concise summation of how superpowers leveraged African states during the Cold War. In terms of diplomacy, African states were forced to align politically with the United States or the Soviet Union. In the case of China, acceptance of the One China principle was a requirement to receive Chinese aid.[29] Alliances like these afforded African states access to "big brother" protection in the international system as the two superpowers avoided direct collision and miscalculations that could have led to nuclear war. Propaganda, in the form of information advocating each opposing ideology, propagated across the continent and the world in general as if humanity's political, social, and economic survival depended on the correct choice.

Soviet and, to a lesser extent, Chinese military assistance supported regimes with host nation training and education, trainers, military equipment. and in some cases proxy forces to engage state enemies on the battlefield. South Africans and Cubans were both used to fight in the Angolan Civil War, representing the United States and the Soviet Union respectively.[30] Finally, superpowers economically assisted regimes that adopted capitalism or the socialist command economy. Without a doubt, some African states benefited from superpower attention, but these proxy relationships, regardless of economic outcomes, reduced African states to little more than leverageable tools in a global struggle.

Neglected but Rediscovered: Third Scramble Period

At the end of the Cold War in 1991, only one superpower remained, the United States. The Soviet Union collapsed after forty years of ideological struggle and devolved into a specter of its former glory.[31] The Russian Federation survived as the largest and most powerful of the post-Soviet states. The termination of the conflict was a watershed moment in world history and marked the beginning of the third scramble period in Africa. After 1976, China reduced contact on the continent to focus on consolidating domestic affairs and international policy. The post-Cold War reality translated immediately into lessened superpower focus on the African continent through circa 2002. In the absence of superpowers, African leaders were left, in a sense, to govern themselves free from the need to select an ideological philosophy in exchange for aid needed to consolidate power and move countries forward on the path to modernization.

With no superpower actively influencing state behavior, violence significantly increased. Africans were tormented by three types of conflicts.[32] First, leaders—feeling threatened—inflicted and suffered violence to secure their regimes. Further, internal and transnational non-state actors threatened peace in Africa. These actors fomented violence to further political objectives and in many cases reap economic benefits.[33] Additionally, neighboring countries at times supported non-state actors or warlords against a state's rivals. In some cases, state-on-state violence occurred over disputes or in support of rebel forces inside the territory of their foes.

The Democratic Republic of the Congo is a good example where Rwanda supported Laurent Kabila in his successful 1997 quest to oust President Mobutu Sese Seko.[34]

Russia, China, and the United States neglected and reduced engagement in Africa for numerous reasons. Primarily, the continent lost its strategic relevance after the Cold War. In fact, the continent was arguably never a priority, rather a peripheral mission for the superpowers and China.[35] Russia was forced to focus internally after the collapse of the Soviet empire. A complete rebuild of political, economic, and social structures was required to revive the ailing former superpower after the cumulative effects of the Cold War and the 1998 Asian financial crisis.[36]

During this period, China focused internally on improving domestic conditions and preparing its "going out" policy to support the state's "peaceful rise."[37] Averse to entanglement in conflict, both politically and militarily, China reserved its strength and grew its economy by 10 percent annually after the end of the Cold War.[38] The United States became the remaining superpower and unipolar hegemon. Immediately, the country was forced to confront Saddam Hussein during Desert Storm in 1991.[39] This conflict likely marked the onset of the country's twenty-year Pax Americana role of continuous conflict and associated expenditures.

By the early 2000s, Russia, China, and the United States rediscovered Africa in the midst of attempting to establish themselves in the new international system. Russia's transition closely mirrored the political fortunes of Vladimir Putin, who began his rise in 2000 as the president of Russia followed by a stint as prime minister then again president.[40] With Putin in power, Russia continued to reverse the combined effects of the collapse of the Soviet Union and the Asian financial crisis.[41] Putin's reforms and reengagement in Africa and throughout the world sought to resurrect Russian pride and influence.

In 2001, Jim O'Neill coined the term BRIC for an emerging association of nations; this was an abbreviation of the original set of countries that included Brazil, Russia, India, and China. South Africa was later added to create BRICS.[42] This new grouping, which represented budding South-South economic and political cooperation, served as a building block for Russia's new engagement approach for Africa. Russia also began a new round of bilateral engagement leveraging old Soviet relationships that formerly provided training, education, arms, and other support to liberation movements during the Cold War.[43] Russian engagement in Africa also focused on natural resources. Energy agreements with Libya and Nigeria in 2008 supported Russia's quest to recreate itself as a global energy superpower. Success in this strategy eventually led to greater control over Europe's energy supply, assuring greater Russian leverage over European affairs.[44] Russia also reinitiated successful arms sales to Africa in 2008 with the government of Libya to the tune of $3.8 billion.[45] Russia's reentry into Africa led to creation and agreement on opportunities unavailable to the United States because of one important reason: America was preoccupied with Pax Americana missions and remaking the global environment free of all perceived threats to its new hegemon status under the banner of the Global War on Terror.[46]

China, after reorganizing internally, launched its "going out" policy in 2003, which followed its 2001 acceptance into the World Trade Organization.[47] A fundamental reason for China's return to Africa was the country's insatiable need for natural resources to fuel its blazing economy.[48] China's non-intervention policy mirrored Russia's, but the country diplomatically leveraged relations with Africans to isolate Taiwan and force them to accept the One China principle espoused by China's leadership.[49] For a continent still recovering from the cumulative effects of over a century of foreign intervention and conflict, China offered appetizing opportunities for Africans to improve their basic living standards. In exchange, African states granted market access to Chinese government-supported businesses. Africans may have felt that granting China access to their markets what the best option available to improve basic living standards, especially for autocratic and poorly governed regimes.[50]

Additionally, China, in concert with Russia, embarked on a long period of ascension to great power status that included indirect challenges to the unipolar world the United States managed as a benign hegemon after the Cold War. Chinese and Russian ideological conflicts with the United States, and belief that America was to blame for all post-Cold War ills, extended the "distance" between the new great powers worldwide. Resulting competitive struggles in Africa and throughout the world portended the steady shift toward a multipolar world.[51]

In reality, the United States never fully left Africa after the Cold War. Rather, the United States drastically reduced and focused on providing low-level support. These efforts included indirect and direct facilitation of resolving conflicts that emanated from Cold War dynamics and internal grievances.[52] There were also definite democratization, human rights, and humanitarian themes throughout the presidencies of Bill Clinton and George W. Bush. These legacy interests remain important parts of African policy. Early in 2002, the United States embarked on a mission to relieve pandemic fear and suffering mounting around the globe. The Global Fund to Fight AIDS, Tuberculosis, and Malaria initiated prevention and treatment in hard-hit areas in Africa.[53] In 2003, President Bush approved the President's Emergency Plan for AIDS Relief (PEPFAR). At the time, over 22.45 million people in sub-Saharan Africa were living with AIDS.[54] By 2008, the PEPFAR program had grown to over $48 billion and represented close to 30 percent of global resources combatting AIDS.[55]

After 2001 and the initiation of the Global War on Terror, America increased its engagement in Africa. Feeling its interests threatened, the United States stepped up support to counter existing and incipient terror and armed groups across the continent.[56] Support included training, equipping, and mentoring of African forces. The country used its overwhelming military technology to target and attack groups, especially in Somalia.[57] To support the military shift to the continent, the United States established a base in Djibouti in 2003.[58] Additionally, the United States European Command transferred the Africa mission to the newly established US Africa Command (AFRICOM) in 2008. This command, envisioned as a non-kinetic command, operationalized the "whole of government" approach to engagement in Africa.[59] Combining representatives from across the spectrum of American power, the United States established itself as the prime purveyor of military cooperation and diplomacy on the continent. AFRICOM inherited missions from US Central Command and US Indo-Pacific Command (formerly Pacific Command) en route to concentrating all continental-wide operations under one command. At initiation, AFRICOM assumed responsibility for a continent with seven United Nations peacekeeping missions and increasing violent extremist activity.[60]

Economically, the United States worked to improve market access to the continent and afforded African textile merchants access to the United States. In 2000, President Bill Clinton, signed the African Growth Opportunities Act. Eventually this act included forty-two African countries, which almost quadrupled African exports to $82 million in 2008 from inception. This initial success led to subsequent extensions scheduled to expire at the end of 2025.[61] Additionally in 2002, the United States named oil as a strategic national interest. At the time, the United States received about 20 percent of its oil from Africa.[62] The percentage of oil imported from Africa was lower in 2020, partly as a result of lower global prices and increased domestic output using the hydraulic fracking technique and downward demand caused by the worldwide COVID-19 virus. The securitization of Africa's oil, nonetheless, highlighted the continent's growing importance at the time. Overall, by the end of the third period in 2010, influential powers were back in Africa competing out of necessity and looking to deepen relationships as the international system continued its path toward a multipolar world.

Engagement in a Multipolar World: Fourth Scramble Period

After the 2008 global financial crisis, the global structure accelerated its shift toward a multipolar world. The great powers—Russia, China and the United States—found themselves recovering and attempting to move forward from the worldwide shock.[63] In this context, engagement in Africa transitioned into the fourth period with the same general themes associated with the later part of the third period. Additionally, there was now an ever-increasing multipolar dynamic that informed engagements. Great power engagement now included increased skepticism among the three main players as well as increased engagement from other actors including states, multinationals, nongovernmental organizations, supranational organizations, and a host of others not directly codified within the Westphalian concept of a state.[64] Although Russia and China had not stepped up engagement to directly antagonize the United States, the perceived adverse impacts of increased engagement in Africa along with the shift from unipolar to a multipolar world contributed to the December 2018 United States decision to promulgate its new Prosper Africa strategy. This new strategy was intended to counter increased influence from Russia and China and advance development and prosperity for all Africans.[65] The Africa strategy synched well with the 2017 *National Defense Strategy*, which identified Russia and China as competitors, and the imperative of ensuring American supremacy.[66]

The fourth scramble did not have definable rules for engagement whereas the first period appeared to have some order. The Berlin Conference of 1884–85 was filled with competitors, including the United States, but it was also a semi-cooperative environment. This environment facilitated elaboration of rules to guide the conquest and colonization of the African continent. Thus far the twenty-first century has been characterized by multilateral bodies that make up the international system like the United Nations, G7, and G20. All great powers have shown varying levels of respect for these international organizations, choosing to use them, ignore them, or recreate them depending on issues and national interests. None of the great powers have been innocent in this respect.

Great powers in the fourth scramble period are compelled to engage with Africa even in an environment filled with different worldviews and suspicions. One driver for all three is the ever-increasing need for resources. China is concerned with supporting its growth while Russia is carving out its global energy superpower niche. Another driver is the economic buffet associated with an advancing Africa. Scrambling for greater market share increases a great power's ability to exert influence on the continent and across the globe. From 2006 to 2016, exports from China and Russia to Africa grew 142 and 233 percent respectively, according to a Brookings Institution report. The same report indicated American exports increased only 7 percent. Even more startling, imports from Africa to the US retreated 66 percent during the same period.[67] Security issues that threaten great power interests also justify increased engagement in Africa. Free flow of goods through strategic chokepoints like the Bab el-Mandeb Strait on the East African coast is an increasing concern. According to the US Energy Information Administration, 9 percent of all seaborne petroleum passed through the strait in 2017.[68]

The absence of a controlling entity to level the playing field between great powers and others that engage in Africa creates an anarchic environment that favors national interests over advancing African security and development. At a glance, this situation seems to render African states relatively defenseless. However, competition does have its advantages. With multiple opportunities from more competitors, African states could exercise greater selectivity and protection of resources. Implementing such a strategy would increase African gains. Maximizing these benefits, however, would require proactive sovereignty accompanied by good governance that limited corruption and prioritized making decisions that enhanced delivery of goods and services. This implies that the state must act as the responsible gatekeeper and remain accountable for all major decisions that affect the greater good of the state.

Future Engagement with Africa: Object or Partner?

To begin to understand how to move from viewing Africa as an object to a more beneficial partnership with Africa, one must consolidate lessons from the four periods of scrambling for African resources and influence. These periods correspond with the transition, which reviewed the evolution of relations as the world transformed from a unipolar to a multipolar world. Figure 6.2 provides a glimpse of how engagement in Africa will continue to evolve in a multipolar world if great power engagement continues along its current trajectory (from lower left to upper right quadrant). The current competitive environment arguably began vigorously around 2010 after the financial crisis. It includes great powers and numerous actors in search of opportunities associated with Africa's future potential.

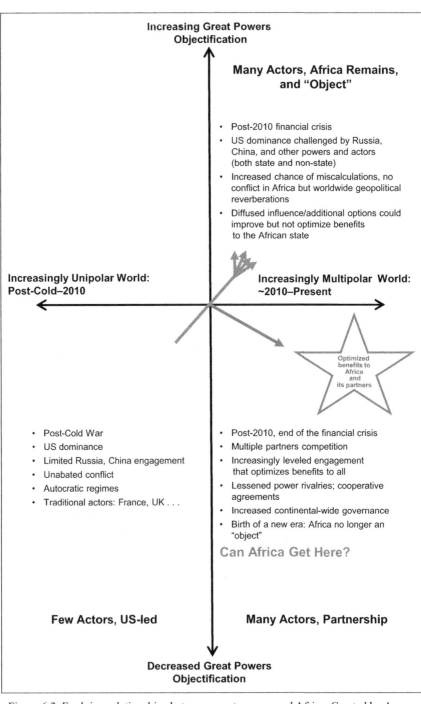

Figure 6.2. Evolving relationships between great powers and Africa. Created by Army University Press based on author drawing.

Increased actors will likely dilute great power influence and encroach upon "quasi-protected" areas once mostly influenced by great powers. The resulting loss of freedom of action by great powers may increase contestation and lead to confrontation short of open hostilities in Africa. However, these clashes may produce secondary effects in other geopolitical hotspots, which could lead to miscalculation and some level of conflict. This vision of the future world maintains the object view of Africa and its potential.

An alternate view embraces Africa and its integration into the multipolar world more as a partner and not as an object to be seized for lopsided gain. The idea involves re-visioning Africa in the multipolar world—even in the midst of concerted efforts by some western powers to hinder or reverse this eventuality. Figure 6.2, bottom right quadrant, depicts a rationalized option that potentially extends the productive lifespan of existing and future relationships, and allows for greater creative initiative between all parties.

The alternate view of Africa is fraught with uncertainty. First, this approach needs dedicated African leaders who truly wish to move their countries forward. These leaders must be convinced that they deserve better deals from engaging powers. To make this work, leaders must be committed to good governance and reducing corruption. Also implied is migration away from ethnic divisions in government that dilute efforts to provide goods and services, and away from the misuse of resources to maintain non-democratized regimes in power. Second, there are definitely roles for regional organizations and the African Union. These organizations could serve as a clearinghouse for best engagement practices and lead in helping shape division of effort and engagement specialization among great powers. Implementation is tricky because states may feel their sovereignty is threatened. Regional and supranational organizations would require staffing and specialized experience. Finally, successful implementation of this alternate view of Africa as a partner in a multipolar world requires Russia, China, and the United States to agree upon engagement in Africa that optimizes state equities and holistically accepts Africa as a partner. Cooperation with reduced harmful competition could occur, but the great powers would need incentives, regimes, and a coordinating body, perhaps like the G7, to begin to consider this alternate view. This option would be difficult to realize but not impossible. Implementation of such an arrangement would not solve all of Africa's engagement issues, but the arrangement would potentially increase gains and state legitimacy as well as, most importantly, terminate Africa's status as an object.

All three levels would reinforce each in a manner that helps ensure Africans receive the best possible deals. This system of checks and balances would increase competition in an orderly manner and give Africans the best possible opportunity to optimize long-term gains.

Conclusion

Great powers over these four periods have viewed Africa as an object. The involved nations and methods have changed, but the primacy of self-interest has guided engagement throughout. In some cases, African leaders justified military violence against civilians, revived authoritarian regimes, and misused Africa's riches after colonial rule ended. Additionally, the way great powers intervened in Africa fostered the destruction of native communities and modes of governance that could have uniquely evolved from interaction with other cultures on the continent. The cumulative effects have clearly singled out African peoples as the real victims of more than a century of treatment as objects.

Perhaps Africa's best chance to profit from this current scramble is to take the necessary steps to positively execute sovereignty—using a definition that includes final authority for all engagements, advancing good governance, low corruption, and internal and external security. A less likely end state is that the great powers will actually set aside their geopolitical squabbles in order to advance the African continent. Rationalized great power engagement in Africa would finally rid the continent of the object status and begin an era of engagement driven by national interests, of course, that consider Africans truly as partners.

Notes

1. Acha Leke and Dominic Barton, "3 Reasons Things are Looking Up for African Economies," World Economic Forum, 5 May 2016, https://www.weforum.org/agenda/2016/05/what-s-the-future-of-economic-growth-in-africa/.

2. "The World Bank in Africa," last updated 23 April 2020, https://www.worldbank.org/en/region/afr/overview.

3. Mohamed Yahya, "Africa's Defining Challenge," United Nations Development Programme Africa, 7 August 2017, http://www.africa.undp.org/content/rba/en/home/blog/2017/8/7/africa_defining_challenge.html.

4. Adam Hochschild, *King Leopold's Ghost* (Boston: Houghton Mifflin Company, 1999), 84–87.

5. For additional information on the scramble for Africa, see Thomas Pakenham, *The Scramble for Africa* (New York: Random House, 1993).

6. Hochschild, *King Leopold's Ghost.*

7. Henry S. Wilson, *The Imperial Experience in Sub-Saharan Africa since 1870* (St. Paul, MN: North Central Publishing, 1997), 74–77.

8. John Stuart Mill, *On Liberty* (Ontario: Batoche Books Limited, 2001), 14.

9. Pierre Englebert and Kevin C. Dunn, *Inside African Politics* (Boulder, CO: Lynne Rienner, 2013), 24–25.

10. Basil Davidson, *Africa in History* (London: Phoenix Press, 1991), 287–89, 302–7, 309.

11. Wilson, *The Imperial Experience in Sub-Saharan Africa,* 144.

12. Davidson, *Africa in History,* 287–89, 302–7, 309.

13. Robert W. July, *A History of the African People,* 5th ed. (Prospect Heights, IL: Waveland Press, 1998), 401–2.

14. July, 421, 436; and Stephen Ocheni and Basil C. Nwaankwo, "Analysis of Colonialism and Its Impact in Africa," *Cross-Cultural Communication* 8, no. 3 (March 2012): 48–50.

15. Guillame Guguen, "Holland Honours African Role in France's WWI Fight," *France 24* (11 August 2013), https://www.france24.com/en/20131108-african-troops-soldiers-world-war-french-hollande-senegal-algeria-tunisia.

16. Myron Echenberg, "'Morts Pour la France'; The African Soldier in France During the Second World War," *Journal of African History* 26, no. 4 (October 1985): 365.

17. Felix Gilbert and David Clay Large, *The End of the European Era 1890 to the Present,* 5th ed. (New York: W. W. Norton & Company, 2002), 397–401.

18. David Birmingham, *The Decolonization of Africa* (Athens: Ohio State Press, 1995), 2.

19. Gilbert and Large, *The End of the European Era,* 545, 590.

20. Birmingham, *The Decolonization of Africa,* 93–96.

21. Christopher Clapham, *Africa and the International System* (Cambridge: Cambridge University Press, 1996), 15–21.

22. William Tordoff, *Government and Politics in Africa,* 4th ed. (Bloomington, IN: Indiana Press, 2002), 74.

23. Liisa Laakso and Adebayo O. Olukoshi, eds., *Challenges to the Nation-State in Africa: The Crisis of the Post-Colonial Nation-State Project in Africa* (Uppsala: Nordiska Afriainstitutet, 1996), 14.

24. Robert H. Jackson and Carl G. Rosberg, "Why Africa's Weak States Persist: The Empirical and the Juridical in Statehood," *World Politics* 35, no. 1 (October 1982): 5–6, https://www.jstor.org/stable/2010277?origin=JSTOR-pdf&seq=1#metadata_info_tab_contents.

25. Clapham, *Africa and the International System*, 81, 52, 180.

26. Clapham, 79.

27. Beth Elise Whitaker and John F. Clark, *Africa's International Relations: Balancing Domestic & Global Interest* (Boulder, CO: Lynne Rienner, 2018), 61.

28. Whitaker and Clark, 65–66.

29. The One China principle emphasizes there is only one China and Taiwan is a part of the country. For more on the One China concept, see Bates Gill, "The Meaning of "'One China,'" Brookings Institution, 23 March 2000, https://www.brookings.edu/opinions/the-meaning-of-one-china/.

30. Whitaker and Clark, *Africa's International Relations*, 70, 72.

31. Gilbert and Large, *The End of the European Era*, 545, 590.

32. Gilbert and Large, 173–76.

33. Gilbert and Large, 173–76.

34. Gilbert and Large, 189.

35. Clapham, *Africa and the International System*, 135, 137.

36. Gilbert and Large, *The End of the European Era*, 84–86, 91–94.

37. Padraig Carmody, *The Rise of the BRICS in Africa The Geopolitics of South-South Relations* (London: Zed Books, 2013), 30–32.

38. Chareles A. Kupchan, *The End of The American Era* (New York: Vintage Books, 2002), 63.

39. Donald E. Nuechterlein, *America Recommitted: A Superpower Assesses Its Role in a Turbulent World,* 2nd ed. (Lexington, KY: University of Kentucky Press, 2001), 209.

40. Pamela Engel, "How Vladimir Putin Became One of the Most Feared Leaders in the World," *Business Insider* (14 February 2017), https://www.businessinsider.com/how-vladimir-putin-rose-to-power-2017-2.

41. Kupchan, *The End of The American Era*, 96.

42. Carmody, *The Rise of the BRICS*, 2.

43. Englebert and Duun, *Inside African Politics*, 353.

44. Daniel Volman, "China, India, Russia, and the United States: The Scramble for African Oil and the Militarization of the Continent," in *Readings in the International Relations of Africa,* ed. Tom Young (Bloomington, IN: Indiana University Press, 2015), 312–13.

45. Volman, 312–13.

46. Alexander Lukin, *China and Russia: The New Rapproachement* (Cambridge: Polity Press, 2018), 3–4.

47. Carmody, *The Rise of the BRICS in Africa*, 23.

48. Carmody, 24.

49. Lukin, *China and Russia*, 343–4.

50. Chris Alden, *China in Africa* (London: Zed Books, 2007), 59–60.

51. Kupchan, *The End of The American Era*, 63, 154, 155.

52. Kupchan, 247, 255–6.

53. Whitaker and Clark, *Africa's International Relations*, 262–65.

54. Max Roser and Hannah Ritchie, "HIV/AIDS," Our World in Data, last updated November 2019, https://ourworldindata.org/hiv-aids.

55. Whitaker and Clark, *Africa's International Relations*, 264.

56. Lyman. *Africa in World Politics Reforming Political Order*, 276–78.

57. Ray Walser and Morgan Lorraine Roach, "Saving Somalia: The Next Steps for the Obama Administration," The Heritage Foundation, 18 May 2012, https://www.heritage.org/africa/report/saving-somalia-the-next-steps-the-obama-administration.

58. Whitaker and Clark, *Africa's International Relations*, 271.

59. Whitaker and Clark, 267.

60. Jerry Lanier, foreword to *African Security and the African Command*, Terry F. Buss, Joseph Adjaye, Donald Golstein, and Louis A. Picard (Sterling, VA: Kumarian Press, 2011), ix, xii; and Feleke, Picard, and Buss, eds., "African Security Challenges and AFRICOM: An Overview," in *African Security Challenges and the African Command*, 9.

61. Whitaker and Clark, *Africa's International Relations*, 261.

62. Volman, "China, India, Russia, and the United States," 313.

63. Carmody, *The Rise of the BRICS in Africa*, 1–2.

64. Dhruv Gandhi, "Figure of the Week: Africa's New Trading Partners," Brookings Institute, 7 March 2018, https://www.brookings.edu/blog/africa-in-focus/2018/03/07/figure-of-the-week-africas-new-trading-partners/.

65. "President Donald J. Trump's Africa Strategy Advances Prosperity, Security, and Stability, Security, and Stability," Fact Sheet, The White House, 13 December 2018, https://www.whitehouse.gov/briefings-statements/president-donald-j-trumps-africa-strategy-advances-prosperity-security-stability/.

66. "National Security Strategy of the United States of America," The White House, December 2017, 2, https://www.whitehouse.gov/wp-content/uploads/2017/12/NSS-Final-12-18-2017-0905-2.pdf.

67. Gandhi, "Africa's New Trading Partners."

68. Justine Barden, "The Bad el-Mandeb Strait Is a Strategic Route for Oil and Natural Gas Shipments," US Energy Information Administration, 27 August 2019, https://www.eia.gov/todayinenergy/detail.php?id=41073.

Chapter 7

Fighting Fire with Water: Low-Cost Ways to Combat Malign Kremlin Influence in Moldova

Stephanie N. Chetraru

In 2012, the Russian Government ended the US Agency for International Development (USAID) presence in Russia.[1] This abrupt closure was foreshadowed by a flurry of foreign agent laws passed by the Russian Duma in the summer of 2012. These laws targeted local organizations that received funding from foreign sources.[2] This was also a preview of what Russia would try to spread to its near abroad, countries that were once part of the Soviet Union and have significant Russian-speaking ethnic minorities.[3]

The previous anthology—*Cultural Perspectives, Geopolitics, & Energy Security of Eurasia: Is the Next Global Conflict Imminent?*—addressed the issue of malign Kremlin influence in its near abroad. Those methods of influence have included Cultural Invasion, meaning Russia uses diaspora, language, entertainment, books, social networks, and the Moscow Orthodox Church to influence targets; Historical Distortion, which includes Russia promoting anti-Western themes; Centralized Media, where Russia monopolizes media and controls messaging; and Information and Psychological Operations.[4] This chapter uses 2013–18 US efforts to combat disinformation and propaganda in Moldova as a case study to show how the US government is actively working to combat this malign influence.

The 2013 Moldova situation was but a test case for the types of malign influence operations Russia rolled out to other parts of Europe and, ultimately, to the United States during its 2016 election season.[5] Acknowledging that the military and intelligence communities play a critical role in combating malign Kremlin influence, these practitioners can benefit from understanding what agencies such as USAID add to the overall US government response. This will save resources—whether that be money or time—as well as enhance coordination of effort. While the US military and intelligence communities can fight fire with fire (i.e., information operations/coordination with tech giants), USAID can fight fire with water.[6] By utilizing USAID's long-term approach to development, the agency can plant a seed, water it, and let it grow over time for sustainable long-term results that last.

Started by President John. F. Kennedy in 1961, USAID has led the US government's international development and humanitarian efforts—and continues to lead these efforts. An independent agency, it follows foreign policy set by the Department of State. USAID programs address a multitude of development issues in more than eighty countries around the world, such as health, democracy, economic growth, education, and food security. The agency's purpose is to implement "US foreign policy by promoting broad-scale human progress at the same time it expands stable, free societies, creates markets and trade partners for the United States, and fosters good will abroad."[7] USAID engages in long-term planning and long-term solutions to a set of development challenges in each country in which it operates.

So, how did USAID tackle the Kremlin's malign influence? How did USAID help counter Cultural Invasion, Historical Distortion, Centralized Media, and Information and Psychological Operations? Moldova experienced tremendous political and economic turbulence from 2014 to 2016, including the 2014 funneling of more than $1 billion out of three Moldovan banks and the replacement of five ostensibly pro-Western governments in 2015 alone. A series of protests rocked the capital in 2015, signaling that Moldovans were tired of the status quo. Their desire for change manifested itself in political shifts for the first time in seven years; anti-corruption/pro-EU candidate Maia Sandu and pro-Russia candidate Igor Dodon ran a tight race for president, with Dodon ultimately winning the election by a close margin.

In subsequent years, Moldovan media remained dominated by media controlled by a handful of oligarchs. This media provided, unfortunately, a steady diet of Russian propaganda. Most Russian-language media was produced by state-controlled Russian outlets that followed the Kremlin line, leaving Russian-speaking Moldovans with few alternative independent news sources. According to USAID partner *Internews*, "Journalists at independent outlets have trouble meeting audience needs due to low professionalism, underdeveloped and outdated technical skills (particularly in investigative and multimedia journalism), and chronic financial concerns due to an economic downturn and an oligarch-dominated advertising market. Even though 51 percent of Moldovans access online news daily, many newsrooms don't have the funds to upgrade platforms to support engaging, interactive content."[8] At the time of publication, the main oligarch's party had lost power in Moldova, but his media empire remained intact.[9]

Media literacy was low in Moldova; 70 percent of respondents in a November 2018 survey stated that they believe the media manipulates, yet only 4 percent indicated they had been manipulated.[10] Those most unaware of media manipulation were the elderly, youth (ages 18 to 29), and rural residents.[11] These groups are particularly vulnerable to the propaganda and unlabeled paid news content that is prevalent in mainstream media. Without the ability to articulate their media demands, Moldovan citizens were also susceptible to Kremlin propaganda, which promoted a political shift away from the European Union. Issues relevant to other marginalized groups such as women, ethnic minorities, and LGBTI (lesbian, gay, bisexual, transgender, and intersex) people were either infrequently addressed or presented using stereotypes.

According to USAID partner Freedom House:

Despite repeated calls for media legislation reform, the Government of Moldova had not made significant efforts to improve access to information and ensure media diversity. Compliance with laws remains weak. Public officials consistently obstruct access to public interest information through refusals, delays, or incomplete answers with impunity, data is available only on a paid basis. Access to public meetings of official bodies has become increasingly limited for representatives of the media.[12]

As other countries in the region adopted restrictive media laws that mimicked those in Russia—for example, over ill-defined "extremist" content or limiting foreign ownership—the Moldovan ruling party followed suit. Moldovan media watchdog groups advocated to prevent similar laws from being adopted in Moldova. Such efforts became ever more crucial.

Power to the (Moldovan) People: How Working with Citizens Affects Change

In 2016, USAID began assisting independent media and cultivating civic leaders and citizens to be more active in informing public policy and monitoring government actions. This directly supported the 2015 USAID Strategy for Moldova, which pledged to support "more effective and accountable democratic governance" by collaborating with Moldovans to bolster a "more effective and sustainable civil society." According to the strategy, these actions would result in "[a] better governed Moldova with improved living standards for its citizens."[13] To support this initiative, USAID's office in Moldova rolled out a five-year, $6.35 million program to promote the development of independent professional media that would give citizens access to a variety of perspectives and help create a media sector that would be more resilient to political and financial pressures. USAID noted the benefits of focusing on the supply of and demand for objective information:

[The program will] strengthen the ability of independent media to fulfill its role as a watchdog over the government and serve as a space for citizens to engage in public policy dialogue. Moreover, the program's focus on the legal enabling environment will reinforce existing protections for freedom of speech, facilitate better implementation of laws, and advocate for media sector regulation in accordance with international norms.[14]

USAID expected the activity to lead to an increased number of independent media producing quality content across a variety of traditional and digital platforms in rural and urban areas, and create a more informed citizenry that would understand the value of fact-based, credible journalism. USAID also expected to see improvements in the capacity of local media support organizations to engender reforms in the media sector and participate as equal partners in their country's democratic development. In addition, USAID pushed to indigenize media development efforts in Moldova so future efforts could be wholly led by Moldovans without donor support to ensure sustainability.

So, was USAID successful? During the first three years of its five-year program, which was started in 2015, USAID achieved impressive results:

With USAID assistance, Moldova's lead independent newspaper increased subscriptions by 150 families per year and won international awards thanks to USAID's targeted assistance—in a news and advertising market that was 80 percent concentrated in the hands of oligarchs.[15]

While election-related disinformation is a worldwide challenge, smaller markets like Moldova have a hard time getting the attention of Facebook and other social media outlets to deal with the issue. As rampant disinformation affected real political discourse in the run-up to the Moldovan presidential elections in 2016, three Moldovan software developers saw a chance to make a difference with future elections. They participated in a 2016 USAID-sponsored hack-a-thon to develop an app that would allow citizens to report fake accounts and misinformation on Facebook in real time. Following the hack-a-thon and with USAID assistance, the developers brought this game-changing product, trolless.com, to fruition. By the 2019 Moldovan election cycle, the software was working well and helped identify 700 problematic social media accounts that could have negatively affected the electoral process. Just before the Moldovan parliamentary elections, reporting through the software prompted Facebook to delete 168 Facebook accounts, 28 Facebook pages, and 8 Instagram accounts active in Moldova for "coordinated inauthentic behavior."[16] This term included the spreading of both fake and manipulative information. According to Facebook, "some of the inauthentic activity could be traced to real Moldovan government employees."[17]

To help improve the legal and regulatory environment for independent media, USAID funded Freedom House Moldova to evaluate, publish, and disseminate legal opinions on a new audiovisual code in Moldova. This helped inform decision-makers and the public alike in a neutral manner.[18]

USAID funded media literacy training to help build Moldovan consumer understanding of and demand for independent and reliable news and information through targeted media literacy activities. Figure 7.1 provides a summary of the more than 200 media literacy workshops, which educated 4,000 Moldovans to combat disinformation and spot fake news.[19]

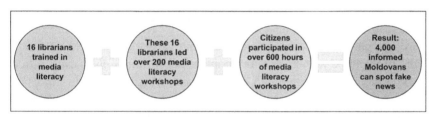

Figure 7.1. USAID-sponsored media literacy training helped 4,000 Moldovans recognize fake news. Created by the author.

Beyond these successes and as part its regional effort to encourage independent media, USAID also supported work by the regional Organized Crime and Corruption Reporting Project (OCCRP) to uncover how Russia laundered money through its near abroad. A 2019 OCCRP report stated: "Three years after the 'Laundromat' was exposed as a criminal financial vehicle to move vast sums of money out of Russia, journalists now know how the complex scheme worked—including who ended up with the $20.8 billion and how, despite warnings, banks failed for years to shut it down."[20] The OCCRP's investigative reporting also helped improve the rule of law in Moldova; in 2016, twenty judges and court officials were arrested for their role in the laundromat scheme.[21] USAID made great strides during a short window of opportunity with America's Moldovan partners—partners from civil society, as well as the government. Additional progress is expected in the future from ongoing USAID efforts to combat the malign Kremlin influence in Moldova.

What Challenges Lie Ahead?

USAID supports the non-profit organization International Research & Exchanges Board (IREX), which produces an annual Media Sustainability Index (MSI). According to the index, there is still much work to do in Moldova. The 2019 overall MSI score for Moldova hovered close to the "near sustainability" category. It did not garner a sustainable score because analysts saw an overall downturn in the application of the country's media laws, an increase in political partisanship, and a media sector still controlled by a select few who use media to influence politics.[22]

What are the next steps? Development practitioners know they do not work in a vacuum. They must contend with real-time forces that affect their well-laid plans. And they are working with small budgets; USAID foreign assistance accounts for less than one-percent of the discretionary federal budget.[23] By comparison, the Department of Defense budget represents more than 50 percent of the discretionary federal budget.[24] USAID is accustomed to planning and implementing low-cost solutions. And while it has broad expertise in development areas, USAID has limited resources more generally. Hence, institutions looking to work with USAID should come to the table with an eye for cooperation. Information sharing is free; USAID has plenty of research and analysis on rising Kremlin influence. The agency's information is also quite accessible since its work is generally available via open source channels. Moldova is but one example; USAID works on media literacy programs that support independent journalism all over the world. USAID can help combat malign Russian influence by planting a seed, watering it, and letting it grow, as it is doing with the media sector in Moldova.

Notes

1. "Russia Expels USAID Development Agency," *BBC News,* 12 September 2012, https://www.bbc.com/news/world-europe-19644897.

2. "Russia: Government vs. Rights Groups," *Human Rights Watch,* 18 June 2018, https://www.hrw.org/russia-government-against-rights-groups-battle-chronicle.

3. William Safire, "On Language; The Near Abroad," *New York Times Magazine,* 22 May 1994, https://www.nytimes.com/1994/05/22/magazine/on-language-the-near-abroad.html.

4. Robert Kurz, "Ukraine's Hidden Battlefield," in *Cultural Perspectives, Geopolitics, & Energy Security of Eurasia: Is the Next Global Conflict Imminent?* ed. Mahir J. Ibrahimov, Gustav Otto, and Col. Lee G. Gentile Jr. (Fort Leavenworth, KS: Army University Press, 2017).

5. Jed Willard, "What Europe Can Teach America About Russian Disinformation*," The Atlantic* (9 June 2018), https://www.theatlantic.com/international/archive/2018/06/what-europe-can-teach-america-about-russian-disinformation/562121/.

6. Elizabeth Bodine-Baron et al., *Countering Russian Social Media Influence* (Monica, CA: Rand Corporation, 2018), https://www.rand.org/pubs/research_reports/RR2740.html.

7. "USAID, Who We Are," USAID, accessed 28 May 2019, https://www.usaid.gov/who-we-are.

8. "National Survey on Perception of Media in Moldova," *InterNews* (November 2018), https://internews.org/sites/default/files/2019-02/03_INTERNEWS_Final%20report_25.10.18_EN-web.pdf.

9. Lyndon Allin and Balázs Jarábik, "Draining the Moldovan Swamp," Wilson Center (blog), 21 June 2019, https://www.wilsoncenter.org/blog-post/draining-the-moldovan-swamp.

10. "National Survey on Perception of Media in Moldova," *InterNews.*

11. "National Survey on Perception of Media in Moldova."

12. "Legal Analysis of the Draft Audiovisual Media Code of Moldova," Freedom House, June 2018, https://freedomhouse.org/sites/default/files/FH%20Legal%20Analysis%20-%20Moldova%20Draft%20AV%20Code.pdf.

13. "USAID Moldova Country Development Cooperation Strategy," USAID, 2013, https://www.usaid.gov/moldova/cdcs.

14. "USAID: Media Enabling Democracy, Inclusion, and Accountability in Moldova," accessed 10 January 2020, https://www.usaid.gov/moldova/governing-justly-and-democratically.

15. "Creative Advertising Boosts Subscribers to Investigative Reporting Outlet in Moldova," *InterNews,* 11 March 2019, https://internews.org/updates/creative-advertising-boosts-subscribers-investigative-reporting-outlet-moldova.

16. "Civil Society Tracks Trolls and Fakes, Prompts Facebook Action in Moldova," *InterNews,* 21 February 2019, https://internews.org/story/civil-society-tracks-trolls-and-fakes-prompts-facebook-action-moldova.

17. "Civil Society Tracks Trolls and Fakes."

18. "Legal Analysis of the Draft Audiovisual Media Code of Moldova," Freedom House.

19. "Media Literacy Can Be Learned at Any Age," *InterNews,* 28 August 2018, https://internews.org/story/media-literacy-can-be-learned-any-age.

20. "The Russian Laundromat Exposed," *OCCRP,* 20 March 2017, https://www.occrp.org/en/laundromat/the-russian-laundromat-exposed/.

21. "Moldova: 20 Judges, Court Officials Accused in Huge Money Laundering Scheme," *OCCRP,* 22 September 2016, https://www.occrp.org/en/daily/5667-moldova-20-judges-court-officials-accused-in-huge-money-laundering-scheme.

22. "Media Sustainability Index 2019," IREX, accessed 28 May 2019, https://www.irex.org/sites/default/files/pdf/media-sustainability-index-europe-eurasia-2019-full.pdf.

23. "The State Department and USAID Budget," USAID, accessed 28 May 2019, https://www.usaid.gov/sites/default/files/documents/9276/FactSheet_StateUSAIDBudget.pdf.

24. "Military Spending in the United States," National Priorities Project, 2015, https://www.nationalpriorities.org/campaigns/military-spending-united-states/.

Chapter 8
Climate Change and US National Security
Michael M. Andregg

In October 2014, the US Department of Defense published an Adaptation Roadmap for climate change that started with: "Climate change will affect the Department of Defense's ability to defend the Nation and poses immediate risks to US national security."[1] Then-Secretary of Defense Chuck Hagel commented: "Climate change does not directly cause conflict, but it can significantly add to the challenges of global instability, hunger, poverty, and conflict. Food and water shortages, pandemic disease, disputes over refugees and resources, more severe natural disasters—all place additional burdens on economies, societies, and institutions around the world."[2] This chapter details what those challenges and burdens are, with emphases on national security implications and consequences for US Army personnel in particular. But it cannot and should not be narrowly focused, because this is a global problem with global consequences that affect the entire US military. It affects alliances, flashpoints, basing issues, geopolitics, and budgets in complex ways I will try to exemplify with specific cases in Syria and South Asia.

Misinformation—or worse, calculated disinformation—can influence assessments in any war zone. It continues to be an especially pernicious problem with climate change.[3] For example, at Minnesota's leading public policy institute we have been discussing and studying climate change since at least 1982.[4] It took thirty-one years before Andy Marshall commissioned the first publicly known Pentagon study of national security implications of climate change in 2003.[5] Yet this author was told personally at the National Intelligence University in 2005 by two participants that officers there had been "ordered not to talk about that subject."[6] This was one small result of a sustained campaign by legacy industries to suppress discussion of something profound that they already knew was guaranteed to occur.[7]

Let me be crystal clear, as a scientist, about a couple of key things up front. First, current climate changes are absolutely real, they are mostly caused by human actions in the modern era, and they are very significant in many ways not least of which are national security effects. Second, scientific consensus on these and many derivative effects was achieved at least a decade ago, but US government reaction to the hundreds of warnings issued has been stalled by that persistent disinformation campaign, and by wishful thinking among some politicians. There is zero real, scientific dispute except on margins such as estimates of how quickly the Arctic and Antarctic ice sheets are melting and how fast, therefore, the oceans will rise.

The rising seas pose immediate and very expensive challenges to the US Navy since, naturally, most of their bases are on seashores. Some very important ones, like Diego Garcia in the Indian Ocean, sit mere feet above current sea levels.[8] Anyone can build a wall to restrain a foot of rising water, but building physical structures to restrain twenty feet of surges during cyclones or hurricanes is an entirely different challenge, as New Orleans learned during Hurricane Katrina. Furthermore, the ocean is becoming more acidic as it rises due to increasing levels of carbon dioxide in the warming water.[9] This, plus the warming water, is killing coral reefs all over the world at this time.[10] Reefs currently protect many other areas like the island of Guam, home to one of America's most important Pacific military bases. Reefs also help to feed a hungry world. When reefs fail, people suffer and some eventually move. When large numbers of desperate people move, smaller conflicts can escalate into major wars.

The US Air Force uses those island bases as much as our Navy, and half of their work supports US Army operations in desert countries far away. There are also major climate change effects much closer to home. MacDill Air Force Base in Tampa Bay, Florida, is home for the US Central Command and remains extremely vulnerable to hurricane damage, as are many other military bases in Florida and along the Gulf coast. US Southern Command was based at Homestead Air Force Base in Miami, until Hurricane Andrew wiped the base off the operational map in 1992. That cost the Air Force billions to rebuild.

Even Offutt Air Force Base in Nebraska, home to Strategic Command, which controls our nuclear forces, had to close in April 2019, because of climate change-enhanced flooding.[11] Yet intelligence personnel with proper clearances were forbidden to discuss this subject in 2005 at the National Intelligence University, then based inside the Defense Intelligence Agency's Defense Intelligence Analysis Center at an Air Force base near Washington, DC. This was not an isolated incident; it is part of a recurring pattern.[12] No doubt there was some progress on the climate change front between 2008 and 2016, like that 2014 roadmap produced when Chuck Hagel was secretary of defense. There were some changes in curricula at war colleges and other adjustments to objective environmental realities, which some say persist to this day.[13] The Environmental Protection Agency began factoring climate change into some of its other long-range assessments, as did the National Aeronautics and Space Administration and the National Oceanic and Atmospheric Administration.[14] Regrettably, much of that positive effort was later reversed by a political campaign to discredit scientists in government service who pressed climate change and other environmental issues.[15]

Figure 8.1. This aerial view of Offutt Air Force Base and surrounding areas affected by March 2019 floodwaters illustrates why Strategic Command had to close for a while. You know a weather event is significant when three major US commands have to adjust in such dramatic and expensive ways. Source: US Air Force photo by Tech. Sgt. Rachelle Blake.

Without digressing further to deal with misinformation and willful ignorance among a variety of vested interests and politicians, let me be blunt about the most important consequences of climate change for the United States of America and the US Army in particular:

• By far the biggest effect is that climate change **drives new conflicts**, especially in desert countries, and **exacerbates existing conflicts**. This is one of several reasons we are currently bogged down in forever wars that do not end.[16]

• **Climate change is expensive**. Some costs are obvious, like the costs of relocating military bases (much less entire cities like Miami someday), and some much less obvious like the costs of crop failures and emergent diseases in more places on earth each day.[17] The COVID-19 pandemic is a dramatic example of the damage that emergent diseases can cause. When national economies suffer, military budgets suffer, and some of those resources must be diverted to increasingly common and expensive "natural" disasters.

• **Mass migrations have already destabilized politics** in Europe and Central America, among other places.[18] Failed or failing states export desperate people to near neighbors, as when Syria disintegrated, sending more than six million people to Turkey, Lebanon, and Jordan.[19] Over one million went on to Europe with huge political consequences. The US Army may not want to be involved in such disasters, but I guarantee it will be.

Among climate change effects observed:

• Increased carbon dioxide and other greenhouse gasses trap heat in the atmosphere, thus increasing average air temperatures worldwide, but with considerable variability.

• Hotter air and infrared radiation warm the oceans, which then expand and slowly rise.[20]

• Increased temperatures also result in ice melting at both poles and almost all glaciers, further increasing the rise of ocean levels. Worst-case scenarios predict much greater consequences, such as a possible twenty-foot rise in sea level noted in the 2003 Marshall Report.[21]

• Hotter air causes more evaporation, which means slowly increasing precipitation and altered high-level wind flows. Both of these effects can dramatically impact agriculture.

• Hotter air and water create more precipitation, and result in more and fiercer storms. Hurricanes and cyclones have especially large effects on US military basing and security.[22]

• The ranges of agricultural pests are moving north (in the Northern Hemisphere), as are optimal zones for growing crops. Large areas are "desertifying" (e.g., regions of Syria and sub-Saharan Africa that once were productive).[23] These result in massive migrations and occasional genocides as we saw in Darfur, or ethnic "cleansings" as in Myanmar.[24]

• There are also major public health implications as once-tropical diseases spread north. Mosquitoes are a significant threat because they are vectors for current endemic diseases like malaria, Zika, and West Nile Virus. But public health professionals also worry about emergent diseases like SARS, MERS, and viral nightmares like Ebola. These can destabilize nations, especially if they become pandemic. Africa will probably be the hardest hit, but Africa connects to everywhere. COVID-19 emerged in Asia from the same family of coronaviruses that produced SARS and MERS. Since it was not contained early on like SARS and MERS,

COVID-19 became a global pandemic with vast economic, public health, and security consequences.[25]

• More and fiercer wildfires are occurring in North America and Southeast Asia, including Australia, especially where forests are stressed for other reasons.[26]

• In desert zones like the Middle East, conflicts over water can result in wars that the US gets involved in but cannot usually end.

• Oceans are also becoming more acidic, with major effects on shell-fish and other foods.[27]

All of these problems are certain to continue, even if population growth stopped tomorrow. But that is not going to stop anytime soon, and population growth is a major driver of climate change. People consume food and water, which uses energy.[28] Growing middle classes in Asia and Africa also want to improve their lives with refrigeration, air conditioning, transportation, and modern medicines, all of which require large amounts of energy to produce.

These ten items, therefore, have national security consequences, not least being increased costs to operate in hostile environments and diversion of military resources to increasing numbers of humanitarian rescue missions. Such disasters often coincide or collocate with armed conflict zones, which wear out equipment and personnel. We have been dealing with **symptoms** of a global crisis for decades, rather than with ultimate **causes**. This is obviously unwise. The military analogue is winning all the battles, but losing the wars.

The Case of Syria

Syria and the rise of ISIS exemplify these difficult problems, particularly discussion focused on the personalities of key leaders like Bashar al-Assad or Abu Bakr al-Baghdadi, and the role of militant Islam. They are relevant, of course, and must be dealt with regardless of efforts to get at ultimate causes. But focusing on obvious things like triggering events and political leaders often obscures the ultimate causes of large-scale armed conflicts.[29]

The case of the ongoing disintegration of Syria since 2011 is particularly vivid and has more reliable metrics than many. In 2010, the population growth rate in Syria was 2.4 percent per year.[30] Based on the accepted formula for population growth, Syria's population could double in under thirty years—with an increasingly "pyramidical" age distribution of many more young people than elders.[31] That matters because pyramidal age distributions have momentum. Even if birth rates plunge suddenly, such populations will continue to grow for decades unless death rates soar. Figure 8.2 shows the Central Intelligence Agency (CIA) estimate of Syria's age distribution for 2018. The researchers also noted a total population that year of 19.5 million. This is many millions LESS than when their civil wars began.

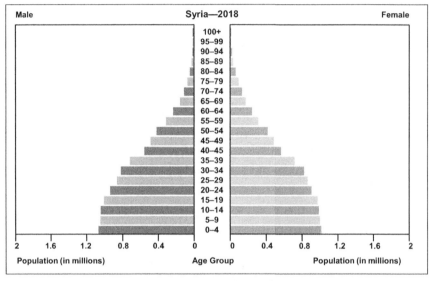

Figure 8.2. This chart from *The World Factbook*, one of the best sources of global demographic data, shows the age distribution of Syria's population in 2018. Source: Central Intelligence Agency, *The World Factbook*, last updated 12 August 2020, https://www.cia.gov/library/publications/the-world-factbook/geos/sy.html.

Mentioned much less often but relevant to climate change issues, the worst drought in Syria's recorded history—from 2006 to 2010—occurred during the four years prior to onset of the war and led to migration of about 1.5 million of Syria's then-24 million people from barren farmlands into overburdened cities.[32] Climate change almost certainly contributed to that drought, and global warming is a substantial and significant consequence of the global increase in human populations and consumption of fossil fuels. Climate change is a **derivative** result of population pressure.

Syrian conflicts began with simple protests, largely of students in Damascus who sought a fairer distribution of job opportunities from the government of Bashar al-Assad.[33] Assad reserved the best opportunities for his Alawite ethno-religious group, with some for minority Christian allies in a predominantly Sunni country (74 percent). Assad followed in his father's footsteps by crushing protests. Such actions introduce two other ultimate causes of war: corruptions of governance and authoritarian law. But this time, the tidal force of population pressure combined with militant religion, which had been growing throughout the region.

Despite many casualties, therefore, protests endured and became more militant and better armed. This morphed over a few years into a hyper-complex and brutal series of civil wars in which ISIS played a prominent role.[34] That led to more than half a million dead, half of the pre-war Syrian population displaced, and at least six million refugees who fled to near neighbors (over one million went on to Europe)—spreading population pressure to all those areas. Burdens were especially great on fragile Lebanon, Jordan, and increasingly militant Turkey.[35] Meanwhile, the Alawite population in Syria grew from 11 percent in 2010 to about 17 percent in 2014.[36]

What do all these demographic numbers mean for US Army operations in desert conflict zones? The most important point is that if the population in distress continues to grow, it can generate almost unlimited numbers of unemployed and largely unemployable teenaged males. Demagogues abound in such places, eager to blame their distress on evil foreign "others" like Americans. Of course, we have the capacity to kill large numbers of these desperate and misguided men. But if we do not get past the tactical level of killing unemployed men (also known as terrorists when their desperation leads to violence) to deal with strategic causes of conflict, we are doomed at best to live with very expensive and painful forever wars.

While the United States was directly involved in defeating ISIS in Iraq, our exposure in Syria was mainly to support local forces. The US declared an official end to ISIS territorial dominance on 23 March 2019 when Baghouz, Syria, was overrun by Kurdish forces supported by US air power and special operations forces.[37] The pros all know, however, that the conditions which gave rise to ISIS remain.[38] The malignant leader of ISIS, Abu Bakr al-Baghdadi, disappeared along with very large sums of money.[39] He was ultimately killed by US Special Forces on 26 October 2019, but economic conditions in the desert that gave rise to those millions of desperate teenaged males will not create new wealth unless someone invests heavily.[40] Unfortunately, rich international donors are scarce during the days of the global COVID-19 pandemic, and the forces of climate change work against current deserts blooming on their own.

Meanwhile, considerable population pressure has transferred to Turkey in recent years in the form of about 3.6 million refugees.[41] They are not going anywhere soon, and Turkey's economy has been struggling with its own issues. Droughts and changing weather patterns that adversely affect agriculture can happen anywhere, and failed states can spread like a contagion. Syria illustrates those dynamics better than most cases but it is not alone in suffering consequences from these long-term, strategic threats to national and global welfare.

Bangladesh, Myanmar, and South Asia

Bangladesh is known for very large numbers of people and abject poverty. But it also contains the largest river delta in the world, and is one of the most fertile agricultural regions on earth. Of greatest relevance to this chapter is the fact that most of that Ganges-Brahmaputra Delta lies within feet of sea level. If sea levels rise significantly, therefore, vast amounts of very productive farmland will be ruined by salt water, and tens of millions of people will need to find new homes in a region already severely overcrowded and prone to conflict.

A much larger area that includes Pakistan, India, Nepal, Bhutan, Myanmar, Vietnam, and China is watered partly by runoff from glaciers and snow deposited on the great Himalayan Mountains and the Tibetan Plateau to the north. Those glaciers have been melting fast, creating additional challenges for the area's combined population, which was about four billion people in 2018. China has a big advantage, because it controls the headwaters of many of the great rivers watering those areas, and of course, it has Asia's largest army.

In 2009, Kenneth Pomeranz discussed this watershed, its vulnerabilities to climate change, and the potential for organized, armed conflict as a result.[42] After noting the other great watersheds of the world, and conflicts in them over water, Pomeranz wrote:

> But none combine the same scale of population, scarcity of rainfall, dependence on agriculture, scope for mega-dam projects and vulnerability to climate change as those at stake within the greater Himalayan region. Here, glaciers and annual snowmelts feed rivers serving just under half of the world's population, while the unequalled heights from which their waters descend could provide vast amounts of hydro-power. At the same time, both India and China face the grim reality that their economic and social achievements since the late 1940s—both "planned" and "market-based"—have depended on unsustainable rates of groundwater extraction; hundreds of millions of people now face devastating shortages.[43]

One of the weakest countries in this complex is Myanmar, which the CIA still calls Burma. Myanmar has been afflicted with small, ethnic-based civil wars for decades. In August 2018, pressure from a rapidly growing Muslim population called the Rohingya angered majority Burmese Buddhists.[44] This resulted in a series of massacres of Rohingya and caused over 700,000 of Myanmar's nearly one million Rohingya to flee into Bangladesh. The United Nations described the military offensive in Rakhine province as a "textbook example of ethnic cleansing."[45] The background reality is that poor populations with high birth rates face continuous pressure over scarce resources even in good times. When climate change increases those pressures, stronger nations or stronger ethnic groups within nations tend to blame their weaker neighbors.[46]

The United States military can stand by while other nations far away conduct ethnic cleansing or even genocide. It certainly cannot solve all the problems of the world, even though some would like us to be a global police force. But our country cannot ignore the fact that three of these countries are nuclear powers: China, India, and Pakistan, all of which have had border wars in the last twenty years. The Pakistan-India dyad has been especially unstable, and if they have a nuclear war, this could damage agriculture worldwide while destroying South Asia's economy.[47]

To the northeast, North Korea is facing off against America over nuclear weapons development, while starvation haunts its people.[48] In mid-2019, North Korea experienced its worst drought in decades, with only 2.1 inches of rain through 16 May. The United Nations warned of an urgent food crisis unless massive food aid appeared from somewhere.[49] No one has been eager to donate food to the most brutal police-state on earth. Desperate nations sometimes do desperate things, and dictators are notorious for starting foreign wars to distract from domestic discontent.[50] When such nations have nuclear weapons, the entire world is at risk. In this setting, classical arms control negotiations are unlikely to succeed, but one cannot know if one does not try.

There are other worst-case scenarios, like Pakistan giving or selling some of its warheads to Islamic extremists in Kashmir or elsewhere.[51] Strategic analysts should be very worried about where all this conflict is headed in a region whose population continues to grow substantially each year, while reliable water sources decline. South Asia is a twenty-first century powder keg with potential to spread its problems worldwide. Climate change, with its underlying cause of population pressure, is one of the conflict drivers that traditional analysts neglect at our peril.

Novel or Exotic Consequences of Climate Change
for Military Professionals

Previous sections of this chapter focused on climate change results that are already visible and easily measurable. There are some more dramatic possible consequences of climate change that serious military professionals should know about as they prepare for rare but high-impact military contingencies.

For example, current estimates are that sea levels may rise about one meter by 2100.[52] That is alarming but manageable unless you are a country like Kiribati in the South Pacific, where islands average only two meters above sea level.[53] More challenging, many of the projections about the pace and scale of climate change have been underestimates. Some have pointed out that if the Antarctic ice shelves collapse completely (the thinnest already have), then sea level rise by 2100 could be as high as twenty feet.[54] That would have big implications for Miami, Manhattan, San Diego, and Honolulu, and much more for countries like Bangladesh.[55] A three-foot sea level rise in Bangladesh would submerge almost 20 percent of the country's farmland, and displace more than thirty million people who are already extremely poor.

The North Pole presents different—and more extreme—dilemmas. First, when ice sheets melt, permafrost melts. That increases decay, releasing potentially vast amounts of methane. Methane is about twenty times more powerful a greenhouse gas than carbon dioxide. That could dramatically increase the pace of climate change through a positive feedback loop.

Second, whether methane becomes important or not, the Arctic ice sheets have already retreated so fast that Canada and Russia in particular are mapping out northern sea routes for trade that were impossible to contemplate before global warming became an issue. This created a large area for many more potential military conflicts than in the past. Russia, for example, has already claimed the North Pole, seeking primacy over mineral resources below it.[56]

As discussed previously, the 2003 Marshall Report was considered an extreme scenario regarding how major changes of ocean currents affect agriculture and much else worldwide. Such scenarios should be considered for the same reasons analysts study potential terrorist attacks at key locations. Likewise, national security implications of emergent, pandemic diseases should be studied carefully. Even ancient killers like the flu and smallpox could become more lethal and impactful. And who wants to deploy into a conflict zone like Eastern Congo during a reemergence of Ebola? The twenty-second outbreak of Ebola since 1977 is spreading rapidly, helped by armed attacks against the medical personnel trying to contain it.[57] If Ebola ever reaches a major population center like Kinshasa, Nairobi, or Lagos, the world will never be the same. COVID-19 showed how even wealthy, first-world, well-developed nations can be devastated by emergent diseases.[58] Such massive public health emergencies can affect the richest as well as the poorest countries on earth, and upset power relations everywhere.

By far the biggest wildcard is Africa. The fundamental reason for that is population growth, the taboo topic that underlies much of the climate change discussion. Africa's fifty-four countries had a population of about 1.3 billion people in 2020. The United Nations estimates that Africa will contain more than 4 billion people by 2100.[59] That is quite a lot of population pressure for an area that already has half of the persistent civil wars on earth. And ISIS—declared dead by any number of experts and politicians—has continued to spread in the Sahara and Sahel of north Africa, despite al-Baghdadi's death in 2019.[60]

US Africa Command may not want more business, but the Russians and especially the Chinese have increased their interactions with African nations. Conflicts are endemic, and some are likely to get worse. It might be nice to build a big wall around Africa and ignore its problems, but that is a fantasy. The world is interconnected and continuing to warm, while the living system that supports it is already in great distress.[61] Civilization itself depends upon that living system. Therefore, it is imperative that sensible people everywhere stop denying climate change, and start the large engineering and constructive biology projects that scientists have been urging for a generation. Otherwise, the global jihads that have caused conflicts since at least 1991 will likely grow even larger, because failing states always seek scapegoats for their failures.

A Good Resource on Climate Change for Military Professionals

While some intelligence professionals were forbidden to discuss this subject, others saw the writing on the wall years ago and began to study military implications of climate change. With a change of administrations in 2008, these professionals gained more freedom to talk seriously about national security implications of climate change and publish subsequent reports. The American Security Project created an effective compilation, their Climate Security Report of 2017, accessible at https://www.americansecurityproject.org/climate-security.[62]

This report's seven major sections included one on solutions plus over fifty subsections on military-relevant topics. Three, in particular, illustrate congruence with my independent assessments. Section two, "Climate Change Threatens National Security," includes subsections on "Climate change threatens South Asian stability," and "Could the Syrian conflict be a symptom of climate change?" My answer to those two cases is an obvious and emphatic yes. Section four, "The Military is Preparing for Climate Change," has several subsections on the Arctic and on the relevant *Quadrennial Defense Review 2014.*[63] Of special interest is the section called "If military sees climate risk, why do we deny?" It is imperative to recognize that organized and well-funded campaigns to deny climate change continue.[64] Some vested interests would rather make maximum profits today no matter how grave the consequences for America's future.[65]

This is neither acceptable, nor wise. But it will continue, because entire civilizations take a long time to learn about difficult new problems, and vested interests are driven by many factors to prioritize their own short-term situations. Garret Hardin called this the "tragedy of the commons" in a landmark 1968 article in *Science.*[66] His basic idea was that when communities depend on communal resources like a common fishery or forest, individuals may be tempted to overuse that resource, depleting it for all others. This ongoing factor distorts clear thinking about a major threat to US national security.

Conclusion

After surviving two world wars, a civil war at home, and a cold war that threatened annihilation of everything, the United States should survive the severe challenges of climate change and emerging pandemic diseases. To move forward with minimal pain, however, will require some paradigm shifts in thinking about strategic threats to our country.

An example specific to the US Army is in how civil affairs units are managed. Not long ago the US Army cut the number of active civil affairs units in half, and put the one remaining brigade under the Special Operations Command.[67] While there is a reasonable rationale for this change if the factors of climate change and global chaos are ignored, Special Operations Command often operates in failed states that could benefit from a little nation building after bad guys have been defeated.

The civil affairs unit reduction has not worked out very well, because rebuilding destroyed nations is extremely expensive, very difficult, and phenomenally frustrating—and will require long-term investments that transcend political administrations. Ensuring long-term financial commitments may be the hardest challenge in today's polarized environments. New terrorist threats are always emerging. It is, therefore, quite natural for forces that are focused on maximum lethality and stealth to look at civil affairs as a kind of junior adjunct to the urgent task of beating today's undoubtedly very dangerous bad guys.

Therein lies a trap that has bogged down the United States in unwinnable forever wars. When the roles of climate change and organized armed conflict in the twenty-first century are factored in, quite a different picture emerges. The only enduring solutions involve dealing with the ultimate causes of such conflicts, not just with the symptoms of terrorism that result.

Nation building becomes far more important no matter how expensive. Therefore, civil affairs units become more important. This does not mean that special forces have no role. All those humanitarian missions need to be protected, because few terrorists have left the field and the demagogues who point them toward us sprout like mushrooms on decaying logs. But more attention must be paid to why the multitudes are so desperate, and how to defeat demagogues through better information operations rather than with better bombs alone.

Another example of a change in strategic focus could be the wisdom, or lack thereof, to major investments in modernizing US nuclear forces. The United States is poised to spend more than $1 trillion to replace all three legs of its nuclear triad.[68] There are many obvious reasons to consider this, not least the fact that every other country with nuclear weapons is modernizing.[69] Some especially loathsome tyrannies want to join that club and proliferate nuclear weapons to their friends. There are, therefore, plenty of valid concerns about nuclear issues today.

Despite shared concerns about a mass attack from China, for example, a bigger danger might be a single nuclear detonation in Tel Aviv accomplished by a terrorist group that bought a nuclear warhead on the black arms market, or was given one by Pakistani sympathizers. Or perhaps a detonation in Washington, DC, or simultaneous detonations in DC and Moscow. The point is what happens after any of these major cities goes up in radioactive smoke? Traditional deterrence is not working well for the long run, according to some of its leading architects.[70]

Escalation chains are easy to describe, but notoriously impossible to predict. Most simulated weapons of mass destruction war games quickly escalate to general thermonuclear war. The US Army has very few tools to influence outcomes if worst-case nuclear scenarios come true. Prevention thus becomes essential. In fact, the Army's most effective tools would apply before disaster strikes, specifically: 1) considerably increased information operations, 2) interdiction of clandestine weapons of mass destruction networks, and 3) nation-building activities by civil affairs units to reduce the chances that conflicts will reignite after conventional or special forces stop an especially dangerous threat.

From this perspective, therefore, it is imperative for the regular Army to **maintain a perimeter between civilization and barbarism**. Terrorists with nuclear weapons are just one obvious example of the manifold types of barbarism that threaten civilization today. But if the Army can hold that perimeter, then other forces can work on the strategic causes of organized, armed conflict in the world today.

A medical metaphor to illustrate why holding such a perimeter is important could be dealing with gangrene. Gangrene is lethal, so ignoring it is not a realistic option. Controlling fever is essential as sepsis spreads, but this deals with a symptom not a cause. The only effective solution is to deal simultaneously with the source of the infection while keeping symptoms from killing the patient. Consider terrorists as a form of gangrene for civilizations.

Unpleasant though these problems are, ignoring the problem of failed states is neither an honorable nor a realistic option for the US Army. The wiser path, when possible, is to rethink allocations of scarce resources away from nuclear Armageddon scenarios and maximum lethality toward actions that contain and then seek to prevent organized, armed conflict. Finding ways to work with adversaries, peer competitors, or even enemies is a good strategic high ground to make the future safer for everyone's children.

Climate change is undoubtedly a significant and dangerous threat to US national security today, as much because it challenges our historic paradigms as because it is huge, expensive, complicated—and cannot be killed directly. It is the duty of everyone who swears to preserve, protect, and defend the US Constitution, however, to figure out how to deal with the emerging challenges of the third millennium of the Common Era, which include degrees of climate change we have never seen before. That will not be easy, but press on.

Notes

1. Office of the Assistant Secretary of Defense (Energy, Installations and Environment) Environment Safety and Occupational Health Directorate, *2014 Climate Change Adaptation Roadmap* (Alexandria, VA: US Department of Defense, June 2014), 1, https://www.acq.osd.mil/eie/downloads/CCARprint_wForward_e.pdf.

2. Chuck Hagel, US Secretary of Defense, remarks delivered to the Halifax International Security Forum on Department of Defense Arctic Strategy, Halifax, Nova Scotia, November 2013.

3. James Hoggan, with Richard Littlemore, *Climate Cover-Up: The Crusade to Deny Global Warming* (Vancouver: Greystone Books, 2009), 2017. This is just one of the more recent and thoroughly researched books and articles on this topic. Others include: Naomi Oreskes and Erik M. Conway, *Merchants of Doubt: How a Handful of Scientists Obscured the Truth on Issues from Tobacco Smoke to Global Warming* (London: Bloomsbury Press, 2010); Niall McCarthy, "Oil and Gas Giants Spend Millions Lobbying to Block Climate Change Policies [Infographic]," *Forbes* (25 March 2019), https://www.forbes.com/sites/niallmccarthy/2019/03/25/oil-and-gas-giants-spend-millions-lobbying-to-block-climate-change-policies-infographic/#9e0917b7c4fb; Matt Hope and Karen Savage, "Global Climate Coalition: Documents Reveal how Secretive Fossil Fuel Lobby Group Manipulated UN Climate Programs," DeSmog Blog, 26 April 2019, https://www.nationofchange.org/2019/04/26/global-climate-coalition-documents-reveal-how-secretive-fossil-fuel-lobby-group-manipulated-un-climate-programs/; and Paula Kehoe, *A Burning Question: Propaganda and the Denial of Climate Change,* a fifty-three-minute educational video produced by Earth Horizons Production, 2012.

4. The Hubert H. Humphrey Public Policy Institute is located at the University of Minnesota, where the author taught in various capacities for thirty-five years.

5. Peter Schwartz and Doug Randall, "An Abrupt Climate Change Scenario and its Implications for United States National Security," 2003 (otherwise known as the "Marshall Report" because legendary Pentagon forecaster Andy Marshall commissioned it), https://grist.org/wp-content/uploads/2004/02/abruptclimatechange2003.pdf.

6. The date of this conference was 29 September 2005, but the names of the participants and organizers are classified.

7. Matthew Taylor and Jonathan Watts, "Revealed: The 20 Firms behind a Third of all Carbon Emissions, New Data Shows how Fossil Fuel Companies Have Driven Climate Crisis despite Industry Knowing Dangers," *The Guardian*, 9 October 2019, https://www.theguardian.com/environment/2019/oct/09/revealed-20-firms-third-carbon-emissions. See also an earlier *Guardian* piece with links to evidence: https://www.theguardian.com/environment/climate-

consensus-97-per-cent/2018/sep/19/shell-and-exxons-secret-1980s-climate-change-warnings.

8. Diego Garcia's average height above sea level is four feet. This major US base supports Naval and Air Force operations throughout the Indian Ocean and as far away as Southeast Asia, Central Asia, and the Middle East.

9. Perrin Ireland, "What You Need to Know about Ocean Acidification," National Resources Defense Council, 13 August 2015, https://www.nrdc.org/stories/what-you-need-know-about-ocean-acidification?gclid=EAIaIQobChMIz-5CAyPeD6QIVENvACh1eJwJQEAAYASAAEgLk3fD_BwE.

10. "What Is Coral Bleaching?," National Oceanic and Atmospheric Administration, last updated 7 January 2020, https://oceanservice.noaa.gov/facts/coral_bleach.html.

11. The Center for Strategic and International Studies is a well-regarded national security think tank in Washington, DC, which sponsors a "Project on Nuclear Initiatives" each year. Their capstone conference for 2019 had to move out of Offutt Air Force Base due to exceptional flooding. The point is that climate change can affect any region on earth, including military bases in the center of America's heartland. More information can be found at https://www.csis.org/programs/international-security-program/project-nuclear-issues/poni-publications.

12. Dana Nuccitelli, "Millions of Times Later, 97 Percent Climate Consensus still Faces Denial," *Bulletin of the Atomic Sciences*, 15 August 2019, https://thebulletin.org/2019/08/millions-of-times-later-97-percent-climate-consensus-still-faces-denial/?utm_source=Newsletter&utm_medium=Email&utm_campaign=Newsletter08192019&utm_content=ClimateChange_ClimateConsensus_08152019.

13. Tara Copp, "Pentagon Is Still Preparing for Global Warming even though Trump Said to Stop," *Military Times*, 12 September 2017, https://www.militarytimes.com/news/your-military/2017/09/12/pentagon-is-still-preparing-for-global-warming-even-though-trump-said-to-stop/.

14. Laignee Barron, "Here's What the EPA's Website Looks Like after a Year of Climate Change Censorship," *Time* (1 March 2018), https://time.com/5075265/epa-website-climate-change-censorship/. "The NOAA Annual Greenhouse Gas Index (AGGI)" is a data-rich chart compiled annually by the US National Oceanic and Aerospace Administration (NOAA) and available at https://www.researchgate.net/profile/Russell_Schnell/publication/267783256_The_NOAA_annual_greenhouse_gas_index_AGGI/links/54d630210cf-24647580b7e2f.pdf.

15. Brad Plumer and Coral Davenport, "Science under Attack: How Trump Is Sidelining Researchers and their Work," *New York Times*, 28 December 2019, https://www.nytimes.com/2019/12/28/climate/trump-administration-war-on-science.html.

16. The most obvious rising power today is China. Harvard professor and Pentagon consultant Graham Allison has been sounding alarms for years through

his much-reviewed book, *Destined for War: Can America and China Escape Thucydides's Trap?* (New York: Houghton Mifflin, 2017). Whether Allison's theory is correct or not, there is zero doubt that China is expanding its leadership positions worldwide and its military strength rapidly while the US spends vast sums and burns up huge amounts of military equipment in wars in the Middle East that have defied resolution for many years.

17. J. A. Patz, P. R. Epstein, and J. M. Balbus, "Global Climate Change and Emerging Infectious Diseases," *Journal of the American Medical Association* 275, no. 3 (1996): 217–23, https://www.ncbi.nlm.nih.gov/pubmed/8604175.

18. Andrew Geddes and Peter Scholten, *The Politics of Migration and Immigration in Europe*, 2nd ed. (Newbury Park, CA: SAGE Publications, 2016); and Peter J. Meyer and Maureen Taft-Morales, "Central American Migration: Root Causes and U.S. Policy," Congressional Research Service Report to Congress, updated 13 June 2019, https://fas.org/sgp/crs/row/IF11151.pdf.

19. Statistics are compiled at "Syria Refugee Crisis," United Nations High Commission for Refugees, accessed 18 August 2020, https://www.unrefugees. org/emergencies/syria/.

20. Ingrid Ahlgren, Seiji Yamada, and Allen Wong, "Rising Oceans, Climate Change, Food Aid, and Human Rights in the Marshall Islands," *Health and Human Rights* 16, no. 1 (June 2014): 69–80, https://www.jstor.org/stable/pdf/ healhumarigh.16.1.69.pdf.

21. Schwartz and Randall, "An Abrupt Climate Change Scenario and its Implications for United States National Security." This report predicted things like sudden twenty-foot rises in sea level if large ice shelves in Antarctica or around Greenland collapse, or if major ocean currents change as in the extreme scenario explored there.

22. Oliver Milman, "Are Hurricanes Getting Stronger – And Is the Climate Crisis to Blame?," *The Guardian,* 20 May 2019, https://www.theguardian.com/ world/2019/may/20/are-hurricanes-getting-stronger-and-is-the-climate-crisis-to-blame?utm_term=RWRpdG9yaWFsX0d1YXJkaWFuVG9kYXllVUy0xOTA-1MjA%3D&utm_source=esp&utm_medium=Email&utm_campaign=Guardian-TodayUS&CMP=GTUS_email.

23. United Nations Development Programme, *Combating Desertification in Kenya: Emerging Lessons from Empowering Local Communities* (New York: The United Nations Development Programme, March, 2013), http://www.undp. org/content/dam/kenya/docs/energy_and_environment/Combating%20Desrtification%20in%20Kenya%20v6%20-4Sep2013.pdf.

24. Darfur is an area in western, desert Sudan that experienced the first genocide of the twenty-first century when as many as a million people were murdered, raped, or expelled from their homelands by forces aligned with Sudan's then-President Omar al-Bashir. The International Criminal Court indicted several people including Bashir for crimes against humanity and other crimes in 2009 and 2010. Rachel Blomquist and Richard Cincotta, "Myanmar's Democratic Deficit: Demography and the Rohingya Dilemma" in *New Security Beat*

(blog), Wilson Center's Environmental Change and Security Program, 12 April 2016, https://www.newsecuritybeat.org/2016/04/myanmars-democratic-deficit-demography-rohingya-dilemma/.

25. University of Cambridge, "COVID-19: Genetic Network Analysis Provides 'Snapshot' of Pandemic Origins," *Science Daily*, 9 April 2020, https://www.sciencedaily.com/releases/2020/04/200409085644.htm.

26. Andrea Thompson, "Yes, Climate Change did Influence Australia's Unprecedented Bushfires," *Scientific American* (4 March 2020), https://www.scientificamerican.com/article/yes-climate-change-did-influence-australias-unprecedented-bushfires/; and "The Connection Between Climate Change and Wildfires," Union of Concerned Scientists (blog), 11 March 2020, https://www.ucsusa.org/resources/climate-change-and-wildfires.

27. National Oceanic and Atmospheric Administration, "Ocean Acidification," updated April 2020, https://www.noaa.gov/education/resource-collections/ocean-coasts-education-resources/ocean-acidification.

28. The United Nations Demographic Division estimated that the earth's human population will reach 11 billion people by 2100, as compared with 7.8 billion today. That is a huge increase in needs for all resources, not least energy, which is why the world agreed to a "Paris Climate Agreement" in 2016. The United Nations "Intergovernmental Panel on Climate Change" (https://www.ipcc.ch/) was created to compile data on these issues in 1988. It publishes a biannual collection of research results from hundreds of studies worldwide. That work resulted in a Nobel Peace Prize in 2007 because of its implications for global security.

29. Michael M. Andregg, *On the Causes of War*, 3rd ed. (St. Paul, MN: Ground Zero Center for the Study of Intelligence and Wisdom, 2007), especially chap. 6, "Causation Is Complex: Ultimate vs. Proximate Causes, and Triggering Events," 22–25, http://hdl.handle.net/11299/209893.

30. CIA, "Syria," *World Factbook*, last updated 12 August 2020, https://www.cia.gov/library/publications/the-world-factbook/geos/sy.html.

31. The rule of thumb formula for doubling times is 70 over the growth rate in percent, so a growth rate of 2.4 percent yields 70/2.4 or a doubling time of 29.17 years. It is very difficult to double economies that fast, even when they are well managed and equitable, which most are not. An excellent reference for age distributions of populations is the CIA's *World Factbook*, https://www.cia.gov/library/publications/the-world-factbook/. The important point about "pyramidal" age distributions is that they develop momentum, so that sudden downturns in, for example, agricultural production can result in immediate social stress and sometimes armed conflict if the agricultural decline is not quickly fixed.

32. Andrea Liverani, "A Syrian Refugee at COP21," World Bank (blog), 21 October 2015, http://blogs.worldbank.org/peoplemove/syrian-refugee-cop21.

33. *Encyclopedia Britannica Online*, s.v., "Syrian Civil War," accessed 28 April 2019, https://www.britannica.com/event/Syrian-Civil-War.

34. ISIS stands for Islamic State in Iraq and Syria but is similar to nearly identical to ISIL (Islamic State in Iraq and the Levant), IS (Islamic State,

preferred by their leaders), or "daesh" (preferred by their Arab and Islamic enemies). There is a rich discussion of these labels and the permutations of "non-state actors" in articles like: https://en.wikipedia.org/wiki/Islamic_State_of_Iraq_and_the_Levant. We will simply use "ISIS" for this chapter.

35. "UNHCR Syria Regional Refugee Response/Total Persons of Concern," *United Nations High Commissioner for Refugees, 29 August 2015,* https://data2.unhcr.org/en/situations/syria.

36. CIA *World Factbook,* section on Syrian population demographics for 2014.

37. Joanne Stocker, "SDF Declares 'Total' Victory over ISIS in Syria," *The Defense Post,* 23 March 2019, https://www.thedefensepost.com/2019/03/23/sdf-victory-isis-syria/.

38. "The ISIS Caliphate has Ended, but its Breeding Ground Thrives," *CNN World Report,* 23 March 2019, https://www.cnn.com/2019/03/23/middleeast/end-of-isis-caliphate-intl/index.html.

39. Frank Gardner, "Abu Bakr al-Baghdadi: Why Is it so Difficult to Track Down IS Leader?," *BBC World News,* 1 May 2019, https://www.bbc.com/news/world-middle-east-48104463.

40. Luis Martinez, "Pentagon Report Says Al-Baghdadi Death had Little Impact on ISIS Leadership and Operations," *ABC News,* 4 February 2020, https://abcnews.go.com/Politics/pentagon-report-al-baghdadi-death-impact-isis-leadership/story?id=68755044.

41. The United Nations High Commissioner on Refugees compiles data on Syrian refugees, by country. Their total for relocated to Turkey was 3,630,767 in April 2019, https://data2.unhcr.org/en/situations/syria/location/113.

42. Kenneth Pomeranz, "The Great Himalayan Watershed: Water Shortages, Mega-Projects, and Environmental Politics in China, India, and Southeast Asia," *The Asia-Pacific Journal: Japan Focus* 7, no. 30 (27 July 2009): https://apjjf.org/-Kenneth-Pomeranz/3195/article.html.

43. Pomeranz.

44. Rachel Blomquist, "Ethno-Demographic Dynamics of the Rohingya-Buddhist Conflict" (master's thesis, Georgetown University, Washington, DC, 2016), 94–117, https://repository.library.georgetown.edu/handle/10822/1029856.

45. "Myanmar Rohingya: What You Need to Know about the Crisis," *BBC World News,* 24 April 2018, https://www.bbc.com/news/world-asia-41566561.

46. Michael T. Klare, *Resource Wars: The New Landscape of Global Conflict* (New York: Holt, 2002).

47. "Nuclear Winter" is a theoretical consequence of even a few score nuclear detonations over large cities. All those burning hydrocarbons could dim light reaching the earth's surface for years, reducing agriculture near and far away. A general nuclear war with hundreds or thousands of nuclear detonations would almost certainly devastate agriculture in at least the Northern Hemisphere.

48. Sang-Hun Choe, "In North Korea, Worst Drought in Decades Adds to Food Crisis," *New York Times*, 16 May 2019, https://www.nytimes.com/2019/05/15/world/asia/drought-north-korea-food-crisis.html?nl=todays-headlines&emc=edit_th_190516.

49. "North Korean Families Face Deep 'Hunger Crisis' after Worst Harvest in 10 Years, UN Food Assessment Shows," *UN News*, 3 May 2019, https://news.un.org/en/story/2019/05/1037831.

50. John George Stoessinger, *Why Nations Go to War, 1975–2010*, 11th ed. (Belmont, CA: Wadsworth Publishing, 2010).

51. Julian Borger, "Pakistani Generals 'Helped Sell Nuclear Secrets,'" *The Guardian*, 7 July 2011, https://www.theguardian.com/world/2011/jul/07/pakistani-generals-helped-sell-nuclear-secrets.

52. "Fourth National Climate Assessment," US Global Change Research Program, 23 November 2018, https://en.wikipedia.org/wiki/Fourth_National_Climate_Assessment.

53. Kiribati includes thirty-three low-lying atolls, three of which support people. Those islands average six feet above sea level at their highest elevation. Residents have already purchased land elsewhere, intending to move their entire 110,000 residents since they know that their own nation is doomed. Denial is not practical when waves wash away your homes.

54. Damian Carrington, "'Extraordinary Thinning' of Ice Sheets Revealed Deep inside Antarctica," *The Guardian*, 16 May 2019, https://www.theguardian.com/environment/2019/may/16/thinning-of-antarctic-ice-sheets-spreading-inland-rapidly-study?utm_term=RWRpdG9yaWFsX0d1YXJkaWFuVG9kYXlVUy0xOTA1MTY%3D&utm_source=esp&utm_medium=Email&utm_campaign=GuardianTodayUS&CMP=GTUS_email; and Ashley Curtain, "'Thinned by Extraordinary Amounts:' Glaciers in Antarctica Melting at Accelerating Rates," in *Nation of Change*, 17 May 2019, https://www.nationofchange.org/2019/05/17/thinned-by-extraordinary-amounts-glaciers-in-antarctica-melting-at-accelerating-rates/. This cites a new study published in *Geophysical Research Letter* by Andy Sheperd et al, which relied on twenty-five years of satellite data from 1992 to 2007.

55. Robert Glennon, "The Unfolding Tragedy of Climate Change in Bangladesh," *Scientific American* (blog), 21 April 2017, https://blogs.scientificamerican.com/guest-blog/the-unfolding-tragedy-of-climate-change-in-bangladesh/.

56. Andrew E. Kramer, "Russia Presents Revised Claim of Arctic Territory to the United Nations," *New York Times,* 9 February 2016, https://www.nytimes.com/2016/02/10/world/europe/russia-to-present-revised-claim-of-arctic-territory-to-the-united-nations.html.

57. "Congo's Ebola Crisis Threatens to Spiral Out of Control," *PBS News Hour*, 20 May 2019, https://www.pbs.org/newshour/show/congos-ebola-crisis-threatens-to-spiral-out-of-control.

58. "Rolling Updates on Coronavirus Disease (COVID-19)," World Health Organization, accessed 28 April 2020, https://www.who.int/emergencies/diseases/novel-coronavirus-2019/events-as-they-happen.

59. Department of Economic and Social Affairs, Population Division, *World Population Prospects – The 2015 Revision: Key Findings and Advance Tables* (New York: United Nations Demographics Division, 2015), https://population.un.org/wpp/Publications/Files/Key_Findings_WPP_2015.pdf.

60. Attia Essawi, "Sahel-Sahara: The next IS Stronghold," *Al-Ahram Weekly*, 21 May 2019, http://weekly.ahram.org.eg/News/27177.aspx.

61. "UN Report: Nature's Dangerous Decline 'Unprecedented'; Species Extinction Rates 'Accelerating,'" United Nations Sustainable Development Goals (blog), 6 May 2019, https://www.un.org/sustainabledevelopment/blog/2019/05/nature-decline-unprecedented-report/.

62. The American Security Project's "Climate Security Report" of 2017 is excellent, comprehensive, and available at https://www.americansecurityproject.org/climate-security. Its prime virtue is over fifty detailed sections on a wide variety of military relevant subtopics.

63. US Department of Defense, *Quadrennial Defense Review 2014* (Washington, DC: US Department of Defense, 2014), https://history.defense.gov/Portals/70/Documents/quadrennial/QDR2014.pdf?ver=2014-08-24-144246-293.

64. Michael E. Mann and Benedetta Brevini, "An Interview with Michael E. Mann: Fighting for Science against Climate Change Denier's Propaganda," in *Carbon Capitalism and Communication: Confronting Climate Crisis*, ed. Benedetta Brevini and Graham Murdock (New York: Palgrave Macmillan 2017), 23–30.

65. Matthew Taylor, "Revealed: Big Oil's Profits since 1990 Total nearly $2 Trillion," *The Guardian*, 12 February 2020, https://www.theguardian.com/business/2020/feb/12/revealed-big-oil-profits-since-1990-total-nearly-2tn-bp-shell-chevron-exxon?utm_term=RWRpdG9yaWFsX0d1YXJkaWFuVG9kYYXl-VUy0yMDAyMTI%3D&utm_source=esp&utm_medium=Email&utm_campaign=GuardianTodayUS&CMP=GTUS_email. Taylor cites another report that the top five firms spent approximately $200 million per year on lobbying against climate change or actions to address it.

66. Garret Hardin, "The Tragedy of the Commons," *Science* 162, no. 3859 (1968): 1243–48, doi:10.1126/science.162.3859.1243.

67. The organization of civil affairs and psychological operations units can be reviewed on the US Army Civil Affairs and Psychological Operations Command (Airborne) headquarters website, https://www.usar.army.mil/Commands/Functional/USACAPOC/USACAPOC-Units/. There are several Reserve Army civil affairs units that supplement the one remaining active-duty brigade, but overall emphasis appears to be weak.

68. Michael Bennett, *Projected Costs of US Nuclear Forces, 2019 to 2028* (report, US Congressional Budget Office, Washington, DC, January 2019), https://www.cbo.gov/system/files/2019-01/54914-NuclearForces.pdf.

69. Senior Defense Officials, "Department of Defense Background Briefing on Nuclear Deterrence and Modernization," transcript, 21 February 2020, https://www.defense.gov/Newsroom/Transcripts/Transcript/Article/2090986/department-of-defense-background-briefing-on-nuclear-deterrence-and-modernizati/.

70. George P. Schultz, William J. Perry, Henry A. Kissinger, and Sam Nunn, "A World Free of Nuclear Weapons," *Wall Street Journal*, 4 January 2007, https://www.wsj.com/articles/SB116787515251566636.

Chapter 9

Human Nature: Fundamental Misunderstandings between East and West

Chaplain (Maj.) Jonathan D. Bailey

During the 2019 US Army Command and General Staff College Ethics Symposium panel "When Things Go Wrong: Genocide, War Crimes, and Mass Atrocities," several panelists asserted that human nature is fundamentally evil at worst and ambiguous at best. None argued for a positive understanding of human nature that identified humanity at its very core as something good. For many in the West, such thoughts and feelings about the nature of humanity are commonplace. In contrast, Livia Kohn noted: "The human condition in [Chinese religion(s)] is normatively seen in an overwhelmingly affirmative mode."[1] Such sentiment echoes throughout Eastern systems of thought that hold much more positive conceptions of human nature.

Philosophical assumptions concerning human nature have profound effects on the ways individuals of one culture interpret—or misinterpret—words and actions by someone from another culture. Foundational assumptions tend to blind us to possibilities and ways of being that are foreign to us. However, we can increase our ability to understand ideas that are foreign to us and enhance our ability to imagine previously unexplored possibilities. This is not to say that such understanding will eliminate all problems; in fact, more problems are likely to arise in the near-term with greater familiarity. But seeking understanding helps guide approaches and strategies as individuals interact and partner with cultures that differ significantly from our own.

Rather than attempting to analyze the whole of Western and Eastern traditions, this chapter begins by exploring specific ideas of human nature developed by Augustine of Hippo in the Christian tradition and Mencius (Mengzi) in the Confucian tradition. Following analysis of both, the aperture expands to look more broadly at how differing Western and Eastern traditions perceive human nature, and how this contributes to frustrations within attempts to build and maintain international relations with East Asian nations. In turn, this chapter offers recommendations on how to revisit personal assumptions in light of how others understand human nature then subsequently learn to ask better questions and discern or imagine more fruitful options in the future.

Realizing that both Christianity and Confucianism traditions are historically significant with numerous variations within—and outside—broader "orthodox" forms, this chapter focuses on thoughts concerning human nature derived from Augustine's *Confessions* within the Christian tradition and the collection of writings and sayings of Mencius within the Confucian tradition. Each thinker made significant contributions to his respective tradition and continues to possess tremendous power and influence across the wider fields of Christianity and Confucianism. In a sense, they epitomize orthodoxy within their traditions, especially on the topic of human nature.

While some Christians would argue that figures like Thomas Aquinas, Martin Luther, or John Calvin hold sway over more recent Christian theories of human nature, Augustine's work was a critical resource for all of them. We have also seen a rise in Augustinian realism linked largely to the popularity and influence of twentieth century American theologian and ethicist Reinhold Niebuhr, who attracted new audiences to Augustinian thought.[2] It should also be noted that even when the Catholic Church has taken issue with Augustine, the church has maintained the essence of his overall contributions and affirmed much of his thinking concerning human nature.

Regarding Mencius, it would be difficult to find a figure more central to the doctrine of innate, unambiguous goodness in Confucianism or elsewhere. Because Confucianism is so focused on past sages and transmission of the Confucian Way, Confucian scholars typically look to those sages for ageless wisdom. While recent figures may have significant relevance in the trajectory of modern Confucianism, Mencius—second only to Confucius—guides the way Confucian scholars think about human nature.

Augustine on Human Nature

Augustine, perhaps best known for his conception of original sin, struggled throughout his *Confessions* to account for the problem of evil and its particular relevance to human beings and human action. In tracing the roots of sin back to the Fall narrative within the Hebrew Bible, Augustine established the transmission of human sin through sexual procreation. As John Toews asserted in *The Story of Original Sin*, due to the fact that sexual passions are related to the sin of concupiscence, "the act of reproduction inevitably stains every child with original sin so that everyone is literally 'born in sin,' that is, in the sin of the parents."[3] For Augustine, sin was a hereditary condition that can only be corrected through salvation, or spiritual rebirth.

Nevertheless, it would be inaccurate to say that Augustine argued that humanity, or creation after the Fall, is evil. Rather, humans are corrupted by sin and the good inherent in their nature has been distorted and broken. To this point he wrote:

> If there were no good in them, there would be nothing capable of being corrupted. Corruption does harm and unless it diminishes the good, no harm would be done. Therefore, either corruption does not harm, which cannot be the case, or (which is wholly certain) all things that are corrupted suffer privation of some good. If they were to be deprived of all good, they would not exist at all.[4]

Augustine maintained a nuanced position that espoused the goodness of creation while also affirming that human beings are fundamentally flawed by sin from birth. It is important to remember that Augustine operated within a Neoplatonic philosophical world where the concepts of substance and privation were perhaps more understandable and widespread. When Augustine referred to evil as a privation of the good, he meant that evil has no substance in and of itself. Therefore, it would be impossible within an Augustinian framework to argue that anything evil exists. As Andrew Flescher stated in *Moral Evil,* "Evil is in its essence a corruption of the initial good with which God has graced the world, and it is this corruption—a diminution of a prior good—for which we are responsible."[5]

In keeping with this example, it would be more accurate to say that the good has become hidden or distorted while still remaining present. In Augustine's description of his own descent into wickedness he wrote, "I had no motive for my wickedness except wickedness itself. . . . I loved the self-destruction, I loved my fall, not the object of my fall but my fall itself."[6] Sin so distorts the goodness in human beings, according to Augustine, that they revel in darkness, selfishness, and self-mutilation. Humans no longer relate to one another properly, but consume one another out of their lusts.[7]

However, the distortion of goodness presented by the problem of sin for Augustine is something that human beings cannot address themselves. There is no fix for sin within the human person. Augustine argued that human beings need salvation that God alone provides through the person of Jesus the Christ, the second person of the Trinity within orthodox Christian thinking. Jesus, God incarnate, assumed our fleshly state, becoming subject to the conditions of our existence, in order to overcome the problem of sin and present a sacrifice to God worthy of rectifying our corrupted state.[8] God is the only one who can restore and heal what was broken by humanity in the Fall. While this is surely an oversimplification of Augustine's Christology and soteriology (doctrine of salvation), it is sufficient to understand the utter helplessness humanity faces responding to the problem of sin.

Human beings then, while not being evil, are unable to rectify themselves in order to embody and habituate their innate, original goodness due to the transmission of sin from humanity's common ancestors. Human activity, even when attempting to do good, is misguided and thwarted by lust and pride. Cultivation, absent transformation by God, is to cultivate a corrupted nature that breeds further corruption. When humans who have not been transformed by God do good, they still fail to achieve goodness either through imperfect deeds or improper motivations. According to Augustine, to be human is to be sinful.

Mencius on Human Nature

While Augustine set the course for the orthodox Christian understanding of human nature as sinful, Mencius's idealism became the standard for orthodox Confucian understanding of human nature as good and perfectible. While one could argue that Confucius maintained a somewhat ambiguous position on whether human nature is inherently good, Mencius clearly held an idealistic view of human nature.[9] In perhaps the clearest expression of Mencius's belief that humans are innately good, he stated:

> Suppose a man were, all of a sudden, to see a young child on the verge of falling into a well. He would certainly be moved by compassion, not because he wanted to get in the good graces of the parents, nor because he wished to win the praises of his fellow villagers or friends, nor yet because he disliked the cry of the child. . . . The heart of compassion is the germ of benevolence; the heart of shame, of dutifulness; the heart of courtesy and modesty, of observance of the rites; the heart of right and wrong, of wisdom. Man has these four germs just as he has four limbs.[10]

Even though he understood that humanity's innate goodness is often clouded or marred by improper cultivation and egoism, Mencius maintained that human nature is still fundamentally good and evidenced by what P. J. Ivanhoe termed "nascent moral 'sprouts.'"[11] While his commitment to innate human goodness **may have been** novel, he affirmed with Confucius and his Confucian contemporary Hsün Tze humanity's ability to cultivate human nature to achieve the Confucian goal of sagehood.[12] Because of his belief in the innate goodness of human beings and his belief in the perfectibility of human nature it might be tempting to identify Mencius as a romantic, but as Tu Wei-Ming illustrated in his *Confucian Thought*:

> [Mencius's] theory of human nature, far from being a romantic advocacy of human perfectibility, calls our attention to our internal resources for spiritual growth. Learning to be human . . . is to refine ourselves so that we can become good, true, beautiful, great, sagely, and spiritual.[13]

Ivanhoe, similar to Tu, saw in Mencius's analysis an identification of resources whereby humanity can fully develop and cultivate those moral sprouts. He wrote:

> Though there is only one moral Way and we are endowed with the beginnings of morality, we do not come into the world as full moral agents. We grow into morality as we exercise each of the various parts according to its Heavenly ordained function. As our nature develops, if it follows the proper course of development, we realize our destiny as moral creatures. For Mengzi, this proper course of development is an essential and defining feature of human nature.[14]

Mencius stressed cultivation of one's moral character and attention or watchfulness over oneself as a means to become a sage and embody *jen*, typically translated as humanity or benevolence. Foregoing such cultivation and attentiveness, one most surely will lose oneself. In original sin, decay is part of birth; however, Mencius commented:

> With proper nourishment and care, everything grows, whereas without proper nourishment and care, everything decays. Confucius said, "Hold it fast and you preserve it. Let it go and you lose it."[15]

From this one can see how Mencius determined that while Heaven endows human nature with goodness, it does not mean that all people will be good. If Mencius had romanticized innate human goodness, he would have spent little time discussing respect, righteousness, filial piety, and humanity since there would have been no need.

Yet, in the spontaneous responses to certain ills, humanity's true nature displays itself—like the man responding to the child about to fall into a well—even when one's nature has not been cultivated properly, which is why Mencius maintained that human nature is good. Mencius went on to say, "Humanity is man. When embodied in man's conduct, it is the Way."[16]

To further clarify what Mencius meant here, when human beings cultivate their true nature to the fullest, according to *The Doctrine of the Mean*, "they can assist in the transforming and nourishing process of Heaven and Earth, they can thus form a trinity with Heaven and Earth."[17] Therefore, in keeping with Mencian idealism, the goodness of human nature and its perfectibility are essential components to develop a solid understanding of orthodox Confucianism.

Toward a Meaningful Comparison

The purpose of meaningful comparison is to cultivate an appreciation of the similarities and differences within the traditions or ideas being compared. Such a project requires a requisite sense of humility because one perspective is simply insufficient to the task; what I may see as meaningful another may see as peripheral. Such humility also acknowledges the ways our own sense of certainty can blind us to errors within our own traditions and ways that we embody those traditions. French novelist Albert Camus discussed the need to maintain humility when talking about matters pertaining to truth and ultimacy: "If absolute truth belongs to anyone in this world, it certainly does not belong to the man or party that claims to possess it."[18]

To help navigate the comparative process with such humility, Stephen Prothero's methodology of comparison in *God Is Not One* provided a simple framework for comparison. His four-step model consisted of identification of the problem to be addressed, the solution to address the problem, techniques to reach the solution, and exemplars of the tradition.[19] Prothero's model intentionally looked at differences in order to view the uniqueness of compared traditions rather than glossing over those differences in order to see or suggest a transcendent unity—that the traditions were just "different paths up the same mountain."[20] Thus, when discussing similarities, the conversation remains rooted in an awareness of the need to discern whether the similarity discussed is in fact similar.

Those trained in navigation learn early about the importance of having the map oriented correctly. Once the map is oriented, you have a clearer picture of where you are, where you are headed, and significant terrain features en route to your destination. When the map is not properly oriented, it's easy to get turned around and go a different direction. In much the same way, orthodox teachings around human nature frame how a significant number of adherents understand the human condition, relevant problems, and solutions to the problems.

As Prothero surmised, if we fail to register real differences across traditions, the problem lies not with map orientation but the map itself. It would make little sense to attempt to navigate China utilizing a map of America. While the principles of navigation are the same, a different map is needed to begin the journey. The same holds true for developing comparative strategies across diverse traditions.

Given that Christianity and Confucianism are solving different problems, the ways they think about the problem and the solutions provided are also markedly different. In a sense, these differences arise from unshared historical narratives. Augustine relied largely on Jewish and Christian texts as an authoritative—literal—account of human history beginning in a primordial paradise with Adam and Eve that is subsequently destroyed by humanity's fall into sin as recorded in the first three chapters of Genesis. Mencius, however, relied on the *Analects of Confucius* and the Five Classics for historical perspective and normative accounts of existence advocates for self-cultivation that nourishes one's moral sprouts to form a harmony with Heaven and Earth.

Those differing histories, narratives, and philosophical traditions provided fertile soil for thinking about the world and engaging the world each of them inhabited. Both Mencius and Augustine constructed beautiful, coherent thought worlds for later generations to explore, develop, and transmit to future adherents. Mencius constructed a vision of human nature that was deeply rooted in an ethico-religious naturalism shaped by Confucius and in conversation with other non-theistic traditions like Taoism and Chan Buddhism. Augustine framed his concept of original sin as a committed Christian heavily influenced by the Greco-Roman world and Pauline interpretations of Hebrew scripture. Both have been praised and castigated throughout history for various reasons, and yet each of them is largely revered within his tradition. The simple fact remains that Mencius and Augustine did not share a common historical heritage, which means that we have to find a way to engage such differences critically while seeking to identify deep, complex similarities.

Having already focused on the differences between the two regarding human nature, there are important similarities in spite of the differences. Briefly, there are three aspects where Mencius and Augustine held similar ideas; namely, the fundamental goodness of nature, the deformities associated with selfishness, and the solution to the problem of corruption as something given and not manufactured. The commonalities identified here are too discordant to be truly similar but hopefully will prove useful in enhancing conversation.

First, Mencius and Augustine shared a sense that nature is fundamentally good and made for goodness. Even though Augustine viewed this through a theistic lens and Mencius did so through a naturalistic lens, both acknowledged the continuity of goodness of nature even when it has been corrupted. They were also committed to working through how goodness was realized here amidst such corruption. Human goodness and its corruptibility are essential facets in varying degrees.

Second, their conceptions of corruption are surprisingly similar. Namely, selfishness is the central corrupting factor for each thinker. The displaced desire to achieve selfish wants deforms the human person and reorients him/her to seek pleasure at the expense of one's true self and his/her inherent goodness. Selfishness causes our moral sprouts to be cut down and brings about dismissal from paradise.

Finally, there are points of agreement even in how they formulated solutions to the problem of human corruption. While Augustine maintained that only God's grace can transform sinful people, he noted that transformation is a particular grace given to humans. Likewise, Mencius identified the moral sprouts in human nature as a gift bestowed by the Mandate of Heaven through *li* (principle). Self-cultivation is only possible because it is an endowment by Heaven. In this sense, the solution is not something that can be manufactured but is remarkable in its givenness.

Why a Discussion on Human Nature Matters

Orientation is an essential part of existence. How we orient ourselves to the world extends beyond mere physiological modes. What we focus on—and how we focus on it—profoundly affects what we see, notice, and experience the world around us.

Western traditions have significant historical connections to Augustinian conceptions on the depravity of humanity; a pessimistic realism of the human condition tends to temper even the most optimistic. While not devoid of hope, Augustine's thoughts formed a dim picture concerning the fates of many, as well as human nature and the utter inability for humans to attain the goodness for which they were made. With such a pessimistic worldview, fear and anxiety are pathological expressions of such an understanding; whereas, healthy embodiments of Augustinian realism create and participate in external structures designed to maintain/enhance peace and security for everyone.

The Confucian tradition—grounded in Mencian idealism—acknowledges that human nature is inherently good and perfectible through human effort; this can create a deep sense of hope and responsibility for the world. Healthy Confucians see education, advisory roles, and key government positions as means to cultivate creative self-transformation and the transformation of others while maintaining proper deference to one's parents, kin, leaders, and others. However, pathological Confucianism can mistake educational aptitude for cultivation and displace filial piety and proper deference with egotistical nepotism.

Revisiting the map metaphor, fundamental perspectives and assumptions tied to deeply held beliefs shaped by religious and philosophical traditions orient how human beings think about navigating life. These traditions provide a guide on how we live before that which we consider ultimate, how we deal with our existential condition, and how we achieve fulfillment in life.[21] They condition adherents to look, think, and act in certain ways and not others. They each possess strengths and weaknesses, and they each have their virtues as well as their failures.[22]

Broader Concerns for Policy

More broadly, Eastern and Western traditions are difficult to translate. One reason is what constitutes valid sources of knowledge. As Tu Wei-Ming acknowledged, "Generally speaking, East Asian thought takes empirical knowledge seriously, while focusing its attention on the supreme value of self-knowledge."[23] Preferencing subjective forms of knowledge differs greatly from the Western bias that favors empirical, objective knowledge.

Such realities make already-complex questions even more complex. Are there conceptions of God that are analogous across traditions? With regard to time, can we overlay a linear understanding of temporality onto a cyclical understanding of temporality? How do we define the self, and what is its importance? What is the nature of revelation, and how do we determine its validity over and against other revelations? How do human beings live in the world? What is the nature of harmony, and do governments have a responsibility to maintain harmony in a global society?

Some might see such questions as unnecessary and instead choose to focus on more concrete matters not so entwined with epistemological baggage. Others might appeal to divinely revealed truth in Jesus Christ, the Quran, Torah, or other examples of revealed religion to dismiss such comparative projects as an attempt to obfuscate the truth of their revelation. Some prefer isolationism and focus on internal societal issues and domestic policies. Nevertheless, these traditions—from Western atheistic Scientism to indigenous traditions across the globe—form how individuals from various societies see the world and how those individuals respond to questions like those posed above.[24]

Authentic engagement requires at least making a concerted effort to understand each other. If we fail to understand certain basic ideas in other cultures, we will never have more than superficial relationships. Beyond that, it is important to take international interests very seriously because so many citizens, schools, banks, and businesses have been and will continue to be considerably affected by what happens across the globe, especially in East Asia.

Today, China poses one of the greatest challenges to the United States of America. Regardless of the state of communism in China, the country has historically been shaped by the Confucian tradition and there has been renewed support and acceptance of the tradition within China. However, Western philosophers have largely overlooked China's philosophical history prior to 1919. As Thomas Metzger wrote:

> Many Western scholars discussing modern Chinese history and politics are not only unacquainted with but also uninterested in China's premodern intellectual history. To take seriously the tradition-rooted aspects of China's quest for modernity would be to reject the premise shared by the most able contemporary Western scholars, men like Leo Strauss, Quentin Skinner, and John Dunn, who all have taken for granted that there is no viable political philosophy outside the pale of Western thought.[25]

By focusing on the discontinuity and continuity of Confucianism throughout China's recent past, Metzger challenged Western assumptions concerning political philosophy. To improve its relationship with China, the West—America in particular—must make a deep commitment to understand Chinese history and Chinese traditions, as well as China's leap to communism rather than another form of Western government and economics. The West might also discover valid and helpful tools to enhance our own political, religious, and philosophical traditions.

This is not to say that the current Chinese government ought to be lauded; rather, by increasing our awareness of Chinese history and traditions, the West can begin to hold the Chinese government more accountable for its actions in and outside of China. To do that effectively, the West must engage our own need for transformation and continued cultivation.

160

Progress, the ability to progress, is rooted in learning. In an age where anyone can access information instantly, let's not waste this opportunity to learn and understand.

Conclusion

First, we need to cultivate awareness. Cultivating awareness takes time and reflection; much like navigation training, we also need tools and training to do it properly. We will require critical comparative courses to increase both our self-awareness and our cultural awareness so we can use that awareness for planning, engagement, and policy decisions that will achieve better outcomes.

Second, we must design programs that cultivate humility. Consistently using the same forms of knowledge, methods of testing, or cultural forms can blind us to possibilities from other cultures. Too often throughout history, human beings have fallen prey to hubris and pride. Rather than cultivating humility and a desire to learn, humans have assured themselves of their own righteousness, truth, and cultural superiority—a practice that has led to innumerable wars and tragedies all over the world since the dawn of human civilization. Humility opens us to the possibility of correction while still allowing us to engage fully, respecting our own histories, traditions, and fundamental beliefs.

Finally, we need renewed emphasis on the humanities to create the necessary breadth to understand complex systems of thought and histories. Science, technology, engineering, and mathematics (STEM) programs offer critical tools for dealing with the material world, but they do not necessarily prepare students to engage with critical issues that help human beings and the world as a whole flourish. Considering that much of the world values self-knowledge, we can discount entire systems of thought by concluding they are not sufficiently informed by "objective" sources of knowledge which would be detrimental to the learning process. Also, STEM programs teach how to measure empirical data utilizing the scientific method and provide solutions to technical problems. The humanities teach us to ask better, life-enhancing questions about the ways we conduct such tests and assess results while also helping us engage matters that lie beyond quantification.

In order to develop meaningful relationships across traditions and cultures, we must understand how foundational concepts like human nature function in traditions and within cultures that embody those traditions. By considering how different our traditions are and then investigating them, we can identify similarities carefully and present them in a nuanced way that affirms the commonalities without sublating difference. By focusing on constructions of human nature from Augustine and Mencius, this chapter has provided a concrete account of divergent opinions, demonstrated their importance within tradition, offered an example comparison, and demonstrated how we are still affected by such aspects in our traditions.

The mystics may very well be right that our various traditions really are representative of the *coincidentia oppositorum*, different sides of the same coin. As Prothero stated, "These differences may not matter to mystics or philosophers of religion, but they matter to ordinary religious people."[26] The project presented to us is how to affirm humanity in and through our differences while working hard to find similarities that connect us and avenues for communication so that we can be more tolerant, accepting, and peaceful. We also need to take stock of ways our own enculturation and foundational assumptions predispose us to see the world and others in certain ways that can be tremendously mistaken. We have to move beyond bumper sticker theology and philosophy to really achieve mutual respect and tolerance that results in a hard-earned, tenuous peace.

Notes

1. Livia Kohn, "Chinese Religion," in *The Human Condition: A Volume in the Comparative Religious Ideas Project*, ed. Robert Cummings Neville (Albany, NY: State University of New York Press, 2001), 21.

2. See Reinhold Niebuhr, *Moral Man and Immoral Society: A Study in Ethics and Politics* (Louisville, KY: Westminster John Knox Press, 2002); and *The Nature and Destiny of Man Vol 1 & 2* (Louisville, KY: Westminster John Knox Press, 1996). For more recent titles related to Christian Realism see Jodak Troy, *Religion and the Realist: From Political Theology to International Relations Theory and Back* (New York: Routledge, 2014); and Guilherme Marques Pedro, *Reinhold Niebuhr and International Relations Theory: Realism Beyond Thomas Hobbes* (New York: Routledge, 2018).

3. John E. Toews, *The Story of Original Sin* (Cambridge, UK: James Clarke & Co., 2013), 82.

4. Augustine, *Confessions*, VII, xii, trans. Henry Chadwick (New York: Oxford University Press, 1991), 124.

5. Andrew Michael Flescher, *Moral Evil* (Washington, DC: Georgetown University Press, 2013) 166.

6. Augustine, *Confessions*, II, iv, 29.

7. Augustine, III, viii, 46–48. Here Augustine describes how lusts pervert human relationality.

8. Augustine, VII, xviii-xxi, 128–32.

9. Wing-Tsit Chan, *A Source Book in Chinese Philosophy* (Princeton, NJ: Princeton University Press, 1963), 49–50.

10. *Mencius*, II, A, 6, trans. D. C. Lau (New York: Penguin Books, 2003), 39.

11. Philip J. Ivanhoe, *Ethics in the Confucian Tradition* (Indianapolis, IN: Hackett Publishing, 2002), 38.

12. The author's emphasis on "may have been novel" is because, as Lau suggests in his introduction to *Mencius*, "Confucius and Mencius repeatedly use the phrase 'delighting in the Way.' . . . This emphasizes the naturalness of morality. Delight and joy are usually experienced when a man pursues a natural activity unimpeded." *Mencius*, xxviii.

13. Tu Wei-Ming, *Confucian Thought: Selfhood as Creative Transformation* (Albany, NY: State University of New York Press, 1985), 12.

14. Ivanhoe, *Ethics in the Confucian Tradition*, 43.

15. *Mencius*, VI, A, 8, translated by Chan in *Chinese Philosophy*, 57.

16. *Mencius*, VII, B, 16, 81.

17. *The Doctrine of the Mean*, 22, translated by Chan in *A Source Book in Chinese Philosophy*, 108.

18. Albert Camus, *Resistance, Rebellion, and Death*, trans. Justin O'Brien (New York: Vintage Books, 1995), 165.

19. Stephen Prothero, *God Is Not One: The Eight Rival Religions that Run the World* (New York: HarperCollins Publishers, 2011), 13–16.

20. Prothero, 5.

21. Robert Cummings Neville, *Ultimates: Philosophical Theology*, vol. 1 (Albany, NY: State University of New York Press, 2013), Kindle, Preface. See all three volumes of *Philosophical Theology* for greater clarity of the ideas introduced here.

22. Aaron Stalnaker, "Comparative Religious Ethics and the Problem of 'Human Nature,'" *The Journal of Religious Ethics* 33, no. 2 (June 2005): 187–224. Stalnaker's piece is another example of comparative studies on the same issue while also considering Hsün Tze (Xunzi) alongside Augustine and Mencius. His piece provides additional context for Augustine's later years and, of course, a divergent lens within the Confucian tradition.

23. Wei-Ming, *Confucian Thought*, 20. See also Sarvepalli Radhakrishnan and Charles A. Moore, *Sourcebook in Indian Philosophy* (Princeton, NJ: Princeton University Press, 1957), xxiv.

24. Thomas Burnett, "What is Scientism?," American Association for the Advancement of Science, accessed 26 June 2019, https://www.aaas.org/programs/dialogue-science-ethics-and-religion/what-scientism.

25. Thomas A Metzger, *The Ivory Tower and the Marble Citadel: Essays on Political Philosophy in Our Modern Era of Interacting Cultures* (Hong Kong: Chinese University Press, 2012), 239.

26. Prothero, *God Is Not One*, 3.

Chapter 10
Culture, Religion, and Weapons of Mass Destruction[1]
Mahir J. Ibrahimov

During military operations in and among indigenous cultures, the protection of civilians should remain a higher priority, an endeavor to attain more popular support rather than repeating the mistakes of unsuccessful British, Soviet, and other experiments.

This chapter examines the methods and techniques of the Iraqi insurgency, its propaganda and influence strategy as well as historical and socio-cultural aspects that might be useful and important for military strategists, policymakers, academics, and others. There are differences between Afghan, Iraqi, and other insurgencies; however, they have one key element in common. The socio-cultural and linguistic aptitude of Iraqi insurgents, the Taliban in Afghanistan, and other insurgencies of the region is an important part of their effective influence operations among their target audiences. Analysis in the chapter is based on Western and regional sources, but primarily on the personal experiences and observations of the author.

The author shares his observations of historical and socio-cultural nuances through detailed descriptions of his time in Iraq. This author believes that while military strategists, policymakers, and regional experts need to understand other indigenous cultures, this appreciation would be very beneficial for ordinary fellow Americans as well.

The real value of this chapter is that it is written by an insider who went with the US military through all the hardships and realities of the war, especially at its most difficult and unpredictable stage when the insurgency started to take shape and develop as a well-organized and -financed movement. Secondly, the author is fluent in Arabic and Turkish—the main languages of the region—and is a qualified expert in Middle Eastern affairs; because of this background, he can base his observations and analysis on his own firsthand experiences. This author has observed firsthand through life experiences over decades about the importance of the human domain. Additionally, he lived through the difficult times of the Soviet empire as a former Soviet soldier in the 1970s, and later witnessed its demise.

As a senior diplomat, the author helped open the first Azerbaijan embassy in the United States during historic global geopolitical changes in the early 1990s and related bloody conflicts that erupted across the post-Soviet, post-Warsaw pact space. As director of the Azerbaijani Foreign Ministry press service, he found himself in the middle of Nagorno-Karabakh conflict, while accompanying Western correspondents to the war zone. His observations in Iraq—while deployed with the US Army in 2004–05 as a cultural advisor and linguist, as well as during a 2016 US Army study trip to Ukraine—contributed to his appreciation of the rapidly changing regional and global geopolitical landscape and helped him more comprehensively share his thoughts and analysis in this chapter. One important aspect which the author shares in his chapter is what he views as the real weapons of mass destruction (WMD): the misuse of religion and God as a

Figure 10.1. The author following his 1974 graduation from Soviet military school in Volgograd City. From the author's personal collection.

means to maintain control and power. The ethnic and religious conflicts in Iraq are disturbingly similar to still-unresolved conflicts the author witnessed in Russia, Azerbaijan, Ukraine, and elsewhere.

The United States never completely understood the nature of the Iraqi and other cultures—or the causes and origins of the regional conflicts. Part of the reason could be its history and geography, simply being across the ocean from European and Eurasian regions that were the main theaters of two devastating global conflicts and are undergoing the first major geopolitical change since the end of the World War Two and Cold War Era.

This chapter describes the real WMD in Iraq, the misuse of religion for political purposes and agendas—exacerbated by corruption and constant US forces missteps because troops lacked appreciation and related training for the history and culture of the region.

The Beginnings of the End

The events in Fallujah seem to have foreshadowed the story of the entire Iraqi conflict. While Fallujah residents did not necessarily welcome the invasion in March 2003, they initially were friendly to Coalition forces, which was of course a good omen. That positive attitude didn't last long. Although sporadically targeted by air, Fallujah had been spared the ground war in March 2003. In what I believe was a misguided effort to maintain the peace, approximately 850 Coalition troops entered the city on 23 April 2003, and approximately 150 of them commandeered the al-Qa'id primary school. Fallujah, known as "the city of mosques," is a religious city populated mostly by Sunnis. It is extremely conservative and has a reverence for the Islamic code of honor. The deteriorating US relationship with the residents of Fallujah was almost inevitable given the predictable clash of cultures and misunderstandings. If US soldiers were briefed regarding proper behavior and the nature of Iraqi culture, they didn't remember much of what they had been taught. Sex and family honor are intimately linked in Iraq, as in most Muslim countries. Relations between men and women are severely constricted. Women are protected while at the same time shunned and dismissed. Even suspicion of lack of propriety can endanger a woman.

For all the repression women face in Iraq, their sensibilities must be protected, and men must not parade in front of them inappropriately dressed. Muslims are quick to find insult from the treatment of their women. It is unacceptable to take pictures of women, and they are not to be spoken to without a male escort. Stories regarding rude behavior by US troops swept through Fallujah and surrounding villages. Salman Safi, my Iraqi counterpart and the man who was to become my best friend during my time there, repeated the stories to me of alleged improprieties by the soldiers toward Iraqi women: soldiers sunning themselves on rooftops without shirts in full view of the women, touching Iraqi women, searching homes while female inhabitants were still in their nightgowns. The Iraqis were further offended by the soldiers' use of night goggles and that they might be using them to spy on women. Iraqi attitudes took a sinister turn as rumors spread of troops using night vision goggles to see through clothing, that children were being detained at their schools and given bubblegum wrapped in paper that contained pornographic pictures. While I am sure some of the accounts were accurate, others obviously were fabricated. They were repeated throughout Iraq, even by local imams in their sermons; ultimately the citizens began treating the stories as unassailable facts. Resentment grew. What sometimes gets lost in all of the rhetoric is the fact that US units are populated with individuals who are barely out of their teens. They are more boys and girls, than men and women. They receive excellent combat training, but nothing can replace life experiences. It is my belief that the soldiers' youth played a significant role in the Fallujah debacle.

The residents resented the soldiers and wanted them out of the school. The US commanders agreed, making plans to vacate the school on 29 April. On the evening of 28 April, approximately 200 protestors approached the school. At this point, reports differ.[2] The protestors insist they were unarmed; soldiers at the scene were equally insistent that the protesters were armed. I am convinced that the initial violence in Fallujah could have been diffused with greater sensitivity to cultural considerations.

Figure 10.2. During a May 2016 visit to Ukraine, the author observes a captured military vehicle that the Ukrainian government views as evidence of Russia's support for pro-Russia rebels in the ongoing conflict in Eastern Ukraine. From the author's personal collection.

The young soldiers definitely heard shots, though some debate whether the shots were fired at them or in celebration some distance away.

Regardless, the soldiers reacted as scared young people would. They fired their weapons; seventeen Iraqi civilians died and more than seventy were wounded. Americans lost one of its first and most important fights for the hearts and minds of the Iraqi people. Any initial euphoria was lost one month into the battle. Violence steadily increased in the city.

Two days later on 30 April, the 82nd Airborne was replaced in the city by 2nd Troop (Fox)/US 3rd Armored Cavalry Regiment (ACR). The 3rd Cavalry was significantly smaller in number and chose not to occupy the schoolhouse where the shooting had occurred two days earlier. On the day they arrived, however, a daytime protest in front of the former Ba'ath party headquarters and mayor's office led to the death of three more protesters.

During the summer, the US Army closed its last remaining base inside the city, which was the former Ba'ath party headquarters at Forward Operating Base Laurie. At this point, the 3rd ACR had all of its forces stationed outside Fallujah in the former Baathist resort, Dreamland. Then on 11 May, the Mujahedin-e-Khalq (MEK) surrendered and the incoming 3rd Infantry Division began using the group's former compound adjacent to Dreamland to accommodate the larger US troop presence in Fallujah.

Approximately one year after the invasion, the city's Iraqi police and Iraqi Civil Defense Corps were unable to establish law and order. Insurgents launched many indiscriminate attacks, including some on police stations in the city that killed at least twenty police officers. Beginning in early March 2004, the Army's 82nd Airborne Division commanded by Maj. Gen. Charles H. Swannack Jr. transferred authority for the al-Anbar province to the I Marine Expeditionary Force commanded by Lt. Gen. James T. Conway.[3]

Figure 10.3. The author (seated) served as a cultural advisor and interpreter for several US military units in Iraq during his 2004–05 deployment. Here he prepares for the next mission with members of his civil affairs unit. From the author's personal collection.

In March 2004, American troops completely withdrew from Fallujah, citing safety concerns. As a result, the city fell under the control of Sunni insurgents led by former members of the Iraqi Army. Then on 31 March 2004, the insurgents overplayed their hand when they ambushed a convoy containing four American military contractors from Blackwater USA, a private security firm. The contractors, Scott Helvenston, Jerko

Zovko, Wesley Batalona, and Michael Teague, were killed when the militants threw grenades through the window of their car. One of the contractors was subsequently decapitated. The insurgents then dragged two of the charred corpses through the streets and hung them over a bridge that crossed the Euphrates River.

I was in Fort Benning, Georgia, at the time, preparing for my own deployment to the region. We all knew beforehand that we would be entering a war zone, but the pictures and the descriptions of increasing violence were sobering. Several people decided the situation was too dangerous and opted to cancel their plans to deploy. Watching the events on television, I noted that the Blackwater contractors swinging from ropes on the bridge were men like me. They were non-military men who had gone to support the rebuilding of Iraq. There was no sense of humanity in the pictures of the dead men or the celebrating crowds. The crowd was a mass of contorted faces, mouths open and twisted; they reminded me of Halloween jack-o-lanterns—the flickering light behind them providing no illumination or warmth.

Though I was apprehensive about the frightening scenes, I never considered quitting. I had a sense of being part of an important mission. Three weeks later our group arrived in Iraq. Those who elected to stay did so for varying reasons. One colleague decided dying in Iraq was better than dying from cancer at home; another saw glory and honor in supporting the fight for freedom. Certainly, none of us would have agreed to take on such a dangerous mission without substantial economic remuneration. Money was one of the reasons I took the job, but no amount of money is worth dying for; of course there had to be something else in it for me. I was a husband and father and had responsibilities to my family, not to mention my desire to grow old with my wife and experience the joys of raising our child and grandchildren. I am not a doctor and was not going to heal bodies, but I speak many languages. Just as musical artists and painters feel a need to express their gifts and share them, I felt a need to share mine. While always gratifying to teach language and culture, in Iraq I could use my talents to affect the quality of people's lives—to interpret between people of different cultures and help build bridges between them.

The Real Weapon of Mass Destruction

The military, UN investigators, and spy planes all missed it. There is a weapon of mass destruction in Iraq: God. I do not mean to speak blasphemy or to impugn any religious belief, but God has been used as a weapon of mass destruction ever since the human mind was able to grasp

Figure 10.4. The author with his daughter at the airport following his 2005 return from Iraq. From the author's personal collection.

the concept of His existence. The insurgents and warring tribes in Iraq are only the most recent abusers. Individual Americans are guilty as well. While sheltering in a bunker during a mortar attack, I met a soldier who insisted the only thing that would save the Iraqis was Jesus. Though words are my business, his comment left me speechless. Jesus may indeed be the savior of mankind and his return may herald peace for the world, but Iraq does not need someone else's definition of God as a solution to the bloodshed. The truth is, wars really aren't about God. God, in fact, is a symbol of love and peace. Wars are about power.

I arrived in Iraq on 21 April 2004 after a four-and-a-half-hour flight from Rhein Main Air Force Base in Germany. Also on the aircraft were three Kurdish Americans who had left Iraq to escape the horrors of the Hussein regime and were returning to help rebuild their country. As we approached Balad, the pilot announced our landing would be delayed due to a sandstorm. One of my traveling companions, a Kurdish Sunni, became visibly upset, certain there was a more sinister reason for the delay. As I tried to calm her fears, the captain again spoke to us—encouraging us to recall the procedures for a parachute evacuation of the aircraft. At that point, my colleague removed her Koran from her backpack and began praying.

In fact, the airplane's landing in Balad was uneventful; that was not true of the helicopter ride to Baghdad to complete my registration. The chopper would bank to the left or right then quickly descend or rise in altitude to avoid ground fire. When we landed at the former Saddam Hussein Zoo—now a military base—soldiers stood on each side of the helicopter, weapons at the ready. Once the pride of Baghdad and the largest zoo in the Middle East, Gulf War sanctions and subsequent looting and battles left it in ruins. Rebuilt and subsequently reopened in 2003 thanks to help from international volunteer organizations, the rejuvenated zoo was a fitting place to begin my journey. I was assigned to the Civil Affairs Unit and transported by jeep back to the Balad base. We were instructed to don civilian clothing and cover our military duffle bags with black plastic for

171

our trip to avoid the attention of insurgents who attacked traffic along the road between Baghdad and Balad.

It is a truism now that, in the end, the war in Iraq is a battle for people's minds. The Civil Affairs Unit was at the forefront of that battle. My job there was to facilitate communication so that the battle could be won. The second battle of Fallujah, dubbed Phantom Fury by the Department of Defense and later renamed Operation al-Fajr (Arabic for Dawn) by the Iraqi Defense Ministry, took place in November 2004, a little more than six months into my tour. Operation Phantom Fury was to re-take the city in advance of the January 2005 elections. Once again, the story turned upon the struggle for power. Between Iraqis, the struggle was about who had power over land and oil, how relationships were defined and regulated between men and women, and who gets to write the history books and who has the right to dictate societal mores and religion. No one ever seriously argued that the United States was engaging in a religious war in Iraq, but the issue of whether the United States was seeking power remained unresolved. The United States government acknowledged one of the initial justifications for the invasion was regime change.[4] Once that was accomplished, there was also little dispute that the United States needed to help Iraq transition to a functioning civil and economic entity.

Figure 10.5. The author (second from right) with local Iraqis during a mission to the village. From the author's personal collection.

172

The Battle for Minds and Hearts

The insurgents—often using God, religious imagery, and even religious artifacts as their shield—claimed a holy right to push Coalition forces out of Iraq. The United States asserted its right to remain in Iraq until a stable democratic government was in place and claimed to be fighting for the liberation of Iraq's people first from the tyranny of the Saddam Hussein regime and then from the tyranny of the insurgents.[5] The stated motives were pure, but there is little logic in the concept that you can liberate a people by destroying their lives. Operation Phantom Fury was the largest combat mission since May 2003. The battle also marked a turning point in the perception of the ongoing conflict. Initially only Hussein loyalists opposed the Coalition occupation; now new and growing groups of insurgents with differing agendas sought to remove all foreign military forces.[6] Tensions were high on the US Balad Air Base in the weeks leading up to the operation. Not one of the Iraqis I spoke to believed military action in Fallujah would solve any problems. Almost immediately after the assault began, mortar attacks on the base—already a common occurrence—increased. In fact, some affectionately called the base "Mortaritasville." The whole tenor of the camp changed. We all listened and watched for the arrival of military medical helicopters, which had also increased dramatically. One soldier huddled in a hardened bunker during an attack simply said, "Why did we have to make it worse?"

Conversations among friends became more intimate. During one extended period in a bunker, the discussion turned to what was the most important thing in our lives. I participated, but mostly I listened and interpreted. I listened to the tone of my friends' voices, to whispers and short choked sounds. Between words you find meaning. Strange friendships grew strong during those attacks, the loquacious became quiet, and others bore the pressure as if it were a typical day. Hunkered in the bunker, it was hard not to visit death, or to at least make its acquaintance; although conversations rarely mentioned death's presence, it was there between the words.

After Operation Phantom Fury, the atmosphere of the entire base became less hopeful. Among coworkers, the generally accepted opinion was that the battle helped insurgents recruit new members. When Colin Powell resigned as secretary of state, the talk in the bunkers was that there was no longer an impediment to US government hardliners and that battles like Fallujah would become the rule rather than the exception. Terror became a business enterprise, with Iraqi entrepreneurs trafficking in stolen weapons and contraband; kidnapping became very profitable.

Many kidnappings were simple commercial transactions: I take your loved one, throw in a little torture to make it look real, and you pay for his return; we are all satisfied. US contractors were particularly profitable victims. Firas, a Shi'ite interpreter, went missing from work for a couple of days, then returned having had $10,000 removed from his savings. Criminals and those seeking political power effectively used fear of American culture as a recruiting tool, swelling their ranks. Better to die the death of a martyr and find paradise than watch as your women walk uncovered, talk to men without the protection of a chaperone, or lose their virginity by choice rather than through the sacred rite of marriage.

Suspicion and distrust shadowed the terror. On one occasion, Americans distanced themselves from local contractors, citing safety concerns. Arabic signs appeared on the base warning Muslims not to enter the dining facility—part of an ill-conceived plan by an ignorant KBR employee. The offered explanation: it was Ramadan, a time of fasting for Muslims. Clearly, it was a poorly concealed ruse. Like Christians and Jews, some Muslims actively practice the faith and others do not. The contractors were working for the Coalition. If they wanted to eat during Ramadan, it was no one's business but their own. True, violence increased during the holy month, but segregation failed as a social policy in the United States, and it was equally destructive in Iraq. It sometimes seemed like the United States was exporting its entire history as a democratic experiment to Iraq, complete with racism and bureaucratic inertia. The Iraqis also carried with them the baggage of history. Because of Baathist propaganda and years of repression and international isolation, many Iraqis were poorly educated and suspicious of foreign influences. Some fervently believed the September 11 attacks were masterminded by Washington, DC, and Israel. Their minds were locked; no amount of evidence could dissuade them. I remain convinced that given a chance, the Civil Affairs Unit could help diffuse the weapon of mass destruction that is the grab for power; and, once Iraq's economy was stable and its infrastructure secure so that the government could supply its population with basic needs, there would be peace. To that end, I spent time with the military on missions to train Iraqis to operate and maintain Coalition-built facilities.

In mid-September 2004, for example, two US officers spent the better part of a day explaining a fuel distribution system to an Iraqi National Guard colonel and major. The system built by the Americans was quite complicated and differed greatly from the former Iraqi system. The Americans also wanted to help their Iraqi counterparts understand the system's vulnerabilities so that they could protect stockpiled fuel deposits—often the target of mortar attacks. The process of educating the Iraqi military was an interesting illustration of the difficulties facing the culture. Iraqi men clearly wanted to learn the intricacies of the system, but their loyalties were never clear. Although they appeared loyal to the new Iraqi Army, they had been similarly loyal to the army under Saddam Hussein. The colonel was a Shi'ite and the major a Sunni, and the two of them seemed to compete for the Americans' attention, each trying to demonstrate his intelligence and bravery.

Because I was the only interpreter in the area who spoke fluent Arabic, English, and Turkish, I became indispensable to the transportation unit, which directed convoys of materials throughout Iraq. I frequently assisted in security screenings of independent transportation contractors. I was proud to undertake the job but also felt an especially heavy responsibility. Few of the local and third country nationals spoke English; those who did, did not speak fluently. I was required to translate and verify their personal information in Arabic and Turkish and convey it to relevant US service members. Aware of horror stories about security breaches that resulted in the deaths of US military and contractors, I made every effort to ensure that the men I interviewed were honest applicants. Several times I alerted military personnel about suspicions and, to my knowledge, was able to prevent those men from being hired.

Figure 10.6. The author (second from left) with a medical unit during a mission to an Iraqi village. From the author's personal collection.

175

The military was acutely aware of the constant danger for transportation contractors, who were obvious and all-too-easy targets. I spent many hours at military convoy staging areas talking with contractors and filing reports and complaints regarding their situation. Some, unfortunately, succumbed to the lure of drugs to numb the fear. Several times I translated for a contractor who was obviously under the influence of a controlled substance and arranged for his transportation to the appropriate authorities. Members of different ethnic groups, though all employed by Coalition forces, were suspicious and distrustful of each other. I remember one instance in the convoy staging area. A tall Saudi Arabian contractor who wore a *dishdaasha* (the white loose and flowing garb of his country) and red and white *shumaagh* (headscarf) with a squared pattern on the fabric held in place with an *'iqaal* or *ra'as*, a thick black cord began yelling obscenities, itself an odd event, and tore at his clothes, kicking the dirt. An Iraqi contractor walked past, creating space and looking down to avoid the Saudi's eyes. The Saudi ran in front of the Iraqi man and faced him, nose to nose, continuing to swear. A second Iraqi pulled the Saudi away and wrestled him to the ground, choking him. When a military policeman arrived and tried to pull the men apart, I stepped in to help translate between the American and the feuding foreign nationals—without further inflaming passions. The hatred between the two men, who knew little of one another, was palpable. Without intervention, they might have fought to the death over nothing. There did not seem to be a specific reason for the fight other than the hardships of the war; ethnic and religious tensions were adding to the animosity between different foreign nationals.

The challenges were varied. Otherwise-healthy contractors who survived insurgent attacks often sought compensation from the various foreign national companies for which they worked. Much of my time was spent helping men write and file the massive amounts of required paperwork—in multiple languages—for the various countries and relevant Coalition forces units. Some of the stories were heartbreaking. One father whose son lost his legs to an improvised explosive device (IED), came at the behest of his son's Turkish employer to seek money from Coalition forces for the truck; in the unlikely event the truck was still on the bridge near the city of Samarra, it was too dangerous for Coalition troops to risk recovery.

Another time an elderly man, or perhaps just a prematurely aged man, came into my office; his hands were shaking, and he had trouble meeting my gaze. His was the only truck of four able to make it to the base following an insurgent attack two months before. Two of his companions had been stabbed and killed during the attack. He sought recovery of the remaining truck so he could take it back to Turkey, a trip he looked too feeble and frightened to make. Still another man needed to complete paperwork confirming that his truck was attacked, leaving his partner dead. Without properly completed paperwork, he would not receive compensation from the Turkish company for his work or injuries.

Figure 10.7. The author during preparations for a mission with a US military intelligence unit. From the author's personal collection.

Independent, non-military commercial contractors have long been part of the landscape of military operations. But the conflict in Iraq represented a paradigm shift given the voluntary nature of the armed forces and the heavy reliance on contractors. According to Peter W. Singer, author of *Corporate Warriors: The Rise of the Privatized Military Industry*, at the end of the Gulf War there was about one contractor to every 100 soldiers; by 2003 the ratio increased to one contractor to every ten soldiers.[7] The non-military transportation contractors were generally from Iraq, Saudi Arabia, Pakistan, and Turkey. Difficulty communicating among and between them was only part of the challenge. Culturally and ethnically, they were different. My studies in Middle Eastern politics and culture were invaluable for interpreting and resolving confusion and disputes between the men. I served not only as an interpreter but also as a referee. When a Kurdish contractor's truck broke down near Balad, for example, I explained in English to the commander that the man needed a ride on another convoy headed to Turkey, where the company he worked for was located. Then I relayed the commander's response to the Kurd in Arabic and arranged for the transport in Turkish.

My translation skills sometimes were required because many foreign national contractors became horribly ill; the health care they received in their country of origin was not up to the standard of American care. One Turkish contractor entered the base during the second Fallujah offensive. He was pale and disheveled, his clothes filthy and walk unsteady. Though the man's speech was slurred, I was finally able to learn he had been sitting in his truck without moving for three days, afraid to leave because of the fighting. The situation escalated as the man ran toward a medic then others, ripping his shirt open to reveal a wet, red rash. A Coalition soldier aimed his weapon at the man as I yelled for both of them to calm down—first in English, then in Turkish, and finally in Arabic. After a medic examined the man and determined his rash was probably an allergic reaction to an insect bite, we "quarantined" the man at an outdoor station and I arranged for some Turkish contractors to transport him back home.

Americans, true to their values and culture, treated the injuries of all who were wounded. I spent innumerable hours in military hospitals assisting medical personnel. Often Americans, Iraqi military, and insurgents would be recovering in the same room—not always a comfortable situation. Salman Safi, who was a local Iraqi Sunni from Taji and contracted as an interpreter by the US Army, was always in awe of the American ethic; he once remarked, "Life is so precious to Americans. Iraqis would let an enemy die, but Americans work to save them." That difference made me proud to be an American.

One evening I helped communicate with a Turkish contractor who had been wounded by an IED on his way to Anaconda Base. The hospital at that time was no more than a tent. As I entered, I saw only one US soldier; most of the wounded were Iraqis and Turkish contractors—some slightly wounded, others more severely. The nurse explained to me that some were Iraqi National Guardsmen and police. In the same room were insurgents receiving medical treatment for injuries suffered while fighting Coalition forces. One of the insurgents, both legs bandaged above the knees, was sleeping. The nurse explained that the man lost his legs because the IED he was setting up on the road exploded prematurely. According to the nurse, once he was strong enough, the man would be interrogated and subsequently jailed. Participants in the war theater have always invented nicknames for their enemies; in this war, insurgents were often called *hajji*. For Muslims, the term describes a person who has made the *hajj*, the pilgrimage to Mecca. For soldiers, the word was derogatory, similar to the word gook during the Vietnam War. It is a way of demystifying and dehumanizing the enemy and perhaps diminishing some of the terror. The handsome young soldier guarding the quiet insurgent said: "Those *hajjis* are all cowards. An IED is a coward's weapon. I don't see why we don't just let them all die." I don't blame him. I knew many soldiers who had lost friends; I assumed he had too. I don't know how I would feel in his place.

Conclusion

Despite previous painful British, Soviet, and other experiences, this author is not surprised by the amount of time it took for the United States to create and refine its cultural and language training. I was the first US Army culture and foreign language advisor hired as a result of US campaigns in Afghanistan and Iraq, so I witnessed the progression first-hand. Cultural and language training once again is becoming a lesser priority with the new Large-Scale Combat Operations (LSCO) concept. According to a Russian proverb: "You do not learn from others' mistakes but you only really learn from your own mistakes." While learning from our own mistakes is definitely desirable, both history and the present show that we fail to learn and continue making the same mistakes over and over again.

Figure 10.8. In appreciation for his service in Iraq, the author (left) received this signed photo from US Senator James Inhofe, chairman of the Senate Armed Services Committee, with the message "You're a great American, Mahir." From the author's personal collection.

Notes

1. The stories and examples are based on the author's personal experiences during his 2004–05 Iraq deployment.

2. Peter Bouckaert and Fred Abrahams, "Violent response: The U.S. Army in Al Falluja," Human Rights Watch, June 2003, https://www.hrw.org/reports/2003/iraqfalluja/.

3. "The Iraq War: Fallujah Before and After," World Press, accessed 8 May 2020, https://articlesfactsstats.wordpress.com/the-iraq-war-fallujah-before-and-after/.

4. Esther Pan, "Iraq: Justifying the War," Council on Foreign Relations, 2 February 2005, https://www.cfr.org/backgrounder/iraq-justifying-war.

5. Austin J. Luckenbach, "Iraq and Afghanistan: Similar, Yet Different," *Small Wars Journal* (30 August 2015), https://smallwarsjournal.com/jrnl/art/iraq-and-afghanistan-similar-yet-different.

6. Ahmed S. Hashim, *Insurgency and Counter-Insurgency in Iraq* (Ithaca, NY: Cornell University Press, 2006).

7. Peter W. Singer, *Corporate Warriors: The Rise of the Privatized Military Industry* (Ithaca, NY: Cornell University Press, 2003).

Chapter 11
Iranian and Turkish Power Projection and Influence in Africa
Michael Rubin

A scramble for Africa is underway. While global and regional powers like China, India, and to some extent the European Union and Great Britain have competed economically across the continent in the twenty-first century, Iran and Turkey saw Africa as fertile ground to exploit for their own ideological and national interests. Nevzat Çiçek, a Turkish journalist close to the Erdoğan government, was blunt: "Although for Turkish society, Africa may seem irrelevant at first glance, the continent is actually the biggest area of struggle in the U.S. and China rivalry. . . . Turkey aims to find a place for itself in this power struggle."[1] In many ways, Turkey's outreach into Africa has been even more calculated and effective than that of the United States.

While Iran has been largely hostile to the United States and, more broadly, the West since its 1979 Islamic Revolution, Turkey has traditionally associated with the West. Mustafa Kemal Atatürk consciously sought to reorient Turkey, going so far as to change Turkey's alphabet and mandate Western dress. Turkey joined the North-Atlantic Treaty Organization (NATO) in 1952 and aspired to join the European Union and solidify its own democracy. While Turkish diplomats still paid lip service to European Union accession and democracy, President Recep Tayyip Erdoğan consolidated control, promoting Islamism and rule without democratic constraints.

The degree of Turkey's anti-Western and Islamist turn has been apparent in the scramble for Africa. Today both Tehran and Ankara have largely pursued the same objectives: acquiring diplomatic support to oppose the West in multilateral organizations, gaining logistical hubs to service or base militaries, securing uranium supplies to fuel nuclear ambitions, and, increasingly, proselytizing as they seek to export their own religious worldviews. They do so with the overarching goal to undermine US and more broadly Western influence within Africa.

Iran's Quid Pro Quo

The 2002 exposure of Iran's covert nuclear program put immense diplomatic pressure on Iran. In 2005, the International Atomic Energy Agency (IAEA) referred Iran's non-compliance with its Nuclear Non-Proliferation Treaty Safeguards Agreement to the United Nations (UN). The UN Security Council subsequently passed a series of sanctions to coerce

Tehran back into compliance.[2] In 2015, after several years of negotiation, Iran agreed to the Joint Comprehensive Plan of Action (JCPOA), the nuclear deal that lifted some but not all sanctions on Iran and empowered the IAEA to resume inspections to confirm Iranian compliance.

The fundamental goal of Iranian diplomacy has been to win favor among the Security Council and IAEA's board of governors—to combat the two entities' outsized roles in sanctioning and policing Iran. Iran has, therefore, sold discounted oil to larger powers. With regard to Africa, however, Iran showered non-permanent members of both bodies with aid in an apparent attempt to establish a quid pro quo for their votes on these bodies.

As successive US administrations have largely ignored Africa, at least in comparison to China and India, the Iranian leadership saw many of Africa's fifty-four countries as diplomatic easy pickings. Discounting the Arab states of North Africa, American presidents made a total of six visits to Africa between 2001 and 2019.[3] Beginning in 2004—as international criticism of Iran's nuclear program crescendoed—first Iranian President Mohammad Khatami and then his successor, Mahmoud Ahmadinejad, began frequently visiting the continent. In October 2004, for example, Khatami visited Sudan.[4] Just three months later, he toured seven African countries.[5] Ahmadinejad visited Africa annually, and often more. Other Iranian ministers visited Africa even more frequently than the two presidents.[6] Soon a procession of African leaders reciprocated with visits to Tehran, although presidential visits to Africa dwindled as negotiations for a nuclear deal with the West progressed.

There is a direct correlation between countries visited and their diplomatic memberships on international bodies. Both the UN Security Council and IAEA normally have African representation. The Security Council, for example, sets aside five non-permanent seats for African and Asian members and so the Council often boasts two or three African states at any given time. From 2010 to 2020, Angola, Chad, Côte d'Ivoire, Egypt, Equatorial Guinea, Ethiopia, Gabon, Morocco, Niger, Nigeria, Rwanda, South Africa, Togo, and Uganda were members, some multiple times. Over the same period, Algeria, Côte d'Ivoire, Egypt. Ghana, Kenya, Morocco, Niger, Nigeria, South Africa, Sudan, and Tanzania also served various terms on the IAEA Board of Governors

The Iranian strategy has paid dividends.[7] While South Africa supported some UN sanctions on Iran, it often diluted them or created loopholes.[8] Despite a February 2008 IAEA report that found that Iran continued to enrich uranium in violation of its Safeguards Agreement and two Security

Council resolutions, the South African government used its position on the Security Council to oppose further sanctions.[9] South Africa subsequently obstructed an IAEA resolution criticizing Iran's failure to comply with Security Council resolutions.[10]

Iran has rewarded South Africa for its defiance. In 2010, Iranian crude provided 25 percent of South Africa's oil, much of it at discounted prices.[11] In October 2017, Iran's ambassador to South Africa predicted bilateral trade could reach $2 billion by 2020.[12] Even though South Africa abided by sanctions on the Iranian oil industry when passed shortly before negotiations began for the JCPOA, South African authorities helped the Islamic Republic in other ways; for example, the US Treasury Department accused South African cell phone company MTN of helping Iran skirt prohibitions on imports of US technology.[13]

Senegal, the target of an intense Iranian courtship in the early 2000s, also demonstrated Iran's quid pro quo on nuclear diplomacy. Shortly after Samuel Sarr, Senegal's energy minister, returned from Tehran with a pledge that Iran would supply Senegal with oil for a year and purchase a 34-percent stake in Senegal's oil refinery, Senegalese President Abdoulaye Wade endorsed Iran's nuclear program.[14] Wade's visit to Iran the following year provided a backdrop for Supreme Leader Ali Khamenei to declare that developing unity between Islamic countries like Senegal and Iran could weaken "the great powers" like the United States.[15]

Togo is another case in point. After the tiny West African country announced its intention to seek a UN Security Council seat, then-President Ahmadinejad met Togolese Foreign Minister Elliott Ohin. Ahmadinejad declared, "An extensive and profound cooperation between Iran and Africa will go a long way to modify international relations and regional balance."[16] Iranian Foreign Minister Manuchehr Mottaki reciprocated the visit the following month.[17] Fourteen months later, in January 2012, Mottaki's successor met Ohin at the eighteenth African Union summit and promised that Iran would help develop Togo.[18] The Togolese government was openly cynical: after successive visits by both US Secretary of State Hillary Clinton and her Iranian counterpart, the Togolese opposition was quite open about the gains their country stood to gain by pitting Washington and Tehran against each other.[19]

The same pattern held true with Gabon. Shortly before Gabon ascended to the Security Council, it became the subject of intense Iranian courtship. In May 2009, the Gabonese culture minister visited Tehran carrying a veritable wish-list of projects for Iran to subsidize or provide.[20] Later that month, Gabonese Foreign Minister Paul Toungui visited Tehran, where he signed a host of agreements to expand and facilitate business.[21] Early the next year, Gabonese President Ali Ben Bongo Ondimba met Mottaki on the sidelines of the African Union conference. Mottaki reiterated Iran's desire to expand political and economic ties with Gabon.[22] Two months later, Gabon used its seat to support Iran's nuclear program.[23]

In the years prior to the JCPOA, when diplomatic tension over Iran's nuclear program was at a high point, Nigeria's role in both the Security Council and the IAEA made it a target of sustained Iranian outreach. Unlike many recipients of Iranian largesse, Nigeria was not oil poor, but its dysfunctional economy left many Nigerians impoverished, and so the Nigerian government welcomed any foreign investment to create jobs. Iran obliged, offering to manufacture Iranian automobiles in Nigeria, providing poorer Nigerians with assembly line jobs and perhaps giving Iranian agents cover to operate in the region given the stranglehold the Khatam al-Anbiya Construction Headquarters held over Iranian manufacturing.[24] Iranian engineers also helped Nigeria bolster its own oil production, lending Iranian engineering expertise to Nigerian efforts to explore offshore gas fields.[25]

With the 2018 election of Niger to a two-year IAEA Board of Governors term, Iranian attention shifted to the landlocked Saharan country. Shortly before the 2017 election—the outcome of which is usually predetermined among African countries—Iranian Foreign Minister Mohammad Javad Zarif traveled to Niamey to launch a bilateral business forum.[26] The Export Development Bank of Iran entered a partnership with Niger and South Africa—also on the Board of Governors—to facilitate aid.[27] Several months later, President Hassan Rouhani reiterated Iran's goal to bolster its relations with Niger.[28]

Turkey's Quid Pro Quo

While the Islamic Republic was adept at leveraging soft power, Turkey was even more so, bringing far more than money to the table in Africa than Iran. This trend will likely continue through the rest of the twenty-first century, as African states increasingly develop their own energy resources and become less dependent on discounted oil from Iran. In 2008, the African Union declared Turkey a strategic partner, and Turkey held its first Turkey-Africa Cooperation Summit in Istanbul, with representatives from forty-nine African states in attendance.[29] For Ankara, the partnership was not a one-off event, but rather the beginning of a series of Turkey-Africa partnership events.[30] By 2018, Erdoğan became the most frequent non-African leader to visit the continent.

Turkey initially embarked on a two-pronged strategy toward Africa, seeking influence through investment and aid. As the United States and European Union largely neglected investment in sub-Saharan Africa, Turkey sought to fill the gap. Between 2008 and 2020, for example, Turkey almost quintupled its permanent diplomatic missions in Africa to forty-nine.[31] In his first five years as president, Erdoğan visited twenty-five African states and hosted even more African heads of state in Turkey. Turkey also inaugurated regular Turkey-Africa summits to keep diplomatic momentum going.[32] The Malabo summit coincided with Equatorial Guinea's 2018 election to the UN Security Council. Turkey appeared most focused on Ethiopia, Chad, Sudan, Somalia, and South Africa, but its Africa outreach went far wider.

Between 2003 and 2017, Turkish trade with Africa tripled to more than $18 billion.[33] By 2015, Turkish investment in Ethiopia alone was $3 billion.[34] Foreign Economic Relations Board Vice Chairman Ayhan Zeytinoğlu explained: "We do not see Africa as a conflict zone but as an area to which humanity owes a great debt."[35] It was not uncommon for Erdoğan to travel with 100 businessmen in tow. The strategy was a success. The Turkish Petroleum Corporation won contacts in Somalia and Sudan, and Yapı Merkezi won a $1.9 billion railway contract in Tanzania.[36]

State-owned Turkish Airlines leapt over competitors to become a dominant airline for Africa, making Istanbul an indispensable hub for African business.[37] In contrast, Iran Air flew briefly to Kenya and Uganda, although it eventually terminated those routes amid sanctions and commercial realities.

In 2014, Davutoğlu and his Ethiopian counterpart Tedros Adhanom helped inaugurate a new regional office for Turkey's state news agency, *Anadolu Agency*.[38] The rapid growth of Turkey's international broadcasts came against the backdrop of severe budget cuts and bureau closings for Islamic Republic of Iran Broadcasting which, even at its peak, largely bypassed Africa.[39]

Turkey's ideological imperatives were subtle but generally revolved around a desire to promote Turkey at the expense of the West and Turkey's vision of Islam. Turkish writing about Africa often contrasted the image of a generous, benevolent Turkey with the damage wrought by centuries of exploitive Western policies and colonialism. For example, the *Daily Sabah*, a Turkish newspaper that has promoted Erdoğan's lines, wrote:

The 16th century was the first time Turks entered Somali territory, when local governors asked Sultan Süleyman the Magnificent to rescue Mogadishu from the Portuguese navy. . . . After three centuries, the Ottomans were in Somalia again to help the local people who were resisting a British invasion and suffering from a humanitarian crisis. . . . Turks again went to Somalia . . . when the Somali government made an international call for help.[40]

Erdoğan himself wrote in its pages, "Turkey, unlike other colonial powers, has a history in Africa with no dark chapters," a claim which the Ottoman-colonized peoples of North Africa and those seized by Ottoman slave traders from the Great Lakes region of Africa might dispute.[41] İlnur Çevik, a favored journalist writing for one of Turkey's main state-controlled assets, elaborated: "The Africans see clearly that the Turks are here as partners, as brothers and sisters, and not as the people who came from the West to exploit their rich resources and oppress them."[42] Çevik also argued that Turkey was a symbol for all who sought to shed the yoke of imperialism: "Mustafa Kemal Atatürk's liberation movement in Anatolia in the twentieth century was the source of inspiration for Africans against the colonialists and oppressors."[43] Historically, the notion that Atatürk inspired Africa was nonsense.

For Turkey's influence operations, allegations of Western exploitation were not limited to the past. They also suggested the rest of the world ignored Somalia's call or, even worse, stole from Somalia. Against the backdrop of the Somali prime minister's visit to Ankara, for example, the state-controlled press suggested that the UN stole or squandered $55 billion that had been donated for Somalia's reconstruction.[44] Cemalettin Kani Torun, a parliamentarian representing Turkey's ruling Justice and Development Party (AKP), argued that while all Turkish aid went to Africa, the UN siphoned off more than 80 percent of donations for its own bureaucracy.[45] Regardless of the grievance, both Erdoğan and the state press depicted Africa as the victim and Turkey as the altruistic savior seeking only to "heal the wounds" caused by Christian powers and the United States, which they maintained had sought to exploit Africa.[46]

Erdoğan used Islam as cement for relations. One court journalist accompanying Erdoğan on a visit to West Africa explained:

The Muslims of Africa see us as the bastion of the Islamic faith and have high expectations of Turkey. We cannot let them down. We have to help them develop their system of educating Muslim clergy who will not only serve the people but also teach the people the true Islam in its purest form.[47]

Turkey, which bragged about being the third-largest donor nation after the United States and Great Britain, prioritized Islamist causes in Africa and elsewhere.[48] When violence erupted in the Central African Republic after Muslim rebels seized power in the majority-Christian country, Turkey offered troops to any European Union humanitarian mission, but only after Turkey coordinated its policies with the Organization of Islamic Cooperation.[49]

Erdoğan's ideological prerogatives were also revealed by his outreach to Sudan when then-leader Omar al-Bashir faced an International Criminal Court war crimes indictment for genocide against the people of Darfur. "A Muslim can never commit genocide," Erdoğan declared, waving off the legitimacy of the warrant facing Bashir.[50] He also absolved Bashir for murders conducted in the name of Islam, noting that Islam strictly forbade "tribalism and nationalism" such as allegedly occurred in Darfur.[51] When the Turkish deputy prime minister arrived in Darfur's Sudan region to inaugurate a hospital, he explained the project symbolized Turkey's desire "to open up to all Arab countries."[52]

The relationship between Erdoğan and Bashir continued, perhaps because Erdoğan was one of few rulers willing to reach out to a leader much of the rest of the world viewed as a pariah. In 2017, Erdoğan visited Bashir in Khartoum and signed twenty-two cooperation agreements, representing a twenty-fold increase in their $500 million bilateral trade volume.[53] The meeting was not merely symbolic. Subsequently, Turkish newspapers periodically reported the opening of projects initiated during the summit.[54]

Islam-oriented outreach also saw Turkey cultivate Chad.[55] Ankara's interest in the country might have been cynical; however, as with Iran, Turkey disproportionately directed its attention to UN Security Council non-permanent members like Chad. When supplying aid to refugees in Chad, Turkish authorities bypassed the Red Cross. Ahmet Kavaş, Turkey's ambassador to Chad, who famously praised al-Qaeda and suggested European peacekeepers were the real terrorists, led a Turkish delegation which included the Humanitarian Relief Foundation (İnsan *Hak ve Hürriyetleri ve* İnsani *Yardım Vakfı*, İHH) to distribute aid to displaced Muslims.[56] Although İHH had long cooperated with al-Qaeda and other radical groups, Mehmet Güllüoğlu, the director-general of the Turkish Red Crescent, acknowledged partnering with İHH.[57] İHH's activities in Africa and internationally increased rapidly under Erdoğan; by 2015, the group boasted 10,000 volunteers available for international missions, mostly in Africa.[58] The group's goal was as much proselytization as aid. While both Turkish and other press sometimes labelled İHH as a charity, the group often subordinated efforts to alleviate poverty and food shortages with more religious goals. *Daily Sabah*, for example, wrote that İHH activities in Somalia helped children "feel the brotherly ties between Muslims."[59] The group also distributed 20,000 Qurans to students in sub-Saharan Africa.[60] Many other Turkish aid delegations targeted Muslims, even sponsoring Eid al-Adha animal sacrifices in refugee and displaced person camps. Musa Ahmet Kaya, a representative for the Cansuyu relief association, bragged they were the first relief body to carry out an Eid al-Adha sacrifice.[61] The İHH subsequently bragged they distributed Eid meat to three million Muslims in 103 countries.[62]

Erdoğan's desire to promote a more orthodox strain of Islam led Turkey to work with other more radical groups around Africa. Turkish organizations, for example, distributed aid in northern Nigeria, where Boko Haram launched a debilitating insurgency and terrorist campaign.[63] At the same time, however, Turkey appeared to covertly distribute arms to the Islamist radicals.[64] Al-Shabab, a Somali militant group affiliated with al-Qaeda, likewise reportedly benefited from covert Turkish largesse.[65]

Somalia became perhaps the greatest focus of Turkish generosity. Turkey opened its largest African embassy in Mogadishu. During Somalia's 2011 famine, Turkey provided emergency relief. Turkey also built schools, hospitals in Somalia, and took over the main international airport in Mogadishu. Between 2011 and 2018, Turkey provided more than $500 million in aid to Somalia.[66] Across Africa, Turkish officials often exaggerated the aid provided; Deputy Prime Minister Mehmet Şimşek, for example, said Turkey provided Somalia almost $1 billion over the same period.[67] Such exaggeration paid dividends as African publics often believed the claims. In January 2019, Somali Security Minister Abukar Hassan Islow told his Turkish counterpart: "We have had a difficult time and our friends didn't let us down. It's impossible for us to forget that, and it is Allah who will reward all the good we have received."[68]

Many Turkish projects that appeared charitable at first glance were quid pro quo. As Erdoğan demanded a permanent seat for Turkey in an expanded UN Security Council, for example, Turkish Foreign Minister Mevlüt Çavuşoğlu pushed Turkey's vision of UN reform to African recipients of Turkish largesse.[69]

After the 2013 break between Erdoğan and his one-time ally theologian Fethullah Gülen, the Turkish government leveraged its largesse and influence in Africa to force African countries to close Gülen-affiliated schools and expel his followers. The *Daily Sabah* explained, "Erdoğan seeks to maximize the effectiveness of Turkey's soft power instruments such as humanitarian and development aid programs and educational institutions within the broader framework of Ankara's fight against the Gülenist Terror Group."[70] Erdoğan was open about this agenda. In June 2016, the parliament created the Maarif Foundation, a pro-AKP organization coordinated by the Education and Foreign Ministries and the sole entity authorized to provide a Turkish education abroad. Ahead of a January 2017 tour of southwestern African nations, his fourth visit to the continent, Erdoğan was blunt: "In this visit, we will—together with the representatives of Maarif Foundation—share our expectations from the respective authorities with regards to the fight against FETÖ . . . and what we can do in order to purge FETÖ from friendly and brother nations."[71] The following year, uprooting his opponents' influence in Africa remained a top priority, according to AKP Foreign Affairs deputy Cemalettin Kani Torun.[72] Turkish newspapers provided regular updates on the Maarif Foundation's progress in assuming control of Gülen schools abroad.[73] *Daily Sabah*, a mouthpiece for the Turkish government, warned African countries that allowing Gülen to operate schools in their countries—often their flagship schools—could lead to a coup.[74] "FETÖ, just like it did in Turkey, tried to brainwash young Sudanese to use against the state for its own purposes," *Daily Sabah* wrote in December 2017.[75] At a February 2017 news conference in Ankara with Ethiopian President Mulatu Teshome, Erdoğan appeared to link preferential trade agreements to Ethiopia's commitment to eradicate the "tumor" of Gülen schools.[76]

Many African countries knew to play along. Chad closed all Gülen schools. Standing alongside Erdoğan after a meeting to discuss aid and trade in his presidential palace in N'Djamena, President Idriss Deby declared that Chad's children would "no longer be educated by terrorists."[77] First Erdoğan won local commitments to shut down or transfer Gülen schools in Guinea, Niger, Somalia, Chad, Sudan, and Senegal—all recipients of Turkish aid—to a pro-AKP foundation; then he visited Tanzania, Madagascar, and Mozambique to seek similar commitments to shutter Gülen schools.[78]

Abdullah Bozkurt, editor of Gülen's now-shuttered flagship paper, was critical of the Turkish government's approach:

Erdoğan was trying to drag Africans into his self-declared war against Gülen who has exposed political Islamists including the chief Islamist Erdoğan for what they are: a bunch of ideological zealots who abuse religion for political purposes and hope to pros-

189

elytize Africa with their own brand of ideology using overseas agencies and state aids as cover.[79]

Some African leaders might have agreed, and so Erdoğan modified his rhetoric to put Africa first, even while staying consistent with his agenda.[80]

Regardless, as much as Erdoğan condemned Gülen, he essentially replicated the exiled theologian's strategy. Not only did the Turkish government build a network of schools, but it also used scholarship programs to bring African students to Turkey and cultivate a new generation of pro-Erdoğan elites.[81] Further, it established a network of Yunus Emre Institutes, named after a thirteenth century Turkish poet, to facilitate educational exchange. By April 2018, the exchange programs had brought 16,000 students from 160 countries to Turkey on full scholarships.[82] As Erdoğan promised Turks he would "raise a religious generation" at home, he also sought to do so abroad; he brought not only university students but also junior high and high school students to Turkey.[83] Pro-AKP newspapers ran glowing stories about African participants who converted to Islam while on the program.[84]

Beyond eviscerating Gülen's financial network, another part of Erdoğan's Africa strategy may have been simply to play to Erdoğan's self-perception as a great leader. When Erdoğan visited the Côte d'Ivoire, for example, President Alassane Ouattara declared, "We know how highly your leadership is appreciated in the world," adding, "We are pleased to host a great statesman here."[85] Somalia named a hospital (built with Turkish funds) after the Turkish president. As Erdoğan's toxicity grew, Ouattara—and many other African leaders—played to Erdoğan's ego in a manner that few Western or Middle Eastern leaders were willing to do anymore.

Quest for Uranium

Both Iran and Turkey also appeared acutely aware of which countries in Africa could one day become suppliers for Iran's nuclear program and Turkey's planned program. The Iranian leadership sought up to sixteen nuclear reactors for civilian energy purposes.[86] Should Iran build such a network, it would deplete its limited indigenous uranium supply within ten years.[87] Turkey's first nuclear plant, meanwhile, was under construction and expected to come online in 2023, and the Turkish government announced plans for three additional nuclear power stations.[88] Both Iran and Turkey have domestic sources of uranium but in amounts insufficient to sustain a full-fledged civilian energy program, let alone any military motivations. This simple fact led both Ankara and Tehran to identify potential sources of uranium in Africa and cultivate them with aid.

A number of African states mine uranium; Namibia, South Africa, and Niger have some of the largest uranium reserves in the world and have become increasingly major players in the international uranium market. Malawi, the Democratic Republic of Congo, and Gabon also operate uranium mines, and deposits exist in several other African countries.[89]

In 2010, a website affiliated with Ange-Félix Patassé, who led the Central African Republic from 1993 until he was ousted in 2003, suggested that Foreign Minister Antoine Gambi had traveled to Tehran to negotiate the Iranian purchase of Central African yellowcake. The website further speculated about "a Bangui-Caracas-Tehran-Pyongyang axis trafficking in uranium" in the making that might both raise anxiety in Western capitals and drag the Central African Republic into dynamics which could further erode its stability.[90]

In theory, international controls prevent African states from exporting uranium absent transparency. In reality, poor infrastructure and corruption enable illicit trade. In 2007, for example, Congolese authorities arrested Fortunat Lumu, director of the Atomic Energy Center, following an investigation of missing uranium.[91] While incidents of uranium and plutonium smuggling declined worldwide, Africa experienced an uptick in illicit yellowcake trade.[92]

In their travels across the continent, Iranian officials often appear to prioritize countries that might serve as uranium sources. Tehran only took significant interest in Guinea, for example, after the country discovered commercially viable uranium deposits in 2007. In the years that followed, Iran-Guinea trade more than doubled, with disproportionate investment in Guinea's mining sector.[93]

Iranian outreach to Gambia, Malawi, Namibia, and Uganda also largely coincided with the discovery of uranium in those countries.[94] Prior to Uganda's announcement of significant uranium reserves, for example, commercial relations between Iran and Uganda remained dormant. Visiting Tehran in 2009, however, Uganda President Yoweri Museveni met not only with his counterpart, but also with Iran's minister of mining. Ahmadinejad reciprocated the trip in 2010. The Kampala-based *Daily Monitor* reported "strong indication that the two leaders discussed prospects of exploiting Uganda's uranium resources, which Mr. Museveni has often said would only be used for the generation of energy."[95] Uganda was not alone.

While the Nigerian government long failed to find commercial success for its uranium mining industry, the discovery of new uranium deposits apparently piqued Iranian interest. In 2019, Iranian Parliamentary

Speaker Ali Larijani suggested that the Nigerian mining sector should be a natural target for Iranian investment and business.[96]

Iran's nuclear quest is more diplomatically sensitive because of suspicions about Iran's covert nuclear ambitions. In 2007, Turkey declared its intention to develop nuclear energy and three years later signed an agreement with Rosatom, the Russian state nuclear company, to build a nuclear power station at Akkuyu along the Mediterranean Coast. Unlike Iran, Turkey has little indigenous uranium supply. Energy Minister Taner Yıldız was quite open about Turkey's intentions in Africa: "Turkey gives importance to the uranium of Niger, as a country building a nuclear plant."[97] Against the backdrop of Turkey's cultivation of Chad as a diplomatic and trade partner, the Turkish press also noted Chad's uranium reserves.[98]

Quest for Bases

If leveraging cash to win adherents to their own ideological and diplomatic priorities was goal number one for both Iran and Turkey and if, to varying degrees, both countries sought to secure a future supply of uranium from African sources, then a future third goal for both Iranian and Turkish outreach to Africa may be to establish their own "string of pearls" as both have aspired to expand their military areas of operation far beyond their immediate neighborhood.

When Mohammed Ali Jafari took over the Islamic Revolutionary Guard Corps (IRGC) in 2007, he reoriented the IRGC land forces inward to defend against internal threats to Iran's revolutionary regime. Supreme Leader Ali Khamenei subsequently delivered a speech to Iranian sailors at Iran's main Persian Gulf port of Bandar Abbas, telling them that their "strategic presence on the high seas . . . is a service to humanity."[99] There followed a number of Iranian port visits and cruises well beyond the Persian Gulf and northern Indian Oceans where the Iranian navy traditionally operated. In 2013, an Iranian flotilla sailed to the Pacific Ocean for the first time in a millennium and, in 2016, two Iranian warships tried to round the Cape of Good Hope before mechanical failure forced them into Durban.[100]

Initially, Iranian authorities cultivated Senegal, with frequent exchanges between Presidents Wade and Ahmadinejad, and also meetings between Wade and Khamenei.[101] The Senegalese foreign and defense ministers also visited their Iranian counterparts.[102] A week after Foreign Minister Cheikh Tidiane Gadio announced he would visit Tehran, Defense Minister Becaye Diop met with the Iranian defense minister to discuss expanding bilateral defense ties between the two states.[103] While Admiral Habibollah Sayyari, chief of the Islamic Republic of Iran Navy, is prone to hyperbole, Senegal could have brought to reality—at least symbolically—his pledge for Iran to establish a presence in the Atlantic.[104] Iranian authorities have no one but themselves to blame that those plans did not move forward. Iran-Senegal bilateral relations suffered a significant setback in 2011 when Senegalese authorities accused Iran of smuggling arms to rebels in southern Senegal's restive Casamance region.[105] If the Senegalese allegations were true—Iranian authorities denied them—then it might illustrate the lack of coordination among various Iranian security elements.[106] Iran's various intelligence services and security wings have, on occasion, run foreign operations at odds with each other and broader Iranian policy.[107] While the two states re-established ties in 2013, that incident and a change in the Senegalese leadership seemingly ended further significant defense ties.[108]

Iran does not have a large enough indigenous navy to justify permanent bases in Africa, but it did at one point try to leverage its aid to Sudan in order to utilize Port Sudan on the Red Sea as a logistical base. Just as Erdoğan sought to embrace Bashir, so too did Ahmadinejad as he visited Sudan before and after Bashir's indictment.[109] Iran's defense minister, meanwhile, called Sudan the cornerstone of the Islamic Republic's Africa policies.[110] That ended when Saudi Arabia outbid Iran for Sudan's loyalty and closed Port Sudan to Iranian naval vessels. The Iranian Navy subsequently made a port call in Djibouti, which has made an industry out of providing port facilities and logistics without respect to sharply diverging diplomatic outlooks; even there it appears that quiet pressure prevented Iran from gaining a toehold.[111]

While Iran's success has been limited, Turkey leveraged its aid into a more ambitious program by extending its military reach and amplifying its influence in Africa. In 2014, for example, four Turkish warships undertook a 102-day sail around Africa, visiting twenty-seven countries, and conducting exercises with many local militaries. Turkish warships traversed the Cape of Good Hope for the first time in almost 150 years.[112] Erdoğan was the first post-Ottoman Turkish leader to establish permanent military bases outside the Anatolian homeland. In 2017, and against the backdrop of Arab efforts to isolate Qatar, the Turkish government announced a permanent base in Qatar. That same year, Turkey inaugurated a forward operating base in Mogadishu then, in 2018, leased Suakin Island, an Ottoman-era embarkation point for pilgrims heading to the Hajj and promised to transform it into a base for civilian and military use.[113] While the acquisition of Suakin was purely strategic, the Turkish press cast it in terms of Turkey's heritage, noting that the island was the residence of the Habesh Eyalat, which occupied much of the Red Sea coast from Sudan down through Somaliland.[114] While Bashir's April 2019 ouster might have hindered Turkish ambitions to transform Suakin into a military base and to create a sphere of political-military influence ranging from the Eastern Mediterranean to the Horn of Africa, Turkey's outlay in Suakin was always a shadow of its investment in Somalia.[115]

Turkey's base in Mogadishu became Turkey's major military center in Africa and an "integral part of Ankara's Africa initiative" to extend Turkish penetration throughout the continent.[116] As headquarters of the Turkish Task Force Command, it hosted a permanent contingent of 200 troops and provided military training for the so-called "African Eagles." At any given time, they trained 500 Somali and other African troops with the aim to train over 10,000.[117] Prior to Bashir's removal from power, Turkey also discussed training Sudanese forces at centers inside Sudan.[118]

The formal base may only be the tip of the Turkish iceberg. SADAT, an Islamist paramilitary and mercenary group founded by Adnan Tanrıverdi—a general once ousted for his Islamist leanings but whom Erdoğan's appointed his military counselor—also operates in Somalia and may be training Somali radicals, much as it has been with Hamas.[119] Regardless, Turkey's 2019 Blue Homeland exercises, the largest naval exercises in its history, demonstrated that Turkey could conduct operations simultaneously in the Black Sea, Aegean Sea, and Mediterranean Sea.[120] Turkey's forthcoming launch of a helicopter carrier promises to further integrate its land and naval strategies and could amplify its influence in Africa.

Conclusion

Both Iran and Turkey have launched deliberate efforts to cultivate Africa to further their own ideological and diplomatic agendas. Their approach is in some ways similar: They maximize use of soft power and seek to pick and then leverage pivotal states on the continent. At best, Tehran appears to be leveraging aid and soft power in exchange for diplomatic favors; at worst, some elements in the Islamic Republic appear to be utilizing Africa as cover for other military or nuclear objectives. Either way, the Iranian government has shown that its self-description as an extra-regional power is no longer rhetorical exaggeration.[121]

The Iranian government has not hesitated to leverage its investment for more malign aims. The 2010 seizure of weaponry in Nigeria and 2018 allegations that Iran and its proxy Hezbollah were training and arming the

Polisario Front against Morocco have exposed Iran's strategy to use Africa as a template to further its objectives by non-diplomatic means.[122]

Turkey is a relative latecomer to Africa, turning to the continent after its previous policies of Zero Problems with Our Neighbors and neo-Ottomanism fell short. While the Iranian threat to Western interests across Africa has been real, the resources Turkey brings to the table in Africa may make it a more potent long-term threat, especially as it encourages a more radical vision of Islam than traditionally embraced by many African countries. Indeed, Turkey's efforts to promote Erdoğan's vision of Islamism in Africa today are similar to Saudi Arabia's efforts to spread Salafism in decades past. This may be Turkey's real legacy in Africa, especially as African diplomatic solidarity will not be enough for Turkey to force UN Security Council expansion or other Turkish efforts to rework the post-World War II order, even if the Erdoğan government does hope to use Africa as a means to push Turkey's agenda through the UN General Assembly.[123]

Turkey may fall short in some of its other objectives. Erdoğan's positioning as an Islamic leader risks alienating the continent's large non-Islamic population. Erdoğan also apparently did not learn the lesson of neo-Ottomanism's failure: Turkish nationalists have a fonder remembrance of Ottoman heritage than do many subject peoples. Erdoğan may see the Ottomans historically as a civilizing force in Africa, for example, but many Africans associate them with the East African *Zanj* slave trade. And while Erdoğan claims Turkey is the pioneer anti-colonial power, there is cognitive dissonance when he embraces an Ottoman past while failing to associate that Ottoman heritage with forced colonization of myriad peoples and countries over the centuries.

Turkish largesse and investment have effectively cultivated African leaders, but loyalty to Turkey's outlook seldom permeates down to ordinary people. Hence, Turkey's diplomatic influence remains shallow and tied almost entirely with the rulers of any particular African state. Turkey, for instance, lost first its footing and then significant investment in Libya and Egypt when Muammar Qadhafi and Mohamed Morsi fell, although it has since sought to reclaim its position in Tripoli by trading military support for the country's besieged Muslim Brotherhood-dominated government in exchange for commercial contracts.

While Erdoğan views Islam as a tool for unity, religion alone has never overcome long-standing disputes such as the one between Somalia and Somaliland, which declared its independence from Somalia in 1991 and has consistently outperformed its neighbor ever since.

Nevertheless, even if Iran and Turkey's strategies for Africa are flawed, they remain more coordinated and comprehensive than those of the United States. While the United States invests militarily in Africa, Africa Command remains based in Europe and there is little coordinated foreign direct investment. Iran and Turkey, on the other hand, embrace a more comprehensive strategy with closely coordinated economic, informational, and diplomatic tools amplifying their relatively small military investments. So long as neither Iran nor Turkey face serious push back for malign activity on the continent, both democracy and stability on the continent will suffer in the long-run.

Notes

1. "Erdoğan in Tunisia to Strengthen Turkey's Win-Win Africa Policy," *Daily Sabah*, 28 December 2017, https://www.dailysabah.com/diploma-cy/2017/12/27/erdogan-in-tunisia-to-strengthen-turkeys-win-win-africa-policy.

2. United Nations Security Council Resolution (UNSCR) 1737, S/RES/1737(2006), https://digitallibrary.un.org/record/589783; UNSCR 1747, S/RES/1747(2007), https://digitallibrary.un.org/record/595373?ln=en; and UNSCR 1803, S/RES/1803(2008), https://digitallibrary.un.org/record/621380?ln=en.

3. "Travels Abroad of the President," Office of the Historian, US Department of State, http://history.state.gov/departmenthistory/travels/president, accessed 3 May 2019; and "George W. Bush," Office of the Historian, US Department of State, accessed 20 February 2013, http://history.state.gov/depart-menthistory/travels/president/bush-george-w. Secretaries of State Colin Powell, Condoleezza Rice, and Hillary Clinton each made four trips to Africa during their respective four-year tenures; John Kerry made five; Rex Tillerson did not make any. See "Travels of the Secretary," Office of the Historian, US Department of State, accessed 3 May 2019, http://history.state.gov/departmenthistory/travels/secretary.

4. "Iran, Sudan Sign Three Cooperation Documents," *Islamic Republic News Agency* (Tehran), 5 October 2004.

5. "Iranian President Terms his 7-Nation African Tour as Fruitful," *Islamic Republic News Agency*, 23 January 2005.

6. "FM: 2008 a Milestone in Iran-Africa Ties." *Fars News Agency*, 30 January 2008; and "Beh Zudi Ijlas Iran va Afriqa dar Tehran Bargazar Mishavad [Tehran Will Soon Host Iran-Africa Summit]," *Mehr News*, 1 February 2008.

7. "SA Commends Iran's Stance on Nuclear Program," *Islamic Republic News Agency*, 14 September 2007.

8. "SA on Wrong Side," *The Citizen* (Johannesburg), 14 March 2007.

9. Director General of the International Atomic Energy Agency (IAEA), *Implementation of the NPT Safeguards Agreement and Relevant Provisions of Security Council Resolutions 1737 (2006) and 1747 (2007) in the Islamic Republic of Iran,* GOV/2008/4 (Vienna: IAEA, 26 May 2008), https://www.iranwatch.org/sites/default/files/iaea-iranreport-052608.pdf; and "Security Council Edges towards Adoption of Iran Sanctions," *The Citizen* (Johannesburg), 29 February 2008.

10. Fredrik Dahl, "South Africa Throws U.N. Nuclear Meeting on Iran into Disarray," *Reuters*, 13 September 2012, http://www.reuters.com/arti-cle/2012/09/13/us-nuclear-iran-iaea-idUSBRE88C0I620120913.

11. "Tamim 25 dar sad Niaz Naft Afirqaye Jonubi Towsat Iran [25 Percent of South Africa's Oil Needs Supplied By Iran]," *Abrar*, 27 January 2010; and "Afzayesh Cheshemgir Vardat Naft-e Kham Afriqaye Jonubi va Iran [The Dramatic Rise in South Africa's Crude Oil Imports from Iran]," *Fars News Agency*, 2 April 2012, http://www.farsnews.com/newstext.php?nn=13910114000938.

12. "Envoy: Iran-South Africa Trade Balance to Hit $2bln by 2020," *Fars News Agency*, 23 October 2017, http://en.farsnews.com/newstext.aspx-?nn=13960801000891.

13. "Special Report: Documents Detail how MTN Funneled U.S. Technology to Iran," *Reuters*, 30 August 2012, http://www.reuters.com/article/2012/08/30/us-mtn-iran-documents-idUSBRE87T05R20120830; and "MTN 'Panicking' over US Treasury Sanctions," *City Press* (Johannesburg), 10 November 2012.

14. "Iran to Supply Crude Oil to Senegal," *Fars News Agency*, 28 August 2007; and "Senegalese President: Nuclear Technology Is Iran's Legitimate Right," *Islamic Republic News Agency* (Tehran), November 25, 2007.

15. "Maqam Mo'azzam-e Rahabari Zaban-e Amrika va Abargodrat-ha ra Zaban-e Tahdid va er'ab Danestand [The Supreme Leader Says America only Knows the Language of Intimidation]," I*slamic Republic News Agency*, 28 February 2008, http://web.archive.org/web/20080301125445/http://www1.irna.ir/fa/news/view/line-1/8612081304213458.htm.

16. "L'Iran, 'partenaire stratégique' de l'Afrique [Iran 'Strategic Partner' of Africa]," RepublicofTogo.com (Lomé), 14 September 2010, http://www.republicoftogo.com/Toutes-les-rubriques/Diplomatie/L-Iran-partenaire-strategique-de-l-Afrique.

17. "Manouchehr Mottaki à Lomé [Manouchehr Mottaki to Lomé]," RepublicofTogo.com (Lomé), 31 October 2010, http://www.republicoftogo.com/Toutes-les-rubriques/Diplomatie/Manouchehr-Mottaki-a-Lome.

18. "Tawse'ah va Gosteresh-e Ravabat Do Keshvar Mavarad Takid Qarar Gereft [Development of Bilateral Relations Emphasized]," *Islamic Republic News Agency*, 30 January 2012.

19. "Visite éclaire de la secrétaire d'Etat Hillary Clinton au Togo : après les questions de trafic de drogue, de blanchiment d'argent et de terrorisme international, le cœur de Faure Gnassingbé balance entre l'Iran et les Usa pour les armes nucléaires et la piraterie maritime [The Visit of Secretary of State Hillary Clinton to Togo Clarifies: After Question of Drug Trafficking, Money Laundering, and International Terrorism, the Heart of Faure Gnassingbe Is the Balance between Iran and the US over Nuclear Arms and Maritime Piracy]," *Le Triangle des Enjeux* (Lomé), 18 January 2012.

20. "Gabon Minister: Iran Source of Honor for Africans," *Fars News Agency*, 4 May 2009.

21. "Minister Welcomes Presence of Iranian Private Sector in Gabon," *Fars News Agency*, 26 May 2009.

22. "Gabonese President Terms Relations with Iran Important," *Fars News Agency*, 1 February 2010.

23. "Iran Renews Calls for N. Disarmament," *Fars News Agency*, 3 April 2010.

24. "Iran dar Nijeria Khodro Misazad [Iran to Build Cars in Nigeria]," *Alef* (Tehran), 31 October 2010.

25. "Hamkari Gazi 156 milliyon dollari Iran va Nijeria [$156 Million Gas Cooperation between Iran and Nigeria]," *Donya-ye Eghtesad* (Tehran), 14 August 2008; and "Dar Ijlas Nijeria Ara'i Shod Pishnahadha-ye Ahmadinejad beh Dey 8 [Ahmadinejad Presents Offer to Developing-8 Countries in Nigeria Meeting]," *Donya-ye Eghtesad*, 11 July 2010.

26. "Zarif Meets with Nigerian Officials on Last Leg of Africa Tour," *Mehr News Agency*, 17 October 2017, https://en.mehrnews.com/news/128981/Zarif-meets-with-Nigerian-officials-on-last-leg-of-Africa-tour.

27. "Iran to Start Broker Ties with South African, Ugandan, Niger Banks," *Fars News Agency*, 27 October 2017, http://en.farsnews.com/newstext.aspx-?nn=13960806001054.

28. "Iran Eager to Boost Ties with Niger," *Tasnim News Agency*, 4 August 2018, https://www.tasnimnews.com/en/news/2018/08/04/1793322/iran-eager-to-boost-ties-with-niger.

29. "III. A New Momentum-Institutionalization of the Relations," Second Turkey-Africa Partnership Summit, n.d., accessed 25 January 2020, http://africa.mfa.gov.tr/turkey_africa.en.mfa.

30. "Turkey-Africa Summit Kicks Off in Equatorial Guinea," *Anadolu Agency*, 19 November 2014.

31. Mohamed Taha Tawakel, "Turkish, Ethiopian FMs Visit AA's new Addis Ababa Bureau," *Anadolu Agency*, 31 January 2014, https://www.aa.com.tr/en/world/turkish-ethiopian-fms-visit-aas-new-addis-ababa-bureau/186256; Andac Hongur and Izzet Taskiran, "Turkey Seeks to Boost Diplomatic Ties with Africa," *Anadolu Agency*, 22 January 2017, https://www.aa.com.tr/en/turkey/turkey-seeks-to-boost-diplomatic-ties-with-africa/732499; "Turkey's Ties with Africa Deeper, Stronger in All Areas," *Daily Sabah*, 24 February 2018, https://www.dailysabah.com/diplomacy/2018/02/24/turkeys-ties-with-africa-deeper-stronger-in-all-areas; and "Turkish Representations," Ministry of Foreign Affairs, http://www.mfa.gov.tr/turkish-representations.en.mfa.

32. "New Missions, Erdoğan Visits Boost Turkey Africa Ties, DRC Envoy Says," *Daily Sabah*, 25 May 2018, https://www.dailysabah.com/diplomacy/2018/05/26/new-missions-erdogan-visits-boost-turkey-africa-ties-drc-envoy-says.

33. Pinar Dost, "Turkey's Growing Presence in Africa, and Opportunities and Challenges to Watch in 2018," The Atlantic Council, 26 March 2018, https://www.atlanticcouncil.org/commentary/event-recap/turkey-s-growing-presence-in-africa-and-opportunities-and-challenges-to-watch-in-2018/.

34. "Erdoğan Set to Kick Off African Tour from Ethiopia," *Daily Sabah*, 20 January 2015, https://www.dailysabah.com/politics/2015/01/20/erdogan-set-to-kick-off-african-tour-from-ethiopia.

35. "CAR Calls on Turkey for Development Assistance," *Anadolu Agency*, 23 June 2014.

36. "Turkish Petroleum to Look for Oil in Sudan," *Daily Sabah*, 18 September 2018, https://www.dailysabah.com/energy/2018/09/19/turkish-petroleum-to-

look-for-oil-in-sudan; and "Local Firm Wins $1.9 Billion Railway Contract in Tanzania," *Daily Sabah*, 2 October 2017, https://www.dailysabah.com/economy/2017/10/03/local-firm-wins-19-billion-railway-contract-in-tanzania.

37. Tawakel, "Turkish, Ethiopian FMs Visit AA's new Addis Ababa Bureau;" Maggie Fick, "Turkish Airlines Profits in Africa, where Others Fear to Fly," *Reuters*, 12 September 2017, https://www.reuters.com/article/us-turkishairlines-africa/turkish-airlines-profits-in-africa-where-others-fear-to-fly-idUSKCN1BN1CZ; and Recep Tayyip Erdoğan, "Burgeoning Ties, Common Future," *Daily Sabah*, 1 March 2016, https://www.dailysabah.com/africa/2016/02/29/burgeoning-ties-common-future.

38. Tawakel.

39. "Ta'atili Dafatar-e Vahed-e Markazi Khabar dar Sarasar Jahan [Closure of Islamic Republic of Iran Broadcasting Central News Units around the World]," *Tabnak.ir*, 14 January 2015, https://www.tabnak.ir/fa/news/466892.

40. "Turkey Seeks Lasting Presence in Somalia via Investments," *Daily Sabah*, 12 June 2014, https://www.dailysabah.com/politics/2014/06/12/turkey-seeks-lasting-presence-in-somalia-via-investments.

41. Recep Tayyip Erdoğan, "Burgeoning Ties, Common Future," *Daily Sabah*, 29 February 2016, https://www.dailysabah.com/africa/2016/02/29/burgeoning-ties-common-future.

42. İlnur Çevik, "World Muslims Looking up to Turkey with Hope," *Daily Sabah*, 1 March 2016, https://www.dailysabah.com/columns/ilnur-cevik/2016/12/29/world-muslims-looking-up-to-turkey-with-hope.

43. Çevik.

44. "Strategic Partnership Basis of Turkish-Somalia Cooperation," *Daily Sabah*, 26 October 2017, https://www.dailysabah.com/diplomacy/2017/10/27/strategic-partnership-basis-of-turkish-somali-cooperation.

45. "Ties with Africa Deeper, Stronger in All Areas," *Daily Sabah*, 24 February 2018.

46. "We Have Been Working to Strengthen our Cooperation with Africa," Presidency of the Republic of Turkey, 10 October 2018, https://tccb.gov.tr/en/news/542/99029/-we-have-been-working-to-strengthen-our-cooperation-with-africa-; and Mehmet Solmaz, "Erdoğan: We Cannot Remain Silent on Africa," *Daily Sabah*, 27 January 2015, https://www.dailysabah.com/politics/2015/01/27/erdogan-we-cannot-remain-silent-on-africa.

47. Çevik, "World Muslims Looking up to Turkey with Hope."

48. "Turkey Third Largest International Donor in Humanitarian Assistance," *Daily Sabah*, 11 September 2014, https://www.dailysabah.com/turkey/2014/09/11/turkey-third-largest-international-donor-in-humanitarian-assistance.

49. "Turkey to Send Aid to CAR to Help People Displaced by Conflict," *Today's Zaman*, 28 February 2014.

50. "Erdogan: 'A Muslim can never Commit Genocide,'" *Hürriyet Daily News*, 8 November 2009.

51. Sahin Alpay, "Sign up to the International Court" *Today's Zaman*, 9 November 2009.

52. Mohamed al-Khatem, "Turkish Deputy PM Arrives in Khartoum to Open Darfur Hospital," *Anadolu Agency*, 29 February 2014.

53. "Turkey Hosts 30 Sudanese Public Servants for Training," *Yeni Şafak*, 14 December 2018, https://www.yenisafak.com/en/news/turkey-hosts-30-sudanese-public-servants-for-training-3469164; and "Vice President in Sudan to Boost Bilateral Ties," *Daily Sabah*, 19 November 2018, https://www.dailysabah.com/diplomacy/2018/11/20/vice-president-in-sudan-to-boost-bilateral-ties.

54. See, for example, "Turkish Health Sciences Academy Opens in Sudan," *Daily Sabah*, 3 December 2018, https://www.dailysabah.com/turkey/2018/12/04/turkish-health-sciences-academy-opens-in-sudan; "Turkish Agriculture Sector to Start Investment in Sudan," *Hürriyet Daily News*, 24 November 2018, http://www.hurriyetdailynews.com/turkish-agriculture-sector-to-start-investment-in-sudan-139155; and "Turkish Firm to Start Building Sudan's 'Biggest Airport,'" *Hürriyet Daily News*, 18 October 2018, http://www.hurriyetdailynews.com/turkish-firm-to-start-building-sudans-biggest-airport-138029.

55. "Turkish Aid Agency TIKA Finishes over 24 Projects in Chad," *Daily Sabah*, 10 November 2015, https://www.dailysabah.com/turkey/2015/11/09/turkish-aid-agency-tika-finishes-over-24-projects-in-chad.

56. Semih Idiz, "Playing with Fire, Turkey Will Get Burned," *Hürriyet Daily News*, 21 February 2013), http://www.hurriyetdailynews.com/opinion/semih-idiz/playing-with-fire-turkey-will-get-burned-41542; and Abdoulaye Adoum, "Turkish Aid Brings Relief to CAR Refugees in Chad," *Anadolu Agency*, 7 March 2014.

57. "Turkish Police Detain 28 in Anti-al-Qaeda Pp, Raid on İHH Office," *Hürriyet Daily News*, 14 January 2014, http://www.hurriyetdailynews.com/turkish-police-detain-28-in-anti-al-qaeda-op-raid-on-ihh-office-61000; "United States of America v. Abdurahman Muhammad Alamoudi," in the United States District Court for the Eastern District of Virginia, Supplemental Declaration in Support of Detention, 22 October 2003; and "Turkish Red Crescent Calls for Aid to Central African Republic," *Daily Sabah*, 11 May 2014, https://www.dailysabah.com/turkey/2014/05/12/turkish-red-crescent-calls-for-aid-to-central-african-republic.

58. "Turkey's İHH Delivers Humanitarian Aid to Refugees in Chad," *Anadolu Agency*, 22 June 2015, https://www.aa.com.tr/en/archive/turkeys-ihh-delivers-humanitarian-aid-to-refugees-in-chad/33840; and "TİKA Charity Project Sends Volunteers All Over the World," *Daily Sabah*, 30 July 2018, https://www.dailysabah.com/turkey/2018/07/30/tikas-charity-project-sends-volunteers-all-over-the-world.

59. "Turkish Aid Agency Puts Smile on Faces of Somali Children, Widows," *Daily Sabah*, 12 April 2018, https://www.dailysabah.com/politics/2018/04/13/turkish-aid-agency-puts-smile-on-faces-of-somali-children-widows.

60. "Turkish Charity Distributes Quran in 8 African States," *Anadolu Agency*, 15 January 2020, https://www.aa.com.tr/en/africa/turkish-charity-distributes-quran-in-8-african-states/1703391.

61. "Turkish Charities Help Needy Muslims in Sudan, Ethiopia," *Anadolu Agency*, 25 September 2015, https://www.dailysabah.com/religion/2015/09/25/turkish-charities-help-muslims-in-need-in-sudan-ethiopia.

62. "Turkish Agency to Send Eid Meat to 3M People Abroad," *Yeni Şafak*, 27 July 2018, https://www.yenisafak.com/en/news/turkish-agency-to-send-eid-meat-to-3m-people-abroad-3437406.

63. Rafiu Ajakaye, "Turkey Pledges Support for Nigeria's Insurgency Victims," *Anadolu Agency*, 23 June 2014, https://www.aa.com.tr/en/health/turkey-pledges-support-for-nigerias-insurgency-victims/148939.

64. "Turkish Airlines Refutes Claims over Arms Shipments," *Hürriyet Daily News*, 19 March 2014, http://www.hurriyetdailynews.com/turkish-airlines-refutes-claims-over-arms-shipments--63791.

65. Abdullah Bozkurt, "Secret Report Reveals how Erdoğan Hushed up Probe into al-Shabab Financiers in Turkey," *Nordic Monitor*, 8 June 2020, https://www.nordicmonitor.com/2020/06/secret-report-reveals-how-erdogan-hushed-up-probe-into-al-shabab-financiers-in-turkey/.

66. "Turkish, Somali Presidents Meet in Istanbul," *Yeni Şafak*, 24 November 2018, https://www.yenisafak.com/en/news/turkish-somali-presidents-meet-in-istanbul-3467235.

67. "Somalia Receives almost $1 Billion Worth of Turkish Aid," *Hürriyet Daily News*, 19 March 2017, http://www.hurriyetdailynews.com/somalia-receives-almost-1-billion-worth-of-turkish-aid---110987.

68. "Turkish Interior Minister Meets Somali Counterpart," *Yeni Şafak*, 16 January 2019, https://www.yenisafak.com/en/news/turkish-interior-minister-meets-somali-counterpart-3471985.

69. "Turkey Wants more 'Politically Active' UN," *Anadolu Agency*, 14 October 2014.

70. Burhanettin Duran, "President Erdoğan's Africa Visit and the Half-Dead Dragon," *Daily Sabah*, 2 March 2018, https://www.dailysabah.com/columns/duran-burhanettin/2018/03/03/president-erdogans-africa-visit-and-the-half-dead-dragon.

71. Andac Hongur and Izzet Taskiran, "Turkey Seeks to Boost Diplomatic Ties with Africa," *Anadolu Agency*, 22 January 2017, https://www.aa.com.tr/en/turkey/turkey-seeks-to-boost-diplomatic-ties-with-africa/732499.

72. "Turkey's Ties with Africa Deeper, Stronger in all Areas," *Daily Sabah*, 24 February 2018, https://www.dailysabah.com/diplomacy/2018/02/24/turkeys-ties-with-africa-deeper-stronger-in-all-areas.

73. "Erdoğan to Inaugurate First Maarif Directorate in South Africa," *Daily Sabah*, 25 July 2018, https://www.dailysabah.com/politics/2018/07/26/erdogan-to-inaugurate-first-maarif-directorate-in-south-africa; and "Turkey Takes

Control of FETÖ-Linked Schools in Ivory Coast," *Daily Sabah*, 2 August 2018, https://www.dailysabah.com/war-on-terror/2018/08/03/turkey-takes-control-of-feto-linked-schools-in-ivory-coast.

74. "FETÖ Network in African Countries Threat to Continent," *Daily Sabah*, 23 January 2017, https://www.dailysabah.com/war-on-terror/2017/01/24/feto-network-in-african-countries-threat-to-continent.

75. "Sun is Rising on Sudan," *Daily Sabah*, 25 December 2017, https://www.dailysabah.com/editorial/2017/12/25/sun-is-rising-on-sudan.

76. "Erdogan Congratulates Ethiopia on Tackling FETÖ 'Tumor,'" *Yeni Şafak*, 8 February 2017, https://www.yenisafak.com/en/news/erdogan-congratulates-ethiopia-on-tackling-feto-tumor-2609520.

77. "Turkey, Chad Vow to 'Stand Together' Against Terrorism," *Hürriyet Daily News*, 27 December 2017, http://www.hurriyetdailynews.com/turkey-chad-vow-to-stand-together-against-terrorism-124804.

78. "FETÖ Schools to be on Agenda during Erdogan's Africa Visit," *Daily Sabah*, 19 January 2017, https://www.dailysabah.com/war-on-terror/2017/01/20/feto-schools-to-be-on-agenda-during-erdogans-africa-visit.

79. Abdullah Bozkurt, "Erdogan's Slight to Africa," *Today's Zaman*, 25 November 2014.

80. Duran, "President Erdoğan's Africa Visit and the Half-Dead Dragon."

81. See, for example, "Turkey to Grant 150 Scholarships to Sudanese Students," *Yeni Şafak*, 18 April 2018, https://www.yenisafak.com/en/news/turkey-to-grant-150-scholarships-to-sudanese-students-3329321.

82. "Turkey to Grant 150 Scholarships to Sudanese Students," *Yeni Şafak*.

83. Recep Tayyip Erdoğan, "Burgeoning Ties, Common Future," *Daily Sabah*, 1 March 2016, https://www.dailysabah.com/africa/2016/02/29/burgeoning-ties-common-future.

84. See, for example, "Ghanaian Student in Turkey Goes Home to Preach Islam," *Yeni Şafak*, 18 April 2018, https://www.yenisafak.com/en/life/ghanaian-student-in-turkey-goes-home-to-preach-islam-3298808.

85. "Cote d'Ivoire Will Be an Important Center of Modern World in Africa," Office of the President of the Republic of Turkey, 1 March 2016, https://www.tccb.gov.tr/en/news/542/39971/cote-divoire-will-be-an-important-center-of-modern-world-in-africa.

86. "Iran Planning to Build More N. Power Plants," *Fars News Agency*, 14 November 2011, http://english.farsnews.com/newstext.php?nn=9007160844; "Qarardad Makanyaye Nirugahha-ye Hastehaye Iran [Agreement for the Placement of Iranian Nuclear Power Plants," *Tabnak.ir* (Tehran), 20 August 2010, http://www.tabnak.ir/pages/?cid=15916; and "Iran Finds New Uranium Reserves," *Kayhan International*, 24 February 2013, http://www.kayhanintl.com/feb24/index.htm.

87. Pacific Northwest Center for Global Security, "Alternative Energy Economics for Iran: Options, Definitions and Evaluation," citing *Uranium 2003 Resources, Production and Demand,* NEA No. 5291, OECD 2004.

88. "Turkey, Japan Sign $22 Bln Deal for Sinop Nuclear Plant," *Hürriyet Daily News,* 3 May 2013, http://www.hurriyetdailynews.com/turkey-japan-sign-22-bln-deal-for-sinop-nuclear-plant-46206.

89. Tshenyo Modibe, "Deployment of Natural Resources for Development in Africa," *The Thinker* (Midrand, South Africa) (December 2012): 24–28; "French Areva Harvests Bumper Uranium," *Eurasia Review* (20 February 2013), http://www.eurasiareview.com/20022013-french-areva-harvests-bumper-uranium/; "Ezulwini Uranium and Gold Mine, Gauteng, South Africa," Mining-Technology.com (London), http://www.mining-technology.com/projects/ezulwini/; and Dumbani Mzale, "Kayelekera Mine Output Jumps 21%," *The Nation* (Blantyre, Malawi), 19 January 2013.

90. "L'uranium centrafricain conduit Bozizé à vouloir jouer dans la cour des grands [Central African Uranium Leads [François] Bozizé to Want to Play in the Big Leagues]," *Centrafrique-Presse* (Paris), 19 April 2010, http://centrafrique-presse.over-blog.com/article-l-uranium-centrafricain-conduit-bozize-a-vouloir-jouer-dans-la-cour-des-grands-48866866.html.

91. Walter Zinnen, "Waar gaat het Congolese uranium heen? [Where Does the Congolese Uranium Go?]," *De Standaad* (Brussels), 7 August 2009, http://www.standaard.be/artikel/detail.aspx?artikelid=4A2DHA72.

92. John-Mark Mutua, "Uranium Yellowcake Trafficking Incidents in Africa," *African Security Review* 24, no. 2 (2015): 162–89, https://www.tandfonline.com/doi/abs/10.1080/10246029.2015.1034737.

93. "Iran-Guinea Trade Exchanges Up By 140%," *Fars News Agency,* 1 May 2010.

94. "President Ahmadinejad Visits Gambia Banjul-Tehran Ties Strengthened," *Daily Observer* (Banjul), 23 November 2009.

95. Emmanuel Gyezaho, "Museveni, Iran Leader Hold Talks," *Daily Monitor* (Kampala), 18 May 2009, http://web.archive.org/web/20090521131952/http://www.monitor.co.ug/artman/publish/news/Museveni_Iran_leader_hold_talks_85022.shtml.

96. "Ground Fertile for Expansion of Iran-Nigeria Trade Ties: Larijani," *Mehr News Agency,* 5 May 2019, https://en.mehrnews.com/news/144893/Ground-fertile-for-expansion-of-Iran-Nigeria-trade-ties-Larijani.

97. "Turkey Eyes Investment in Niger's Uranium Supplies," *Anadolu Agency,* 11 March 2014.

98. "Chad Visit Showcases Turkey's Aim to Reinforce Cooperation in Africa," *Daily Sabah,* 26 December 2017, https://www.dailysabah.com/economy/2017/12/27/chad-visit-showcases-turkeys-aim-to-reinforce-cooperation-in-africa; and "Oil-Rich Chad Invites Turkish Companies to Invest after Erdoğan Visit," *Hürriyet Daily News,* 29 December 2017, http://www.hurriyet-

dailynews.com/oil-rich-chad-invites-turkish-companies-to-invest-after-erdogan-visit-124933.

99. "Leader: Iran's Naval Presence in High Seas Beneficial to All Human Beings," *Fars News Agency*, 24 July 2011.

100. "Navhaye Artesh Farda Varud Aqiyanus-e Aram Meshavand [Tomorrow Navy Ships Will Enter Pacific]," *Fars News Agency*, 25 February 2013, https://www.farsnews.com/news/13911207000046/; and "Iranian Navy Logistics Vessel Undergoing Repairs in Durban," DefenceWeb (Johannesburg), 16 January 2017, https://www.defenceweb.co.za/sea/sea-sea/iranian-navy-logistics-vessel-undergoing-repairs-in-durban/.

101. "Communiqué conjoint de la visite officielle de Son Excellence Me Abdoulaye Wade, président de la République du Sénégal en République Islamique d'Iran : du 26 au 28 juin 2006 (du 5 au 7 Tir 1385 de l'Hégire solaire), *Le Soleil* (Dakar), 29 June 2006, http://fr.allafrica.com/stories/200606290749.html; and "Leader Urges Muslim Unity Against Israel," *Press TV* (Tehran), 16 May 2010, http://www.presstv.ir/detail/126703.html.

102. "Senegalese DM Meets Iranian Counterpart," *Fars News Agency*, 28 January 2008; and "Senegal FM Describes Iran as 'Friend of Africa,'" *Fars News Agency*, 13 December 2010, http://english.farsnews.com/newstext.php?nn=8909221177.

103. "FM: 2008 a Milestone in Iran-Africa Ties," *Fars News Agency*, 30 January 2008, http://english.farsnews.com/newstext.php?nn=8611100422; and "Najjar Meets Senegalese President, DM," *Fars News Agency*, 2 May 2009, http://english.farsnews.com/newstext.php?nn=8802121304.

104. "Farmandeh-e Niruye-e Darya-ye Artesh az Barnameh Navgan-e Darya-ye Artesh-e Iran dar Nazdiki Morzha-ye Abi Amrika dar Aqiyanus Atlas Khabar Dad [The Commander of the Navy Announces the Program of Deploying the Iranian Navy in the Atlantic Ocean near the Waters of America]," *Nasim* (Tehran), 27 September 2011, http://nasimonline.ir/TextVersion/Detail/?Id=275914&Serv=9.

105. "Biyanieh-e Vizarat-e Kharajeh dar Mavarad Qata'ye Kemal Ravabat-e Diplomatik Senegal ba Tehran [Statement of the Ministry of Foreign Affairs on the Severing of Diplomatic Relations between Senegal and Tehran]," *Fararu.com*, 21 February 2011, http://fararu.com/vdciuraq.t1a3r2bcct.html.

106. "Tehran Gives Senegal Second Chance to Decide on Ties with Iran," *Fars News Agency*, 26 February 2011, http://english.farsnews.com/newstext.php?nn=8912070878.

107. For example, see the Said Hajjarian interview with *Andisheh Pouya*: "Sayyid Hajjarian az bi E'temadi Hashemi O va Dostanesh Miguyad [Said Hajjarian Speaks of Hashemi's Lack of Trust toward Him and His Friends]," excerpted in *Khabar Online* (Tehran), 25 June 2012, http://www.khabaronline.ir/print/237993/politics/parties. Kuwait authorities also say a similar dynamic was in play in the incident referred to in "Kuwait Condemns Iran Rejection of Court

Verdict," *Gulf News* (Dubai), 31 May 2012, http://gulfnews.com/news/gulf/kuwait/kuwait-condemns-iran-rejection-of-court-verdict-1.1030132.

108. "Iran-Senegal Resume Severed Diplomatic Relations," *Islamic Republic News Agency*, 7 February 2013, http://www.irna.ir/en/News/80533391/Politic/Iran-Senegal_resume_severed_diplomatic_relations.

109. "Ahmadinejad to Leave for Sudan," *Fars News Agency*, 27 February 2007; and "Ahmadinejad Arrives in Sudan," *Fars News Agency*, 26 September 2011, http://english.farsnews.com/newstext.php?nn=9007040020.

110. "Sudan, noqteh-ye ateka-ye rivabat-e Iran va Africa ast [Sudan Is the Cornerstone of Iran's Relations with Africa]," *Aftab-e Yazd*, 7 March 2008, http://web.archive.org/web/20080307111644/http://www.aftab-yazd.com/textdetalis.asp?at=3/6/2008&aftab=8&TextID=37476.

111. "Rebels: Sudan, Iran Agree to Set Up Military Base in Red Sea," *Fars News Agency*, 11 December 2012; "Etehad-e Iran va Sudan dar Moqabal Doshman-e Moshtarak [Iran and Sudan United Against a Common Enemy]," *Fars News Agency*, 9 May 2013, http://www.farsnews.com/newstext.php?nn=13920219000189; and "Navgarueh Bist va Nahom Niru-ye Darya-ye Artesh dar Bandar Djibouti Pehlu Gereft [The 29th Battle Group Docked in the Port of Djibouti]," *DefaPress.com*, 7 April 2014, http://www.defapress.com/Fa/News/15283.

112. Sidi Ould Abdel-Malek, "Turkish Warships Sail to Dakar as Part of Africa Tour," *Anadolu Agency*, 3 April 2014; Mohamed al-Khatemi, "Turkish Warships Dock Off Sudanese Coast," *Anadolu Agency*, 16 June 2014.

113. "Vice President in Sudan to Boost Bilateral Ties," *Daily Sabah*, 19 November 2018, https://www.dailysabah.com/diplomacy/2018/11/20/vice-president-in-sudan-to-boost-bilateral-ties.

114. "Vice President in Sudan to Boost Bilateral Ties."

115. "Turkey Leaving its Military Footprint Overseas," *Yeni Şafak*, 1 August 2017, https://www.yenisafak.com/en/news/turkey-leaving-its-military-footprint-overseas-2769879.

116. "Turkey Leaving its Military Footprint Overseas."

117. "Defense Minister Akar Visits Turkish Task Force Command in Somalia," *Daily Sabah*, 9 November 2018, https://www.dailysabah.com/diplomacy/2018/11/09/defense-minister-akar-visits-turkish-task-force-command-in-somalia; "Turkey Leaving its Military Footprint Overseas;" and "Turkey's First Overseas Military Base to Open in Africa," *Yeni Şafak*, 30 September 2016, https://www.yenisafak.com/en/news/turkeys-first-overseas-military-base-to-open-in-africa-2539457.

118. "Turkey's Plan to Set Up Military Training Centers in Sudan," Justice and Development Party (AKP), 6 November 2018.

119. "SADAT eski askerlere ne teklif ediyor," *OdaTV*, 5 March 2019, https://odatv.com/sadat-eski-askerlere-ne-teklif-ediyor-05031916.html; and Judah Ari Gross, "Shin Bet Accuses Turkey of Allowing Hamas to Raise, Launder Money," *The Times of Israel*, 12 February 2018, https://www.timesofisrael.com/arab-israeli-man-turkish-citizen-arrested-for-helping-to-fund-hamas/.

120. Can Kasapoğlu, "'The Blue Homeland': Turkey's Largest Naval Drill," *Anadolu Agency*, 27 February 2019, https://www.aa.com.tr/en/analysis/-the-blue-homeland-turkey-s-largest-naval-drill/1404267.

121. For example, see "Tahdid, Tahrim, va Teror, Khalali dar 'Dafa'e Muqa-das Hastehha-ye' Ijad Namikonad [Threats, Sanctions, and Assassinations Won't Interfere in 'Core Sacred Defense']," *Fars News.com,* 11 January 2012, http://www.farsnews.com/newstext.php?nn=13901021001600.

122. Nick Tattersall, "Weapons Seized in Nigeria Came from Iran: Shipping Company," *Reuters*, 30 October 2010, https://www.reuters.com/article/us-ni-geria-weapons/weapons-seized-in-nigeria-came-from-iran-shipping-company-idUSTRE69T1YT20101030; and "Morocco Severs Ties with Iran, Accusing It of Backing Polisario Front," *Reuters*, 1 May 2018, https://www.reuters.com/article/us-morocco-iran/morocco-severs1-ties-with-iran-accusing-it-of-backing-polisario-front-idUSKBN1I23VF.

123. "Africa Central to Turkey's Push for New World Order," *Daily Sabah*, 24 August 2018, https://www.dailysabah.com/diplomacy/2018/08/25/africa-cen-tral-to-turkeys-push-for-new-world-order.

Chapter 12
International Law as a Tool of Strategic Soft Power
Kevin G. Rousseau

International law has become an increasingly relevant component of soft power.[1] Soft power relies on shaping preferences and promoting the superior attractiveness of one's values as expressed by institutions and culture. Joseph S. Nye Jr., who coined the term soft power, pointed out that non-state actors and nongovernmental organizations (NGOs) contribute directly and indirectly to developing new norms and "altering public perceptions of what governments and firms should be doing."[2] These groups typically raise public awareness of laws and criticize governments for their failures to abide by these rules. Perceptions of who holds the moral high ground can improve or detract from a culture's reputation and attractiveness on the world stage, and the potential costs associated with actual or alleged violations of the law can be detrimental to the effective exercise of soft power.

There is nothing new about using law to legitimize one's claim to moral superiority. Shakespeare's King Henry V, before setting out to seize the throne of France, called upon the archbishop of Canterbury to "kindly explain to us the legal and religious grounds for why this French Salic law either should or shouldn't bar me in my claim."[3] The king was careful to warn his advisor not to "invent, twist, or distort your interpretation, or burden your conscience by subtly arguing for false claims. For God knows how many healthy men will shed their blood in support of whatever you persuade me to do."[4] In today's operational environment, states look toward international laws, treaties, and tribunals for the contested moral high ground rather than to archbishops. US adversaries in these contests use international law to support aspects of their respective strategies—sometimes with reasonable arguments, but sometimes with some twists and distortions of their own.

This chapter examines how non-state actors and states use international law as a soft power tool. Both use law to portray their actions as legitimate, promote their reputation as a rule-abiding organization, and persuade others that their values and culture are superior to their adversaries. Some states work to alter the prevailing international system to better align it with their preferred norms and modes of behavior. These trends influence the use of soft power and affect the use of military power. A subtle shift in emphasis in international law from sovereignty to humanitarian principles has helped create gaps between peace and war that state and non-state actors exploit through various measures short of war.

In the words of Philip Bobbitt: "Fundamental innovations in war bring about fundamental transformations in the consitutional order of states, while transformations in the constitutional order bring about fundamental changes in the conduct and aims of war."[5] Bobbitt also noted that the very success of democracies in the twentieth century "created the conditions for a new kind of conflict."[6] The outcome of wars can affect the prevailing international system, but changes in the international system can also affect the character of war.

Non-State Actors and Weak States

Growing emphasis on human rights and democratic values places international pressure on some states to conform to the new norms. These internationally imposed values are often at odds with the actor's own domestic values or threaten the power of the ruling regime. Some states have figured out how to balance internal concerns against this external pressure. These states have found that by enacting and paying a minimal amount of lip service to token measures, such as laws to protect minorities, they can manage a certain degree of exploitation of these same minorities without outside interference. By avoiding the most outrageous acts that would trigger intervention, these governments articulate policies with enough rhetorical support to international humanitarian values to ensure they have a relatively free domestic hand.

One way Central Asian states balanced international demands with domestic concerns was by conflating democratization with regime integrity in the wake of the Color Revolutions. As Alexander Cooley wrote:

In reacting to the perceived threat to regime integrity posed by so-called Western-style democracy and human rights appeals, the Central Asian states grafted a set of alternative norms, practices, and institutions, supported by Moscow and Beijing, which stressed the importance of sovereignty and cultural relativism.[7]

Kazakhstan's President Nursultan Nazarbayev was "one of the leading proponents of this cultural relativism."[8] Turkmenistan's president "painted with a broader brush, accusing all external efforts to raise issues of democracy or human rights as unacceptable infringements on Turkmen sovereignty."[9] By cloaking their interests in the language of international norms and values, these states sowed enough confusion over the true nature of their programs to block negative international reactions.

Central Asian states "strategically and expediently used the norms and justifications provided by foreign powers to guard and support their own domestic political practices."[10] Besides "cultural relativism," Central Asian countries also added "sovereign democracy" to their list of normative shields. Originally a Russian idea, sovereign democracy argues that democratic reforms must be enacted incrementally and modified to fit the domestic political culture.[11] These regimes protected themselves by exploiting the confusion in international law over whether sovereignty or human rights have primacy; "by grafting their own domestic pushback against Western democratic standards onto Russia's 'sovereign democracy' concept, Central Asian elites mounted an ideological and normative counteroffensive against the West."[12]

Central Asian countries used the sovereign democracy concept to justify crackdowns on NGOs that allegedly threatened their unique domestic form of developing democracy and, therefore, managed to "de-universalize democratic standards and values."[13] For example, Central Asian governments enacted laws to prevent foreign NGOs from mobilizing political opposition. Primary targets were NGOs such as Freedom House and Amnesty International.[14] Uzbekistan criminalized unapproved gatherings, to close approximately 300 NGOs between 2004 and 2007.[15] Kazakhstan passed new tax and security laws to close over thirty NGOs.[16] Using these measures, Central Asian states barred external non-state actors they considered politically destabilizing.

Such instrumentalization of law to achieve security objectives has come to be termed "lawfare." Lawfare is defined as "the strategy of using—or misusing—law as a substitute for traditional military means to achieve an operational objective."[17] Lawfare is a deliberate strategy "to gain advantage from one side's greater allegiance to international law and its processes."[18] Also considered as lawfare is the abuse of international humanitarian law (IHL) to destroy public support for military operations while "making the US fight with one hand tied behind its back."[19] Lawfare is also described as the use of law as a weapon of war and an obstacle to the state's legitimate use of armed force.[20]

Successful strategic performance requires an appreciation for the role of politics in war, and because law is an intensely political matter it is an integral part of the operational environment. In one of the first major works in English on the practice of lawfare, legal scholar Orde F. Kittrie analyzed the increasing effectiveness of using law to achieve objectives that previously might only have been achievable using force. Kittrie traced the first attempts at lawfare back to 1609 when Grotius used legal arguments to bolster Dutch maritime power.[21] Kittrie attributed the recent rise of lawfare to three factors: the increased number and reach of international laws and tribunals, the rise of NGOs focused on the law of armed conflict (LOAC), and the advance of globalization and economic interdependence.[22] Compliance-leverage disparity—defined as "the phenomenon of law and its processes (or particular laws and their processes) having greater leverage over some states or non-state actors (including individuals) rather than over others"—also drives lawfare.[23] Lawfare offers advantages that let weak powers compete in the courtroom with strong powers that they could not match on the battlefield.

Of course not all legal advantages lie with the weaker powers; some question whether labeling adverse legal actions as lawfare is an attempt by stronger states to intimidate weaker powers. To these critics, the lawfare concept is used by some governments to cast legitimate causes of action in a negative light. These critics view lawfare as a politically charged word "coined within the United States military and subsequently adopted by right-wing ideologues as a way of stigmatizing legitimate recourse to legal remedies, particularly within an international law context."[24] From this perspective, the term lawfare, "is being mobilized by neoconservatives to reframe liberal human rights NGOs as a security threat."[25] Labeling a legitimate cause of action as lawfare implies an improper abuse of the law, and blacklisting as lawfare what might be a legitimate grievance "runs counter to the right for a remedy, a firmly established principle of international law."[26]

The US government, according to these critics, depicts some valid legal procedures with which it disagrees as somehow unpatriotic by stigmatizing them as lawfare. Critics charged that:

> Lawfare has been developed to buttress this attitude. Lawfare, as it has been applied recently, is intended to intimidate and silence lawyers; it equates them with the enemy and suggests that their arguments contain at least a seed of treason."[27]

These critics argued that labeling legal actions designed to challenge the state's use of force as lawfare is, in reality, a public information campaign against valid accusations of excessive government force. Discouraging lawfare is contrary to the purpose of law, because to "insinuate that advancing such arguments is lawfare, and hence illegitimate, is to insinuate that law should never constrain armed might. Thus the radical critique of lawfare amounts to an assault on international humanitarian law and international criminal law as such."[28] One study found the threat of lawfare over-politicized and concluded that "litigation lawfare is largely a myth" and that the "threat of lawfare was overstated and was adequately handled by our judicial system."[29]

Others claim that the term lawfare abuses the law because it is a blanket term for acts that are already plainly illegal, and do not represent any essential change in the way law is perceived. To these observers, "manipulation by belligerents of the law—for instance by hiding amongst the civilian population and leading the other party to commit possible violations of [international humanitarian law]—is better described as a war crime than an act of lawfare."[30] The act of using civilians as a shield may be taking advantage of an opponent's respect for IHL, but that act is already considered a LOAC violation. According to these critics, it is unnecessary to create a new lawfare category because these violations represent nothing new or unique.

Weaker powers, however, have effectively targeted the legitimacy of military operations by alleging battlefield IHL violations. Examples of this type of lawfare have been used against Israel and its operations in the Gaza Strip. Israel, in turn, has responded with its own forms of lawfare. The use of lawfare evolved to such an extent in the Israeli-Palestinian conflict that Kittrie described it as "the closest thing the world has to a lawfare laboratory."[31]

For example, Hamas used lawfare on the battlefield against Israel by hiding among the civilian population and using protected sites as shields. Hamas counted on Israel's greater need to comply with the protections to civilian populations, such as those proscribed in Article 48, 51, and 52 of Additional Protocol I to the Geneva Conventions requiring the parties in a conflict to distinguish between military and civilian persons and objects.[32] Hamas's IHL violation—placing civilians at risk by using them as shields—puts Israel in the position of potentially violating international law by targeting sites where civilians will be killed.[33]

Various international investigations have become mired in controversy over whether investigators emphasized Israeli IHL violations while failing to address Hamas's inappropriate use of protected objects such as hospitals. For example, Israel launched a three-week 2008 military offensive in the Gaza Strip that killed approximately 1,300 Palestinians and wounded over 5,000 persons.[34] These military operations led to allegations of war crimes and IHL violations against both Israel and Hamas. The UN set up a fact-finding mission on the Gaza Conflict led by international lawyer Richard Goldstone that came to be known as the Goldstone Mission. The mission report—called the Goldstone Report—concluded that "both Israel and Hamas committed international law violations by indiscriminately targeting civilians."[35]

The controversial Goldstone Report had some far-reaching strategic implications. First, it placed what some criticized as disproportionate blame on the Israelis. Second, it provided Hamas an opportunity to attack the legitimacy of Israel's military operations and claim the moral high ground. Finally, the report's conclusions set a potential precedent that could affect the military practices of other states facing a similar dilemma as Israel. Regardless of whether or not the report was biased, the controversy itself helped weaken domestic and international support for Israeli military operations in the Gaza Strip.

Critics complained that the report unjustly placed the blame and culpability for human rights violations heavily upon the Israelis. The report was simply "far more willing to draw adverse inferences of intentionality from Israeli conduct and statements than from comparable Palestinian conduct and statements."[36] According to the report, "Israel used the rocket attacks on its citizens as a pretext, an excuse, a cover for the real purpose of the operation, which was to target innocent Palestinian civilians—children, women, the elderly—for death."[37]

UN investigators laid the blame for war crimes squarely upon the Israeli leadership rather than Hamas. The report concluded that Israel's "failure to distinguish between combatants and civilians appears to the Mission to have been the result of deliberate guidance issued to soldiers, as described by some of them, and not the result of occasional lapses."[38] Furthermore, "responsibility lies in the first place with those who designed, planned, ordered, and oversaw the operations."[39] In contrast, investigators found no evidence that Hamas fighters donned civilian clothes or fought from protected sites such as mosques, and concluded that Hamas "was not guilty of deliberately and willfully using the civilian population as human shields."[40]

Hamas, in effect, exploited compliance-leverage disparity to take advantage of Israel's greater interest in abiding by IHL. The less militarily capable side had successfully gained an edge over its opponent because of its willingness to "openly violate the law of war to gain a tactical advantage in specific operations by handicapping the ability of the IHL-compliant military to carry out its mission within the bounds of the law."[41] Hamas succeeded in casting doubt on the legitimacy of Israel's military actions by targeting public and international opinion critical to political support for Israel's war effort. Hamas's exploitation of IHL exemplified a strategy where the "technologically and militarily disadvantaged forces target public support and seek to force a political end to the fighting."[42]

Supporters of the Goldstone Report fired back against these critics by denouncing the accusations of lawfare and arguing that the report served a useful purpose. Supporters objected to the way critics cast the report as an example of lawfare, claiming that the term lawfare itself was being "used abusively to attack critics who invoke the illegality of the behavior of certain military forces, including those of Israel and the United States."[43] To its supporters, the Goldstone Report deterred future Israeli excesses because it "heightened the risk for Israel that another sovereign state will choose to prosecute its political or military leaders."[44]

Israel learned from the Goldstone Report experience that it needed to play a stronger role in shaping the strategic narrative. Part of the reason the report was so harsh on Israel was that Israel was uncooperative with investigators, leaving the Palestinian Authority (PA) to supply most of the evidence.[45] During military actions in Gaza in 2008 to 2009, and in 2014, Israel undertook an extensive information recording and media campaign to "push back against accusations that its uses of force violated the laws of war."[46] For example, the Israeli military posted a 2014 online briefing that documented evidence it collected of Hamas firing from protected sites, concluding that Hamas's tactics "flagrantly violate international law."[47] Israel also instituted new methods to limit civilian casualties, such as dropping leaflets warning about upcoming attacks, making recorded warning telephone calls, and firing warning rounds.[48] Nevertheless, the June 2015 UN investigation report, although arguably more balanced than the Goldstone Report, "failed to address, and thus had the effect of encouraging, Hamas's battlefield lawfare."[49]

Lawfare is a characteristic of an emerging world order where international courts and international law have a stronger role in matters concerning the use of force. Israeli legal scholar Yoram Dinstein warned not to underestimate the power of international law and lawfare because it is a "weapon of mass disinformation, attuned to the peculiarities of the era in which we live."[50] As some observers note, international investigations such as the Goldstone Report may suggest emerging trends in how some basic LOAC principles will be applied to the future use of force.[51]

Leveraging the legal system to influence public opinion in a conflict is not limited to legal actions against states. Individuals have also been subject to lawsuits intended to intimidate a group's critics and garner public support for a cause. Perhaps the most notable examples have been Islamist groups that some claim used lawsuits as a weapon to indirectly augment military force. One observer, Brooke Goldstein, labeled such lawfare as the "new jihad."[52]

Goldstein emphasized two goals of Islamist supporters within the legal system. The first goal was to "abolish public discourse critical of Islam."[53] The second objective was "to impede the free flow of public information about the threat of Islamist terrorism thereby limiting our ability to understand and destroy it."[54] She argued that lawfare emerged as a legal campaign in domestic and international courts that complemented terrorism and asymmetric warfare. The method employed was "often predatory, filed without serious expectation of winning, and undertaken as a means to intimidate, demoralize, and bankrupt defendants."[55] One primary example was "the libel tourist," Khalid bin Mahfouz, who often sued American researchers and authors in British courts for libel against Islam.[56] The intent was to instill a fear of resource-draining lawsuits against publishing material offensive to Islam, thereby "creat[ing] a detrimental chilling effect on open public dialogue about issues of national security and public concern."[57]

Other examples of Islamists using lawfare to promote their cause include the London Muslim Brotherhood, which "employed a dream team of internationally renowned British lawyers . . . to start legal proceedings against the Egyptian government, potentially in the International Criminal Court."[58] Islamists have long used this approach—working within the existing institutions of a non-Islamic entity to prepare the way for the eventual introduction of an Islamic system—against secular regimes.

The use of Western norms and institutions against the West itself is not new to Islamists. For example, the so-called Project memorandums—notes from a 1991 Muslim Brotherhood meeting outlining their strategic goals for North America—advocated gradually using the West's own institutions against it, and "frequently uses the Western-based international legal system."[59] Islam is flexible enough to reconcile alien legal systems with its own, as evidenced by past multicultural Islamic societies such as the Ottoman Empire.

Some interpretations of Islam consider such an accommodation as but a temporary step toward the recreation of a new Islamic-based system modeled on the caliphate. Supporters of the caliphate narrative, such as the Islamic State, find credibility in an interpretation of Islam that historically "refused to recognize legal systems other than its own."[60] For example, "the modern international system, born of the 1648 Peace of Westphalia, relies on each state's willingness to recognize borders, however grudgingly. For the Islamic State, that recognition is ideological suicide."[61] The Islamic State's rejection of the modern secular world takes these beliefs further and "looks nonsensical except in light of a sincere, carefully considered commitment to returning civilization to a seventh-century legal environment and ultimately to bringing about the apocalypse."[62] If this is lawfare, it is lawfare at its most extreme.

State Actors: The Major Powers

Major powers also use international law in a conflict and do so with more strategic effect. Strong states are able to extract enduring strategic advantages from international law, although some states are more inclined to exploit these advantages than others. Major powers are strategically more resilient and remain capable of exhibiting rapid innovation and novel adaptations in the changing international legal environment because strong states can draw upon greater legal resources.

First, stronger states have the potential to use more sophisticated legal tools, such as financial law, as part of their lawfare. For example, China and Russia "view themselves as victims of hegemonic power wielded by the West, in particular by legal power exercised through international law, sometimes in the form of unfair treaties."[63] International law is an arena where these states can seek to increase their relative influence without using military power. Like weaker powers and non-state actors, larger and more powerful states are also poised to take advantage of the transition in international law by alternatively emphasizing different principles to benefit themselves.

Second, citing humanitarian ideals couched under IHL can provide convenient political cover and legitimacy to state interventions. Some legal scholars have even argued that IHL has become an unexpected threat to peace because it weakens the protections traditionally granted to sovereign states and provides new justifications for the use of military force. "The idea is powerful. States are not fully sovereign when they are violating human rights. Powerful, but with deleterious effects for other international legal norms."[64] Rather than international law serving as a tool to discourage war, strong states can use international law as part of their own narrative to justify using military force.

Recent interventions in Syria, for example, arguably further relaxed international prohibitions on the use of force. United Nations Charter 2(4) forbids the "threat or use of force against the territorial integrity or political independence of any state."[65] However, the humanitarian crisis in Syria became a major justification for the use of force, an arguable departure from the principles of Article 2(4). Such departures are frought with risk: "Many in the West assume that we—meaning the West—can set the rules for the appropriate departures from Article 2(4). Russia has made clear in Eastern Europe that it will use those departures to its own ends. China may be next."[66] States have also developed alternatives to state-sponsored military forces—witness Russia's use of private security forces in Syria—that allow them to further exploit these openings in international law, granting them greater flexibility in the use of these forces.[67]

The Strategic Use of Lawfare

Lawfare likewise is not restricted to weaker powers and non-state actors; "modern State military forces do legitimately use the law to achieve military outcomes."[68] To depict lawfare solely as a weapon for the weaker side neglects half the phenomenon and "gives a one-sided perspective on the role of law in contemporary conflicts. It largely neglects the many ways in which governments and the military use law strategically and presents the recourse to law and legal procedure as something negative."[69] Carl von Clausewitz's insights are relevant here, because he "was keenly aware of the political dimension, and this is the linkage to today's understanding of lawfare."[70] In today's international legal environment, strong states recognize that law—like war—can also be used to compel an enemy to do their will.

Many states, with some notable exceptions, have yet to fully embrace the concept of lawfare. Exceptions include China, which systematically wages lawfare across the operational environment, to include maritime and aviation lawfare, space lawfare, and cyberspace.[71] As China opened up to the world in the post-Mao era, its ability to engage with international law suffered as a result of suppressing lawyers during the Cultural Revolution. In the last decade, however, China's lawyers have become increasingly more active and proficient on the international scene.[72] China has now incorporated law into its strategic thinking and developed a comprehensive approach to lawfare that is coordinated across the Chinese government. For example, China used maritime law to justify denying access to international navigation in the South China Sea.[73] China has developed a concept of lawfare it calls "falu zhan" or "falu zhanzheng," or "legal warfare," as part of its strategic thought.[74]

A 1999 treatise published by the People's Liberation Army (PLA) titled *Unrestricted Warfare* provided some insight into Chinese conceptual

218

thinking on lawfare. Written by two PLA colonels, this study showed that Chinese thinkers draw inspiration from foreign practices, including those of the United States. The authors observed that "non-military war operations" were "being waged with greater and greater frequency."[75] Among the examples cited were trade wars waged "with particularly great skill in the hands of the Americans, who have perfected it to a fine art."[76] The treatise listed various measures such as "the use of domestic trade law on the international stage; the arbitrary erection and dismantling of tariff barriers; the use of hastily written trade sanctions; [and] the imposition of embargoes on exports of critical technologies."[77] One lesson the Chinese authors drew from studying these non-military measures was that "these means can have a destructive effect that is equal to that of a military operation."[78]

China demonstrates the potential for law to shape strategy when approached from a more aggressive perspective by also treating international law "as an offensive weapon capable of hamstringing opponents and seizing the political initiative."[79] China's version of lawfare is more "instrumental" and focused on positive results, while "Western military legal experts appear more focused on ensuring that their forces and commanders are not liable to war crimes charges than they are on undertaking offensive legal warfare."[80] Kittrie provided several examples of Chinese lawfare, including its deliberately inaccurate interpretations of international law to force changes in the customary Law of the Sea.[81]

For example, the Chinese assert that the UN Convention on the Law of the Sea (UNCLOS) provides broad powers over rights of passage and that "foreign naval operations within another nation's 200 nautical mile Exclusive Economic Zone (EEZ) should be subject to the approval of the owning state."[82] This is a deliberate misinterpretation of UNCLOS. However, Chinese claims of broad powers within the EEZ, if left unchallenged, can eventually bear fruit because "customary international law can be nullified or even changed through state practice with an assertion that such practice is consistent with international law."[83] By using international law, China can potentially expand its area of control in the South China Sea without using force.

Another adept practitioner of lawfare is Israel, which has been forced to develop a number of lawfare countermeasures to include pre-strike warnings and other changes to its battlefield operations.[84] Israel's experience with lawfare also provides an example of how the state can draw upon its superior legal resources and more sophisticated legal tools to achieve a military objective without using force. In May 2010, Israeli forces intercepted a flotilla of ships from Turkey attempting to violate a blockade of the Hamas-controlled Gaza Strip, killing nine people. A UN fact-finding mission subsequently criticized Israel for its handling of the incident. Faced with a similar flotilla leaving Greece in June 2011, Israeli lawyers used legal measures to stop the ships from leaving port. The measures included threatening legal action against companies providing the ships essential services such as maritime insurance. In letters to these companies, Israeli lawyers referenced the US Supreme Court case of *Holder v. Humanitarian Law Project* to argue that providing services to the flotilla was illegal because it supported terrorism. The legal letters proved persuasive. By rendering the ships unable to secure the necessary services to gain permission to leave their Greek ports, Israel succeeded in stopping the 2011 flotilla without firing a shot.[85]

Another phenomenon arguably resulting from the shifting international legal environment has been the use of international law as a component of so-called hybrid warfare. Russia is a leading example of using "legal arguments as a means to support hybrid warfare."[86] One way to do this is to cast doubt on whether an act is legitimate under international law and cause indecision and hesitation among opponents until it is too late to act. The uncertain relationship between sovereignty and humanitarian law leaves ample room to sow confusion and shape a convincing narrative.

The concept of self-determination and its relationship with humanitarian interventions was central to Russia's justifications for intervening in Ukraine. The self-determination debate arose earlier when NATO intervened in Kosovo. NATO used legitimate humanitarian concerns as justification for trumping Serbia's sovereignty. The West's argument would later be turned on its head and used by Russia with respect to the Crimean crisis.

The Kosovo experience was an instructive one for Moscow. In his Kremlin speech on 18 March 2014, Russian President Vladimir Putin cited the "Kosovo precedent—a precedent our Western colleagues created with their own hands in a very similar situation, when they agreed that the unilateral separation of Kosovo from Serbia, exactly what Crimea is doing now, was legitimate."[87] Moscow criticized the West over its legal justifications for the Kosovo war at the time and its subsequent independence, but found the arguments useful and "Russia adopted this rhetoric itself, regarding Crimea."[88]

The shifting nature of international law provided an opportunity for Russia "to construct its own 'legal' framework."[89] This legal framework allows Russia to use noble-sounding ideals to justify interventions, portraying these actions as legitimate and securing public support. Russia's strategic approach to "Crimea and eastern Ukraine has been an amalgamation of stealth invasion and quasi-legal rhetoric. The stealth part of the invasion was to maintain a fig-leaf of deniability and to make the uprising in eastern Ukraine seem homegrown, as opposed to Russian-led."[90] Russia used the rhetoric of self-determination and effectively exploited international law to mask its true motivations and further its interests in the Crimea. This strategy "interlocks with Russia's rhetoric, a quasi-legal/ nationalist amalgamation that attempts to persuade those who can be persuaded and befuddle those who cannot."[91]

Russia is taking advantage of the shift in sovereignty's priority under international law. Russia used the rhetoric of self-determination to shift the emphasis it traditionally placed on state sovereignty. For Russia "sovereignty moved from being the core value that was protected by international law, to simply a fact that may or may not come into play in a particular circumstance."[92] Russia appears to have recognized that the evolving international legal environment has provided an opportunity for justifying interventions that earlier would have been clear sovereignty violations. Framing the Crimea issue in these terms "gave Russia the opportunity to use the persuasive rhetoric of self-determination to frame its perspective of what was and was not allowed under international law."[93]

Hybrid warfare may not be new, but the expanded opportunities presented under international law are a recent phenomenon, and exploitation of these gaps in international law allowed Russia to frame the strategic narrative. Russia's arguments are well-crafted to take advantage of the coalitional nature of NATO because "the use of international legal rhetoric in general, and framing an issue as a self-determination struggle in particular, can put other actors, such as the United States and the EU, on the wrong foot, making it difficult to marshal an effective response."[94] For example, Russian opportunism and disregard for international law pose a looming dilemma for NATO by threatening the integrity of Article 5 of the North Atlantic Treaty because the "use of the rhetoric of self-determination can be used to befuddle and confuse treaty obligations and military strategy."[95] NATO faces a potential dilemma in considering how it will respond to an unclear Russian threat to seize a small slice of a NATO ally because to ignore such an act undermines Article 5, but to respond with force risks escalation over ambiguous stakes.

The use of alternatives to the state-sponsored military force, whether through proxies, by contractors, or via mercenaries, is another increasing phenomenon since the end of the Cold War. Russia also used proxy forces in the Crimea and Ukraine and concealed the use of its own military forces to sow confusion and obscure its actions. Russia's motives probably were to obscure its involvement in what it wanted to depict as an internal uprising and exploit the gap between peace and war long enough to forestall a more decisive NATO response. By using proxy forces and denying the role of Russian troops, Russia succeeded in depicting the situation in Ukraine as a civil war such that Western media often referred to Kiev's opponents as rebel forces without acknowledging the presence of Russian personnel.[96] Russia strove to "create doubts and anxieties on the part of western governments and the public whom they serve, knowing that no democratic country commits readily to support a cause fraught with ambiguity."[97] Russia's legal arguments didn't need to be completely convincing to everyone; they merely needed to foster enough uncertainty over the true nature of the conflict long enough to create facts on the ground that favored its preferred outcome.

Exploiting the Law's Gaps and the Importance of Legitimacy

Strong states and weaker actors seek to use international law to further military objectives but in different ways. There are at least three major differences. First, strong states have more at stake in terms of using international law to legitimize their actions. Non-state actors often have alternative sources of legitimacy, and view legitimacy derived from international law as a state vulnerability that can be exploited. Second, strong states are better equipped to extract long-term advantages from international law. States tend to exploit more sophisticated legal areas such as financial regulations that leverage a non-state actor's greater vulnerability to the disparate costs and benefits of compliance. States have the strategic culture to incorporate international law into their strategic thinking. States control the international law venue that makes the rules. Finally, strong states and weaker actors are both willing to manipulate, change, or simply ignore international law if necessary to further their vital interests. The unintended consequences of this behavior for the international order probably place strong states at risk more than other actors in the system.

Central to how states and non-state actors leverage international law are their different approaches to legitimacy. International law is a system created by states and it is natural for states to pin their legitimacy to compliance with the agreed-upon rules. States, whether strong or weak, are more concerned with appearing to act in accordance with international law and to depict their use of force as justified and legitimate. Non-state actors use international law to cast doubt on the legitimacy of their state opponents rather than to bolster their own.

Use of international law by non-state actors in these terms is almost entirely offensive. It is more difficult for states to use IHL in offensive lawfare against non-state actors, for many non-state actors do not consider all international norms as entirely valid. They find legitimacy through other means such as popular support, leading to a compliance-leverage disparity with respect to international law. At one extreme are the jihadists who dream of an entirely new system of international order based on Islam, and on the other extreme are those who push for humanitarian considerations to trump more traditional concepts of international law.

Chinese thinkers have already contemplated the different approaches various actors take toward lawfare. *Unrestricted Warfare* noted that whether or not states acknowledge the law "often depends on whether or not they are beneficial to themselves." Another difference is that small states "hope to use the rules to protect their own interests, while large nations attempt to utilize the rules to control other nations. When the rules are not in accord with the interests of one's own nation, generally speaking, the breaking of the rules by small nations can be corrected by large nations in the name of enforcers of the law."[98] Weak powers, however, have little inherent power to enforce the rules, and look more often to the growing influence of international tribunals or to the court of public opinion for leverage over stronger powers.[99]

The use of international law by non-state actors to undermine the legitimacy of state military actions has immediate strategic implications. For example, media reports on "civilian casualties caused by state forces, whether in Gaza, Iraq, or Afghanistan, produce an immediate outcry and debates about the lawfulness of the military operation, the motives of the state forces, and the potential for criminal liability."[100] Non-state actors can exploit civilian deaths against the state on a strategic level to undermine popular and international support for the state's military campaign. In addition to opportunistically exploiting civilian casualty situations, opponents "unconstrained by humanitarian ethics now take the strategy to the next level, that of orchestrating situations that deliberately endanger noncombatants. Civilians thus become a pawn at the strategic level as well, because they are used not only for tactical advantage (e.g., shelter) in specific situations, but for broader strategic and political advantage."[101]

States derive strength from legitimacy, so it is also a potential vulnerability. Announcing that one has a just cause for war and claiming moral superiority puts one at risk of forfeiting legitimacy by losing the moral high ground. Lawfare "can be effectively canvassed to corrode the indispensable home-front support for a given war."[102] Conflict legitimacy is vulnerable to public opinion, and when that legitimacy is based on following the humanitarian aspects of international law then any perceived moral failure undermines that legitimacy.

Strong states have proved adept at exploiting the gaps in the international legal order as well as, perhaps better than, weak powers and non-state actors. NATO and the West successfully intervened in Kosovo and secured its independence. Russia has manipulated international law to justify absorbing part of a neighboring country. China is using lawfare to try to force changes in the customary international Law of the Sea. States have proved able to successfully use legal measures to help secure their strategic objectives.

Some argue that the US has yet to fully tap into its potential lawfare capabilities. The US does not possess a comprehensive approach to lawfare strategy as China or Israel have developed. Kittrie described how parts of the US government successfully used legal techniques to achieve strategic results, such as the US Treasury and its use of international financial laws against Iran.[103] Also, some of the most effective US lawfare has been the work of private sector attorneys. Kittrie provided several examples of litigation using the Anti-Terrorism Act of 1990. A significant case was *Boim v. Holy Land Foundation*, in which attorneys working on behalf of the family of a US victim of terrorism secured a judgment against Islamic fundraising organizations, drying up a significant source of financial support to Hamas.[104]

Given the vast experience of the US legal community, "the United States has the potential to be the dominant lawfare superpower."[105] However, the US has refrained from incorporating law into its national strategy, with the exception of a mention in the 2005 National Defense Strategy that Kittrie noted unfortunately seemed to dismiss lawfare as a strategy of the weak that was of little use to the United States.[106] The US government has yet to fully tap into the national reservoir of legal talent to maximize its advantages in legal skills and abilities, advantages already being demonstrated by US private sector attorneys.[107]

US private sector expertise can inform potential military uses of lawfare. Kittrie described how Special Operations Command Pacific reached out to the University of Pennsylvania's Law School for research on foreign criminal laws that could be used to detain and prosecute foreign fighters supporting the Islamic State.[108] In Kittrie's assessment, if the US properly leveraged its extensive legal expertise to support a national lawfare strategy, the "US advantage in sophisticated legal weapons has the potential to be even greater than its advantage in sophisticated lethal weapons."[109]

International law has come to play an expanded role in the use of force. This expanded role elevated evolving humanitarian law concepts over the longstanding preference for sovereignty, and contributed to the state losing its uncontested control over the direction of war. The "state therefore has an interest in re-appropriating the control and direction of war." As Hew Strachan noted, "that is the purpose of strategy."[110] Arguments about international law are part of diplomacy, and "diplomatic arguments are a means to an end. They are part of a strategy."[111] For this reason, in the tight relationship between law and politics, law has a Clausewitzian link to war. Competitors such as Russia that view international law as a weapon show that "to simply ignore legal argument is to cede a strategy, to concede multiple positions."[112] As one study of Russian legal maneuvers on Ukraine concluded, "to shape the legal environment unchecked is to concede that lawfare can adversely shape the battlefield without hindrance from those whose interests are undermined."[113] To leave legal arguments unchallenged not only cedes a strategy and a soft power tool, it cedes taking a guiding hand in shaping the operational environment, and perhaps in shaping the nature of contemporary strategy itself.

Notes

1. Portions of this article were derived from the author's previously published work: Kevin G. Rousseau, "International Law and Military Strategy," *Journal of National Security Law and Policy* 9, no. 1 (2017): 1–27.

2. Joseph S. Nye Jr., *Soft Power: The Means to Success in World Politics* (New York: Perseus Books, 2004), 90.

3. *Henry V*, Act 1 Scene 2.

4. *Henry V*, Act 1 Scene 2.

5. Philip Bobbitt, *Terror and Consent: The Wars for the Twenty-First Century* (New York: Anchor Books, 2009), 23.

6. Bobbitt, 11.

7. Alexander Cooley, *Great Games, Local Rules* (New York: Oxford University Press, 2012), 98.

8. Cooley, 112.

9. Cooley, 112.

10. Cooley, 9.

11. Cooley, 112.

12. Cooley, 114.

13. Cooley, 112.

14. Cooley, 109.

15. Cooley, 109.

16. Cooley, 109.

17. Charles Dunlap, "Lawfare Today: A Perspective," *Yale Journal of International Affairs* (Winter 2008): 148.

18. Orde F. Kittrie, "Lawfare and U.S. National Security," *Case Western Reserve Journal of International Law* 43, no. 1 & 2 (Fall 2011): 396.

19. Kittrie, 396.

20. Kittrie, 393.

21. Kittrie, 4.

22. Kittrie, 40.

23. Kittrie, 20.

24. William A. Schabas, "Gaza, Goldstone, and Lawfare," *Case Western Reserve Journal of International Law* 43, no. 1 & 2 (Fall 2011): 309.

25. Neve Gordon, "Human Rights as a Security Threat: Lawfare and the Campaign against Human Rights NGOs," *Law and Society Review* 48, no. 2 (2014): 312.

26. William J. Aceves, "Litigating the Arab-Israeli Conflict in US Courts: Critiquing the Lawfare Critique," *Case Western Reserve Journal of International Law* 43, no. 1 & 2 (Fall 2011): 313.

27. Scott Horton, "The Dangers of Lawfare," *Case Western Reserve Journal of International Law* 43, no. 1 & 2 (Fall 2011): 168.

28. David Luban, "Carl Schmitt and the Critique of Lawfare," *Case Western Reserve Journal of International Law* 43, no. 1 & 2 (Fall 2011): 462.

29. John Swanberg, "Lawfare: A Current Threat or Much Ado about Nothing?" (master's thesis, US Army War College, Carlisle Barracks, PA, 2013), 16.

30. Jamie A. Williamson, "The Knight's Code, Not His Lance," *Case Western Reserve Journal of International Law* 43, no. 1 & 2 (Fall 2011): 448.

31. Kittrie, "Lawfare," 197.

32. Kittrie, 290.

33. Kittrie, 288.

34. Milena Sterio, "The Gaza Strip: Israel, Its Foreign Policy, and the Goldstone Report," *Case Western Reserve Journal of International Law* 43, no. 1 & 2 (Fall 2011): 229.

35. Sterio, 229.

36. Alan Dershowitz, *The Case Against the Goldstone Report: A Study in Evidentiary Bias* (Boston: Harvard University Law School Public Law & Legal Theory Working Paper Series, Paper No. 10-26, February 2010), 1, http://nrs.harvard.edu/urn-3:HUL.InstRepos:3593975.

37. Dershowitz, 2.

38. United Nations, General Assembly, Human Rights Council, *Report of the United Nations Fact-Finding Mission on the Gaza Conflict* (12th sess., A/HRC/12/48, 25 September 2009), 407, http://www2.ohchr.org/english/bodies/hrcouncil/docs/12session/A-HRC-12-48.pdf.

39. United Nations, 408.

40. Dershowitz, *The Case Against the Goldstone Report*, 3.

41. Laurie R. Blank, "Finding Facts but Missing the Law: The Goldstone Report, Gaza, and Warfare," *Case Western Reserve Journal of International Law* 43, no. 1 & 2 (Fall 2011): 283.

42. Blank, 283.

43. Schabas, "Gaza, Goldstone, and Lawfare," 307.

44. Sterio, "The Gaza Strip," 253.

45. Sterio, 304.

46. Sterio, 304.

47. Israeli Defense Force, "Hamas War Tactics: Attacks from Civilian Centers," 14 August 2014, http://acdemocracy.org/wp-content/uploads/2014/08/Hamas-Urban-Warfare-Tactics.pdf.

48. Kittrie, *Lawfare,* 297.

49. Kittrie, 288.

50. Yoram Dinstein, "Concluding Remarks: LOAC and Attempts to Abuse or Subvert It," in *International Law and the Changing Character of War,* ed. Raul Pedrozo and Daria Wollschlaeger (Newport, RI: International Law Studies 87, 2011), 484.

51. David E. Graham, "The Law of Armed Conflict in Asymmetric Urban Armed Conflict," in *International Law and the Changing Character of War,* 302.

52. Goldstein and Meyer, "Legal Jihad," 395.

53. Brooke Goldstein and Aaron Eitan Meyer, *Lawfare: The War against Free Speech. A First Amendment Guide for Reporting in an Age of Islamist Lawfare* (Washington, DC: The Center for Security Policy, 2011), 15.

54. Goldstein and Meyer, 15.

55. Goldstein and Meyer, 16.

56. Goldstein and Meyer, 155.

57. Goldstein and Meyer, 16.

58. Bel Trew, "London Underground," *Foreign Policy* (27 September 2013), http://foreignpolicy.com/2013/09/27/london-underground/.

59. Clarion Project, *The Muslim Brotherhood*, 16, accessed 22 November 2015, http://www.clarionproject.org/sites/default/files/Muslim-Brotherhood-Special-Report.pdf.

60. Majid Khadduri, *War and Peace in the Laws of Islam* (New Jersey: The Lawbook Exchange, 2010), vii.

61. Graeme Wood, "What ISIS Really Wants," *The Atlantic* (March 2015): 88, http://www.theatlantic.com/magazine/archive/2015/03/what-isis-really-wants/384980/.

62. Wood, 80.

63. Ingrid Wuerth, "International Human Rights Law: An Unexpected Threat to Peace," 101 *Marquette Law Review* (2018): 803–19.

64. Wuerth, 810.

65. United Nations Charter, Art 2, (4).

66. Wuerth, "International Human Rights Law," 813.

67. Thomas Gibbons-Neff, "How a 4-Hour Battle Between Russian Mercenaries and U.S. Commandos Unfolded in Syria," *New York Times*, 24 May 2018, https://www.nytimes.com/2018/05/24/world/middleeast/american-commandos-russian-mercenaries-syria.html.

68. Dale Stephens, "The Age of Lawfare," in *International Law and the Changing Character of War*, 327.

69. Wouter Werner, "The Curious Career of Lawfare," *Case Western Reserve Journal of International Law* 43, no. 1 & 2 (Fall 2011): 71.

70. Charles Dunlap, "Lawfare: A Decisive Element of 21st Century Conflicts?," *Joint Force Quarterly* 54 (3rd Quarter 2009): 35.

71. Kittrie, "Lawfare," 165.

72. Kittrie, 186–87.

73. Kittrie, 165–68.

74. Dean Cheng, *Winning Without Fighting: Chinese Legal Warfare* (report, Heritage Foundation, 18 May 2012): 2, http://report.heritage.org/bg269.

75. Qiao Liang and Wang Xiangsui, *Unrestricted Warfare* (Beijing: PLA Literature and Arts Publishing House, February 1999), 50, https://www.oodaloop.com/documents/unrestricted.pdf.

76. Liang and Xiangsui, 51.

77. Liang and Xiangsui, 51.

78. Liang and Xiangsui, 51.

79. Cheng, *Winning Without Fighting*, 1.

80. Cheng, 7.

81. Kittrie, "Lawfare," 166.

82. Cheng, *Winning Without Fighting*, 9.

83. Kittrie, "Lawfare," 166.

84. Kittrie, 284.

85. Kittrie, 313–14.

86. Christopher J. Borgen, "Law, Rhetoric, Strategy: Russia and Self-Determination Before and After Crimea," *International Law Studies* 91 (2015): 268, http://stockton.usnwc.edu/ils/vol91/iss1/7/.

87. "Crimea Crisis: Russian President Putin's Speech Annotated," *BBC*, 19 March 2014, http://www.bbc.com/news/world-europe-26652058.

88. "Crimea Crisis."

89. Borgen, "Law, Rhetoric, Strategy," 262.

90. Borgen, 266.

91. Borgen, 266.

92. Borgen, 260.

93. Borgen, 266.

94. Borgen, 269.

95. Borgen, 270.

96. Thomas Grant, "Russia's Invasion of Ukraine: What Does International Law Have to Say?," Lawfare blog, 25 August 2015, https://www.lawfareblog.com/russias-invasion-ukraine-what-does-international-law-have-say.

97. Grant.

98. Qiao and Wang, *Unrestricted Warfare*, 130.

99. The Palestinian Authority's April 2015 accession to the International Criminal Court exemplified how international tribunals and organizations can allow weak actors to punch well above their weight in the international arena. See Kittrie, "Lawfare," 208.

100. Blank, "Finding Facts but Missing the Law," 304.

101. Blank, 304.

102. Dinstein, "Concluding Remarks: LOAC and Attempts to Abuse or Subvert It," 485.

103. Kittrie, "Lawfare," 111.

104. Kittrie, 54–60.

105. Kittrie, 343.

106. Kittrie, 30.

107. Kittrie, 38.

108. Kittrie, 107.

109. Kittrie, 32.

110. Hew Strachan, *The Direction of War: Contemporary Strategy in Historical Perspective* (Cambridge: Cambridge University Press, 2013), 42.

111. Borgen, "Law, Rhetoric, Strategy," 263.

112. Borgen, 278.

113. Michael A. Newton, "Illustrating Illegitimate Lawfare," *Case Western Reserve Journal of International Law* 43, no. 1 & 2 (Fall 2011): 261.

Chapter 13
Narrative in Culture, Center of Gravity, and the Golden Azimuth
Brian L. Steed

The source of conflict can be characterized as a problem in communication between parties.[1] In the absence of clear communication, a competition or conflict develops between the wills of opponents. The objective of conflict should be to change the will of the opponent to be more in line with one's preferences, which is in line with what Carl von Clausewitz stated: "War is thus an act of force to compel our enemy to do our will."[2]

This act of force is a form of communication—an expression of intent, commitment, and objective. Communication is difficult between people and societies even when those people and societies share a common perspective. When those involved in communicating come from significantly different cultural perspectives the problems of effective communication are only exacerbated.

The reasons, purposes, or necessary forces to compel an opponent are dependent, in large measure, on cultural values, norms, and identities. One of the fundamental problems that arises from trying to assess the communications of another person from another culture is mirror imaging. I perceive in another's actions that which I would have intended under the same circumstances. This introspection allows me to imagine what I might intend to communicate in response.

In trying to understand the other by conducting mirror imaging, the problem is that I cannot see another in a mirror. This is visualized in Figure 13.1 as the blue figure tries to understand the red figure, but only really sees itself in the mirror.

In an earlier work, I used a metaphor of a pyramid to capture these thoughts. What one sees when looking at a three-dimensional pyramid is determined by the angle of perspective. From one direction, the observer sees a square. From another direction, the observer may see a triangle. What is seen is dependent on the direction or angle from which the pyramid is viewed.[3]

Symbolically speaking, people from one culture see squares and their counterparts from other cultures see triangles. The square is no more accurate a way to envision the pyramid than is the triangle and the triangle is no less accurate a way to describe the pyramid than is the square. Neither perspective captures the entirety of the shape and both have accuracies and inaccuracies built into their perspective. Thus, one cannot assume that equal information conveys equal understanding, acceptance, or advocacy, nor can one assume that equal effort generates equal influence as one communicates from one culture to the next.

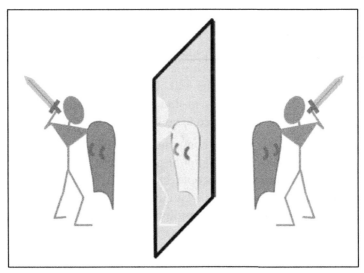

Figure 13.1. Mirror imaging. Created by the author.

Different cultures have different perspectives or directions of view. The determination of acceptance or rejection of different ideas is influenced by these directions of view. How one perceives facts and data is determined by one's narrative. The US military addresses an understanding of narrative as follows:

> A narrative is an organizing framework expressed in story-like form. Narratives are central to representing identity, particularly the collective identity of religious sects, ethnic groupings, and tribal elements. They provide a basis for interpreting information, experiences, and the behavior and intentions of other individuals and communities. Stories about a community's history provide models of how actions and consequences are linked. Thus, narratives shape decision making in two ways: they provide an interpretive framework for a complicated and uncertain environment and offer idealized historical analogies that can serve as the basis for strategies.[4]

This chapter addresses narrative as an environment within a geologic or terrain metaphor where narrative has shape. The shape of narrative space terrain differs with general and specific audiences as there are a variety of perspectives.[5] Obviously, leaders and policymakers cannot account for each individual perspective; however, the large, societal-based perspectives must be considered to adequately understand the terrain and its relationship to the actor's interactions with the opponent, counterpart, or partner.

Mirror Imaging

Mirror imaging happens at every level of strategy and thought (technical or behavioral, tactical or doctrinal, strategic cultures, strategy, cultural, values or morality, historical or educational), and problems exist in the process at each level. The following is a simple example of mirror imaging challenges from the violent US and Iranian clashes in Iraq in late 2019 and early 2020.

On 27 December 2019, an Iranian-backed Iraqi Shia militia attacked a military site in Iraq where US personnel stayed and killed a US military contractor. Two days later, the US retaliated with a strike against a camp used to house and train the militia group and killed twenty-five. Then on 31 December, a mob of Iraqis demonstrated outside the US embassy, broke into an entry point, and set the entry point and adjacent areas on fire. On 3 January 2020, the US fired missiles from a drone aircraft to kill Iranian Maj. Gen. Qasem Soleimani and Abu Mahdi al-Muhandis, the leader of the Iranian Quds Force and the leader of the Iraqi Shia militia Kataib Hezbollah respectively.

The recounting of these events demonstrates flawed mirror imaging. When looking at the *Al-Jazeera* website, it is clear that the limited series of events included here is not the story as understood from another part of the world.[6] That site included many references to US economic actions that neither appear in the description above, nor do they typically appear in American media outlets. American reports tend to emphasize issues that are violence-related in the action-counteraction-counter-counteraction that occurred rather than looking beyond those events.

Iranians saw the contest with the US as one that existentially threatened both the Islamic Revolution and the Iranian state.[7] In this sense, economic sanctions were as much acts of conflict as firing rockets, burning embassies, and drone attacks. Additionally, Iran cannot compete with the US in terms of military-technical capability and must conduct the conflict with asymmetries with respect to weapons (improvised explosive devices and inexpensive rockets and mortars), organizations (proxies), strategy (exhaustion), and cultural appeals of a war against Islam. This example deserves a lot more space, but the point is that the difficulties of mirror imaging even affect how we characterize events and their causes and effects.

Another example of the difficulties in seeing one's own and the enemy's perspective comes from the reflections of Ambassador Maxwell Taylor referring to the problems with understanding Vietnam. The "dirty business" to which he referred was war, or, for the sake of this argument, conflict:

> First, we didn't know ourselves. We thought we were going into another Korean war, but this was a different country. Secondly, we didn't know our South Vietnamese allies. We never understood them, and that was another surprise. And we knew even less about North Vietnam. Who was Ho Chi Minh? Nobody really knew.
>
> So, until we know the enemy and know our allies and know ourselves, we'd better keep out of this kind of dirty business. It's very dangerous.[8]

In this regard, one must refer to the dictum of Sun Tzu to "know the enemy, know yourself; your victory will never be endangered. Know the ground, know the weather; your victory will then be total."[9] It is critical to recognize that there may be little to no correlation between knowing oneself and knowing the opponent as expressed by Sun Tzu. Seeing oneself through the mirror of introspection doesn't mean that the mirror provides any degree of accuracy for knowing the other. This brings to light the constant and considerable problem of cultural and personal bias. It may be impossible to remove bias, but it is possible to be conscious of that bias and aware of how it shapes the perception of both the square and the ability to see the triangle. Consciousness with respect to how one sees the metaphorical pyramid also exerts influence on how effectively one understands the narrative space terrain. Narrative is not solely a cognitive domain, which is why it is described as more than story. It is the environment, the experience, and the associated cognition.

Influence

Using force to compel is more coercion than influence. Influence, as used throughout this chapter, is about the results rather than the means. The means may be violent, tangible, and direct, or they may be passive, unobserved, and circuitous. The emphasis in this section of the chapter is on using those directly coercive, manipulative, and even converting actions to develop a comprehensive program of thought that leads to direct and indirect influence in its broadest sense.[10]

The 2016 movie *The Founder* included a scene in which Ray Kroc, the "founder" of McDonald's, talks with Harry J. Sonneborn, lawyer and future chief executive officer of McDonald's Corporation. Sonneborn asks questions to understand why Kroc is financially struggling. After sum-

234

ming up the problems in Kroc's relationship with the McDonald brothers, Sonneborn shifts to the topic of land purchases. After understanding the company's financial bases, Sonneborn makes the following profound statement: "You don't seem to realize what business you're in. . . . You're not in the burger business; you're in the real estate business."[11] This scene and quote provide an impetus for reassessment of purpose that can help those concerned with conflict.

It is common to hear military people say that the army, or the military, exists to kill people and break things. Such statements tend to have two purposes: either to motivate soldiers with the "spirit of the bayonet" (kill-kill-kill) or to explain why soldiers should not focus on enemy attitudes and motivations. Such things, so the reasoning goes, are not important, because it is too difficult to win hearts and minds. The military's job, in this vein, is to inflict violence.

The military purpose isn't to win hearts and minds. The military purpose also isn't to kill people and break things. Those who emphasize violence as a purpose have forgotten the words of Sun Tzu: "For to win one hundred victories in one hundred battles is not the acme of skill. To subdue the enemy without fighting is the acme of skill."[12] Sun Tzu, in this statement, expressed the power of influence which comes from positioning, planning, and understanding.

The purpose of killing people and breaking things in war is to influence others to move in the direction you desire. To paraphrase Harry Sonneborn in *The Founder*, the military is not in the killing business; it is in the influence business.

Recognizing war as primarily influence becomes even more important when a country seeks to fight an opponent by, with, and through a partner as the complexity of influence increases. The actor needs to understand more than what it takes to influence the opponent. The actor also needs to know what it takes to influence the partner to, in turn, influence the opponent. Influence happens within cognition, or the narrative space.

An example comes from the game of pool, which is played on a smooth and flat surface (see Figure 13.2). A player does not intend to hit the cue ball into a pocket. The intent is to hit another ball into a pocket by using the cue ball—influencing one ball through the action and interaction with another ball. If the player wants to sink the eight ball, then the player must influence the eight ball through the cue ball—that is conflict with the opponent.[13]

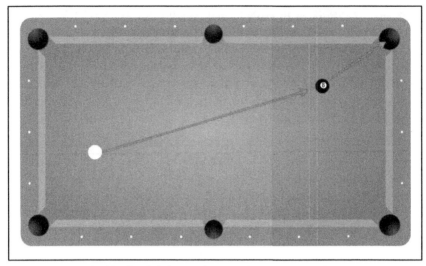

Figure 13.2. Pool table simple influence image. Adapted by the author.

Conflict that is by, with, and through a partner, such as that seen in Libya in 2011 or in the 2014 to 2020 fight against ISIS in Iraq and Syria, is a combination shot where the player influences the eight ball into the pocket by using the cue ball to, in turn, influence the four ball to then influence the eight ball (see Figure 13.3).

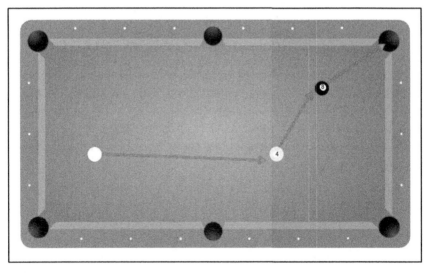

Figure 13.3. Pool table complex influence image. Adapted by the author.

In Libya and in the fight against ISIS, the US did not put boots on the ground as the intent was to have the ground combat conducted by local fighters—by, with, and through Libyans, Iraqis, and Syrians. They become, in this analogy, the four ball. Such a combination shot is difficult on a standard pool table with a smooth, flat surface. Imagine the difficulty when the surface is neither smooth nor flat. Narrative space is neither flat nor featureless. It has terrain and shape (see Figure 13.4).

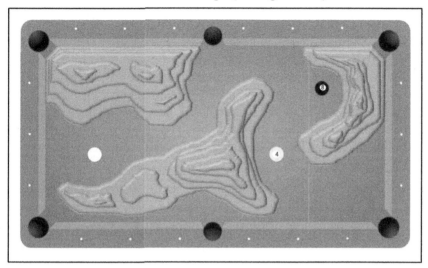

Figure 13.4. Pool table complex infuence with narrative space terrain. Adapted by the author.

To influence a partner and/or opponent requires understanding the basic narrative landscape on which influence happens. Ignorance of that landscape condemns an actor to the possibility of an endless Sisyphean effort of trying to influence the partner or opponent up an impossible mountain when there may be a more appropriate option—directing the eight ball toward a different pocket. Much of the actions in Afghanistan, Iraq, Syria, and unfortunately many other countries associated with the Global War on Terrorism have become Sisyphean efforts born out of ignorance of the narrative space landscape. In that ignorance, the US military has reverted to being in the burger business and, like Ray Kroc, it runs the risk of fiscal insolvency.

Sun Tzu told us that "an army prefers high ground to low," and he further advised commanders to "fight downhill; do not ascend to attack," and his final warning was "do not attack an enemy who occupies key ground."[14] Each of these simple, fortune-cookie aphorisms provides the profound truth that trying to fight on the narrative space landscape that one does not understand will lead to frustration at best, and empire-collapsing failure at worst. The military profession needs to reorient toward the influence business. It needs to stop focusing on killing people and blowing up buildings and place much greater emphasis on influencing partners and opponents through understanding the narrative space in which it lives and functions.

Center of Gravity

Victory comes from one of two primary strategies: annihilation or exhaustion. So argued German historian and theorist Hans Delbruck. In an 1890 work, Delbruck expressed two great challenges to the conceptualization of the great captains of war as masters of the offense. First, he addressed the conflict dialectic as annihilation and exhaustion rather than offense and defense.[15] Second, he posited that Frederick the Great did not win through annihilation; rather he won through exhaustion. Though controversial, this interpretation helped others reevaluate the options available for victory.[16]

Delbruck, in his explanation of his term *ermattungsstrategie* (literally fatigue strategy and hereafter referred to as exhaustion) explained how the Greek political/military leader Pericles convinced the Athenian people to endure the pain of having their territory destroyed while they simultaneously blockaded the Peloponnesus. This was a war without battle, or nearly so, a "nonconduct of war."[17]

The distinction between attrition and exhaustion is critical in that attrition implies reduction of physical force through losses whereas exhaustion implies, for the purposes of this argument, a reduction in will from physical, morale, economic, or ideological losses.

According to contemporary US military thought and doctrine, maneuver should be directed toward the center of gravity.[18] Clausewitz explained first and best its central importance to achieve victory:

One must keep the dominant characteristics of both belligerents in mind. Out of those characteristics, a certain center of gravity develops, the hub of all power and movement, on which everything depends. That is the point at which all our energies should be directed.[19]

Clausewitz described in this ideal world a single center of gravity that can be understood if one fully understands both self and the opponent as earlier illuminated by Sun Tzu. Elsewhere, Clausewitz both stated and implied that there may be more than one center of gravity.[20] He typically identified the army as a center of gravity, but he also included cities and infrastructure as possible options.

A center of gravity is that thing which, if threatened, will cause a change in behavior of the opponent. It is the thing which the opponent cannot dare risk and will make adjustments to protect. This expression of center of gravity necessitates significant intellectual effort to understand. It is necessary to understand the opposing actor as he sees himself. What can the enemy not risk? What does he value to such a degree that he will change his behavior to protect that thing when threatened?

The complexity of modern state and non-state actors calls into question the existence of such a thing as a center of gravity. In short, can one win a war by winning a battle or battles? This was possible in the times of Clausewitz and Delbruck, but maybe not now. In that same era, theorists like Clausewitz and Delbruck conceived of conflict as only or primarily existing in the physical space. Hence, a center of gravity needed to be a physical thing like an army or a capital. Like the question about whether a center of gravity exists, it may exist but not be in the physical space. Despite this uncertainty, the term center of gravity is regularly used in planning and execution of conflict actions.[21] Center of gravity most succinctly captures the ideal of maneuver—a position so vital as to lead to an overthrow of the opponent.[22] Such a thing is truly a position of advantage: the purpose of maneuver.

For center of gravity to be influential in maneuver, a series of assumptions must be played out in full. First, we must assume (as we have) that a center of gravity does, in fact, exist. Second, the actor must be able to identify the center of gravity. It isn't enough that it exists, but the actor must also understand it well enough to know the right way to attack or undermine it. Third, the center of gravity must be able to be targeted. In the case of a physical center of gravity as part of a violent or kinetic centric military campaign, the actor is able to deliver some weapon against the target. Fourth, resources targeting the center of gravity must be able to reach the target. In World War II, this was particularly dangerous as numerous bombers were destroyed on the way to targets and the targets were often not engaged as a result. Fifth, the resources, once at the target area, must accurately engage the target. In World War II, it was not sufficient to get the bombers over the target; the bombs had to be accurate enough to hit the target. This was not a certainty. Sixth, the center of gravity must be targeted enough times to achieve desired effect. Rarely does one blow achieve desired results—the overthrow of the enemy. For this to work, sufficient blows must be delivered. Finally, the opponent must be prevented from developing effective countermeasures.[23]

A critical addendum to assumption number seven is provided from the 1950s fighting in Algeria between the French army and Algerian separatists. Roger Trinquier, a French soldier and counterinsurgency theorist from the period, implied that the opponent, if allowed to remain with and throughout the population, would continue to employ countermeasures to any form of messaging or propaganda.[24] Thus, to effectively apply the center of gravity-focused targeting model, one needs to separate the populace either physically or narratively from the opponent.

The Islamic State or the Islamic State in Iraq and al-Sham (ISIS from here forward) provides an excellent example for this discussion of center of gravity. If ISIS has a center of gravity, and this is open for debate, then this center of gravity does not exist in the physical space; rather it exists in the narrative space (see Figure 13.5). Thinking of it this way: what can ISIS not afford to risk or lose? Salvation.[25] ISIS has declared a caliphate, and that caliphate must control some terrain to have validity, but in today's world, it is possible to imagine terrain controlled in cyberspace or small areas of a remote island in some distant archipelago. A present conception of governed space isn't necessarily linked to cities or deserts or mountains in Iraq or Syria. Taking away terrain may not overthrow ISIS, as it has not. What happens to ISIS if one takes away its definition of salvation? If no one believes the ISIS salvation narrative, will anyone flock to its banner or conduct attacks around the globe in its name? The answer is no. Therefore, this must be their center of gravity.

Understanding the importance of salvation as a center of gravity can be seen in how ISIS responds to those who attack its religiously motivated actions. This exists in exchanges between ISIS followers and Muslims, especially *salafi-jihadi*, detractors. These debates are heated and long. The ISIS followers, in tweets or official publications, provided detailed explanations to challenge the attacks on their spiritual legitimacy. A couple of examples are ISIS efforts to explain the burning of the Jordanian pilot and justification for taking and selling sex slaves. Both of these ISIS actions were attacked by respected clerics and needed vigorous defense.[26]

How does this possible ISIS center of gravity play out using the previously discussed seven assumptions? For the purpose of this argument, the actor is the United States government. The seven assumptions are addressed in brief. This is a linked series. If any one of the series fails, then the likelihood of achieving the success promised by Clausewitz is minimal.

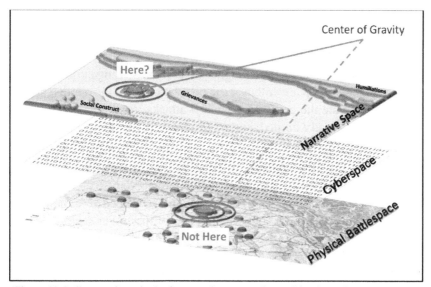

Figure 13.5. Center of gravity in the narrative space. Created by the author.

First, the center of gravity is the ISIS-defined notion of salvation.

Second, can the US government understand this center of gravity? The answer here is problematic as few people are trained to grasp the Koranic and hadithic exegesis necessary to fully understand the argument.

Third, can the US government target salvation? How could it? This isn't something delivered by a bomber or tank or even through a speech or series of internet ads or satellite television commercials. The US government is probably not deemed credible in the religious debate as it is typically seen in the Middle East and among Muslims as either a Christian or secular nation.[27]

Fourth, assuming that the US can target the center of gravity through messaging, how can those messages reach the target audience—fighters or potential fighters who believe in the salvation message? Will they believe the message delivered? If the intended recipients are those yet to decide which side to support, it is more likely that US messages will reach them. Audience definition is crucial in this assumption.

Fifth, will the message be accurate enough to actually achieve target effects—in this case fighters leaving the ISIS army or potential recruits remaining at home and peaceful?

The sixth and seventh assumptions are linked in that it is likely that ISIS will develop countermeasures to prevent the message from having effect before it can happen often enough.

Here is where Trinquier's thoughts are crucial. So long as the believers of the opposing group are amongst the population, then the opponents will strive to inoculate the population against attacks. As the population may not be geographically limited, but may instead be virtually connected, this becomes even more challenging.

The ISIS example is central to understanding maneuver in the narrative space. The linked assumptions explain the problems with understanding both the position and the relative advantage gained by holding that position. This also provides the relationship of maneuver with respect to a specific enemy. It is unlikely that al-Qaeda, for example, has the exact same center of gravity as ISIS. Therefore, it is unlikely that the position of advantage—the objective of the maneuver—is the same. Just as for each enemy on each different terrain on battlefields around the world, there is no one pre-designated position of advantage. Each battlefield and opponent must be understood independent of previous battlefields and opponents.

Though the discussion on center of gravity seems negative with specific respect to ISIS, this should not be interpreted as an assertion that a center of gravity should not be either identified or understood. It is only after both have happened that an actor can properly assess the potential efficacy of a maneuver. In following the terrain analogy, one must identify the mountaintop and the approaches to it before assessing whether the peak is climbable.

Why Exhaustion?

Delbruck laid out two options (annihilation and exhaustion) that are similar to present US military uses of decision or decisive operations and attrition. Achieving annihilation or decisive operation requires some combination of three things: the existence of a center of gravity, an overwhelming physical force advantage, and/or an asymmetrical approach. A center of gravity requires the presence of all of the steps in the center of gravity path described above. Overwhelming force can be seen most clearly in operations against Japan late in World War II when the US Navy could employ dozens of aircraft carriers in a single campaign. An asymmetric approach is applying strength against weakness. Operation Desert Storm was an excellent example of this as the US military used global positioning systems to provide both precision fires and conduct maneuver through a near featureless desert against an unexpected flank of the enemy force. Sometimes having one condition is not enough. The US had overwhelming technological superiority in both Korea and Vietnam and yet was not successful in decisive operations or annihilation.

A center of gravity does not exist if any part of the chain of assumptions fails. In contemporary conflict, there is rarely a center of gravity. Modern states, and most non-state actors, are too complex for there to be a simple center of gravity. Overwhelming force is rare given the nature of all-volunteer forces which tend to be small, technologically advanced, and expensive. Asymmetry is difficult to achieve, as most opponents seek to deny their weakness to attack. It is not enough to simply have one element; annihilation typically requires more. If these three elements do not exist, then annihilation or decisive operations cannot work. This means that modern conflict tends to be either exhaustion or attrition.

Is decision or annihilation a preferred option? Is it actually better to win quickly, or is it better to cause attrition or exhaustion? As noted in the following section, the US military seeks for rapid and decisive victory. Lewis Coser, on the other hand, suggested the value of an attrition/exhaustion approach:

Trial by attrition may thus serve to reveal the relative strength of the parties and, once relative strength has been ascertained, it may be easier for the parties to arrive at new accommodations with each other.[28]

As an exercise in communication and influence or compulsion of will, conflict informs each side of the relative strengths and weaknesses. An opponent who has been defeated solely through a stratagem or trick may be inclined to believe that next time the opposing actor may not get so "lucky." This thinking may lead to more conflict or a perpetual environment of instability. If completely exhausted, an opponent may be forced to realize that future conflict serves little purpose.

If this is true, then students and practitioners of conflict need to understand how to exhaust opponents and what attrition actually accomplishes. Yet, we neither train nor educate for successful attrition, because we are drawn to the impressive victory based on attacking a center of gravity.

The Golden Azimuth and the Variants

Modern action-adventure and science fiction movies and television programs tend to show the existence of a center of gravity. The invading

243

aliens have one weakness that if properly attacked destroys the invading force. *Ender's Game* (2013) had a queen ship that, once destroyed, caused the entire fleet to die. *Independence Day* (1996) had a mother ship to which all other ships were linked. Once the computer virus was uploaded, all of the enemy ships were infected and open to attack. The Death Star in the original *Star Wars* (1977) film had a thermal exhaust port that, when properly attacked, caused a chain reaction that destroyed the entire moon-sized threat. In the movie *Armageddon* (1998), oil drillers needed to get a nuclear device to a single spot on an earth-killing asteroid. If the weapon detonated at a depth of 800 feet, the asteroid would split and no longer threaten earth. Every *Terminator* movie (1984, 1991, 2003, 2009, 2015, 2019) and the associated television series (2008–9) was based off the idea that destroying or stopping the creation of Skynet would change the future and save the human race. The Avengers only needed to collect the gems and reform a gauntlet so that one of them could snap his fingers and reconfigure the universe in *Avengers: Endgame* (2019).

These pop culture references are extreme examples of a center of gravity. They convey the notion that attacking a single thing, killing a single leader, destroying a single ship, results in total victory. When combined with US military doctrine and broader military theory that emphasizes decisive victory as the ideal and acme of combat leadership, the importance of the center of gravity and its association with decisive operations and annihilation becomes a powerful intellectual attractor. Annihilation/decision is good and exhaustion/attrition is bad.[29]

This simple notion leads to an idealized vision that conflict can be won cleanly and quickly. This is the military Utopia toward which a conceptual course is charted along a prescribed intellectual azimuth.

Precise control as demonstrated during Operation Desert Storm (1991) established for the US military, specifically, and many other participants and observing states, generally, that the way of warfare changed. For the US, this produced a new definition of the American way of war—a Golden Azimuth—promising to lead practitioners to surgical levels of success in future conflicts (see Figure 13.6).[30] An entire generation of thinkers espoused the importance of knowledge and speed to fight and end wars rapidly, precisely, and in terms of previous wars, relatively cleanly. In thinking about this concept, one cannot divorce the successes of Operation Desert Storm from the end of the Cold War which occurred with near simultaneity.[31]

In these two companion successes, the Golden Azimuth was plotted for both an ideological opponent and a battlefield opponent. The paradigm

Figure 13.6. The Golden Azimuth. The image provides a top-down view of soldiers holding compasses and following azimuths. Created by the author.

for fighting ideologies was information. The idea was that providing information in the form of news, entertainment, and economic and material success would and did break down ideological barriers and led to success. The second victory was in Operation Desert Storm where the US confirmed its way of war as a way of battle in which targeting equaled strategy.[32] The two nearly simultaneous achievements confirmed the azimuth that had been corrected and adjusted by the US military nearly continuously since Vietnam and the institution of the all-volunteer force. These successes essentially created a myth of this progressive path being the Golden Azimuth that would continue to bring success in the future—winning wars through clean and quick success on the battlefield.[33] Emphasis on precision targeting, decisive maneuver, and counterinsurgency decapitation continued in Afghanistan (2001–present), Iraq (2003–11 and 2014–present), and many more nations associated with the Global War on Terrorism.

Operation Desert Storm was significant to other actors in addition to the United States. It was the most widely broadcast war to that time. The coalition against Saddam Hussein went to great lengths to show how effective the new technology and approach was as the world watched. From

245

those observations, different powers drew different lessons. State actors, like Russia and China, appreciated that they were not in a position to compete with the space-based global positioning system centered approach to precision.[34] The well-publicized Gerasimov Doctrine had its origins in the immediate aftermath of Operation Desert Storm as the Russians were determined to compete militarily, but not in the same game or by the same rules. Their answer was to change the environment such that in any conflict between the US and Russia, the US would not be the global good guy. This was a policy based on perception and narrative.[35]

China had similar concerns, but a different approach.[36] The strategy game *Go* has allusions to Chinese strategy. This is a game based on creating walls to protect territory rather than on capturing opposing pieces (though that may occur). The placing of pieces on the board is about creating future opportunities as much as it is about the current decision. This means that the strategy is based on potential opportunity rather than immediate or near-immediate success.[37] In addition, the Chinese sought to expand the strategic field to more than military and, specifically, military technology. This was unrestricted warfare or warfare that wasn't solely about the American conceptions of military exchanges or violent coercion.[38] Economic power, strategic asset control, and general spatial positioning with respect to positions of importance drove Chinese thought.

Non-state actors were more aggressive in their movement away from the vision of conflict offered by Operation Desert Storm. In many cases, the best-known non-state actors are ones in the Middle East who connect to some ideology associated with faith and religion: Hezbollah, Hamas, al-Qaeda, Taliban, and ISIS. In their adjusted azimuth for conceptualizing conflict, these groups vary significantly from previous revolutionary non-state actors as demonstrated in the Chinese civil war and the French Indochina and Vietnam wars. Revolutionary war was originally espoused as secular and progressive. Progressive means that the non-state actor began in a position of limited relative power with respect to the state opponent and intended to develop political efforts and insurgent and terrorist activities to a point where the disadvantage was minimal or erased and the non-state actor could then challenge the state actor in a conventional military struggle.[39]

Though the Maoist Revolutionary War phases existed with the religiously motivated groups, the conception of victory through conventional engagement was very different. Victory came from God and within God's timeline or phases. Victory might not require actual battlefield success. Victory might mean something as simple as non-defeat or existence. So long as the non-state actor existed and continued in the struggle, it was victorious.[40]

The very idea of an existential fight leads one away from the notion of decision or annihilation or quick or clean victories. Such conflict is, by definition, attrition or exhaustion based. The idea is most thoroughly articulated in *The Management of Savagery: The Most Critical Stage Through Which the Umma Will Pass*. In this 2004 book, the author, who goes by the pseudonym Abu Bakr Naji, explained that attacking a resort in a Muslim country frequented by foreign tourists would force the regime to protect all similarly frequented resorts. The security burden placed upon the state would ultimately cause it to collapse from the economic exhaustion imposed by relatively few attacks.[41]

The intent behind the warfare theories articulated by these groups follow this path: God will win; we are on the side of God; we do not have the power to fight the US militarily or technologically; our strength is in our belief, which cannot be defeated; the Americans are weak as their beliefs are based on materialism (consider the US approach to military success as an example); and success is to remain in the battle and wait for God to bring the victory.

Conclusion

For those inclined to scoff at this approach to warfare, consider the competing Battles of Mosul. One was led by ISIS and one by the Iraqi Army (see Figure 13.7). ISIS, using an exhaustion-based and narrative-led model, took the city in a handful of days and defended it against attack for 278 days. The focus of the Iraqi military, supported by the US and dozens of other anti-ISIS coalition countries, was to use technological advantage to retake the city with limited casualties to friendly forces. The stark difference in terms of casualties and physical destruction vividly demonstrates the power of narrative and the failure of the Golden Azimuth. The ISIS method caused little damage to the city, and its residents were able to continue living in their homes while the coalition effort rendered significant portions of the city virtually uninhabitable.

The irony of the Mosul examples was that the narrative-led and exhaustion-focused strategy took less time on the battlefield though more time to prepare than the kinetic-led strategy. The effort to exhaust the opponent's morale created an environment that caused the opponent to collapse once the attack occurred. This kind of success comes from significant understanding of the narrative space as well as the center of gravity and sources of power, and a commitment to a long-term vision of success communicated inside and outside the organization. The people of northern Iraq knew ISIS believed it was the army of the righteous. They knew ISIS was determined to control their villages, their livelihood, and their lives. They also knew ISIS was in the battle all the way. This narrative and commitment, clearly communicated through videos and social media, allowed ISIS to achieve tremendous results.

Russian television personality Dmitry Kiselyev contended, "If you can persuade a person, you don't need to kill him."[42] Modern exhaustion warfare is based on persuasion and understanding and use of narrative more so than the Operation Desert Storm paradigm that continues to enthrall US military and political leaders.

Roger Trinquier stated that state militaries were not studying the type of war that mattered—the wars they lost in French Indochina and Algeria rather than the large-scale war that they won in World War II:

We still persist in studying a type of warfare that no longer exists and that we shall never fight again, while we pay only passing attention to the war we lost. . . . The result . . . is that the army is not prepared to confront an adversary employing arms and methods the army itself ignores. It has, therefore, no chance of winning.[43]

Fully appreciating his concern is the beginning of the solution.

We need to study the types of warfare that matter: narrative, exhaustion, attrition, persuasion. We need to pay attention to conflicts against different social cultures as well as different military cultures. By so doing, we may be prepared to confront current and future adversaries effectively and successfully.

Battles of Mosul

Narrative-Led 2014		Kinetic-Led 2016–17
6 (4+ years prep)	Days	278
1,000	Attacking Force	110,000
60,000	Defending Force	9,000
1:60	Ratio of Attacker to Defender	12:1
105+	Attacking Force Killed	1,400
6,500	Defending Force Killed	8,000
1:65	Infrastructure Damaged/Destroyed	1:7
<1%	Civilians Killed	<60%
Unknown	Civilians Displaced	25,000
500,000		900,000

Figure 13.7. Statistics from the battles of Mosul based on estimates from multiple sources. Reports vary widely, because each side retains details to help protect itself from criticism. Compiled by the author.

Notes

1. Sociologist George A. Lundberg made the assertion, as discussed by Lewis Coser, that "communication is the essence of the social process and since 'abstinence from communication is the essence of conflict situation,' conflict must be a purely dysfunctional behavior." Coser explained that conflict between humans and societies is not aberrant nor is it solely dysfunctional. Conflict is part of how people interact. Lewis A. Coser, *The Functions of Social Conflict* (Glencoe, IL: The Free Press, 1956), 23.

2. Carl von Clausewitz, *On War*, ed. and trans. Michael Howard and Peter Paret (Princeton, NJ: Princeton University Press, 1976), 75.

3. Brian L. Steed, *Bees and Spiders: Applied Cultural Awareness and the Art of Cross-Cultural Influence* (Houston, TX: Strategic Book Publishing and Rights, 2014).

4. Department of Defense, Joint Publication 3-24, *Counterinsurgency* (Washington, DC: 25 April 2018), II-13.

5. The most comprehensive explanation of narrative space terrain is found in Brian L. Steed, "Maneuvering within Islam's Narrative Space," *Strategic Review: The Indonesian Journal of Leadership, Policy and World Affairs* 8, no. 1 (January–March 2018): 16–35.

6. "US-Iran Tensions: Timeline of Events Leading to Soleimani Killing," *Al Jazeera*, 8 January 2020, https://www.aljazeera.com/news/2020/01/iran-ten-sions-timeline-events-leading-soleimani-killing-200103152234464.html.

7. International Institute for Strategic Studies, *Iran's Networks of Influence in the Middle East* (strategic dossier, International Institute for Strategic Studies, November 2019); Seth G. Jones, *Containing Tehran: Understanding Iran's Power and Exploiting Its Vulnerabilities* (Lanham, MD: Center for Strategic and International Studies, January 2020), https://csis-prod.s3.amazonaws.com/s3fs-public/publication/200106_Jones_ContainingIran_WEB.pdf?vcq9T-KxKsEizo0lf.tJ5ZpUcOssC_3qK; and US Defense Intelligence Agency, *Iran Military Power: Ensuring Regime Survival and Securing Regional Dominance* (Washington, DC: US Government Publishing Office, 2019), https://www.dia.mil/Portals/27/Documents/News/Military%20Power%20Publications/Iran_Mili-tary_Power_LR.pdf.

8. Stanley Karnow, *Vietnam: A History* (New York: Viking Press, 1983), 19.

9. Sun Tzu, *The Art of War*, trans. Samuel B. Griffith (New York: Oxford University Press, 1963), 129.

10. The genesis of this definitional emphasis comes from Howard Gambrill Clark who argued that most of what is called influence is actually coercion. Howard Gambrill Clark, "Defining Influence," *Narrative Strategies Journal* 2 (24 January 2019): 1–6.

11. B. J. Novak, *The Founder,* directed by John Lee Hancock (2016; The Weinstein Company, 2016), DVD.

12. Sun Tzu, *The Art of War*, 77.

13. These thoughts and images were also expressed and addressed in greater detail in another work by the author. Brian L. Steed, "Maneuvering within Islam's Narrative Space," *Strategic Review: The Indonesian Journal of Leadership, Policy and World Affairs* 8, no. 1 (January–March 2018): 16–35.

14. Sun Tzu, *The Art of War*, 117, 116, 131.

15. "Delbrück made a theoretical distinction between two basic strategies for conducting war: *niederwerfungsstrategie*, the strategy of annihilation (literally translated as the "thrashing" strategy); and *ermattungsstrategie*, the strategy of exhaustion (literally translated as the "fatigue" strategy, alternately translated as a strategy of attrition by Walter J. Renfroe). The basis for these strategies was found in Clausewitz's *On War*, which deeply influenced Delbrück, according to Randall G. Bowdish. "Military Strategy: Theory and Concepts" (PhD diss., University of Nebraska, Lincoln, NE, June 2013), 76–77, http://digitalcommons.unl.edu/poliscitheses/26. Annihilation is the effort to achieve victory through a decisive attack, battle, or campaign that forces the enemy to accept terms. Exhaustion achieves victory through the dissipation of the opponent's will. These brief definitions are a synthesis from Clausewitz, Delbruck, Craig, Bowdish, and others.

16. Gordon A. Craig, "Delbruck: The Military Historian," in *Makers of Modern Strategy: Military Thought from Machiavelli to Hitler* (Princeton: Princeton University Press, 1944), chap. 11, 260–83; Hans Delbruck, *History of the Art of War, Volume I: Warfare in Antiquity*, trans. Walter J. Renfroe Jr. (repr. 1920; Lincoln, NE: University of Nebraska Press, 1990).

17. Delbruck, 136.

18. Antoine Henri Jomini used the term *decisive point* rather than center of gravity. Baron de Jomini, *Summary of the Art of War*, trans. Capt. G. H. Mendell and Lt. W. P. Craighill (1861; repr., Westport, CT: Greenwood Press, 1992), 461. "A center of gravity is the source of power that provides moral or physical strength, freedom of action, or will to act." Department of Defense, Joint Publication (JP) 5-0, *Joint Planning* (Washington, DC: 16 June 2017), xxii; and Department of the Army, Field Manual 3-0, *Operations* (Washington, DC:, October 2017), 1-18–1-19, 2-5.

19. Clausewitz, *On War*, 595.

20. Clausewitz, 596.

21. Department of Defense, JP 5-0, xxii, IV-23–IV-28, IV-31–IV-34, V-25.

22. Clausewitz, *On War*, 69.

23. Modified from "Essential Assumptions to Air Corps Strategic Bombing Doctrine" created by Dr. Donald "Scott" Stephenson as adapted from Williamson Murray, "Strategic Bombing: The British, American, and German experiences," *Military Innovations in the Interwar Period* (New York: Cambridge University Press, 1996), 127.

24. Bruno C. Reis, "David Galula and Roger Trinquier: Two Warrior-Scholars, One French Late Colonial Counterinsurgency?," in *The Theory and Practice*

of Irregular Warfare: Warrior-Scholarship in Counter-insurgency (New York: Routledge, 2014), 48.

25. President Donald J. Trump directly attacked the notion of salvation as a center of gravity for ISIS in his speech in Riyadh, Saudi Arabia; he called on those present to essentially attack the center of gravity of groups like ISIS. He said, "A better future is only possible if your nations drive out the terrorists and extremists. Drive. Them. Out. Drive them out of your places of worship. Drive them out of your communities. Drive them out of your holy land, and drive them out of this earth. . . . Religious leaders must make this absolutely clear: Barbarism will deliver you no glory—piety to evil will bring you no dignity. If you choose the path of terror, your life will be empty, your life will be brief, and your soul will be condemned." Donald J. Trump, "President Trump's Speech to the Arab Islamic American Summit, Riyadh, Kingdom of Saudi Arabia," 21 May 2017, https://www.whitehouse.gov/the-press-office/2017/05/21/president-trumps-speech-arab-islamic-american-summit; and Ronald Tiersky, "ISIS's Deadliest Weapon Is the Idea of Heaven," *Real Clear World,* 19 September 2016, http://www.realclearworld.com/articles/2016/09/19/isiss_deadliest_weapon_is_the_idea_of_heaven_112051.html.

26. In this excellent piece, the author provides specific information on counter-narratives used against ISIS by Muslim clerics. He then provides twelve claims ISIS makes and gives arguments against them. This is one of the best single-source references with respect to counter-narratives. Alex P. Schmid, *Challenging the Narrative of the "Islamic State,"* ICCT Research Paper (The Hague, Netherlands: International Centre for Counter-Terrorism – The Hague, June 2015), http://icct.nl/wp-content/uploads/2015/06/ICCT-Schmid-Challenging-the-Narrative-of-the-Islamic-State-June2015.pdf. "The Burning of the Murtadd Pilot," *Dabiq* 7 (12 February 2015): 5–8. The discussion in this article is on the historical and religious precedents for execution through burning, which is normally forbidden in Islamic law. The article includes a quote from Abu Sayyaf ash-Shalabi, who attacked the execution. The author used this quote as an opportunity to point out Abu Sayyaf's ignorance of the circumstances and the true reading of the law. Umm Sumayyah al-Muhajirah, "Slave-Girls or Prostitutes?" *Dabiq* 9, "They Plot and Allah Plots" (21 May 2015): 44–49. The article's author is a woman and her name is given, both of which are unusual for *Dabiq* articles. Fewer than half of the articles in any *Dabiq* issue have named authors and, of those, it is extremely rare for the author to be a woman. In this explanation the author gives hadithic support, historical precedent, as well as cultural and religious justification for the practice of enslaving captives in war and then the acceptability of female slaves for sex. Women captured from unbelievers are essentially blessed to be so enslaved as they are treated better by a believer then by an idolater and their potential for salvation is greater.

27. President Obama, for example, was seen by many ISIS followers as an unbeliever who apostatized from the Islam of his father to become a Christian. Thus, when he declared ISIS to be non-Islamic, it was viewed as ironic

and lost any narrative power both against the target audience and more broadly. See Graeme Wood, "What ISIS Really Wants," *AP/The Atlantic* (March 2015), http://www.theatlantic.com/features/archive/2015/02/what-isis-really-wants/384980/.

28. Coser, *The Functions of Social Conflict*, 136–37.

29. Secretary of Defense Caspar W. Weinberger, "The Uses of Military Power," speech given to the National Press Club, 28 November 1984; referred to as the Weinberger Doctrine.

30. Two books do an excellent job of explaining the evolution to and pursuit of what this author terms the Golden Azimuth. Neither of the book authors use that term, but the intent is similar. Frederick W. Kagan, *Finding the Target: The Transformation of American Military Policy* (New York: Encounter Books, 2006); and Adrian Lewis, *The American Culture of War: The History of U.S. Military Force from World War II to Operation Enduring Freedom*, 2nd ed. (New York: Routledge, 2012).

31. The author's book *Armed Conflict: The Lessons of Modern Warfare* addresses the transformation in thought following Operation Desert Storm and prior to the 11 September 2001 attacks. See also US Army Training and Doctrine Command, *Knowledge and Speed: The Annual Report on the Army After Next Project to the Chief of Staff of the Army* (Fort Monroe, VA: US Army Training and Doctrine Command, 1997).

32. Antulio J. Ecvhevarria wrote that the US really has a way of battle more than a way of war in that the focus is on linking together successful battlefield victories rather than crafting a strategic vision of war. Two places where this argument is most clearly explained are the "Principles of War or Principles of Battle?" chapter in McIvor, *Rethinking the Principles*, 58–78, and in *Toward and American Way of War* (Carlisle Barracks, PA: US Army War College, Strategic Studies Institute), 2004.

33. Daniel P. Bolger, "The Ghosts of Omdurman," *Parameters* (August 1991): 28–39.

34. Stuart Kaufman, "Military Doctrine: Lessons from the 1991 Gulf War and Russian Military Doctrine," *The Journal of Slavic Military Studies* 6, no. 3 (September 1993).

35. Valery Gerasimov, "The Value of Science is in the Foresight," *Military Review* (January–February 2016): 23–29; and Nicholas Fedyk, "Russian 'New Generation' Warfare: Theory, Practice, and Lessons for U.S. Strategists," *Small Wars Journal*, 4 May 2017, http://smallwarsjournal.com/jrnl/art/russian-%E2%80%9Cnew-generation%E2%80%9D-warfare-theory-practice-and-lessons-for-us-strategists.

36. James P. Farwell, "Adversarial Tactics to Undercut US Interests in New Generation Warfare 2019," Strategic Multilayer Assessment (SMA) Future of Global Competition & Conflict (Boston, MA: NSI, 3 May 2019), https://nsite-am.com/social/wp-content/uploads/2019/05/Farwell_Adversarial-Tactics.pdf.

37. David Lai, *Learning from the Stones: A Go Approach to Mastering China's Strategic Concept, SHI* (Carlisle Barracks, PA: Strategic Studies Institute, 1 May 2004).

38. Qiao Ling and Wang Xiangsui, *Unrestricted Warfare* (Beijing: PLA Literature and Arts Publishing House, 1999).

39. Mao wrote about his conduct and views on revolutionary warfare in several major works. The reference here is an example of the theory of conduct of revolutionary or guerilla warfare that he espoused. Note the title. This is a play on Carl von Clausewitz's work, *On War*, of which Mao was a big fan. Mao Tse-Tung, *On Guerilla Warfare*, trans. Samuel B. Griffith II (1961; repr., Champaign, IL: University of Illinois Press, 2000).

40. Itai Brun's ideas were interwoven throughout this paragraph and the preceding one. His ideas were best captured in Itai Brun, "'While You're Busy Making Other Plans'—The 'Other RMA,'" *Journal of Strategic Studies* 33, no. 4 (20 August 2010): 535–65, http://dx.doi.org/10.1080/01402390.2010.489708.

41. Abu Bakr Naji, *The Management of Savagery: The Most Critical Stage through Which the Umma Will Pass*, trans. William McCants (Cambridge, MA: John M. Olin Institute for Strategic Studies, 2006), 46. This idea was expressed in multiple places in the cited work, but the referenced page gives the specific link to a resort.

42. Timothy B. Lawn, "Narrative Landmines and Combatting Foreign Influence," *Narrative Strategies Journal* 2 (24 January 2019): 15.

43. Roger Trinquier, *Modern Warfare: A French View of Counterinsurgency*, trans. Daniel Lee (1964; repr., Westport, CT: Praeger Security International, 2004), 3.

Chapter 14
Tweets from Tahrir's 2011 Egyptian Arab Spring: Fast-Moving Revolutions through the Lens of Content Analysis[1]
Lt. Col. Rafael E. Linera Rivera

The 2011 Egyptian Arab Spring protests, locally known as the 25 January Revolution, transcended geographical boundaries. Activists and demonstrators from a wide range of socio-economic backgrounds united locally, digitally, and globally to achieve one goal: immediate removal of Egyptian President Hosni Mubarak. As comments and images emanated from Tweets and Facebook, local protesters and the press kept the world abreast of the situation as it evolved. Such real-time messaging presented rich themes disseminated through both social and traditional media. Protesters' ability to rally in one area (i.e., Cairo's Tahrir Square) facilitated dissemination, as social media and conventional live-news coverage shaped public sentiment locally and abroad.

Social media discourse played a role in Mubarak's 2011 removal. Indeed, scholars such as Zeynep Tufekci and Christopher Wilson highlighted how information through social media was "crucial in shaping how citizens [in Tahrir] made individual decisions about participating in protests, the logistics of protest, and the likelihood of success."[2] This chapter instead explains how this revolution evolved by employing content analysis to reflect on time, space, and motivational aspects based on collected Tweets such as those that Alex Nunns and Nadia Idle explored in *Tweets from Tahrir: Egypt's Revolution as It Unfolded, in the Words of the People Who Made It.*[3] The first part of this analysis explores the themes at the level of the Twitter feed for the activists. To establish a basis of comparison, this chapter compares the Twitter feed of the activists with the thematic structure of George Friedman's *Stratfor* article, "Egypt: The Distance between Enthusiasm and Reality."[4] Friedman's article summarized the events in Egypt right after the revolution ended.

In contrasting the book and the article, results suggest two main points. First, by analyzing the proximity (space) of Tweets describing the events as they occurred (time)—aside from effectively constructing a consistent (motivational) social reality—the 2011 Egyptian Arab Spring protests played a minimal role in Mubarak's removal from power by the military. Second, the reigning situation before, during, and after the 25 January Revolution did not change; the military remained the arbiter of who governed Egypt. This chapter ends by discussing US national-level values and interests at stake during the revolution, and how they affected the outcome.

Understanding Twitter Content and Motivation through the Ego-Alter-Object Triad

Twitter messages were limited to 140 characters during the Arab Spring, making it one of the most compacted social media platforms at the time. And even with Twitter's 2017 increase to 280 characters, many ask and continue to study how people can get so much out of so little when engaging in Twitter conversations or exchanges. The question becomes even more interesting when activists communicate the vicissitudes of an ongoing event that is unfolding, dynamically, as was the case with Tahrir Square and the 25 January Revolution. The interaction between the ego (I, or self) and alter (other) while defining the object (sign, symbol, representation) is a simple but effective way to understand the relationship between Twitter dialogue and subsequent behavior.[5] As described in Ivana Marková's February 2000 *Theory & Psychology* article:

The "other" in a triad can represent a group, a subgroup, a culture, and so on. Therefore, one can consider various kinds of a triadic relationship. For example, I-you-object (local situation) versus I-you-object in a cultural context, with the third movement being a newly co-constructed meaning.[6]

Along with social categorization and identity, including the concept of themes to appreciate the structure and formation of public opinion, this triad can assist in understanding the content in today's saturated media forums. Themes structure how people view the world, as they reveal the latent content that underpins public opinion. In essence, themes mold and direct the content of public opinion. Exploring themes on platforms such as Twitter can reveal structuring of public opinion within the studied population or sample. Such focus offers an opportunity to help understand latent content, or latent drivers, of public opinion and behavior.

Of note, the relationship between the self-other is pivotal at the time of defining the object through dialogue. It becomes a dynamic conflict and tension to define the issue at hand and the identity of those involved. Such triad application facilitates understanding the 2011 Egyptian Arab Spring protests' discourse, used platforms, and themes. Adapting the triad helps depict the Egyptian population's (self) and Mubarak's (other) positions related to Egypt (object). This will also facilitate the transformation of both the Egyptian population and Mubarak himself as they continue to define Egypt throughout this rapidly evolving revolution. To examine and extract their motivation to action, this chapter uses content analysis of Tweets from the population (self) during the protests (space and time) as its main method of inquiry. Here, a comparison of Tweet content with Egypt's contemporary political reality using *Stratfor's* article will expand the understanding of this reality; that is, the results of the 2011 Egyptian Arab Spring protests in terms of Mubarak's already planned departure and subsequent ratification of the military as the party in charge.

Analyzing the 2011 Egyptian Arab Spring Protests

The 25 January 2011 Egyptian revolution can be classified into six turning points (time):

• *25 to 28 January 2011.* Unarmed protesters clashed with police and Mubarak's security forces, resulting in rubber bullets, tear gas, concussion grenades, and water cannons fired at the crowd.

• *29 January to 1 February 2011.* The Egyptian army stepped in as police withdrew. The military allowed protesters to rally, with some military personnel exhibiting support for the revolution.

• *2 to 3 February 2011.* Armed Mubarak supporters fired at protesters as violence erupted when the former forced their way into the square. The Army did not intervene during this clash.

• *4 to 7 February 2011.* Egyptian protesters set up tents, food stalls, and health clinics in Tahrir Square (space), while the military assisted in splitting the pro- and anti-government sides. Wael Ghonim, a Google executive who had taken leave from Google to join the protest, was released on 7 February after being secretly detained for eleven days by the Mubarak government. He subsequently was interviewed by Dream TV. Ghonim cried while talking about Egyptians who died during the protests.

• *8 to 10 February 2011.* Protests picked up momentum after Ghonim's release and TV interview. Ghonim encouraged the crowd on 8 February as new protesters crowded the square.

• *11 February 2011.* Soon after Mubarak hinted that he was not going to step down, then-Vice President Omar Suleiman confirmed that Mubarak had been removed as president.

Regarding the selection of Tweets, Idle and Nunns gathered protester comments dating from 14 January to 20 February 2011 for their book; the only comments opposing the revolution were Mubarak's epic Tweets—to include his 13 February message: "You people are hypocrites! You talk about democracy, but you won't let me run for president? Where's the freedom?! #VoteHosni #Egypt."[7] Furthermore, their comments selection only considered English-language Tweets by Egyptians in Cairo. In contrast, the study in this chapter is based on the previously identified turning points and thus sampled 1,108 of the 1,168 Tweets that Idle and Nunns compiled in their book. Of note, while demonstrators came from both affluent and poor backgrounds, Idle and Nunns primarily selected Tweets from a more privileged group. This chapter's content analysis factors additional criteria for locality, time, and motives.

In contrast, Stratfor's article—published after Mubarak's removal—analyzed views throughout the protests and its outcome. Such analysis painted Egypt's distance between the crowd's enthusiasm and their political reality. This chapter uses a twofold approach: comparing the article's analysis with the themes reflected from the Tweets and also providing a holistic perspective of the events and outcomes.

To effectively compare the differing perspectives, we used Leximancer, an automated program that provides quantitative and qualitative tools to analyze text. Leximancer identifies high-level concepts, providing key insights into the data through interactive visualizations (e.g., concept maps) and a theme concepts summary that depicts their correlation. To take full advantage of those features, the Tweets were divided into separate files and folders based on the six turning points criteria. Next, the sampled Tweets were uploaded into Leximancer. In the initial pass, the "Merge word variants" option was selected to cut down on concepts being listed separately. On the second pass, we merged identified concept seeds that referred to matching ideas such as "Tahrir" to "square," "tear" with "gas," "#Jan25" with "#jan25," "Mr. Mubarak" with "Hosni Mubarak," "Gamal Mubarak" with "son," and "protesters" with "demonstrators." This technique permitted to categorize similar contexts, allowing for better extraction of themes, motives, and identification of actors involved throughout this fast-moving revolution.

Results of the Idle and Nunns Book Analysis

1. 172 Tweets from 25 to 28 January 2011—Tweets such as "Tahrir got broken up by police using tear gas, rubber bullets, water hoses, & rock-throwing" described the clash between protesters and the police.[8] The self-other-object triad is exposed with protesters (self), police, and Mubarak's forces (others), and Egypt (object)—all identified in the "Jan25" theme.

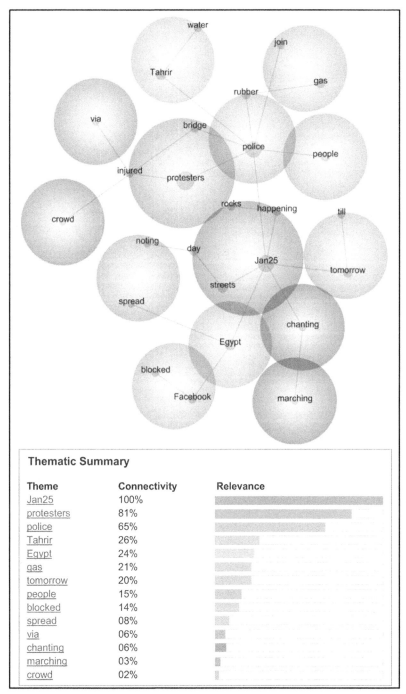

Thematic Summary

Theme	Connectivity	Relevance
Jan25	100%	
protesters	81%	
police	65%	
Tahrir	26%	
Egypt	24%	
gas	21%	
tomorrow	20%	
people	15%	
blocked	14%	
spread	08%	
via	06%	
chanting	06%	
marching	03%	
crowd	02%	

Figure 14.1. Leximancer Concept Map and Thematic Summary graphs for 172
Tweets dated 25 to 28 January 2011. Created by the author.

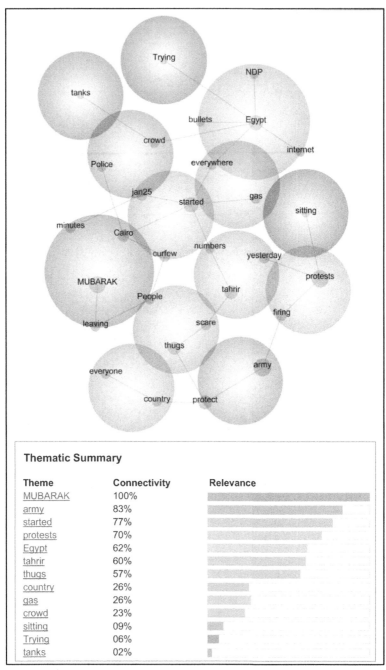

Thematic Summary

Theme	Connectivity	Relevance
MUBARAK	100%	
army	83%	
started	77%	
protests	70%	
Egypt	62%	
tahrir	60%	
thugs	57%	
country	26%	
gas	26%	
crowd	23%	
sitting	09%	
Trying	06%	
tanks	02%	

Figure 14.2. Leximancer Concept Map and Thematic Summary graphs for 187 Tweets dated 29 January to 1 February 2011. Created by the author.

These events took place locally (mainly in Tahrir) and digitally (Facebook and Twitter), as both platforms were temporarily blocked by Mubarak's government obstruction of the internet and in the streets of Cairo's Tahrir Square. On 26 January, Mubarak confirmed the blockage: "I blocked Twitter and Facebook so you could focus on your work, not run around the streets shouting. #jan25."[9] Yet, a day later he Tweeted that "Habib just sent me a bbm. He says I should prepare a farewell speech for my citizens. Where are you guys going? #jan25."[10] Mubarak's Tweets demonstrate his mixed contradictory feelings of angst and disregard of the situation.

2. 187 Tweets from 29 January to 1 February 2011—Tweets like "will the army be with the people? I think they will never shoot at the people, they are there only to protect" depicted the existing conflict.[11] The self-other-object triad can be identified with "crowd" "protests" (self), pro-Mubarak forces A.K.A. "thugs" (others), and "Egypt" (object); all were branded in the main theme "MUBARAK." At this juncture, the army had physically replaced the police, taking an active stance initially.

3. 198 Tweets from 2 to 3 February 2011—Tweets like "Pro-Mubarak thugs are police" and "When protesters capture thugs . . . they protect them from being beaten all the way till they hand them to the military #Jan25" reveal pro-Mubarak's forces (other) resolving to physically fight against the revolution (self) while defining Egypt (object).[12] Notice how the military continues to define its role in the streets. Simultaneously, the "Jan25" revolution continues to take place online. Demonstrators Tweeted words such as "bravery" and "resistance" to describe their nonviolent approach to attain their goal of removing Mubarak from the presidency. Such words incited others to continue Tweeting, as well as plan other ways to attain their ultimate goal—an Egypt without Mubarak.

4. 237 Tweets from 4 to 7 February 2011—An individual other than Mubarak takes center stage. Wael Ghonim's release and 7 February interview by Dream TV show host Mona el-Shazly played a pivotal role in the revolution. This emotional interview "undercut two weeks of relentless state propaganda."[13] At this point, Ghonim symbolized the protesters (self) sense of unity through Tweets such as "Wael @Ghonim cries when he sees the pictures of the people who died #Jan25 #Egypt."[14] Ghonim's words and actions condemning pro-Mubarak supporters' (others) violence and abuses against the Egyptian people (self) continued to define Egypt (object) during this turning point of the revolution.

5. 183 Tweets from 8 to 10 February 2011—Fueled by Ghonim's presence, protesters (self) were defined by the themes of "crowd" and "rev-

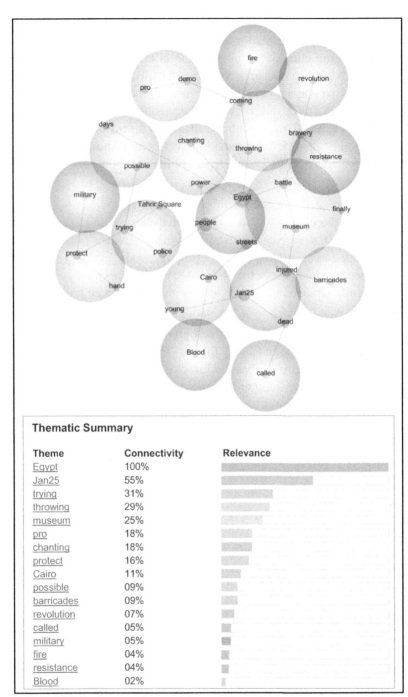

Thematic Summary

Theme	Connectivity	Relevance
Egypt	100%	
Jan25	55%	
trying	31%	
throwing	29%	
museum	25%	
pro	18%	
chanting	18%	
protect	16%	
Cairo	11%	
possible	09%	
barricades	09%	
revolution	07%	
called	05%	
military	05%	
fire	04%	
resistance	04%	
Blood	02%	

Figure 14.3. Leximancer Concept Map and Thematic Summary graphs for 198 Tweets dated 2 to 3 February 2011. Created by the author.

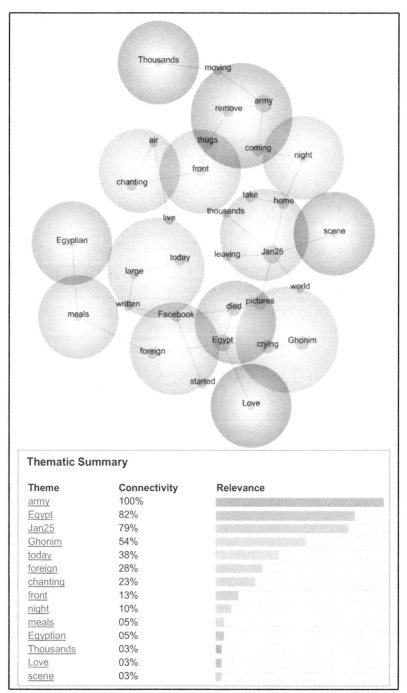

Thematic Summary

Theme	Connectivity	Relevance
army	100%	
Egypt	82%	
Jan25	79%	
Ghonim	54%	
today	38%	
foreign	28%	
chanting	23%	
front	13%	
night	10%	
meals	05%	
Egyptian	05%	
Thousands	03%	
Love	03%	
scene	03%	

Figure 14.4. Leximancer Concept Map and Thematic Summary graphs for 237 Tweets dated 4 to 7 February 2011. Created by the author.

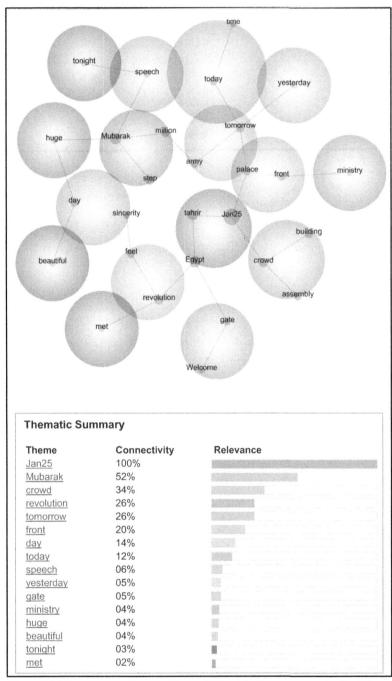

Thematic Summary

Theme	Connectivity	Relevance
Jan25	100%	
Mubarak	52%	
crowd	34%	
revolution	26%	
tomorrow	26%	
front	20%	
day	14%	
today	12%	
speech	06%	
yesterday	05%	
gate	05%	
ministry	04%	
huge	04%	
beautiful	04%	
tonight	03%	
met	02%	

Figure 14.5. Leximancer Concept Map and Thematic Summary graphs for 183 Tweets dated 8 to 10 February 2011. Created by the author.

olution." Tweets like "The regime & the army know they can't handle the 20 million estimated to march tomorrow which is why Mubarak will hopefully step down #EGYPT" depicted Mubarak and the army (together as "others" in the triad) facing each other to define Egypt (object).[15] This presented a defining moment for the Army, as they were given the opening to be a central actor in the revolution.

On 10 February, Mubarak addressed the nation on state TV, hinting that he would not step down. His deceptive intentions to cause confusion and fear in the crowd were reflected both before and after his address. Prior to his address, Mubarak Tweeted "#reasonsmubarakislate: I'm aiming for an Oscar for the best suspense movie. #Jan25 #Egypt."[16] After his address, he ratified his intentions by Tweeting "Ha! Gotcha, again! Come on, you can't be that stupid. #Jan25 #Egypt."[17] Yet, his attitude fueled the masses even more, as demonstrated by Tweets like this one: "Anger swelling after mubarak's arrogance 5000 protesters surround state tv building also close to tahrir #Jan25."[18]

6. 131 Tweets from 11 February 2011—Tweets like "I think it's an excellent time to call and annoy all people who have been telling us to leave the square. :) #Egypt #Jan25" and Mubarak's "You're welcome. #Egypt #Jan25" response summarized the sense of accomplishment for the revolution (self) as they "finally" ended their struggle with Mubarak (other) in terms of defining the dream of a better, more democratic Egypt (object).[19] This so-called closure and final transformation of this tale of the people versus Mubarak was reflected through their societal emotions (i.e., "crying," "screaming" and "free") as well as committing to be a part of Egypt reform (i.e., "clean") both on the streets and for their governing institutions.

Results of the *Stratfor* Article Analysis

Using Leximancer for content analysis provides a great start to consider emergent concepts and themes grounded within the Tweets collected. The next step is to review published analysis from experts in the field during or shortly after the revolution. This will assist understanding (a) the nuances of how the story evolved (sampling taken from the Tweets); (b) how it was retold as it transitioned from the original to the other reacting Tweets; and (c) how successful the revolution was, based on the themes and concepts in comparison with Egypt's reality.

The *Stratfor* analysis highlighted that the military was the backbone of the regime after Col. Gamal Abdel Nasser Hussein took the uniform off and became prime minister in 1954, followed by his 1956 to 1970 presidency. As Friedman commented: "Nasser believed that the military

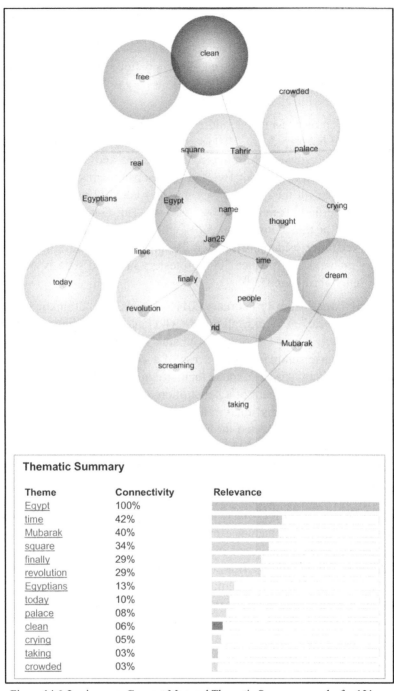

Thematic Summary

Theme	Connectivity	Relevance
Egypt	100%	
time	42%	
Mubarak	40%	
square	34%	
finally	29%	
revolution	29%	
Egyptians	13%	
today	10%	
palace	08%	
clean	06%	
crying	05%	
taking	03%	
crowded	03%	

Figure 14.6. Leximancer Concept Map and Thematic Summary graphs for 131 Tweets dated 11 February 2011. Created by the author.

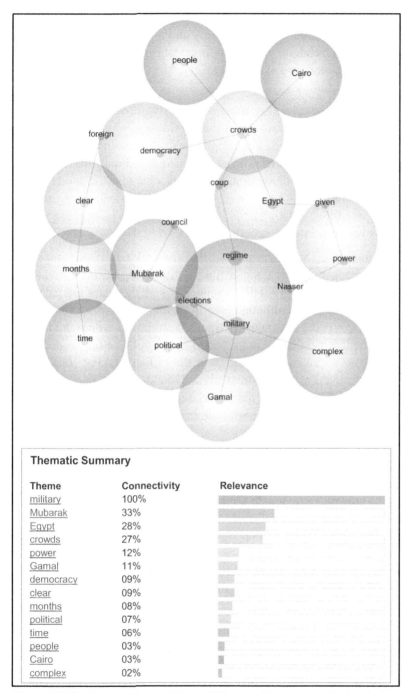

Thematic Summary

Theme	Connectivity	Relevance
military	100%	
Mubarak	33%	
Egypt	28%	
crowds	27%	
power	12%	
Gamal	11%	
democracy	09%	
clear	09%	
months	08%	
political	07%	
time	06%	
people	03%	
Cairo	03%	
complex	02%	

Figure 14.7. Leximancer Concept Map and Thematic Summary graphs that depict analysis of George Friedman's *Stratfor* article. Created by the author.

was the most modern and progressive element of Egyptian society and that it had to be given the responsibility and power to modernize Egypt."[20] This became a trend, as succeeding presidents (i.e., Anwar Sadat in 1970 and Hosni Mubarak in 1981), while elected by the people, were officers in the Egyptian military.

Friedman's article also presented the issue of "Gamal" Mubarak, Hosni's son and potential heir of the presidency, who struggled because he lacked military service and rapport with the institution. On the latter, Gamal was notorious for his banking background and financial reforms that prevented the military from habitually obtaining its funds from the Egyptian banking system. Indeed, while Gamal's dealings presented no overt signs of illegal activity, "his investments show how deeply the family is woven into Egypt's economy."[21]

Furthermore, "the corruption of the Mubarak family was not stealing from the budget, it was transforming political capital into private capital."[22] And, with foreign aid diminishing through the years, Gamal's action against the institution, although creating a mortgage system for the regular Egyptian to take advantage of, created animosity within the military's ranks. Such detachment, compounded by Egypt's failing economy and empowering social media, resulted in the military taking sides with the 2011 revolution. Lastly, Friedman argued that the situation, once Mubarak was out of the presidency, did not change. The military dismantled the government, took over, and abolished the constitution.

Discussion and Conclusion

The 25 January Revolution's outcome, although effectively constructing a cohesive social perception based on rich themes, played a minimal role in Mubarak's previously arranged departure from the presidency. The peoples' campaigns helped remove Mubarak immediately; yet, the short- and long-term effect was that the military was in charge. Furthermore, asking what system or person was to blame could have been a better way to frame the argument against the regime. In short, protesters generalized, failing to blame the regime's ideology and the individuals that supported the system (the military).

First, the people believed Mubarak was the only one responsible; they did not touch the institution that placed him in power. The military, as an institution, was and remained in charge of Egypt. And second, Gamal's banking sector accomplishments, aside from his lack of prior military service, remained a fundamental element of the military's disdain toward him. Both gaps worked well for the military; the press also antagonized

Mubarak, partaking with Egyptian's public opinion explicitly and the army's agenda implicitly. Although this evil versus good dichotomy identified Mubarak as the former and the Egyptian people as the latter, the reality presented another facet: the military, as this chapter has shown, used the digital and physical existence of the 2011 Egyptian Arab Spring protests to both feed the audience's immediate wants and speed up the existing transition to maintain the status quo.

Note that such transition did not happen in a vacuum. This chapter does not address international factors such as US involvement. At the time, US national values at risk included America's commitment to democracy and human rights. Indeed, "American values naturally side with protesters against autocracy in the call for freedom and democracy."[23] The United States kept "promoting freedom and human rights and showing the Arab world we were not ruthless and hypocritical supporters of authoritarianism," and condemned "Ben Ali of Tunisia, Mubarak of Egypt, and Saleh of Yemen . . . [all] explicit American allies."[24]

US national interests at risks were security and, subsequently, the international order. Egypt's security, as well as regional stability in the Middle East, was at risk due to the unrest. This situation did not allow for rule-based international order to be established. By condemning Mubarak's oppressive regime, the United States advanced national interests to expand human rights to all Egyptians, and collaboration with the new Egyptian government dominated by the Muslim Brotherhood to improve regional security and stability.

Still, the military became the ultimate winner. Mubarak and his cabinet also won. Despite his sudden removal in 2011 and adjudicated charges in 2012 for human rights violations during the revolution, Mubarak was exonerated on 29 November 2014.[25] Today, Egyptians have another president who took the uniform off to take the executive branch. This final transition did not happen overnight. A year after winning the 2012 elections, then-President Mohamed Morsi, from the Muslim Brotherhood, was ousted by his appointed defense minister, General al-Sisi. Initially, the Muslim Brotherhood had a good human rights record.[26] Nevertheless, Morsi became more authoritarian than Mubarak himself. Right after Morsi's removal, al-Sisi ran and won the executive in 2014, building his coalition that included "other remnants of the Hosni Mubarak regime."[27] Egyptian politics came full circle.

Notes

1. The opinions and characterizations in this piece are those of the author and do not necessarily represent official positions of the US government.

2. Zeynep Tufekci and Christopher Wilson, "Social Media and the Decision to Participate in Political Protest: Observations from Tahrir Square," *Journal of Communication* 62, no. 2 (2012): 363.

3. Alex Nunns and Nadia Idle, eds., *Tweets from Tahrir: Egypt's Revolution as It Unfolded, in the Words of the People who Made It* (New York: Or Books, 2011).

4. George Friedman, "Egypt: The Distance between Enthusiasm and Reality," *Stratfor,* 14 February 2011, https://worldview.stratfor.com/article/egypt-distance-between-enthusiasm-and-reality.

5. Ivana Marková, "The Individual and Society in Psychological Theory," *Theory & Psychology* 10, no. 1 (February 2000): 107–16.

6. Marková, "The Individual and Society in Psychological Theory," 113.

7. Nunns and Idle, *Tweets from Tahrir,* 234.

8. Nunns and Idle, 43.

9. Nunns and Idle, 49.

10. Nunns and Idle, 52.

11. Nunns and Idle, 69.

12. Nunns and Idle, 110, 113.

13. Kareem Fahim and Mona El-Naggar, "Emotions of a Reluctant Hero Galvanize Protesters," *New York Times*, 9 February 2011, A14, https://www.nytimes.com/2011/02/09/world/middleeast/09ghonim.html?_r=1&scp=1&sq=Mona%20El-Nagger&st=cse.

14. Nunns and Idle, *Tweets from Tahrir,* 171.

15. Nunns and Idle, 199.

16. Nunns and Idle, 201.

17. Nunns and Idle, 204.

18. Nunns and Idle, 204.

19. Nunns and Idle, 223, 216.

20. Friedman, "Egypt."

21. Neil MacFarquhar, David Rohde, and Aram Roston, "Mubarak Family Riches Attract New Focus," *The New York Times*, 13 February 2011, https://www.nytimes.com/2011/02/13/world/middleeast/13wealth.html.

22. MacFarquhar, Rohde, and Roston.

23. Vaughn Shannon and Joshua Cummins, "US-Egyptian Relations since the Arab Spring: Balancing Interests and Values." *The DISAM Journal* (2014): 2. https://corescholar.libraries.wright.edu/political_science/9.

24. Shannon and Cummins.

25. Jason Hanna, Sarah Sirgany, and Holly Yan, "Egypt: Prosecutors to Appeal after Mubarak Verdict," *CNN World*, 1 December 2014, https://www.cnn.com/2014/12/01/world/meast/egypt-mubarak-trial/.

26. Shannon and Cummins, "US-Egyptian Relations since the Arab Spring."

27. Robert Springborg, "The Resurgence of Arab Militaries," *The Washington Post*, 5 December 2014, https://www.washingtonpost.com/news/monkey-cage/wp/2014/12/05/the-resurgence-of-arab-militaries/?noredirect=on.

Chapter 15
Soft Power, Influence Operations, and the Middle East Experience

Gary R. Hobin

Joseph S. Nye Jr., writing in 2004, described soft power as the power of attraction, "the ability to shape the preferences of others."[1] Soft power is not coercive; it is the power to get others to want the same outcome "we" do, regardless of who that "we" might be. Soft power coopts people; soft power is persuasive and does not rely on an explicit threat or an exchange of material things. Soft power depends on context: what might be attractive to one group at a specific time may not be attractive to another group, or at a different time. Nye asserted that "soft power is not merely the same as influence . . . influence can also rest on the hard power of threats or payments."[2]

Most nation-states use multiple instruments of national power to achieve what they perceive to be their interests. The hard powers of military action and economic muscle tend to be the most noticeable, and have the quickest effect, but as they are coercive rather than persuasive, their effects tend to be shorter duration. The soft power resources of a society or culture, the things that persuade others to agree that the interests of that society's members are things the others would like as well, generally take longer to have an effect, but seem to have greater staying power.

This chapter focuses on whether Russia, Iran, and others are using soft power to achieve their interests in the Middle East. That Russia and Iran (and others) are using influence operations is clear; whether this is a soft power application or not is an open question. If we accept Nye's proposition that soft power is the power of attraction, then the evidence from Syria indicates Russia is using hard power to achieve influence; Iran uses mostly hard power with some softer approaches; the United States likewise is using hard power at present. Comparing the civil war situation in Syria with the relative calmness in neighboring Jordan should demonstrate the distinctions.

Russia has a long-standing interest in the wider Middle East, and in particular in Syria, dating back to the days of the tsars. One of the friction points leading to the Crimean War of 1854 was the Russian demand to be recognized as the protector of all Orthodox Christians in the Ottoman Empire; another, the tsars' long-term quest for warm water ports and access to the Mediterranean Sea.[3] Where the Tsarist Russian Empire was stymied, the Soviet Union achieved some success by supporting the Assad regime, not to protect Orthodox Christians, but to gain access to port facilities on the Syrian Mediterranean coast at Tartus. The post-Soviet Russian Federation retains the interest in warm water ports as well as the interest in engaging Western powers, particularly the United States, in regions as far away from the Russian near abroad as possible. Supporting the current Assad regime in Syria serves these interests well. Equally, it demonstrates to regional actors that Russia is back as a significant player in Middle Eastern affairs.

Russian influence operations are the ways for achieving the ends of access and distracting the West. Russia's influence in Syria comes not because of an attractiveness of the Russian experience, which from the Syrian perspective is the failure of the Soviet socialist economy. It comes from the hard power of military assistance: equipment, advisors, technicians and contractors, and economic support. To a lesser extent, Russian influence in Syria is the result of Russia's ability to "play the diplomatic card," such as vetoing United Nations Security Council resolutions that condemned the Assad regime's tactics in the civil war or called for sanctions against the regime. That Russia has achieved influence in Syria is unquestioned, but this influence is not through the use of soft power.

Iran has a long history of influence in the Middle East. To understand the basis for contemporary influence, recall that the Persian Empire, five centuries before the current era, and the Sassanian Empire, about 1,100 years later, both controlled most of the Middle East; the imperial heartland of both empires was the Iranian plateau.[4] This influence has been, in effect, a two-way transaction. The Shi'i branch of Islam was imported in the sixteenth century to be the state ideology of the Safavid rulers in Iran; the clerics the Safavid rulers imported came from Mount Lebanon, in the western part of Greater Syria.[5]

For Iran in the twenty-first century, reestablishing its influence throughout the Middle East is, therefore, a return to its perceived historic legacy. As expected of any state, Iran uses its influence to achieve its interests: to demonstrate Iran's prominence as a key player and champion of Shi'i Muslims throughout the world; support friendly Muslim states—in this case Syria and Lebanon; undermine the international sanctions regime; and, importantly, undermine the influence of its greatest rival—the Kingdom of Saudi Arabia. Iran, like Russia, uses hard power to achieve influence: advisors from the Quds Force, the special operations element of the Iran Revolutionary Guard Corps; military equipment supplied to Syrian and Lebanese sub-state military organizations; and diplomatic tools to demonstrate Iran's purpose in finding a political solution to the Syrian civil war—albeit on terms highly favorable to Iran.

Iran also has a soft power advantage not shared with Russia: the attractiveness to at least a significant minority within the Middle Eastern population of its Shi'i faith. Shi'i Muslims, who arguably include the Alawites—the ruling party in Syria—make up about 12 percent of the Syrian population, and about 27 percent of Lebanon's population. This connection gives Iran a soft power advantage not available to either the Russians or the United States. Significantly, two mosques of particular reverence to Shi'i Muslims and an ancient cemetery are all located in the vicinity of Damascus; for generations, Iranian Shi'i Muslims have made pilgrimages to visit them. This ongoing connection, at least prior to the current civil war, gave Iran a means of exerting soft power influence. For a Shi'i Muslim—whose history is as a small minority in a sea of Sunni Muslims with few perceived open paths to economic or political leadership—having the example of a Shi'i-led nation-state just a few hundred miles to the east is likely to be attractive. Equally, the perception that Iran has expanded its influence—and Shi'i political leadership—to its neighbor, Iraq, is also likely to be attractive at least on some levels. Whether one agrees with Iranian politics is of lesser importance.

The potential soft power advantage that Iran might have with Shi'i communities in the region must be balanced with the realization that few of these communities have extensive political, economic, or diplomatic power. The so-called Shi'i arc stretching from Iran and eastern Iraq along the Tigris-Euphrates River valleys and through Syria to reach the Mediterranean in southern Lebanon is certainly an impressive graphic on the map but may not survive critical scrutiny.

While the current civil conflict in the Republic of Syria is attracting international attention for a variety of reasons, the Bashar al-Assad regime's connection to the Islamic Republic of Iran has less to do with soft power than with the hard power of military assistance and diplomatic support. President Assad's Alawite clans seem to be more interested in survival than in expanding Iranian influence; the fact that the 'Alawis consider themselves to be a branch of Twelver Shiism is less important in Syria than the fact that Iran has military and diplomatic resources that they are willing to use to support the regime.

In this regard, consider that the 'Alawis make up only about 11 percent of Syria's population; of the remainder, more than 70 percent are Sunni. Bernard Lewis, in discussing the interface of Islamic religion and law, remarked that historically, the Sunni majority's tolerance of unorthodox interpretation of Islam, that is Shi'i interpretations, "is extended at the present day to such marginal groups as the 'Alawis and the Druze in the Levant."[6]

The 'Alawis as a marginal group gained political, and more importantly military, prominence in Syria under the French Mandate after World War One. The French sought to maintain their control through isolating and fragmenting communities; by giving relative prominence to the 'Alawi minority, the French reasoned they would tie its members to their administration. Under the mandate, Syrian society—most notably in cities like Damascus and Aleppo—took on an increasingly westernized coloration, to include sidewalk cafés and secular publications. The organization of the Arab Socialist Ba'ath Party as a secular Arab nationalist movement has more connection to European rationalism than to an ideological link with Shi'i Iran.

Given the 'Alawi's history of being a minority group ruling over a larger majority with whom they have significant ideological differences, President Assad's looking farther eastward for support makes sense: his northern neighbor, Turkey, is both heavily Sunni and a traditional adversary; the Hashemite Kingdom of Jordan, his southern neighbor, is also majority Sunni and closely linked to the United States and the West. Lebanon, Assad's western neighbor, has a significant Shi'i population but also significant internal fractures making it an uncertain ally. Iraq, Syria's immediate eastern neighbor, has a similar secular-oriented, Arab-Shi'i government, but long-standing rivalries between Iraq and Syria as well as Iraq's continuing internal rebuilding efforts limit the potential for significant support from there. That leaves Iran. One has to suspect, however, that the image of Bashar al-Assad taking on the role of an Iranian-style cleric and politician would not sit well with him, with his 'Alawi supporters, or with the wider Syrian population. Iran's attractiveness, its soft power advantage, is limited; its hard power-based influence, on the other hand, is significant.

As a player in the contemporary Middle Eastern "great game," the United States has both soft and hard power pieces on the chessboard. The hard power pieces are clear even to the most casual observer: military advisors, close air support for US allies and coalition partners, and foreign aid and economic support to countries in the region. The United States' hard power buys influence; how much influence and for how long is hard to determine.

Equally difficult to quantify is US soft power influence in the region. Artifacts of US attractiveness are easily found: things like Levi's jeans,

Kentucky Fried Chicken restaurants, and New York Yankees baseball caps. Artifacts themselves might be indicators; however, they are not measures of influence.

One measure of US attractiveness—its soft power influence—is the number of people waiting in lines to apply for travel visas to the United States. The common experience of consular officers at US embassies in the Middle East seems to be that regardless of the weather, long lines form each day at the embassy's consular section door with people applying for travelers' visas, whether for tourism, for business, or for immigration.[7] I observed no equivalent lines at the embassies of the Soviet Union (and later of Russia) or Iran. The implication: many more people living in the Middle East were attracted to the United States than were attracted to Russia or Iran.

Without question, anecdotal evidence is hardly definitive, but can be indicative. Having served in several US embassies in the region, both as an Army officer and as a consular officer, I can attest to the attractiveness of the United States as a travel destination and to the popularity of artifacts of US influence. Contacts in every country in which I served commented favorably on previous visits to the United States, or spoke of their plans to visit the United States in the future. In some cases, these comments were shaped by the understanding that, after all, I was an American and would not take kindly to criticism of my country, but after continued contact, hospitality gave way to greater frankness.

The Kingdom of Jordan can be characterized as both heavily westernized and strongly traditional. The Jordanian military relies heavily on Western—primarily American—technologies; many officers from the different services attend US military schools for basic and advanced education. The average number of Jordanians studying at civilian institutions in the United States routinely tops 2,000 (2,330 in 2016, the last year for which figures are available).[8] While this number is dwarfed by the similar number of students from, say, Saudi Arabia, nonetheless it is a significant part of Jordan's population of approximately 9.5 million in 2016. Based on my personal observations, many Jordanians identify the United States as the place they would most like to visit.

Syria, prior to 2011, was similarly westernized, albeit with a more authoritarian government. Syrian officers who traveled out of the country for military education routinely went to Russian schools; Syrian military services were armed mainly with Russian equipment. Figures for Syrian civilian students currently studying abroad are unreliable, but the comparable number of Syrian students studying in the United States in 2016 was "almost 800."[9] It is highly likely that this small number relates more to an inability for students to get to the United States rather than a lack of attractiveness of the idea of studying in the United States. Anecdotal evidence, admittedly subject to varied interpretations, indicates the United States is—or at least was before the civil war erupted—a popular destination.

The challenge for the United States, then, if these anecdotal indicators are relevant, is to capitalize on means to take advantage of soft power attractiveness. Soft power tools relating to the informational instrument of national power are already in place: print and electronic media, public and private educational institutions, cultural exchange programs that showcase American art forms like jazz, among others. Soft power elements of the diplomatic instrument of national power are continuously at work: face-to-face interactions among diplomats during which they develop mutual trust and confidence; participation in international fora during which US delegates express the humanitarian ideals on which the United States was founded, as examples. Similarly, soft power aspects of the economic instrument of national power influence these populations, but analysis of these effects is beyond the scope of this article.

Soft power attraction generates influence, an influence that is likely to remain effective for the long term. Soft power also is more difficult to focus than hard power, and takes longer to have a measurable effect. In contrast, hard power (military actions, economic measures) can be more focused and is likely to have a clearly measurable impact. Hard power actions definitely generate influence, for good or ill. Russia and Iran are relying primarily on hard power to exert influence in the Middle East; there is very little that is truly "attractive" to the majority of a Middle Eastern audience from either. The United States has a soft power advantage in the Middle East, but generally sacrifices it in favor of using hard power to achieve rapid results that are clearly measurable in the short term. Syria, as the theater in which Russia, Iran, and the United States (among others) are exerting influence, demonstrates these distinctions.

Notes

1. Joseph S. Nye Jr., *Soft Power: The Means to Succeed in World Politics* (New York: Public Affairs, 2004), 5.

2. Nye, 6.

3. Peter Mansfield, *A History of the Middle East*, 4th ed. (New York: Praeger Books, 2013), 76; and Bernard Lewis, *The Middle East: A Brief History of the Last 2,000 Years* (New York: Scribners, 1995), 279.

4. Lewis, 21, 29.

5. Lewis, 278.

6. Lewis, 228.

7. Note: These observations were prior to the COVID pandemic.

8. "Largest Number of Jordanians Ever Studying in the United States," US Embassy in Jordan, accessed 2 May 2019, https://jo.usembassy.gov//largest-number-jordanians-ever-studying-united-states/.

9. "EducationUSA Syria: An Update," NAFSA: Association of International Educators, accessed 2 May 2019, https://www.nafsa.org/Professional_Resources/Browse_by_Interest/International_Students_and_Scholars/Network_Resources/International_Enrollment_Management/EducationUSA_Syria__An_Update/.

Conclusion

Strategic Implications of Wars and America's Emerging Role in the Geopolitical Landscape[1]

Mahir J. Ibrahimov

The chapters of this anthology—which cover Eurasia, the Western Hemisphere, Africa, the Middle East, Southwest and Central Asia, and other regions—reveal a steady trend of challenges for US national security and national defense strategy objectives.

The geopolitics of regional and global affairs continue to change at a rapid pace. Military decisions rely heavily on understanding the operating environment and regional cultures of America's allies and adversaries. New political and military alliances are under construction, and are already challenging US interests and influence across the globe. The operational challenges addressed in this anthology are profound. Leading experts in their respective areas emphasize the importance of appreciating socio-cultural and historical lessons learned. This appreciation is particularly important for US policymakers and military leaders as they shape the right strategy to achieve success. Understanding other indigenous cultures and histories during potential conflict, including large-scale combat operations (LSCO), remains as important today as it was during the counterinsurgency operations that dominated the last decade. Research and analysis of emerging global and regional adversaries will help predict their behavior during the years to come. Developing an appreciation of the social structure, culture, and history of our joint, interagency, and multinational partners is equally important, because it will enable the United States to achieve our shared geopolitical objectives.

Based on careful review of the global and regional literature and thorough analysis, Iraq, Afghanistan, and Syria could be the US military's final overseas conflicts for a while. Based on current trends, the United States will no longer be the sole superpower by the time these major conflicts end. These trends are clearly indicated by the gradual yet steady fall of the US dollar, America's huge budget deficit, the colossal and unexpected expenses of the various wars, and, most importantly, the undefined nature of current US strategy and steady decrease of support at home. Leaders of insurgent and terrorist organizations have indicated they intentionally pulled the US military into the Afghanistan and Iraq conflicts to help undermine America's power. In at least two statements,

Osama Bin Laden acknowledged a plan to make the US economy "bleed" like they made the former Soviet Union "bleed" before its demise.[2]

It is becoming increasingly clear that no country can completely defeat insurgencies and terrorism. If their cells are destroyed and financial support cut off, similar organizations will emerge unless geopolitical issues that drive the insurgencies and terrorism are resolved. History tends to repeat itself to a certain extent. For example, America's 2019 agreement in principle with the Taliban to withdraw 5,000 US troops within five months" was consistent with follow-on US administration steps taken since then.[3]

Tension in the Middle East, including in Syria, continues to affect regional and global security. The unresolved Israeli-Palestinian conflict continues to be directly and indirectly in the center of many of that region's conflicts. Defusing the tension there would require a more balanced policy toward Israel and its Arab neighbors. Part of the solution of the Israeli-Palestinian conflict should be the creation of two states: Israel and Palestine. The full-scale war between Azerbaijani and Armenian forces over the Nagorno-Karabakh region, which recently erupted in the South Caucasus, is the latest test of the emerging regional and global security architecture. The outcome of the war could have significant long-lasting geopolitical implications for regional and global powers, as well as for international organizations such as the Organization for Security and Cooperation in Europe (OSCE) in the South Caucasus and the entire post-Soviet and post-Warsaw pact space.

The futures of Iraq and Afghanistan should be decided by the local people, with the help of international and community organizations. Otherwise, the unilateral involvement of other countries will always be perceived as interference, resulting in further alienation and encouraging insurgency and terrorism. Terms such as insurgency and terrorism—and the differences between them—need to be clearly defined and leveraged in the right narrative and context to avoid confusion and the emergence of new violent groups and organizations with their own political agendas.

Given all these factors, the next few decades will most likely see the United States lose its sole grip on world affairs; new superpowers will emerge. One likely candidate is China, which has successfully modified its political and economic systems to meet present-day requirements. In the new era, the most influential factors will be economic "soft" power rather than traditional military means. Russia is another superpower candidate. For the past several years, leaders there have effectively used a combination of economic expansionist policy, soft power, and military capabilities to target Russia's neighbors in the former Soviet Republics as well as in the Middle East, the Western Hemisphere, and other regions of the world.

The research by this group of knowledgeable authors indicates that America's position cannot be taken for granted. The world is approaching a very sensitive historical juncture with multiple regional and global conflicting interests. The emerging situation raises several questions: how will the global security architecture be structured in the next five to ten years, what role will the United States play in that environment, and finally, will we witness another major global conflict—possibly one disastrous for mankind?

Notes

1. The opinions and characterizations in this piece are those of the author and do not necessarily represent official positions of the US government.

2. Mahir Ibrahimov, *Life Looking Death in the EYE: The Iraqi War as Experienced by A U.S. Army Contactor* (New York: Global Scholarly Publications, 2012). See also Osama Bin Laden, "Nass Bayan al-Jabhah al-Islamiyah al-Alamiyah li-Jihad al-Yahud wa-al-Salibiyin [World Islamic Front for Jihad Against Jews and Crusaders]," *al-Quds al-Arabi*, 23 February 1998.

3. Deirdre Shesgreen et al., "'Agreement in Principle' Reached with Taliban to Withdraw 5,000 US Troops within Five Months," *USA Today*, 3 September 2019, https://www.usatoday.com/story/news/world/2019/09/02/agreement-principle-reached-taliban-end-afghanistan-war-withdraw-us-troops/2141480001/.

About the Authors

Michael M. Andregg

Michael M. Andregg has a PhD in genetics from the University of California, Davis. He studied monkeys in Morocco and taught thirty-five years at the University of Minnesota; his main academic home is now the University of St. Thomas in St. Paul, where he teaches in the Aquinas Scholars Honors program. Andregg's book *On the Causes of War* won a National Peace Writing Award in 1999. He has authored or edited several other books, including *Democratization of Intelligence* (2015), and has published more than fifty articles in peer-reviewed journals worldwide as well as a 2007 reader on intelligence ethics and a 2014 textbook on global demographics. He is a trustee of the Workable World Trust and vice president for the International Society for the Comparative Study of Civilizations.

Jonathan D. Bailey

Chaplain (Maj.) Jonathan D. Bailey is an ethics instructor at the US Army Command and General Staff College (CGSC). His civilian education includes a bachelor's in history and religious studies from Stetson University and master's degrees in divinity and sacred theology in ethics from Boston University School of Theology. He has served as a chaplain in the US Army for thirteen years.

Robert F. Baumann

Robert F. Baumann is a Ministry of Defense advisor representing the Defense Security and Cooperation Agency as senior faculty and education advisor at the Armed Forces Academy of Uzbekistan. Previously, he served as professor of history and director of degree programs for the CGSC from 2003 to 2020. Baumann joined the CGSC faculty in 1984 and served for nineteen years as a member of the Department of Military History/Combat Studies Institute. He received a BA in Russian from Dartmouth College as well as an MA in Russian and East European studies, a Master of Philosophy degree in history, and a PhD in History from Yale University. Baumann wrote *Russian-Soviet Unconventional Wars in the Caucasus, Central Asia, and Afghanistan* (1993) and more than twenty scholarly articles and book chapters and has been a frequent contributor to *Military Review*. He was coauthor of *Invasion, Intervention, Intervasion: A Concise History of the U.S. Army in Operation Uphold Democracy* (1998), *My Clan Against the World: A History of US and Coalition Forces in Somalia 1992–1994* (2004), and *Armed Peacekeepers in Bosnia* (2004).

Anna L. Borshchevskaya

Anna L. Borshchevskaya is a senior fellow at The Washington Institute. In addition, she is a contributor to Oxford Analytica and a fellow at the European Foundation for Democracy. She previously was with the Atlantic Council and the Peterson Institute for International Economics. A former analyst for a US military contractor in Afghanistan, she also served as communications director at the American Islamic Congress. Her analysis is published widely; until recently, she conducted translation and analysis for the US Army's Foreign Military Studies Office and its flagship publication, *Operational Environment Watch*, and wrote a foreign affairs column for *Forbes*. She is the author of the February 2016 Washington Institute monograph *Russia in the Middle East*. She has a doctorate from George Mason University.

Stephanie N. Chetraru

Stephanie N. Chetraru is chair of the CGSC's Department of Development Studies. She has been a US foreign service officer with the US Agency for International Development (USAID) since 2004, serving US embassies in El Salvador, Israel, Pakistan, Russia, and Moldova. Most recently, she managed USAID's Countering Malign Kremlin Influence in Moldova portfolio from 2013–18. Chetraru, who is seeking a PhD in security studies from Kansas State University, also wrote the USAID/Russia Performance Management Plan (2012–16).

Gregory J. Cook

A retired US Army lieutenant colonel, Greg Cook is an assistant professor at the CGSC. He served in the Army as a Eurasian foreign area officer and was a liaison officer to the Russian airborne brigade in Bosnia. Cook graduated from Ukrainian reconnaissance school and the Russian Ministry of Foreign Affairs Diplomatic Academy. He was an intelligence analyst at the National Ground Intelligence Center; a strategist at US Army, Europe headquarters; an arms control inspector in the Defense Threat Reduction Agency; a military observer in the Organization for Security and Cooperation in Europe; and worked in the US Embassy in Moldova. His last active duty assignment was at the George C. Marshall European Center for Security Studies in Germany. Cook has an MA in foreign affairs from the University of Virginia and a BA in history from the Citadel.

Nicole L. Hash

Maj. Nicole Hash is an active duty US Army military intelligence officer. She served in Operation Iraqi Freedom and Operation Enduring Freedom, and in and various military intelligence assignments. Hash has a bachelor's in Spanish and Russian from the US Military Academy, a master's in international relations from St Mary's University of San Antonio, a master's in Russian and East European studies from Indiana University-Bloomington, and a master of military arts and science from the CGSC.

Gary R. Hobin

Gary R. Hobin is an assistant professor in the Department of Joint, Interagency, and Multinational Operations at the CGSC, where he has taught for more than sixteen years. He previously was a civilian contractor with the Battle Command Training Program (now Mission Command Training Program) and before that was a US State Department foreign service officer at US embassies in Damascus, Syria, and Riyadh, Saudi Arabia. He also was a US Army infantry officer, retiring after more than twenty years' service. His active duty Army service included tours in Germany and the Hashemite Kingdom of Jordan and ended with deployment to Saudi Arabia for Operations Desert Shield and Desert Storm. He has a bachelor's in history from Dartmouth College and a master's in Middle Eastern studies from the University of Chicago.

Mahir J. Ibrahimov

Mahir J. Ibrahimov is director of US Army Cultural and Area Studies Office (CASO) and previously was the first senior Army culture and foreign language advisor. He served in the Soviet Army and witnessed the breakup of the Soviet Union. He helped open the first embassy of Azerbaijan in Washington, DC, and served as senior diplomat. Ibrahimov also provided vital assistance to US forces as multi-lingual cultural adviser during Operation Iraqi Freedom II. He supported the Army chief of staff's Russian New Generation Warfare Study, which required him to travel to Ukraine and provide follow-on recommendations to Army leaders. Ibrahimov is the author of several books and numerous other publications, including in foreign languages. His books gained significant international traction among scholars, the general public, the movie industry, and Army leaders. He is fluent in multiple languages and cultures and has a PhD in international relations from Academy of Social Sciences, Moscow, and a master's in international journalism and linguistics (Arabic and English) from Peoples' Friendship University, Moscow. Additionally, Ibrahimov attended the MA in International Public Policy Program for Mid-Career Professionals, School of Advanced International Studies, Johns Hopkins University, and the Joint Program in Public Diplomacy of the Institute of World Politics and Boston University, Washington, DC.

Roderic C. Jackson

Roderic Jackson is the defense intelligence chair at the CGSC as well as the Defense Intelligence Agency (DIA) representative to the Combined Arms Center/Army University. He has more than thirty years' experience in national security affairs with long-term interest in African security. Jackson has worked more than sixteen years for DIA, including as a defense attaché and policy advisor to Africa Command, Central Command, and European Command military leaders. He has a bachelor's in mathematics and master's degrees in international relations, international business, and strategic intelligence.

Rafael E. Linera Rivera

Lt. Col. Rafael "Rafa" E. Linera Rivera was commissioned as a second lieutenant in the Infantry branch when he graduated from the University of Puerto Rico in 1997. Prior to serving in the CGSC as a Department of Joint, Interagency, and Multinational Operations instructor, Linera Rivera was US Army Special Operations Command (USASOC) chief, G-39 Information Operations, where he co-authored the command's information operations, cyber, electronic warfare, and military deception policies. He has a PhD and MA in psychology from Fielding Graduate University, an MA in finance from Webster University, and a BBA from the University of Puerto Rico. He has written several white papers and articles for the Strategic Multilayer Assessment Office at the Office of the Secretary of Defense, Army University Press, and *Small Wars Journal*.

Kevin G. Rousseau

Kevin G. Rousseau has been the distinguished chair for national intelligence studies at CGSC since July 2017. He retired from the US Army as a lieutenant colonel, having served as a military intelligence officer with the 82nd Airborne Division, the 3rd Armored Division, the Defense Intelligence Agency, and the National Ground Intelligence Center, as well as deployments to Bosnia, Kosovo, and Afghanistan. He was an assistant general counsel at the National Geospatial-Intelligence Agency as well as an analyst, an instructor, and manager at the Central Intelligence Agency. Rousseau has a bachelor's from the US Military Academy, a master's in strategic intelligence from National Intelligence University, a JD from the George Mason University School of Law, and a master's in strategic studies from the School of Advanced Military Studies Advanced Strategic Leadership Studies Program.

Michael Rubin

Michael Rubin is a resident scholar at the American Enterprise Institute in Washington, DC; senior lecturer at the Naval Postgraduate School in Monterey, California; and senior editor of the *Middle East Quarterly*. Between 2002 and 2004, he was a staff advisor for Iran and Iraq in the Office of the Secretary of Defense at the Pentagon. Rubin has a bachelor's in biology and a PhD in history from Yale University. Rubin lectured on Iranian history at Yale University, Johns Hopkins University, and three universities in northern Iraq. Additionally, he lived and conducted research in Yemen, the Islamic Republic of Iran, and with the Taliban in Afghanistan pre-9/11. Rubin was co-editor of *Seven Pillars: What Really Causes Instability in the Middle East?* (2019) and author of *Kurdistan Rising* (2016), *Dancing with the Devil: The Perils of Engagement* (2015), *The Shi'ites of the Middle East* (2014), and two earlier books examining Iranian history.

Brian L. Steed

Brian L. Steed is an associate professor of military history at the CGSC. A retired US Army lieutenant colonel, he has more than thirty years' active duty and civilian experience, including as a Middle East foreign area officer. He was both an officer in the Jordanian Armed Forces and a liaison to the Israel Defense Forces. Steed wrote and edited nine books, including *Iraq War: The Essential Reference Guide* (2019) and *ISIS: The Essential Reference Guide* (2019), as well as numerous articles and papers on military theory, military history, and cultural awareness. He has a bachelor's degree in history from Brigham Young University, a master's in international relations from Vermont College of Norwich University, and a PhD in political science-history from the University of Missouri-Kansas City.

Mark R. Wilcox

Mark Wilcox is an associate professor and the William E. Odom chair of joint, multinational, and interagency studies at the CGSC. He served in the United States Army from 1980 until retiring as a lieutenant colonel in 2005. He served in tactical and strategic-level counterintelligence assignments and politico-military posts at the operational and strategic levels, including as a politico-military staff officer at the US European Command headquarters in Stuttgart, Germany; a Joint Chiefs of Staff representative to the United States Mission to the Organization for Security and Cooperation in Europe in Vienna, Austria; and a security cooperation liaison officer representing US Central Command in the Republic of Uzbekistan.

He is a graduate of the Defense Language, the US States Army Russian Institute, and the CGSC. He has a bachelor's in foreign service from Georgetown University, a master's in Soviet and East European studies from the University of Kansas, and a PhD in security studies from Kansas State University.

Made in United States
North Haven, CT
01 November 2022